THE A-Z OF POLITICALLY INCORRECT JOKES

Ollie Tabooger

Illustrations: Euro Snotball

National Library of Australia Cataloguing-in-Publication entry

Creator: Tabooger, Ollie, author.

Title: A-Z of politically incorrect jokes / Ollie Tabooger;
         illustrator, Ms. Euro Snotball.

ISBN: 978-1-925181-62-3 (paperback)

Subjects: Wit and humor.

Other Creators/Contributors:
   Ms. Euro Snotball, illustrator.

Dewey Number: 808.882

A-Z of politically incorrect jokes
Copyright 2015 Ollie Tabooger

Important disclaimer

Without limiting the rights under copyright reserved above, no part of this publication may be reproduced, stored, or transmitted in any form or by any means, without prior written permission of both the copyright owner and the above publisher of this book.

The information in this book is of a general nature and is intended to be (at least for some) humorous. It is not intended to be professional advice.

The book is a collection of jokes provided to the author over time and no offence is intended in relation to any aspect of the book.

Contents

Chapter 1: A is for Australia 1
Chapter 2: B is for Beer 27
Chapter 3: C is for Cricket 44
Chapter 4: D is for Darwin Awards 52
Chapter 5: E is for Education. 73
Chapter 6: F is for Females 159
Chapter 7: G is for Golf 224
Chapter 8: H is for Heaven 236
Chapter 9: I is for Irish 251
Chapter 10: J is for Jerk 270
Chapter 11: K is for Kiwi 279
Chapter 12: L is for Lethally Blonde 289
Chapter 13: M is for Male. 320
Chapter 14: N is for Nude 370
Chapter 15: O is for One Liners 378
Chapter 16: P is for Police 429
Chapter 17: Q is for Queensland. 447
Chapter 18: R is for Rugby 462
Chapter 19: S is for Sex 472
Chapter 20: T is for Tax. 502
Chapter 21: U is for Urban Myths 512

Chapter 22: V is for Virgin 567
Chapter 23: W is for Work 576
Chapter 24: X is for Xenophobia 606
Chapter 25: Y is for Youth 626
Chapter 26: Z is for Zoo 645

CHAPTER 1

A is for Australia

At an international woman's conference the topic for discussion was how to empower women in the home.

The first speaker was the British representative. She stood up and said; "I decided to make a stand against my husband's oppression and so I told him that I would no longer be doing the washing. After the first day I saw no result; after the second day I saw nothing; but after the third day he did his own washing."

The delegates applauded this brave stand for women's rights.

The second speaker was from America. She stood up and said; "I told my husband that I was no longer prepared to cook for him as it was a form of enslavement. After the first day I saw no result, after the second day I saw no result; but after the third day he cooked a meal for the both of us."

Again the conference applauded.

Next came the Australian delegate. She said; "I told my husband that I would no longer be doing the shopping. After the first day I saw nothing, after the second day I saw nothing; but after the third day I could see a little bit out of my left eye."

Tim Ferguson 'And you call that a preamble?'

The prime minister and the poet have had their go. Now here's what they should have said.

We, the people of the broad, brown land of Oz, wish to be recognised as a free nation of blokes, sheilas and the occasional trannie. We come from many lands (although a few too many of us come from New Zealand) and, although we live in the best little country in the world, we reserve the right to bitch and moan about it whenever we bloody like.

We are one nation but we're divided into many states. First, there's Victoria, named after a queen who didn't believe in lesbians. Victoria is the realm of Massimo turtlenecks, café latte and grand final day. Its capital is Melbourne, whose chief marketing pitch is that it's liveable.

Next there's NSW. It is the realm of pastel shorts, macchiato with sugar, thin books read quickly and millions of dancing gay boys. Its mascots are Bondi lifesavers who pull their Speedos up their cracks to keep the left and right sides of their brains separate.

Down south we have Tasmania, a State based on the notion that the family that bonks together stays together. In Tassie, everyone gets an extra chromosome at conception. Maps of the State bring smiles to the sternest faces.

South Australia is the province of half-decent reds, a festival of foreigners and bizarre axe murders. They had the grand prix, but lost it when the views of Adelaide sent the Formula One drivers to sleep at the wheel.

Western Australia is too far from anywhere to be relevant in this document;

The Northern Territory i.e. the red heart of our land. Outback plains, sheep stations, kangaroos, Jackaroos, emus and dusty kids with big smiles. Although the Territory is the centrepiece of our national culture, few of us live there and the rest prefer to fly over it on our way to Bali.

And there's a Queensland. While any mention of God seems silly in a document defining a nation of half-arsed agnostics, it is worth noting that god probably made Queensland. Why he filled it with dickheads remains a mystery.

We, the Lullaby League of Oz, are united, primarily by the Pacific Highway, whose treacherous twists and turns kill more of us each year than die by murder.

We are united in our lust for international recognition so desperate for praise we leap in joy when a ragtag gaggle of corrupt IOC officials tells us Sydney is better than Beijing. We are united by a democracy so flawed that a political party, albeit a redneck gun-toting one, can get a million votes and still not win one seat in Federal Parliament. Desirable, sure. But fair? Not when you consider Brian Harradine can get 24.000 votes and run the bloody country. Not that we're whingeing.

We've chucked out the concept of "fair go" in the downsized '90s. Instead we want to make "no worries" our national phrase. We love sport so much our newsreaders can read the death toll from a sailing race and still tell us who's winning, in the same breath

We the brain, the heart and the nerve of Oz want the world to know we have the biggest rock, the tastiest pies and the worst dressed Olympians in the known universe. We don't know much about art but we know we hate the people who make it. We shoot, we vote. We are girt by sea and pissed by lunchtime.

And even though we might seem a racist closed minded sports obsessed little people, at least we're better than the Kiwis.

Now bugger off, we're sleeping.

These are actual questions taken from the Sydney Olympics web site.

Answers have been added where necessary.

1. Does it ever get windy in Australia? I have never seen it rain on TV, so how do the plants grow? (UK) (Up- wards, out of the ground, like the person who asked

this question, who themselves will need watering if their IQ drops any lower...)

2. Will I be able to see kangaroos in the street? (USA) (Depends on how much beer you've consumed...)

3. Which direction should I drive—Perth to Darwin or Darwin to Perth to avoid driving with the sun in my eyes? (Germany) (Excellent question, considering that the Olympics are being held in Sydney) I want to walk from Perth to Sydney, can I follow the railroad tracks? (Sweden) (Sure, it's only seven thousand miles, so you'll need to have started about a year and a half ago to get there in time for this October...)

4. Is it safe to run around in the bushes in Australia? (Sweden)(And accomplish what?)

5. It is imperative that I find the names and addresses of places to contact for a stuffed porpoise. (Italy) (I'm not touching this one...)

6. My client wants to take a steel pooper-scooper into Australia. Will you let her in? (South Africa) (Why? We do have toilet paper here...)

7. Are there any ATMs in Australia? Can you send me a list of them in Brisbane, Cairns, Townsville and Hervey Bay? (UK) (Which Bank?)

8. Where can I learn underwater welding in Australia? (Portugal) (Who do you want to sabotage?)

9. Do the camels in Australia have one hump or two? (UK) (Is this for comfort sake?)

10. Can I bring cutlery into Australia? (UK) (Why bother? Use your fingers like the rest of us...)

11. Do you have perfume in Australia? (France) (No, everybody stinks.)

12. Do tents exist in Australia? (Germany) (Yes, but only in sporting supply stores, people's garages, and most national parks...)

13. Can I wear high heels in Australia? (UK) (This has to have been asked by a blonde...)

14. Can you tell me the regions in Tasmania where the female population is smaller than the male population? (Italy) (Yes, Gay nightclubs.)

15. Do you celebrate Christmas in Australia? (France) (Only if you're Christian...)

16. Can I drive to the Great Barrier Reef? (Germany) (Sure, if your vehicle is amphibious.)

17. Are there killer bees in Australia? (Germany) (Not yet, but we'll see what we can do when you get here.)

18. Can you give me some information about hippo racing in Australia? (USA) (What's this guy smoking, and where do I get some?)

19. Are there supermarkets in Sydney and is milk available all year round? (Germany) (Another blonde?)

20. Please send a list of all doctors in Australia who can dispense rattlesnake serum. (USA) (I love this one. there are no rattlesnakes in Australia, but plenty others that are more deadly!)

21. Which direction is North in Australia? (USA) (Face north and you should be about right)

22. Can you send me the Vienna BOYS' Choir schedule? (USA) (Americans have long had considerable trouble distinguishing between Austria and Australia.)

23. I have a question about a famous animal in Australia, but I forget its name. It's a kind of bear and lives

in trees. (USA) (It isn't a Kodiak that's for sure—but sounds familiar!)

24. I have developed a new product that is the fountain of youth. Can you tell me where I can sell it in Australia? (USA) (From Liz Taylor, perhaps?)

25. Are there places in Australia where you can make love outdoors? (Italy) (Yes, outdoors.)

26. I was in Australia about 30 years ago on R;plR, and I want to contact the girl dated while I was staying in Kings Cross. Can you help? (USA)(Well, then there was AIDS!)

27. Will I be able to speak English most places I go? (USA) (Yes, provided it's not Marrickville in Sydney or Sunnybank in Brisbane!)

Subject: FW: Anti-Terrorism Rally

Do It for your Country!

Since the Taliban cannot stand nudity and consider it a sin to see a naked woman that is not a wife. This Saturday afternoon at 2:00 pm Eastern Standard Time. All Australian women are asked to walk out of their house completely naked to help weed out any neighbourhood terrorists. Circling your block for one hour is recommended for this anti-terrorist effort. All men are to position themselves in lawn chairs in front of their house to prove they think it's okay to see other women in the nude. And since the Taliban also does not approve of alcohol. An Esky containing a cold slab is to be at your side as further proof of your anti- Taliban sentiment. Australia appreciates your efforts to root out terrorists and applauds your participation.

God Bless Australia! Come on all Aussie men. Get out there and support the girls as they weed out the terrorists hiding in YOUR neighbourhood!!

Yours.

The Prime Minister.

An Australian guy goes into a bar in the Greek Islands. Jill, the barmaid takes his order and notices his Australian accent. Over the course of the night they talk quite a bit. At the end of the night he asks her if she wants to have sex with him.

Although she is attracted to him she says no. He then offers to pay her $200 for the deed. Jill is travelling the world and because she is short of funds she agrees.

The next night the guy turns up again and after showing her plenty of attention throughout the night he asks if she will sleep with him again for $200. She figures in for a penny in for a pound, and it was fantastic the night before so she agrees.

This goes on for 5 nights. On the sixth night the guy comes into the bar.

But this night he orders a beer and just goes and sits in the corner. The girl is disappointed and thinks that maybe she should pay him more attention.

She goes over and sits next to him.

She asks him where he is from and he tells her Melbourne." So am I" she says. "What suburb in Melbourne."

"St Kilda" he says.

"That's amazing" she says, "so am I—what street?"

"Cameo Street" he says.

"This is unbelievable" she says, "what number?"

He says "Number 20" and she is astonished.

"You are not going to believe this" she says, "I'm from number 22 my parents still live there!"

"I know" he says "your father gave me $1,000 to give you."

To:

The Indonesian Foreign Minister

From

The Australian Prime Minister

My Dear Sir,

May I thank you, on behalf of the Australian people, for your country's kind declaration of war, received in my office at 8pm last night. With sincere regret, I must decline your invitation to fight. If you could delay your invasion of our northern coastline for, say, the 15 years, I'm sure we'd be able to give you a terrific scrap.

But at the moment I doubt we could even field a team. Our P111s are grounded again, and, because of their age (ours are the ones with the gearshift on the steering column, and those indicators that flip out of the door pillars), spare parts are available only at wrecking yards and swap meets in Kentucky and Tennessee. Also, try as we might, we just can't seem to get them to run properly on unleaded.

The Chinook helicopters in Townsville are grounded, too. Now losing the choppers is bad news, as our fixed-wing capacity in the north is presently in tatters. Why? A night kerfuffle over my good friend Warren Entsch's concreting business has left our Raap base at Weipa short of a number of desirable features like a runway.

Our Defence Minister, Mr Moore, sends his apologies, but insists that a war is presently out of the question as we don't have a Defence Secretary. Well we have one, but he's currently trying to wrestle Mr Moore to death in the Federal Court, for wrongful dismissal. It would be a little unfair on Mr Moore to begin a war while nobody in the Defence Department will speak to him.

You will probably know that the Chief of Navy isn't getting a new contract either but, even if he was, I could not possibly commit our senior service to any conflict. Our two Collins-class submarines, Drowning and Waving, have just returned from sea trials off Fiji to assess their design targets of silence and stealth. Every time they went into reverse, normal conversation became impossible across most of Chile and Peru.

It is also disheartening that Drowning ran aground, especially as this mishap somehow snapped off her periscope. Think about it! Not that we have enough submariners to man the boats anyway. Attracting career sailors to our modern professional navy has not been helped by recent revelations on prime time television that recruits are routinely stripped naked, smeared with food scraps and excrement, and flogged on the buttocks. I take no comfort from the flood of applications this publicity drew from Tasmania.

The Army is still the bulwark of Australia's security, but even there things are difficult. Changes following the Women in Combat report, and same-sex relationship rulings, have, in my opinion, compromised our flexibility. For example, both the First Heavy Armoured (Dykes With Pykes) and the Gay Fusiliers (The Queens Light Foot) Divisions refuse to fight for a fortnight either side of the Sydney Mardi Gras. Other soldiers are insisting, these days, on owning the conflict and have begun to enrol in regular workshops to engage their aggression.

High Court rulings may also mean, with no offence Dr Alatas that we cannot engage in a battle against a racially-selected enemy force. Can you recruit a sprinkling of Europeans next time? By all means take as many of ours as you want.

It is a good indication of the quality of our Defence Intelligence Organisation that I am unable to send this transmission in code. The code books were stolen by an unstable steroid-abuser, Jean-Phillippe Wispelaere, shrewdly recruited by the 010, and entrusted with most of our defence secrets. So now we don't have any Mr Wispelaere sold them all in Bangkok. If you have any secrets you don't need any more, we would be most grateful for them. I should have the code books back soon. Christies are auctioning them in Havana next week. In the meantime, our secret intelligence advisers suggest we do the old a;eqb, b;eqc, c;eqd code. They swear by it.

I know our refusal will be a considerable disappointment to you, but can I suggest that you consider invading New Zealand instead? Their only significant defence capability lies with their two Anzac-class frigates, Mulk and Lemb. I have no doubt you'll cream them, and I should know. They were both built in Australia.

Best wishes, The Prime Minister

Two blokes bump into each other in the supermarket. Sorry mate, says the first one, I am a bit nervous, I lost my wife, can't find her anywhere. Second bloke replies; gee, I can't find mine either, how about we go and look for them together? Sure, says the first one, what does your wife look like? Eh well, she's blonde, long hair, tall slim body, well-tanned, large breasts and she's wearing a tight fitting low cut black dress. What does your wife look like? Forget about my wife, says the other bloke, let's go and look for yours!

Sheila wants an all over suntan but is not quite sure how to go about it, so she says to Bruce, you reckon I should go sunbathing in the nuddy in the backyard? Yeah, no worries, says Bruce, go for it. But what if the neighbours see me naked, what will they think? Bruce; that I married you for your money.

Kiwi, Aussie and a West Indian

Three men in a delivery waiting room, a Kiwi, an Aussie and a West Indian.

Matron comes to tell them that all 3 wives have given birth but that there's been a mix-up and they're not quite sure which baby belongs to which father and could they please come to the nursery and work it out between them.

The 3 men go into the nursery and after 30 seconds the Australian comes out and says to matron: This one's mine.

The matron looks at the baby and says: But this baby looks West Indian.

The Australian says: I know, but one of the other two is a Kiwi and I'm not taking any chances.

An Australian, Irishman and an Englishman were sitting in a bar. There was only one other person in the bar. The three men kept looking at this other man for he seemed terribly familiar. They stared and stared, wondering where they had seen him before when suddenly the Irishman cried out: 'My God! I know who that man is—it's Jesus!"

The others looked again, and sure enough, it was Jesus himself, sitting alone at a table.

The Irishman calls out across the lounge: "Hey! Hey you! Are you Jesus? "

Jesus looks over at him, smiles a small smile and nods his head. "Yes, I am Jesus," he says.

Well, the Irishman calls the bartender over and says to him: "I'd like you to give Jesus over there a pint of Guinness from me. The bartender pours Jesus a Guinness.

Jesus looks over, raises his glass, thanks and drinks.

The Englishman then calls out: "Er, excuse me Sir, but would you be Jesus?" Jesus smiles and says "Yes, I am Jesus". The Englishman beckons the bartender and tells him to send over a pint of Newcastle Brown Ale for Jesus, which the bartender duly does. As before, Jesus accepts the drink and smiles over at the table.

Then the Australian calls out: "Oy you! D'ya reckon you're Jesus or what?" Jesus nods and says "Yes, I am Jesus". The Australian is mighty impressed and has the bartender send over a schooner of VB for Jesus which Jesus accepts with pleasure.

Sometime late, after finishing the drinks, Jesus leaves his seat and approaches our three friends. He reaches for the hand of the Irishman and shakes it, thanking him for the Guinness. When he lets go, the Irishman gives a cry of amazement: "Oh God! The arthritis is gone! The arthritis I've had for years is gone! It's a miracle!"

Jesus then shakes the Englishman's hand, thanking him for the Newcastle. Upon letting go, the Englishman's eyes widen in shock: "By Jove, the migraine! The migraine I've had for 40 years is completely gone! It's a miracle!!!"

Jesus then goes to approach the Australian who says: "Back off mate! I'm on compo!!"

AND JUST A LITTLE NOTE TO REMIND US WHERE WE ARE FROM!

- It would be Un-Australian not to have a few beers on Australia Day.
- It would be Un-Australian not to observe one minute's silence on ANZAC Day.
- It would be Un-Australian stick it to the Poms as possible, but secretly like the majority of them.
- It would be Un-Australian not to try and drink every Irishman you meet under the table.
- It would be Un-Australian not to have owned a Speedwell or Malvern Star pushbike at some stage in your life.
- It would be Un-Australian not to love a bet—on anything, anything at all.
- It would be Un-Australian not to have had a chill run up your spine every time you see the scene in The Man from Snowy River, where man and horse careen down that steep, slippery slope at break neck speed.
- It would be Un-Australian not to secretly love the stereotypical image Paul Hogan has portrayed for all of us.
- It would be Un-Australian not to tell foreign visitors that, yes indeed I do have a kangaroo in my back yard.
- It would be Un-Australian not to like that endless series of VB advertisements on television.
- It would be Un-Australian not to have squinted at the horizon, in the face of another burning summer sunset.
- It would be Un-Australian not to have been drenched by a sudden summer thunder storm.

- It would be Un-Australian not to have swallowed a fly at some stage in your life.
- It would be Un-Australian not to enjoy beating the Poms at cricket, whether you are a cricket fan or not.
- It would be Un-Australian not to know the words to Advance Australia Fair and Waltzing Matilda.
- It would be Un-Australian not to proudly proclaim your nationality, no matter where you were in the world.
- It would be Un-Australian not to be able to decipher "Ava go ya bloody mug why don't ya".
- It would be Un-Australian not to have a jar of vegemite in the cupboard.
- It would be Un-Australian not to be able to laugh at ourselves.
- It would be Un-Australian not to take advantage of our God given right to the sickie.
- It would be Un-Australian not to do circle work
- It would be Un-Australian not to have a Hills Hoist in the backyard
- It would be Un-Australian not to love VB's
- It would be Un-Australian not to call any successful New Zealanders "Aussies" and the rest 'sheep rooters'".
- It would be Un- Australian to have not swung from a piece of rope tied to a tree into the local river.
- It would be Un-Australian not to own a pair of thongs.
- It would be Un-Australian not to have a street sign with your name on it in your bedroom. Or at least a flashing road work sign.

- It would be un-Australian not to loudly pronounce to everyone in England that Darren Gough is the only English cricketer for ten years that would make the Tasmanian Sheffield Shield side.
- It would be Un-Australian not to tell every foreigner that "Land Down Under" is the national anthem.
- It would be Un-Australian not to tell everybody that the national anthem of New Zealand is "God Loves New Zealand—He Gave Them Boiling Mud".
- It would be un-Australian not to tell people that New Zealand is still constitutionally the 7th State.
- It would be Un-Australian to actually eat Jaffas in the cinema.
- It would be Un-Australian not to have a pub where you are on a first name basis with the staff and they don't have to ask what you are drinking.
- It would be Un-Australian not to try the hardest ski slopes or rapids even though you are a complete novice.
- It would be Un-Australian not to have said the line "don't worry about me, I can handle my drink" at least once.
- It would be Un-Australian not to have thrown up, 2 hours after saying the previous line.
- It would be Un-Australian not to have thrown up on shoes you don't own.
- It would be Un-Australian not to tell everybody in England about the healthy state of all Australian sport, while sitting on your arse in a pub drinking beer and contributing nothing to it.

- It would be Un-Australian to agree with the gentleman at the door as to the state of your inebriation.
- It would be Un-Australian to leave quietly.
- It would be Un-Australian not to stop during the Melbourne Cup, ideally for the entire day.
- It would be Un-Australian not to have been to a day at the races and not remember seeing a horse, at least once.

LETTER FOUND IN A "PERSONAL PROBLEMS" ADVICE COLUMN OF AN AUSTRALIAN MAGAZINE

From Jeremy of Sydney, Australia.

I am a sailor in the Australian Navy.

My parents live in the suburb of Redfern and one of my sisters, who lives in Canberra, is married to a Kiwi. My father and mother have recently been arrested growing and selling marijuana and are currently dependent on my other two sisters, who are prostitutes in Kings Cross.

I have two brothers, one who is currently serving a non-parole life sentence in Long Bay Jail, Sydney, for the murder of a teenage girl in 1994, the other is currently being held in the Parramatta remand centre on charges of incest with three children.

I have recently become engaged to marry a former Thai prostitute who lives in Chatswood and indeed is still a part time "working girl" in a brothel, however, her time there is limited as she has recently been infected with an STD. We intend to marry as soon as possible and are currently looking into the possibility of opening our own brothel with my fiancée utilising her knowledge of the industry working as the manager.

I am hoping my two sisters would be interested in joining our team.

Although I would prefer them not to prostitute themselves, it would at least get them off the streets and hopefully the heroin.

My problem is this: I love my fiancée and look forward to bringing her into the family and of course I want to be totally honest with her. Should I tell her about my brother-in-law being a Kiwi?

The local bar was so sure that its barman was the strongest man around that they offered a standing $1,000 bet. The barman would squeeze a lemon until all the juice ran into a glass, and hand the lemon to a patron.

Anyone who could squeeze one more drop of juice out would win the money.

Many people had tried over time (weight lifters, oil rig workers, builders' labourers etc.) but nobody could do it.

One day a scrawny little man came in, wearing thick glasses and a polyester suit, and said in a tiny, squeaky voice, "I'd like to try the bet."

After the laughter had died down, the barman said "okay", grabbed a lemon and squeezed away. He then handed the wrinkled remains of the rind to the little man.

But the crowd's laughter turned to total silence as the little man clenched his fist around the lemon and six drops fell into the glass.

As the silence turned to cheers, the barman paid the $1,000, and asked the little man, "What do you do for a living? Are you a gym instructor, a weight lifter, or what?"

The man replied, "No, I work for the Australian Taxation Office."

Aussie Idiots—a sub-grouping of the Darwin Award.

BROOKVALE IDIOT

The North Shore Times News crime column reported that a man walked Into Brookvale McDonalds at 8:50AM, flashed a gun and demanded cash. The clerk turned him down because she said she couldn't open the cash register without a food order. When the man ordered a Big Mac, the clerk said they weren't available until 10:30 am as only the breakfast menu was on offer. Frustrated, the man walked away.

ADELAIDE IDIOTS

Two men tried to pull the front of an ATM machine in Adelaide's Henley Street by running a chain from the machine to the bumper of their Toyota Landcruiser, but instead of pulling the front panel off the machine, they pulled the bumper off their 4WD, scared, and attracting attention from oncoming traffic, they left the scene and drove home, with the chain still attached to the machine, their bumper still attached to the chain, and their vehicle's license plate still attached to the bumper. No, they did not use a stolen car.

WOLLONGONG IDIOT

A man walked into a Seven-Eleven, put a $20 bill on the counter and asked for change. When the clerk opened the cash drawer, the man pulled a gun and asked for all the cash in the register, which the clerk promptly provided. The man took the cash from the clerk and fled, leaving the $20 bill on the counter. The total amount of cash he got from the drawer? Fifteen

ROOTY HILL IDIOT

Seems this guy wanted some beer pretty badly. He decided that he'd just throw a brick through a liquor store window, grab some booze, and run. So he lifted the brick and heaved it over his head at the window with all his might. The brick bounced back and hit the would-be thief on the head, knocking him unconscious. Apparently, the liquor store window was made of Plexi-Glass. And the whole event was caught on videotape, which the store owner consequently sold for use on TV.

CAMPBELLTOWN IDIOT

As a female shopper exited the Campbelltown K-Mart in Queen Street, a man grabbed her purse and ran. A shop assistant at K-Mart called the police immediate and the woman was able to give them a detailed description of the snatcher. Within minutes, the police had apprehended the snatcher, trying to mingle in the shopping crowd on Queen Street. They put him in the car and drove back to the K-Mart store. The thief was then taken out of the car and up to the K-Mart front desk and told to stand there for a positive ID. To which he replied; "Yes, Officer, that's her. That's the lady I stole the purse from."

PORT MACQUARIE IDIOT

When a man attempted to siphon petrol from a motor home parked on a Port Macquarie Street, he got much more than he bargained for. Police arrived at the scene to find an ill man curled up next to a motor home near spilled sewage. A police spokesman said that the man admitted to trying to steal petrol and plugged his hose into the motor home sewage tank by mistake. He had tried to siphon the petrol by first sucking it up the hose. The owner of the vehicle declined to press charges, saying that it was the best laugh he'd ever had.

Two Aussies, Bruce and Jimbo, were adrift in a lifeboat. While rummaging through the boat's provisions, Bruce stumbled across an old lamp. He rubbed the lamp vigorously and a genie came forth. This genie, however, stated that he could only deliver one wish, not the standard three.

Without giving much thought to the matter, Bruce blurted out, "Make the entire ocean into VB!"

The genie clapped his hands with a deafening crash, and immediately the entire sea turned into the finest brew ever sampled by mortals. The genie then vanished. Only the gentle lapping their circumstances.

Jimbo looked disgustedly at Bruce whose wish had been granted. After a long, tension-filled moment: "Nice going Bruce! Now we're going to have to piss in the boat."

A guy from Auckland is having a quiet drink in a Sydney Bar. He leans over to the big guy next to him and says, "Do you wanna hear an Aussie joke?"

The big guy replies, "Well, mate, before you tell that joke you should know something: I'm six feet tall, 105kgs and I'm a Wallaby forward.

The guy sitting next to me is 6'2", weighs 115kgs and he's an ex-Wallaby lock.

Next to him is a bloke who's 6'5", weighs 120kgs and he's a current Wallaby second-rower.

Now, do you still want to tell that Aussie joke?"

The Kiwi says, "Nah...not if I'm going to have to explain it three times."

Sheila didn't come home one night. When Bruce asked her where she'd been she said she spent the night at a girl friend's house. Bruce was a bit suspicious she'd been rooting around so rang her ten closest friends, but none of them had seen her.

Next week Bruce didn't come home one night. Sheila asks him where the hell he'd been. Bruce says he got a bit drunk at a mate's place and thought it was safer not to drive and crash out there. Sheila thinks he's been rooting around so rings his ten best mates. Eight of them say he spent the night there and two claim he's still there.

Save the Bogan (Maximum us tight black jean us with mullet us) First identified as a sub-species during the mid-70s, the Bogan is thought to be a close relation of the Booner (found in Canberra's Eastern suburbs) and the Westie (spread throughout Western Sydney).

It is believed the initial Brisbane population was introduced to purpose-built habitats such as Ipswich, Inala and Woodridge. However by the mid-80s, the species had multiplied to plague proportions, spreading though much of Redbank and Goodna. While authorities considered a culling program, they need not have bothered, as the regional population began a rapid decline from the early 90s onwards. The situation has now reached a critical point, with Bogans rarely sighted in the inner Brisbane suburbs, and those remaining cling to the region's outskirts.

The species is now officially endangered. Identifying a Bogan is genetic, while others argue it is a product of nurture, as extremely young males seem coerced by parents to adopt the growth.

Other distinguishing male characteristics include tight black denim covering on the hind limbs and bright flannelette markings on the forepaws and belly.

Males adopt a dominant status within the community, with a vague sense rank defined by the ownership of aging Ford and Holden motor vehicles.

Female Bogans are entrusted with the raising of multiple offspring, a role they perform from a young age and often without the presence of the male.

They may be similarly identified though distinctive denim markings, though the colour is usually "stonewash". In warmer weather, females have been known to shed the lower layer of denim to just below the genital area, resulting in a "cut-off" effect.

Both males and females have been known to cover their lower hind-limbs with furry pouches called "ugg-boots". While the wild population of Bogans is dwindling, it is still possible to view them in their natural environment. The species have been known to congregate around regional "shopping malls", where family units often come to settle domestic issues using high-pitched wailing sounds. After sunset, younger males and females meet in small dark enclaves known as "Taverns", where they consume large amounts of liquid called "Bourbon".

There are numerous factors attributed to the decline of the local Bogan population. Scientists have identified the unpopularity of 'The Village' as a contributing cause, while the development of adequate social infrastructure (i.e. schools, medium density housing) may have fragmented the species. More controversial theories suggest many Bogans may have removed their mullets, purchased "cargo pants" and attempted to integrate themselves in Brisbane's mainstream population, but these claims are yet to be substantiated.

At present there seems little hope of restoring the Bogan population to its previous levels. Recent attempts included the development of a new artificial habitat named "Forest Lake", but it seems this area may be far from Ipswich to attract large numbers of the species. More successful is an enclosed breeding program called "Archerfield Raceway". The program has proven highly effective, combining aggressive behaviour, beer and occasional displays of female sexuality. Authorities recently have attracted Bogan elders AC/DC for a brief visit.

In the beginning..............

In the beginning God created day and night. He created day for footy matches, going to the beach and barbies. He created night for going prawning, sleeping and barbies. God saw that it was good. Evening came and morning came and it was the Second Day.

On the Second Day God created water—for surfing, swimming and barbies on the beach. God saw that it was good. Evening came and morning came and it was the Third Day.

On the Third Day God created the Earth to bring forth plants—to provide tobacco, malt and yeast for beer and wood for barbies. God saw that it was good. Evening came and morning came and it was the Fourth Day.

On the Fourth Day God created animals and crustaceans for chops, sausages, steak and prawns for barbies. God saw that it was good. Evening came and morning came and it was the Fifth Day.

On the Fifth day God created a bloke—to go to the footy, enjoy the beach, drink the beer and eat the meat and prawns at barbies. God saw that it was good. Evening came and morning came and it was the Sixth Day.

On the Sixth Day God saw that this bloke was lonely and needed someone to go to the footy, surf, drink beer, eat and stand around the barbie with. So God created mates, and God saw that they were good blokes. God saw that it was good. Evening came and morning came and it was the Seventh Day.

On the Seventh Day God looked around at the twinkling barbie fires, heard the hiss of opening beer cans and the raucous laughter of all the Blokes, smelled the aroma of grilled chops and sizzling prawns and God saw that it was good. Well almost good. G od saw that the blokes were tired and needed a rest.

So God created Sheilas—to clean the house, bear children, wash, cook and clean the barbie. God saw that it was not just good, it was better than that, it was bloody great! IT WAS AUSTRALIA!!

An American decided to write a book about famous churches around the world. So he bought a plane ticket and took a trip to Orlando, thinking that he would start by working his way across the USA from South to North.

On his first day he was inside a church taking photographs when he noticed golden telephone mounted on the wall with a sign that read "$10,000 per call". The American, being intrigued, asked priest who was strolling by what the telephone was used for.

The priest replied that it was a direct line to heaven and that for $10,000 you could talk to God. The American thanked the priest and went along his way.

Next stop was in Atlanta. There, at a very large cathedral, he saw the same golden telephone with the same sign under it. He wondered if this was the same kind of telephone he saw in Orlando and he asked a nearby nun what its purpose was. She told him that it was a direct line to heaven and that for $10,000 he could talk to God. O.K., thank you," said the American. He then travelled to Indianapolis, Washington DC, Philadelphia, Boston, and New York. In every church he saw the same golden telephone with the same "$10,000 per call" sign under it.

The American, upon leaving Vermont decided to travel to Australia to see if Australians had the same phone. He arrived in Australia, and again, in the first church he entered, there was the same golden telephone, but this time the sign under it read "40 cents per call." The American was surprised so he asked the priest about the sign.

Father, I've travelled all over America and I've seen this same golden telephone in many churches. I'm told that it is a direct line to Heaven, but in the US the price was $10,000 per call. Why is it so cheap here?"

The priest smiled and answered, "You're in Australia now, mate—it's a local call".

The Sydney Morning Herald conducted a poll of male readers to see what exactly each enjoyed from having oral sex performed on them.

Seven percent said they most enjoyed the sensations.

Five percent confessed that their chief enjoyment came from the sense of domination.

A staggering 88 percent said that they really enjoyed the peace and quiet.

CHAPTER 2

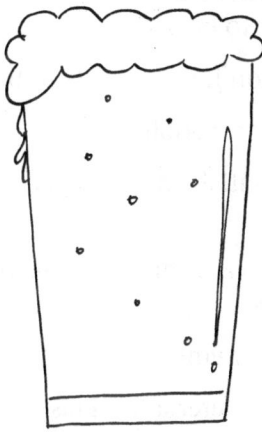

B is for Beer

REASONS WHY BEER SHOULD BE SERVED AT WORK...

1. It's an incentive to show up.
2. It reduces stress.
3. It leads to more honest communications.
4. It reduces complaints about low pay.
5. It cuts down on time off because you can work with a hangover.
6. Employees tell management what they think, not what management to hear.
7. It helps save on heating costs in the winter.
8. It encourages carpooling.
9. Increase job satisfaction because if you have a bad job, you don't care.
10. It eliminates vacations because people would rather come to work.
11. It makes fellow employees look better.
12. It makes the cafeteria food taste better.
13. Bosses are more likely to hand out raises when they are wasted
14. Salary negotiations are a lot more profitable.
15. Suddenly, burping during a meeting isn't so embarrassing.
16. Employees work later since there's no longer a need to relax at the bar
17. It makes everyone more open with their ideas.
18. Everyone agrees the work is better after they've had a couple of drinks

19. Eliminates the need for employees to get drunk on their lunch break

20. Employees no longer need coffee to sober up.

21. Sitting on the copy machine will no longer be seen as "gross".

22. Babbling and mumbling incoherently will be common language.

Due to increasing product liability, beer manufacturers have accepted Medical Association's suggestion that the following warning labels be placed immediately on all beer containers.

- Warning: consumption of beer may make you think you are whispering when you are not.
- Warning: consumption of beer is a major factor in dancing like a wanker.
- Warning: consumption of beer may cause you to tell the same boring story over and over again until your friends want to smash your face in.
- Warning: consumption of beer may lead you to believe that ex-lovers are really dying for you to telephone them at 4 in the morning.
- Warning: consumption of beer may leave you wondering what the hell happened to your trousers.
- Warning: consumption of beer may make you think you can logically converse with other members of the opposite sex without spitting.
- Warning: consumption of beer may make you think you possess mystical Kung Fu powers.

- Warning: consumption of beer may cause you to rollover in the morning and see something really scary (whose species, and/or name you can't remember).
- Warning: consumption of beer is the leading cause of inexplicable rug burns on the forehead.
- Warning: consumption of beer may lead to traffic signs and cones appearing in your home.
- Warning: consumption of beer may lead you to believe you are invisible.
- Warning: consumption of beer may lead you to believe that people are laughing with you.
- Warning: consumption of beer may cause an influx in the time-space continuum, whereby small (and sometimes large) gaps of time may seem to literally disappear.
- Warning: consumption of beer may actually cause pregnancy.

Please ensure all fellow staff members are made aware of these pending damages to our Liquor Licensing Laws.

- I feel sorry for people who don't drink. When they wake up in the morning, that's as good as they're going to feel all day.—Frank Sinatra
- The problem with some people is that when they aren't drunk, they're sober.—William Butler Yeats
- An intelligent man is sometimes forced to be drunk to spend time with his fools.—Ernest Hemingway
- Always do sober what you said you'd do drunk. That will teach you to keep your mouth shut.—Ernest Hemingway

- You're not drunk if you can lie on the floor without holding on. -Dean Martin
- Drunk is feeling sophisticated when you can't say it. -Anonymous
- No animal ever invented anything as bad as drunkenness—or as good as drink.—G.K. Chesterton
- Crime is never wasted when you're wasted all the time.—Catherine Zandonella
- Abstainer: a weak person who yields to the temptation of denying himself a pleasure.—Ambrose Bierce
- Reality is an illusion that occurs due to lack of alcohol.—Anonymous
- Work is the curse of the drinking classes.—Oscar Wilde
- When I read about the evils of drinking, I gave up reading.—Henny Youngman
- Life is a waste of time, time is a waste of life, so get wasted all of the time and have the time of your life.—Anonymous
- I'd rather have a bottle in front of me, than a frontal lobotomy.—Tom Wait.
- 24 hours in a day, 24 beers in a case. Coincidence?—Stephen wright
- When we drink, we get drunk. When we get drunk, we fall asleep. When we fall asleep, we commit no sin. When we commit no sin, we go to heaven. So, let's all get drunk, and go to heaven—Brian O'Rourke
- You can't be a real country unless you have a beer and an airline—it helps if you have some kind of a football team, or nuclear weapons, but at the very least you need a beer.—Frank Zappa

- Always remember that I have taken more out of alcohol than alcohol has taken out of me.—Winston Churchill
- He was a wise man who invented beer.—Plato
- Beer is proof that God loves us and want us to be happy.- Benjamin Franklin
- If you ever reach total enlightenment while drinking beer, I bet it makes beer shoot out your nose. -Deep Thought, Jack Handy
- The problem with the world is that everyone is a few drinks behind.—Humphrey Bogart
- I drink to make other people interesting.—George Jean Nathan
- All right, brain, I don't like you and you don't like me. Let's just do this and I'll get back to killing you with beer.—Homer Simpson.

Proverb of the day.

"Sometimes when I reflect on all the beer I drink I feel ashamed. Then I look into the glass and think about the workers at the brewery and all of their hopes and dreams. If I didn't drink this beer, they might be out of work and their dreams would be shattered. Then I say to myself, it is better that I drink this beer and let their dreams come true than be selfish and worry about me health.

A drunk staggers into a church after a heavy night of beer consumption and sits down in a confessional and says nothing. The bewildered priest coughs to attract his attention, but still the man says nothing. The priest knocks on the wall three times in a final attempt to get the man to speak.

The drunk replies: "No use knocking' mate, there's no paper in this one either.

Scary virus on the loose . . .

After worldwide strike of the "I LOVE YOU VIRUS", reports are already coming in that the virus is mutating into several stages.

Within the next few hours, expect to see:

- The original "I love you" virus
- The "I like you a lot" virus
- The "You're nice, but I just want to be friends" virus
- The "It's not you, it's me" virus
- The "Look, it was just a date ...don't get clingy" virus
- The "Okay, I think it's best if we don't have any more contact" virus
- The "It was late, I was drunk, you were easy" virus
- The "Stop calling me, you unfeeling prick" virus

Plus:

- The "No, I Really Like You" Virus ... usually hits around midnight
- The "You're Beautiful ....." virus. usually hits about 2am
- The "Nothing has to happen. I just want to wake up with you in my arms" virus careful, it's a sly one.

- The "You're OK but I was wondering if your friend is single" virus
- The "Of course I'll phone you. Now do you want me to call a cab for you?".......... Hmm, that'll hit anytime between 3am & noon.

The following is an actual excerpt from this month's Forbes Magazine:

A herd of buffalo can only move as fast as the slowest buffalo, and when the herd is hunted, it is the slowest and weakest ones at the back that are killed first. This natural selection is good for the herd as a whole because the general speed and health of the whole is maintained or even improved by the regular culling of the weakest members.

In much the same way, the human brain can operate only as fast as the slowest brain cells through which the electrical signals pass.

Recent epidemiological studies have shown that while excessive intake of alcohol kills off brain cells, it attacks the slowest and weakest brain cells first.

Thus, regular consumption of beer helps eliminate the weaker cells, constantly making the brain a faster and more efficient machine.

The result of this in-depth study verifies and validates the causal link between all-weekend parties and job related performance. It also explains why, after a few short years of leaving university and getting married, most professionals cannot keep up with the performance of the new graduates.

Only those few that stick to the strict regimen of voracious alcoholic consumption can maintain the intellectual levels that they achieved during their university years.

So, this is a call to arms. As our country is losing its technological edge we should not shudder in our homes. Get back into the bars quaff that pint your company and country need you to be at your peak, and you shouldn't deny yourself the career that you could have.

Take life by the bottle and be all that you can be. Cheers

Yesterday scientists revealed that beer contains small traces of female hormones. To prove their theory, the scientists fed 100 men 12 pints of beer and observed that 100% of them gained weight, talked excessively without making sense, became emotional, couldn't drive, couldn't think, and refused to apologize when wrong.

No further testing is planned.

A couple of drinking buddies, who are airplane mechanics, are in the hanger at JFK New York; it's fogged and they have nothing to do.

One of them says to the other, "Man, have you got any bee' to drink?"

The other one says, "Nah, but I hear you can drink jet fuel, that will kind of give you a buzz." So they do drink it, get smashed and have a beautiful time; like only drinking buddies can do.

The following morning, one of them wakes up and he knows his head will explode if he gets up, but it doesn't. He gets up and feels good, in fact, he feels great- No hangover!

The phone rings, it's his buddy. The buddy says, "Hey, how do you feel?"

He said, "I feel great!!" The buddy says, "I feel great too!! You don't have a hangover?" He says, "No, that jet fuel is great stuff, no hangover, we ought to do this more often."

"Yeah, we could, but there's just one thing." "What's that?"

"Did you fart yet?" "No."

"Well, Don't, because I'm in Phoenix!"

Declan the humble crab and Kate the Lobster Princess were madly deeply and passionately in love. For months they enjoyed an idyllic relationship, until one day Kate scuttled over to Declan in tears.

"We can't see each other anymore," she sobbed. "Why?" gasped Declan.

"Daddy says that crabs are too common," she wailed." He claims you, a mere crab, and a poor one at that, are the lowest class of crustacean and that no daughter of his will marry someone who can only walk sideways."

Declan was shattered, and scuttled away into the darkness and to drink himself into a filthy state of aquatic oblivion.

That night the great Lobster ball was taking place. Lobsters came from far and wide dancing and merry making, but the lobster Princess refused to join in, choosing instead to sit by her father's side, inconsolable. Suddenly the doors burst open, and Declan the crab strode in. The Lobsters all stopped their dancing, the Princess gasped and the King Lobster rose from his throne.

Slowly, painstakingly, Declan the crab made his way across the floor and all could see that he was walking forward, one claw after another! Step by step he made his approach towards the throne, until he finally looked King lobster in the eye. There was a deadly hush.

Finally, the crab spoke. "Fuck, I'm pissed."

A man and his wife were sitting in the living room and he said to her, "Just so you know, I never want to live in a vegetative state, dependent on some machine and fluids from a bottle. If that ever happens, just pull the plug."

His wife got up, unplugged the TV and threw out all of his beer.

The five stages of drunkenness:

Stage 1—SMART

This is when you suddenly become an expert on every subject in the known universe. You know you know everything and you want to pass on your knowledge to anyone who will listen. At this stage you are always RIGHT. And of course, the person you are talking to is very WRONG. This makes for an interesting argument when both parties are SMART.

Stage 2—GOOD LOOKING

This is when you realise that you are the BEST LOOKING person in the entire bar and that people fancy you. You can go up to a perfect stranger knowing they fancy you and really want to talk to you. Bear in mind that you are still SMART, so you can talk to this person about any subject under the sun.

Stage 3—RICH

This is when you suddenly become the richest person in the world. You can buy drinks for the entire bar because you have an armoured truck full of money parked behind the bar. You can also make bets at this stage, because of course you're still SMART, so naturally, you will win all your bets. It doesn't matter how much you bet 'cos you are RICH. You will also buy drinks for everyone that you fancy, because you are now the BEST LOOKING person in the world.

Stage 4—BULLET PROOF

You are now ready to pick fights with anyone and everyone, especially those with whom you have been betting or arguing. This is because nothing can hurt you. At this point you can also go up to the partners of the people who you fancy and challenge them to a battle of the wits or money. You have no fear of losing this battle, because you are SMART, you're RICH and Hell, you're Better Looking than them anyway!

Stage 5—INVISIBLE

This is the final stage of Drunkenness. At this point you can do anything, because NO ONE CAN SEE YOU, You dance on a table to impress the people who you fancy because the rest of the people in the room cannot see you. You are also invisible to the person who wants to fight you. You can walk through the street singing at the top of your lungs because no one can see or hear you and because you're still SMART you know ALL the words.

The Five stages of Hangover

Stage 1—Stupid

As you regain consciousness and begin to enjoy a flood of sensations only dimly remembered from previous hangovers, such as the pneumatic drill headache, cloying nausea and Guinness/ Tetley/ Baileys/[add tipple most consumed night before] two-Step, you realise that you have lost not only several hours of your life but the ability to concentrate on anything. You are now officially stupid and will probably stay stupid until you get onto your third bacon sandwich.

Stage 2—Ugly

Never entirely happy with the comic effects of the bathroom mirror first thing you are horrified to discover that you have now become even less attractive than you thought previously possible. Not only has the combined effect of the booze and smoky/sweaty atmosphere given you a glorious collection of spots but you've either left your makeup on overnight or are shaking so much that you now look like you've shaved with a sanding block! Unfortunately you are still too stupid to know better than to try paper over the cracks.

Stage 3—Poor

Having crawled out of bed and got dressed you are about to shamble out the door when you discover that the money you got from the cashpoint to last you the entire week is missing. You have no idea what happened to it but the smell of curry on your coat/duvet leads you to suspect that you may have treated an entire rugby team to curry and lagers at some point, alternatively your pocket will have been picked or you will have given the taxi driver a $50 note by mistake. Rationalising that you couldn't possibly have been that stupid and that you would remember being mugged, you come to believe that you were the only one who bought any drinks all night and start to loathe all humanity.

Stage 4—Made of Glass

As you are now a stupid, ugly and poor sociopath, you embody most of the characteristics you hate in other people and your self-respect plummets. Your already fragile physical condition is made worse by this until you think you are likely to melt or shatter if handled at all roughly.

Stage 5—Circus Freak

Luckily, any non-hung-over person can spot this condition and its cause from a great distance. Even better, they know that they can complete your misery by parading you in front of your colleagues/family/friends, shouting at you and insisting that you drink things with whole eggs and Worcestershire sauce in or eat greasy food as "it's the only thing that will make you feel better". You are too stupid to know where to hide and too conspicuously ugly to get away with it, too poor to buy alka seltzer and too fragile to hit them.

"DRINKING" WEEK—PART III the Official Drinking Scale

The starting phases are applicable to both lads and lasses but after about stage 7 the lads are on their own. Lasses would have gone home weeks earlier.

THE OFFICIAL DRINKING SCALE

0—Stone cold sober. Brain as sharp as an army bayonet.

1—Still sober. Pleasure senses activated. Feeling of wellbeing.

2—Beer warming up head. Chips are ordered. Barmaid/Barman complimented on choice of blouse/shirt.

3—Crossword in newspaper is filled in. After a while blanks are filled with random letters and numbers.

4—Barmaid/Barman complimented on choice of bra/undies. Partially visible when bending to get packets of crisps. Try to instigate conversation about bras/underwear. Order half a dozen packets of crisps one by one.

5—Have brilliant discussion with a guy/gal at bar. Devise foolproof scheme for winning lottery, sort out cricket/tennis/football/boyfriend/diet/problems. Agree people are same world over except for the bloody French.

6—Feel like a demigod. Map out rest of life on beer mat. Realise that everybody loves you. Ring up parents and tell them you love them. Ring girlfriend/boyfriend to tell her/him you love her/him and he/she still has an amazing arse.

7—Send drinks over to woman sitting at table with boyfriend. No reaction. Scribble out message of love on five beer mats and Frisbee them to her across the room. Boyfriend asks you outside. You buy him a Long Island Iced Tea. (Only applicable for fellows—girls just don't do things like this.)

8—Some slurring. Offer to buy drinks for everyone in room. Lots of people say yes. Go round the pub hugging them one by one. Fall over. Get up.

9—Headache kicks in. Beer tastes off. Send it back. Beer comes back tasting same. Say "that's much better". Fight nausea by trying to play fruit machine for ten minutes before seeing out of order sign.

10—Some doubling of vision. Stand on table shouting abuse at all four barmen. Talked down by barmen's wives, who you offer to give a baby to. (Again a very bloke thing—girls would be doing this to barman). Fall over. Get up. Fall over. Impale head on corner of table. Fail to notice oozing head wound.

11—Speech no longer possible. Eventually manage to find door. Sit and take stock. Realise you are sitting in pub cellar, having taken a wrong turn. Vomit. Pass out.

12—Put in taxi by somebody. Give home address. Taken home. Can't get key in door. Realise you've given address of local football club. Generally pleased at way evening has gone. Pass out again.

TOTALLY SOBER.

---

starkle starkle little twink

who the hell you are I think

I'm not under what you call

the alcofluence of incohol

I'm just a little slort of sheep
I'm not drunk like tinkle peep
I don't know who is me yet
but the drunker I stand here
the longer I get
Just give me one more drink
to fill me cup
'coz I got all day sober
to Sunday up

---

25 Reasons why beer is better than women

1. You can enjoy a beer all month long
2. Beer stains wash out
3. You don't have to wine and dine a beer
4. Your beer will always wait patiently for you in the car while you play football
5. When your beer goes flat you toss it out and get another one
6. Beer is never late
7. A beer doesn't get jealous when you grab another beer
8. Hangovers go away
9. Beer labels come off without a fight
10. When you go to a bar you know you can always pick up a beer
11. Beer never has a headache

12. After you're finished with a beer the bottle is still worth five cents
13. A beer won't get upset if you come home with another beer
14. If you pour a beer right you'll always get good head
15. A beer always goes down easy
16. You can always share a beer with friends
17. You know you're always the first one to pop a beer
18. Beer is always wet
19. Beer doesn't demand equality
20. You can have a beer in public
21. A beer doesn't care what time you come home
22. A frigid beer is a good beer
23. You don't have to wash a beer before it tastes good
24. If you change beers you don't have to pay maintenance

CHAPTER 3

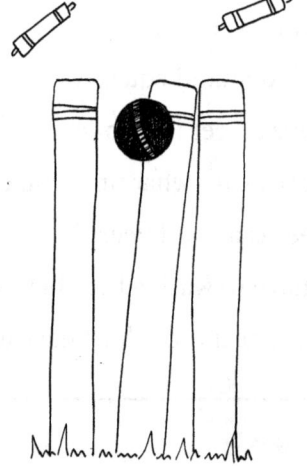

C is for Cricket

News just in.....

In a shock move England cricket selectors have called up Paula Yates as the new team coach. Outgoing coach David Lloyd said "Her experience of screwing Australians and bringing home the ashes will be invaluable".

Q. What is the height of optimism?

A. An Indian batsman putting on sunscreen.

Q. What would Australia's 11 batsman be if he was an Indian?

A. An all-rounder.

Q. What is the main function of the Indian coach?

A. To transport the team from the hotel to the ground.

Q. What's the Indian version of a hat-trick?

A. Three runs in three balls.

Q. When does the cricket ball travel at its fastest in this Tour?

A. An Indian bowler's delivery flying towards the boundary.

Q. Why don't Indian fielders need pre-tour travel injections?

A. Because they never catch anything.

Q. What's the Indian version of LBW?

A. Lost, Beaten, Walloped.

Q. What do you call an Indian with 100 runs against his name?

A. A bowler.

Q. What's the most proficient form of footwork displayed by Indian batsmen?

A. The walk back to the pavilion.

Q. What did Tendulkar say after the India-Australia match?

A. Shaken but not stirred

Q. What did Tendulkar say after the India-Pakistan match?

A. Massacred but not killed ....we're not worried

Q. What do Indian batsmen and drug addicts have in common?

A. Both spend most of their time wondering where their next score will come from.

Q. Who spent the most time on the crease of anyone in the Indian touring party?

A. The lady who ironed the cricket whites.

Q. What do Indian bowlers put in their hands to make sure the next ball almost always takes a wicket?

A. A bat

Q. Why are Indian cricketers cleverer than Houdini?

A. Because they can get out without even trying.

Q. Why were Indian batsmen looking forward to the new millennium?

A. So they can at least say they passed a century.

Edward took his blonde girlfriend to a test match. Not only did she not understand the game, she was completely bored. After tea, a batsman hit a powerful six over the long on boundary. "Thank heavens! Now they got rid of the ball!" she shouted in delight. "Now we can all go home!"

Billy was at school this morning and the teacher asked all the children what their Father's did for a living. All the typical answers came out, Fireman, Policeman, Salesman, Chippy, Captain of Industry, etc. but Billy was being uncharacteristically quiet, and so the teacher asked him about his Father.

'My Father is an exotic dancer in a gay club and takes off all his clothes in front of the other men. Sometimes if the offer is really good he'll go out with a man, rent a cheap hotel room and let them sleep with him'.

The teacher quickly set the other children some work and took little Billy aside to ask if that was really true. 'No' said Billy 'he plays cricket for England, but I was just too embarrassed to say'.

BOOKIES PAID BRADMAN TO THROW HIS LIFE

Mumbai, Thursday

The cricket world is again in turmoil following reports that Sir Donald Bradman accepted money from bookmakers to throw his own life.

The world-renown batsman was looking very comfortable on 92 when he suddenly died. The death has raised the suspicions of Indian police who thought it was unusual for Bradman not to reach 100.

"If you watch replays of the death very closely," said one police investigator, "you'll notice how dubious it looks. In all his life, he'd never once died before. It's completely out of character."

The international Cricket Committee has questioned whether the coroners were too quick to attribute the death to pneumonia. The ICC thinks they should instead have called on the third coroner to give the decision.

The possibility that Bradman was involved in death-fixing has indelibly shaken the Australian Test team. "I always thought I was our county's only corruptible player," said Mark Waugh.

It's believed Waugh recently received some new cash payments in return for providing corruption information to police. Waugh was interviewed extensively last night about a man who approached Bradman shortly before his death, and who only identified himself as "James." Police were told by Waugh that this was just the Prime Minister.

Spin bowler Shane Warne was also approached by the police, but declined to answer their questions. He told them he had nothing but the utmost respect for Bradman, whom he described as Australia's greatest ever f*cking arsey c*nt.

Former Text captain Mark Taylor also paid tribute to the late Sir Donald, vowing to kill himself when he turns 92 so as to never outdo the Bradman legacy.

MUMBAI, Thursday:

Following the crushing defeat of India in the first test, the International Cricket Council has imposed a new set of rules to make the contest more even. The new rules were formulated in conjunction with James Miller, 9, of Haberfield and his school friends.

As a result, India has been granted an electric wicketkeeper, freeing up wicket keeper Nayan Mongia to defend the boundary. Under the rule, Australian batsmen will be deemed out "caught behind" if the ball snicks their bat and lands in the immediate area behind the wicket.

The rule is a compromise from the original Indian proposal which had pushed for electric slips as well. The ICC refused that request on the grounds that "someone has to go and get the ball when an Australian misses it."

In addition, Australia is under strict "tip and run" restrictions which require they take a run off every ball they hit. Following his performance in the first test Australian wicketkeeper Adam Gilchrist has "six and out" restrictions imposed on him. As well, following complaints from Indian fielder, Gilchrist will have to get the ball if it goes across the road.

Instead of using a bat, Hayden will now be obliged to use his arm with jumper wrapped around it.

New rules for India include "one hand, one bounce" while they are fielding, and the provision of "last man carries" when they are batting. Australian captain Steve Waugh has vigorously opposed the "last man carries" rule and has launched an appeal. Waugh says Australia will only agree to the rule if there are electric wickets at the end, allowing Aussie fielders to throw to the stumps at either end.

A spokesperson for the ICC also announced that following six successive ducks "from now on Ajit Agarkar can't get out for a duck and no Indian batsman can get out in their first over at the crease". Indian medium pacer Ajit Agarkar will also be allowed to wrap the ball's seam with electrical tape in the second innings. The spokesperson added there will be "no LBW" for Indian batsmen unless it is really obvious."

Glenn McGrath has conceded that it's "fair enough" that he has to bowl underarm to India's tail end as long as they're not molly grabbers. Despite the changes, Australia remains firm favourites going into the Second Test, paying $112, while an Indian win is currently paying $13 trillion.

Michael Vaughan and Andrew [Freddie] Flintoff, now elderly, 85 and 82 years old, are sitting on a park bench outside Lord's cricket ground feeding pigeons and talking about cricket, past Ashes series, and tours like they do every day.

Michael turns to Freddie and asks, 'Do you think there's cricket in heaven?'

Flintoff thinks about it for a minute and replies, 'I don't know. But let's make an agreement: if I die first, I'll come back and tell you if there's cricket in heaven, and if you die first, you do the same.' They shake hands on it. Sadly, a few months later, poor Freddie passes on.

One day soon afterward, Vaughan is sitting there feeding the pigeons by himself when he hears a voice whisper, 'Michael................Michael'

Vaughan responds, 'Freddie, is that you?' Yes it is, Michael, 'whispers Freddie's ghost.

Vaughan, still amazed, enquires, 'So, is there cricket in heaven? 'Well, 'says Freddie, 'I've got good news and bad news.'

'Give me the good news first, 'says Vaughan.

Freddie opines, 'Well... there is cricket in heaven.'

Vaughan says, 'That's great! What news could be bad enough to ruin that?'

Freddie sighs and whispers, 'You are going to open the innings this Friday.'

A blonde woman ran into a police station wailing. She claimed that she had been raped. After she stopped sobbing, the Police Officer requested her for a description of the rapist. "He was tall and dressed in white. He was wearing all sorts of protective pads, gloves and helmet." "Hmmm... he appears to be a cricketer," concluded the policeman. "Ah officer!" she confirmed, "then he must have been an English cricketer." "What makes you think that he was English? From the accent?" asked the officer. "No sir," she replied, "he just didn't stay in very long."

CHAPTER 4

D is for Darwin Awards

A man in Alabama died from rattlesnake bites. Big deal you may say, but there's a twist here that makes him a candidate. It seems he and a friend were playing catch with a rattlesnake. You can guess what happened from here. The friend (a future Darwin Awards candidate) was hospitalized.

Not much was given to me on this unlucky fellow, but he qualifies nonetheless.

You see, there was a gentleman from Korea who was killed more or less. He was doing the usual "walking and by talking his cell phone" when he walked into a tree and managed to somehow break his neck.

Keep that in mind the next time you decide to drive and dial at the same time.

Several years ago, in a west Texas town, employees in a medium-sized warehouse noticed the smell of a gas leak. Sensibly, management evacuated the building, extinguishing all potential sources of ignition—lights, power, etc.

After the building had been evacuated, two technicians from the gas company were dispatched. Upon entering the building, they found they had difficulty navigating in the dark. To their frustration, none of the lights worked.

Witnesses later described the vision of one of the technicians reaching into his pocket, and retrieving an object that resembled a lighter. Upon operation of the lighter-like object, the gas in the warehouse exploded, sending pieces of it up to three miles away. Nothing was found of the technicians, but the lighter was virtually untouched by the explosion. The technician that was suspected of causing the explosion had never been thought of as "bright" by his peers.

When a 40-year old man turned up at a hospital asking to see a doctor specialising in men's troubles, he was shown into a cubicle, where he gingerly unwrapped three yards of foul smelling stained gauze from around his scrotum, which had swollen to twice the size of a grapefruit.

On further inspection, it was discovered that his left testicle was missing completely, and, embedded within the swollen, tender and weeping wound, were a number of dark objects which the patient confessed were one inch staple nails from an industrial staple gun.

It transpired that the man spent his lunchtimes alone in his workshop, where he regularly enjoyed the sexual thrill of placing his penis on the moving canvas fan-belt of a piece of machinery. One day, the excitement had caused him to lose his concentration, and the fan-belt had snatched his scrotum into the fly-wheel, throwing him several feet across the floor tearing off his left nut.

Rather than go to the hospital, he performed first-aid on himself with the stapling gun, then went back to work when his colleagues returned. It was two weeks before he got around to visiting the hospital.

- WILL THE REAL DUMMY PLEASE STAND UP?

AT&T fired President John Walter after nine months, saying he lacked intellectual leadership. He received a $26 million severance package.

Perhaps it's not Walter who's lacking intelligence.

- WITH A LITTLE HELP FROM OUR FRIENDS!

Police in Oakland, California spent two hours attempting to subdue a gunman who had barricaded himself inside his home. After firing ten tear gas canisters, officers discovered that the man was standing beside them, shouting out to give himself up.

- WHAT WAS PLAN B?

An Illinois man, pretending to have a gun, kidnapped a motorist and forced him to drive to two different automated teller machines. The kidnapper then proceeded to withdraw money from his own bank account.

- SOME DAYS, IT JUST DOESN'T PAY!

Fire investigators on Maui have determined the cause of a blaze that destroyed a $127,000 home last month—a short in the homeowner's newly installed fire prevention alarm system." This is even worse than last year," said the distraught homeowner "when someone broke in and stole my new security system ..."

- THE GETAWAY

A man walked into a Topeka, Kansas Kwik Shop and asked for all the money in the cash drawer. Apparently, the take was too small so he tied up the store clerk and worked the counter himself for three hours until police showed up and grabbed him.

- DO-IT-YOURSELF BRAIN SURGERY?

In Ohio, an unidentified man in his late twenties walked into a police station with a 9-inch wire protruding from his forehead and calmly asked officers to give him an X-ray to help him find his brain, which he claimed had been stolen. Police were shocked to learn that the man had drilled a 6-inch deep hole in his skull with a Black & Decker power drill and had stuck the wire in to try and find the missing brain.

- DID I SAY THAT?

Police in Los Angeles had good luck with a robbery suspect who just couldn't control himself during a line-up. When detectives asked each man in the line-up to repeat the words,

"Give me all your money or I'll shoot", the man shouted, that's not what I said!

- OUCH, THAT'S SMART

A bank robber in Virginia Beach got a nasty surprise when a dye pack designed to mark stolen money exploded in his Fruit-of-the-Looms. The robber apparently stuffed the loot down the front of his pants as he was running out the door." He was seen hopping and jumping around with an explosion taking place inside his pants," said police spokesman Mike Carey. Police have the man's charred trousers in custody.

- ARE WE COMMUNICATING?

A man spoke frantically into the phone, 'My wife is pregnant and her contractions are only two minutes apart!" "Is this her first child? The doctor asked." No, you idiot!" the man shouted, "this is her husband"

- NOT THE SHARPEST KNIFE IN THE DRAWER!

In Modesto, CA, Steven Richard King was arrested for trying to hold up a Bank of America branch without a weapon. King used a thumb and a finger to simulate a gun but unfortunately be failed to keep his hand in his pocket.

Latest Darwin Award nominees:

- A young Canadian man, searching for a way of getting drunk cheaply because he had no money to buy alcohol, mixed gasoline with milk. Not surprisingly, this concoction made him ill, and he vomited into the fireplace in his house. The resulting explosion and fire burned his house down, killing both him and his sister.

- A 34 yr. old white male found dead in the basement of his home died of suffocation, police said. He was approximately 6' 2" and 225 lb. He was wearing a pleated skirt, white bra, black and white saddle shoes, and a woman's wig. It appeared that he was trying to create a schoolgirl's uniform look. He was also wearing a military gas mask that had the filter canister removed and a rubber hose attached in its place. The other end of the hose was connected to a hollow wooden section of bedpost approximately 12 inches long and 3 inches in diameter. This bedpost was inserted into his rear end for reasons unknown, and was the cause of his suffocation. Police found the task of explaining the circumstances of his death to his family members "very awkward".

- Three Brazilian were flying in a light aircraft at low altitude when another plane approached. It appears they decided to "moon" the occupants of the other plane, but lost control of the plane and crashed. They were all found dead in the wreckage with their pants around their ankles.

- A police officer in Ohio responded to a call that was made to 911. She had no details before arriving except that someone was reporting that his father was not breathing. Upon arrival, the officer found the man face down on the couch, naked. When she rolled him over to check for a pulse and to start CPR if necessary, she noticed burn marks around his genitals. After the ambulance arrived and removed the man (who turned out to be dead on arrival at hospital), the police made a closer inspection of the couch, and noticed that the man had made a hole between the cushions. Upon flipping the couch over they discovered what caused his death. Apparently the man had a habit of putting his penis between the cushions, down into the hole and between two electric sanders (with the sandpaper removed for obvious reasons). According to the story, after his orgasm the ... ahem ... discharge shorted out one of the sanders, electrocuting him to death.

- LOS ANGELES—Police officials would not release the name of a Pacoima man who was found dead yesterday after responding to complaints from neighbours that a bad smell was coming from his apartment. Upon entering the apartment, officers were surprised to see that every square inch of the apartment, including appliances and even the inside of the toilet were covered with pornographic images cut from magazines. "The visual effect was very unsettling," said Officer Hardy of the Pacoima Police." Because everything looked the same, you could not tell where one wall ended and a doorway began. "The surprises did not end there, however. Police described the man as having "concocted a wire frame around his head" upon which he had taped various pornographic images, apparently so he could freely move about his apartment without ever losing his close-up view of nude bodies. Small slits had been cut into the paper so he could find his way, but according to Hardy, "He had almost no peripheral vision. He could barely see a thing. "The man was found nude with this wire frame entangled in a hanging lamp." We think he had been dusting," said another police officer, "because a feather duster was lying nearby, and his head gear had somehow become caught in the lamp, which was chained to the ceiling." The man allegedly choked to death trying to extricate himself from his predicament. According to his apartment manager, the white male in his mid-30s never left his apartment, and had food delivered weekly. Funeral services are planned for next week. His next of kin requested that his name be withheld.

- A 27 year-old French woman lost control over her car on a highway near Marseilles and crashed into a tree, seriously injuring her passenger and killing her. As a commonplace road accident, this would not have qualified for a Darwin nomination were it not for the fact that the driver's attention had been distracted by her Tamagotchi key ring, which had started urgently beeping for food as she drove along. In attempting to press the correct buttons to save the Tamagotchi's life, the woman lost her own.

- A 22-year-old Reston man was found dead yesterday after he tried to use occy straps (the stretchy little ropes with hooks on each end) to bungee jump off a 70-foot railroad trestle, police said. Fairfax County police said Eric A. Barcia, a fast-food worker, taped a bunch of these straps together, wrapped an end around one foot, anchored the other end to the trestle at Lake Accotink Park, jumped and hit the pavement. Warren Carmichael, a police spokesman, said investigators think Barcia was alone because his car was found nearby. "The length of the cord that he had assembled was greater than the distance between the trestle and the ground" Carmichael said. Police say the apparent cause of death was "major trauma."

- Three young men in Oklahoma were enjoying the coming fourth of July holiday and wanted to apparently test fire some fireworks. Their only problem was that their launch pad and seating arrangement reveal hundred thousand gallon fuel distillation storage tank. Oddly some fumes were ignited, producing a fireball seen for miles and miles. They were launched, no doubt, countless thousands of feet into the air and were found dead 250 yards from their respective seats.

The long awaited return of this year's idiots. Yes, the one we've all been waiting for the Darwin Awards.

The candidates have finally been released! For those not familiar with the Darwin Award, It's an annual honour given to the person who provided the Universal human gene pool the biggest service by getting KILLED in the most extraordinarily stupid way.

As always, competition this year has been keen again. Some candidates appear to have trained their whole lives for this event!

DARWIN AWARD CANDIDATES

1. In September in Detroit, a 41-year-old man got stuck and drowned in two feet of water after squeezing head first through an 18-inch-wide sewer grate to retrieve his car keys.

2. In October, a 49-year-old San Francisco stockbroker, who "totally zoned when he ran," accidentally jogged off a 100-foot-high cliff on his daily run.

3. Buxton, NC: A man died on a beach when an 8-foot-deep hole he had dug into the sand caved in as he sat inside it. Beach goers said Daniel Jones, 21, dug the hole for fun, or protection from the wind, and had been sitting in a beach chair at the bottom Thursday afternoon when it collapsed, burying him beneath 5 feet of sand. People on the beach, on the outer banks, used their hands and shovels, trying to claw their way to Jones, a resident of Woodbridge, VA, but could not reach him. It took rescue workers using heavy equipment almost an hour to free him while about 200 people looked on. Jones was pronounced dead at a hospital.

4. In February, Santiago Alvarado, 24, was killed in Lompoc, CA, as he fell face-first through the ceiling of bicycle shop he was burglarizing. Death was caused when the long flashlight he had placed in his mouth

(to keep his hands free) rammed into the base of his skull as he hit the floor.

5. According to police in Dahlonega, GA, ROTC cadet Nick Berrena, 20, was stabbed to death in January by fellow cadet Jeffrey Hoffman, 23, who was trying to prove that a knife could not penetrate the flak vest Berrena was wearing.

6. Sylvester Briddell, Jr., 26, was killed in February in Selbyville, Del, as he won a bet with friends who said he would not put a revolver loaded with four bullets into his mouth and pull the trigger.

7. In February, according to police in Windsor, Ontario, Daniel Kolta, 27, and Randy Taylor, 33, died in a head-on collision, thus earning a tie in the game of chicken they were playing with their snowmobiles.

DARWIN AWARD HONORABLE MENTIONS

1. In Guthrie, Okla., in October, Jason Heck tried to kill a millipede with a shot from his 22 calibre rifle, but the bullet ricocheted off a rock near the hole and hit pal Antonio Martinez in the head, fracturing his skull.

2. In Elyria, Ohio, in October, Martyn Eskins, attempting to clean out cobwebs in his basement, declined to use a broom in favour of a propane torch and caused a fire that burned the first and second floors of his house.

3. Paul Stiller, 47, was hospitalized in Andover Township, NJ, and his wife Bonnie was also injured, when a quarter-stick of dynamite blew up in their car. While driving around at 2 AM, the bored couple lit the dynamite and tried to toss it out the window to see what would happen, but apparently failed to notice the window was closed.

RUNNER UP

TACOMA, WA—Kerry Bingham, had been drinking with several friends when one of them said they knew a person who had bungee-jumped from the Tacoma Narrows Bridge in the middle of traffic. The conversation grew more heated and at least 10 men trooped along the walkway of the bridge at 4:30 am.

Upon arrival at the midpoint of the bridge they discovered that no one had brought a bungee rope. Bingham, who had continued drinking, volunteered and pointed out that a coil of lineman's cable lay nearby. One end of the cable was secured around Bingham's leg and the other end was tied to the bridge.

His fall lasted 40 feet before the cable tightened and tore his foot off at the ankle. He miraculously survived his fall into the icy river water and was rescued by two nearby fishermen. "All I can say," said Bingham is that God was watching out for me on that night.

There's just no other explanation for it. Bingham's foot was never located.

AND THE WINNER

PADERBORN, GERMANY—Overzealous zookeeper Friedrich Riesfeldt fed his constipated elephant Stefan 22 doses of animal Laxatove and more than a bushel of berries, figs and prunes before the plugged-up pachyderm finally let it fly, and suffocated the keeper under 200 pounds of poop!

Investigators say ill-fated Friedrich, 46, was attempting to give the wailing elephant an olive oil enema when the relieved beast unloaded on him. The sheer force of the elephant's unexpected defecation knocked Mr. Riesfeldt to the ground, where he struck his head on a rock and lay unconscious as the elephant continued to evacuate his bowels on top of him," said flabbergasted Paderborn police detective Erik Dern." With no one there to help him, he lay under all that dung for at least an hour before a watchman came along, and during that time he suffocated. It seems to be just one of those freak accidents that happen."

Fire Authorities in California found a corpse in a burnt out section of dive forest while assessing the damage done by a forest fire. The deceased male was dressed in a full wet suit, complete with a tank, flippers, and face mask. A post-mortem examination revealed that the person died not from burns but from massive internal injuries.

Dental records provided a positive identification. Investigators then set about determining how a fully clad diver ended up in the middle of a forest fire.

It was revealed that, on the day of the fire, the person went diving trip off the coast of the forest.

The firefighters, seeking to control the fire as quickly as possible, called in a fleet of helicopters with very large buckets. The buckets were dropped into the ocean for rapid filling, then flown to forest some 20 miles away from the fire and emptied.

You guessed it. One minute our diver was making like Flipper Pacific, the next he was doing a breaststroke in a fire bucket feet in the air. Apparently, he extinguished exactly 5'10" of fire.

Every year the US FBI is asked investigate over 36000 serious crimes including Murder/Homicides. Every year the Homicide Investigations unit puts out its "Top Homicides of the Year" – some recent examples:

1. Alex Mijtus, 36 years old, is killed by his wife, armed with a 20" long vibrator. Mrs Mijtus had had enough of her husband's strange sex practices and one night during a

prolonged evening of "fun" she snapped, pushing all of the vibrator into Alex's anus until it ruptured several internal organs and caused severe bleeding.

2. Debby Mills-Newbroughton, 99 years old, was killed as she crossed the road. She was to turn 100 the next day, but crossing the road with her daughter to go to her own birthday party her wheel chair was hit by the truck delivering her birthday cake.

3. Peter Stone, 42 years old, is murdered by his 8 year old daughter, who he had just sent to her room with no dinner. Young Samantha Stone felt that if she couldn't have dinner no one should, and she promptly inserted 72 rat poison tablets into her father's coffee as he prepared dinner. The victim took one slip and promptly collapsed. (Samantha Stone was given a suspended sentence as the judge felt she didn't realise what she was doing, until she tried to poison her mother using the same method one month later.)

4. David Danil, 17 years old, was killed by his girlfriend after he attempted to "have his way with her" his unwelcome advance was met with a prompt kick in the chest and then 4 shots from a doubled barrelled shotgun Charla's (the girlfriends') father had given to her an hour before the date started, just in case.

5. Xavier Halos, 27 years old, was killed by his landlord for failing to pay his rent for 8 years (yes 8 years). The Landlord Kirk Weston clubbed the victim to death with a toilet seat after he realised just how long it had been since Mr Halos paid his rent.

6. Mary-Lee Cooper, 11 years old, was killed by her 1 year old sister who climbed on top of her while she was sleeping, suffocating her.

7. Meegan Fri, 44 years old, was killed by 14 state troopers after she wandered onto a live firing, fake town simulation. Seeing the troopers all walking slow down the street Meegan

Fri has jumped out in front of them and yelled. "Boo!" The troopers, thinking she was a pop up target fired 67 shots between them, over 40 of them hitting their target. "She just looked like a very real looking target." One of the troopers stated in his report.

8. Louis Zaragoza, 68 years old, was killed as he prepared to drive to work. Lee Zaragoza, had been plotting to kill him for over a year, and had cut the brakes on his car 4 times previously. On this attempt Lee was just about to cut the brakes again when Louis snuck up behind her, he grabbed her and spun her around, as he did she lost her footing and stumbled into him, stabbing him in the lower ventricle of the heart, killing him instantly

9. Mummod Foli, 22 years old, was killed by an unknown member of the Russian Mafia, after he accidentally took away the gangsters drink too soon at the nightclub he worked in. The gangster was so upset he forced the waiter to drink over 27 litres of 'coca cola' (the drink he had taken away) until Mummod drowned.

10. Julia Smeeth, 20 years old, was killed by her brother Michael because she talked on the phone too long, Michael clubbed his sister to death with a cordless phone, then stabbed her several times with the broken aerial.

11. Helena Sinnns, wife to the famous American Nuclear Scientist Harold Sinnns was killed by her husband after she had an affair with the neighbour. Over a period of 3 months Harold substituted Helena's eye shadow with a Uranium composite that was highly radioactive, until she died of radiation poisoning. Although she suffered many symptoms, including total hair loss, skin welts, blindness, extreme nausea and even had an ear lobe drop off the victim never attended a doctor's surgery or hospital for a check-up.

12. Military sergeant John Joe Winter killed his two-timing wife by loading her car with Trinitrate explosive (similar to

C4) the Ford Taurus she was driving was filled with 750 000 kgs of explosive, forming a force twice as powerful as the Oklahoma Bombing. The explosion was witnessed by several persons, some up to 14 kilometres away. No trace of the car or the victim were ever found. Only a 55 metre deep crater, and 500m of missing road.

13. Patty Winter, 35 years old, was killed by her neighbour in the early hours of a Sunday morning. Her neighbour, Falt Hame, for years had a mounted F6 phantom jet engine in his rear yard. He would fire the jet engine, aimed at an empty block at the back of his property. Patty Winter would constantly complain to the local sheriff's officers about the noise and the potential risk of fire. Mr Hame was served with a notice to remove the engine immediately. Not liking this he invited Miss Winter over for a cup of coffee and a chat about the whole situation. What Winter didn't know was that he had changed the position of the engine, as she walked into the yard he activated it, hitting her with a blast of 5000 degrees, killing her instantly, and forever burning her outline into the driveway.

14. Michael Lewis, angry at his gay boyfriend used the movie, Diehard, with a Vengeance, as inspiration. He drugged his boyfriend, Tony Berry, into an almost catatonic state, then dressed him only in a double sided white board that read Death to all Nigers! On one side, and God love the KKK. On the other, Lewis then drove the victim to down town Harlem and dropped him off. Two minutes later Berry was deceased.

15. Jay Newton was killed after a co-worker at Sea World Florida dropped a 20 tonne killer whale on him. The whale had been hoisted out of his tank by a Master Tonne Crane, when the victim swam underneath to inspect the harness his colleague, Brian Hartley released the whale, crushing the victim instantly, (and emptying 1/4 the water from the pool)

16. Carl Densinter, 34 years old, was killed by a fellow worker trying to prove a point. The worker, San Amote Pet,

disconnected the internal landing gear settings on a Boeing 747 test plane, the planes gear automatically retracked after take-off. But come landing time wouldn't re-engage, the helpless Densinter couldn't do a thing as the plane ran out of fuel, in an attempt at an emergency landing the 747 exploded. Densinter was killed instantly.

17. Mary Dridely, Joseph Coles and Haven Gillies were killed as they walked past a New York apartment building, David Smee, 7 old, and his 6 year old sister were left alone in their 27th floor hotel room by their parents as they went to the hotels gaming room. Bored, the kids thought it'd be fun to try to squish the "Ant looking things on the foot path below." (i.e—people). They started by throwing fruit, then quickly graduated to chairs, televisions, even the drawers from the bedroom dresser.

18. Conrad Middleton, 26 years old, was killed by his twin brother Brian after a disagreement over who should take the family home after their parents past away. Conrad had a nasal problem, and had no sense of smell. After the argument Brian stormed out of the house, then snuck back later, and turned on the 3 gas taps in the house, filling it with gas. Then left out a box of cigars, a lighter and a note saying, "Sorry for the spree, have a puff on me, Brian". Conrad promptly lit a cigar, destroying the house, and himself in the process.

19. Gail Queens, 23 years old, was killed by her Zoo keeper boyfriend Matthew Kellaway after she refused sex. He 'invited her' to the zoo to see the lion feeding, and at feeding time lead her into a room that had a large slide away panel. He explained to her that it was a large glass viewing window to watch the lions devour their prey. He 'ducked out for a quick smoke' and locked her in the room. Suddenly the slide away panel opened to reveal many persons starring at her, she was just about to yell and tell them that they were on the wrong side of the glass when she realised that it was her on the wrong side. Another panel opened and 3 hungry lions

were let into the pen. Gail survived for 2 days in hospital before dying of massive internal injuries.

The true high point of the email year has arrived, yes it is the Darwin Awards. For those sheltered few of you who are not fully aware of the Darwin Awards. These awards are given annually (and posthumously) to those individuals who did the most for the human gene pool by removing themselves from it.

AND THE DARWIN AWARD WINNER IS ..."

THOMPSON, MANITOBA, CANADA.

Telephone relay company night watchman Edward Baker, 31, was killed early Christmas morning by excessive microwave radiation exposure. He was apparently attempting to keep warm next to a telecommunications feed-horn. Baker had been suspended on a safety violation once last year, according to Northern Manitoba Signal Relay spokesperson Tanya Cooke. She noted that Baker's earlier infraction was for defeating a safety shut-off switch and entering a restricted maintenance catwalk in order to stand in front of the microwave dish. He had told co-workers that it was the only way he could stay warm during his twelve-hour shift at the station, where winter temperatures often dip to forty below zero. Microwaves can heat water molecules within human tissue in the same way that they heat food in microwave ovens. For his Christmas shift, Baker reportedly brought a twelve pack of beer and a plastic lawn chair, which he positioned directly in line with the strongest microwave beam. Baker had not been told about a tenfold boost in microwave power planned that night to handle the anticipated increase in holiday long-distance calling traffic. Baker's body was discovered by the daytime watchman, John Burns, who was greeted by an odour he mistook for a Christmas roast he thought Baker must have prepared as a surprise. Burns also reported to NMSR company officials that Baker's unfinished beers had exploded.

DARWIN AWARD RUNNERS—UP:

#1—LOS ANGLES, CA. Ani Saduki, 33, and his brother decided to remove a bees' nest from a shed on their property with the aid of a pineapple. A pineapple is an illegal firecracker which is the explosive equivalent of one-half stick of dynamite. They ignited the fuse and retreated to watch from inside their home, behind a window some 10 feet away from the hive/shed. The concussion of the explosion shattered the window inwards, seriously lacerating Ani. Deciding Mr Saduki needed stitches, the brothers headed out to go to a nearby hospital. While walking towards their car, Ani was stung three times by the surviving bees. Unbeknownst to either brother, Ani was allergic to bee venom, and died of suffocation en-route to the hospital.

#2—Derrick L. Richards, 28, was charged in April in Minneapolis with third-degree murder in the death of his beloved cousin, Kenneth E. Richards. According to police, Derrick suggested a game of Russian roulette and put a semiautomatic pistol (instead of the more traditional revolver) to Ken's head and fired.

#3—PHILLIPSBURG, NJ. An unidentified 29 year old male choked to death on a sequined panty he had orally removed from an exotic dancer at a local establishment. "I didn't think he was going to eat it," the dancer identified only as "Ginger" said, adding "He was really drunk."

#5—MOSCOW, Russia-A drunk security man asked a colleague at the Moscow bank they were guarding to stab his bulletproof vest to see if it would protect him against a knife attack. It didn't, and the 25-year-old guard died of a heart wound. (It's good to see the Russians getting into the spirit of the Darwin Awards.)

#6—In FRANCE, Jacques LeFevrier left nothing to chance when he decided to commit suicide. He stood at the top of a tall cliff and tied a noose around his neck. He tied the other end of the rope to a large rock. He drank some poison and set fire to his clothes. He even tried to shoot himself at the last moment. He jumped and fired the pistol. The bullet missed him completely and cut through the rope above him. Free of the threat of hanging, he plunged into the sea. The sudden dunking extinguished the flames and made him vomit the poison. He was dragged out of the water by a kind fisherman and was taken to a hospital, where he died of hypothermia.

#7—RENTON, WASHINGTON, USA. A Renton, Washington man tried to commit a robbery. This was probably his first attempt, as suggested by the fact that he had no previous record of violent crime, and by his terminally stupid choices as listed below:

1. The target was H&J Leather & Firearms—a gun shop.
2. The shop was full of customers, in a state where a substantial portion of the adult population is licensed to carry concealed handguns in public places.
3. To enter the shop, he had to step around a marked Police patrol car parked at the front door.
4. An officer in uniform was standing next to the counter, having coffee before reporting to duty. Upon seeing the officer, the would-be robber announced a holdup and fired a few wild shots. The officer and a clerk promptly returned fire, removing him from the gene pool. Several other customers also drew their guns, but didn't fire. No one else was hurt.

Larry Walters of Los Angeles is one of the few to contend for the Darwin Awards and live to tell "I have fulfilled my

20-year dream," said Walters, a former truck driver for a company that makes TV commercials. "I'm staying on the ground. I've proved the thing works."

Larry's boyhood dream was to fly. But fates conspired to keep him from his dream. He joined the Air Force, but his eyesight disqualified him from the job of pilot. After he was discharged from the military, he sat in his backyard watching jets fly overhead.

He hatched his weather balloon scheme while sitting outside in his "extremely comfortable" Sears lawn chair. He bought 45 weather balloons from an Army-Navy surplus store, tied them to his tethered lawn chair dubbed the inspiration I the 4' diameter balloons with helium. Then he strapped himself into his lawn chair with some sandwiches, Miller Lite pellet gun. He figured he would pop a few of the many balloons when it was time to descend.

Larry's plan was to sever the anchor and lazily float up to a height of about 30 feet above his back yard, where he'd enjoy a few hours of flight before coming back down. But things didn't work out quite as Larry planned.

When his friends cut the cord anchoring the lawn chair to his Jeep, he did not float lazily up to 30 feet. Instead, he shot into the LA sky as if shot from a cannon, pulled by the lift of 42 helium balloons holding 33 cubic feet of helium he did not level off at 100 feet, nor did he level off at 1000 feet. After climbing and climbing, he levelled off at 16,000 feet.

At that height he felt he couldn't risk shooting any of the balloons, lest he unbalance the load and really find himself. So he stayed there, drifting cold and frightened with his beer and sandwiches, for more than 14 hours. He crossed approach corridor of LAX, where Trans World Airlines and Delta Airlines pilots radioed in reports of the strange signal.

Eventually he gathered the nerve to shoot a few balloons, and slowly descended. The hanging tethers tangled and in a power line, blacking out a Long Beach neighbourhood for 20 minutes. Larry climbed to safety, where he was met by waiting members of the LAPD. As he was led away in handcuffs, a reporter dispatched to cover the daring rescue and asked him why he had done it. Larry replied nonchalantly, "A man can't just sit around."

The Federal Aviation Administration was not amused. Safety Inspector Neal Savoy said, "We know he broke some of the Federal Aviation Act, and as soon as we decide which part it is, a charge will be filed."

Larry's efforts won him a $1,500 FAA fine, a prize from the Bonehead Club of Dallas, the altitude record for gas-filled clustered balloons, and a Darwin Awards Honourable Mention. He gave his aluminium lawn chair to admiring neighbourhood children, abandoned his truck driving job, and went onto the lecture circuit. He enjoyed some success as a motivational speaker, but said he never made much money from his innovative flight. He never married and had no children. Larry hiked into the forest and shot himself in the heart. He died at the age of 44.

CHAPTER 5

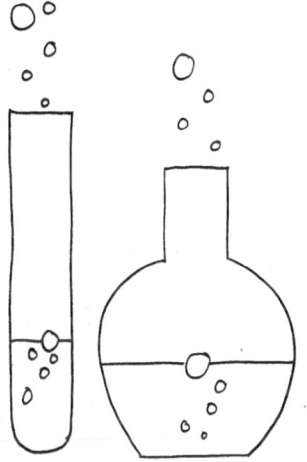

E is for Education

College entrance exam—football player version

Time Limit: 3 wks

1. What language is spoken in France?
2. Give a dissertation on the ancient Babylonian Empire with particular reference to architecture, literature, law and social conditions -OR- give the first name of Pierre Trudeau.
3. Would you ask William Shakespeare to:
   a. build a bridge
   b. sail the ocean
   c. lead an army or
   d. Write a Play
4. What religion is the Pope?
   a. Jewish
   b. Catholic
   c. Hindu
   d. Polish
   e. Agnostic

(check only one)

5. Metric conversion. How many feet is 0.0 meters?
6. What time is it when the big hand is on the 12 and the little hand is on the 5?
7. How many commandments was Moses given? (approximately)

8. What are people in America's far north called?
   a. Westerner
   b. Southerner
   c. Northerner
9. Spell Bush, Carter and Clinton
10. Six kings of England have been called George, the last one being George the Sixth. Name the previous five.
11. Where does rain come from?
    a. Macy's.
    b. 7-11
    c. Canada
    d. the sky
12. Can you explain Einstein's Theory of Relativity?
    a. yes
    b. no
13. What are coat hangers used for?
14. The Star Spangled Banner is the National Anthem for what country?
15. Explain Le Chateliers Principle of Dynamic Equilibrium -OR- Spell your name in BLOCK LETTERS
16. Where is the basement in a three story building located?
17. Which part of America produces the most oranges?
    a. New York
    b. Florida
    c. Canada
    d. Wisconsin

18. Advanced math. If you have three apples, how many apples do you have?

19. What does NBC (National Broadcasting Corporation) stand for?

20. The University of Pennsylvania's tradition for efficiency began when (approximately)?
    a. B.C.
    b. A.D.

21. Extra Credit—What is your name? (Please print clearly)

22. You must answer at least 3 questions correctly to qualify for this school.

An English teacher was explaining to his students the concept of gender association in the English language. He stated how hurricanes at one time were given feminine names and how ships and planes were usually referred to as "she." One of the students raised their hand and asked "What 'gender' is a computer?" The teacher wasn't certain which it was, so he divided the class into two groups, males in one, females in the other, and asked them to decide if computer should be masculine or feminine. Both groups were asked to give four reasons for their recommendation.

The group of women concluded that computers should be referred to in the masculine gender because:

1. In order to get their attention, you have to turn them on.
2. They have a lot of data but are still clueless.

3. They are supposed to help you solve your problems, but half the time they are the problem.

4. As soon as you commit to one, you realize that, if you had waited a little longer, you could have had a better model.

The men, on the other hand, decided that computers should definitely be referred to in the feminine gender because:

1. No one but their creator understands their internal logic.

2. The native language they use to communicate with other computers is incomprehensible to everyone else.

3. Even your smallest mistakes are stored in long-term memory for later retrieval.

4. As soon as you make a commitment to one, you find yourself spending half your pay check on accessories for it.

The following is an actual question given at a University of Washington midterm chemistry test. The answer was so "profound" that the professor shared it with colleagues, which is why we now have the pleasure of enjoying it as well.

Bonus Question: Is Hell exothermic (gives off heat) or endothermic (absorbs heat)?

Most of the students wrote proofs of their beliefs using Boyle's Law, (gas cools off when it expands and heats up when it is compressed) or some variant. One student, however, wrote the following:

First, we need to know how the mass of Hell is changing in time. So we need to know the rate that souls are moving into Hell and the rate they are leaving. I think that we can safely assume that once a soul gets to Hell, it will not leave. Therefore, no souls are leaving.

As for how many souls are entering Hell, let's look at the different religions that exist in the world today. Some of these religions state that if you are not a member of their religion, you will go to Hell. Since there are more than one of these religions and since people do not belong to more than one religion, we can project that all souls go to Hell.

With birth and death rates as they are, we can expect the number of souls in Hell to increase exponentially.

Now, we look at the rate of change of the volume in Hell because Boyle's Law states that in order for the temperature and pressure in Hell to stay the same, the volume of Hell has to expand as souls are added.

1. If Hell is expanding at a slower rate than the rate at which souls enter Hell, then the temperature and pressure in Hell will increase until all Hell breaks loose.

2. Of course, if Hell is expanding at a rate faster than the increase of souls in Hell, then the temperature and pressure will drop until Hell freezes over.

So which is it? If we accept the postulate given to me by Ms. Teresa Banyan during my Freshman year, "that it will be a cold day in Hell before I sleep with you", and take into account the fact that I still have not succeeded in having sexual relations with her, then, #2 cannot be true, and thus I am sure that Hell is exothermic and will not freeze.

The student received the only "A" handed out.

PROFESSIONAL QUIZ

This quiz consists of four questions that tell you whether or not you are qualified to be a professional.

SCROLL DOWN FOR THE ANSWERS

There is no need to cheat. The questions are not that difficult. You just need to think like a professional.

1. How do you put a giraffe into a refrigerator?

Correct answer is: Open the refrigerator, put in the giraffe and the door. This question tests whether or not you are doing simple things in a complicated way.

2. How do you put an elephant into a refrigerator?

Incorrect answer: Open the refrigerator, put in the elephant and shut the refrigerator.

Correct answer: Open the refrigerator, take out the giraffe, put in the elephant and close the door. This question tests your foresight.

3. The Lion King is hosting an animal conference. All the animals attend except one. Which animal does not attend?

Correct answer: The elephant. The elephant is in the refrigerator, you just put him there. This question tests your memory.

4. There is a crocodile invested river that you must cross, however you may not use a boat or canoe—how do you do it?

Correct Answer: Simply swim through it. All the crocodiles are attending the animal meeting! This question tests your reasoning ability.

SO... If you answered four out of four questions correctly, you are a true professional. Wealth and success await you.

If you answered three out of four, you have some catching up to do but there's hope for you. If you answered two out of four, consider a career as a hamburger flipper in a fast food joint. If you answered one out of four, try selling some of your organs. It's the only way you will ever make any money. If you answered none correctly, consider a career that does not require any higher mental functions at all, such as law or politics.

Rejected greetings cards submitted by school children

So your daughter's a hooker

And it spoiled your day.

Look at the bright side,

She's a really good lay.

My tire was thumping....

I thought it was flat.

When I looked at the tire.

I noticed your cat ... Sorry

You had your bladder removed

And you're on the mends

Here's a bouquet of flowers

And a box of Depends.

You've announced that you're gay.

Won't that be a laugh?

When they find out you're one

Of the Joint Chiefs of Staff.

Happy Vasectomy!

Hope you feel zippy!
Cause when I had mine
I got real nippy.
Heard your wife left you.
How upset you must be.
But don't fret about it
She moved in with me
Your computer is dead...
It was once alive ...,
Do you regret installing
Win 95?
You totalled your car...
And can't remember why
Could it have been
that case of Bud Dry?

Subject: Chinese Proverbs

1. Passionate kiss like spider's web, soon lead to undoing of fly.
2. Virginity like bubble, one prick all gone.
3. Man who run in front of car get tired.
4. Man who run behind car get exhausted.
5. Man with hand in pocket feel cocky all day.
6. Foolish man give wife grand piano, wise man give wife upright organ.

7. Man who walk thru airport turnstile sideways going to Bangkok.
8. Man with one chopstick go hungry.
9. Man who scratches ass should not bite fingernails.
10. Man who eat many prunes get good run for money.
11. Baseball is wrong, man with four balls cannot walk.
12. War doesn't determine who is right, war determines who is left.
13. Wife who put husband in doghouse soon find him in cathouse.
14. Man who fight with wife all day get no piece at night.
15. It take many nails to build crib but one screw to fill it.
16. Man who drive like hell bound to get there.
17. Man who stand on toilet is high on pot.
18. Man who lives in glass house should change clothes in basement.
19. Man who fishes in other man's well often catches crabs.
20. Man who farts in church sits in own pew.

- IDIOTS AT WORK ...

I was signing the receipt for my credit card purchase when the clerk noticed that I had never signed my name on the back of the credit card. She informed me that she could not complete the transaction unless the card was signed. When I asked why, she explained that it was necessary to compare the signature on the credit card with the signature I just signed on the receipt. So I signed the credit card in front of her. She carefully compared that signature to the one I signed on the receipt. As luck would have it, they matched.

E is for Education

- ADVICE FOR IDIOTS

An actual tip from page 16 of the HP "Environmental, Health & Safety Handbook for Employees: "Blink your eyelids periodically to lubricate your eyes."

- IDIOTS IN THE NEIGHBOURHOOD

I live in a semi-rural area. We recently had a new neighbour call the local township administrative office to request the removal of the Deer Crossing sign on our road. The reason: Many deer were being hit by cars and he no longer wanted them to cross there.

- IDIOTS IN FOOD SERVICE

My daughter went to a local Taco Bell and ordered a taco. She asked the individual behind the counter for "minimal lettuce."

He said he was sorry, but they only had iceberg.

IDIOT SIGHTINGS

- Sighting #1:

I was at the airport, checking in at the gate, when the airport employee asked, "Has anyone put anything in your baggage without your knowledge?' I said, 'If it was without my knowledge, how would I know?" He smiled and nodded knowingly, 'That's why we ask."

- Sighting #2:

The stoplight on the corner buzzes when it is safe to cross the street. I was crossing with an intellectually challenged co-worker of mine, when she asked if I knew what the buzzer was for. I explained that it signals to blind people when the light is red.

She responded, appalled, 'What on earth are blind people doing driving?"

- Sighting #5:

When my husband and I arrived at an automobile dealership to pick up our car, we were told that the keys had been accidentally locked in it. We went to the service department and found a mechanic working feverishly to unlock the driver's side door. As I watched from the passenger's side, I instinctively tried the door handle and discovered it was open. "Hey," I announced to the technician, 'It's open!'

"I know," answered the young man. "I already got that side."

FINALLY A CHAIN LETTER THAT I LIKE!

Hello, my name is Basmati Kasaar. I am suffering from rare and deadly diseases, poor scores on final exams, extreme virginity, fear of being kidnapped and executed by anal electrocution, and guilt for not forwarding out 50 billion fucking chain letters sent to me by people who actually believe that if you send them on, then that poor fucking 6 year old girl in Arkansas with a breast on her forehead will be able to raise enough money to have it removed before her redneck parents sell her off -to the traveling freak show.

Do you honestly believe that Bill Gates is going to give you and everyone you send his email to $1000?

How stupid are you?

Oh, look here! If I scroll down this page and make a wish, I'll get laid by every Playboy Bunny in the magazine! What a bunch of fucking bullshit.

So basically, this message is a big FUCK YOU to all the people out there who have nothing better to do than to send me stupid chain mail forwards.

Maybe the evil chain letter leprechauns will come into my apartment and sodomize me in my sleep for not continuing the chain which was started by Jesus in 5 A.D. and was brought to this country by midget pilgrims on the Mayflower and if it makes it to this year, it'll be in the Guinness Book of World Records for longest continuous streak of blatant stupidity.

Fuck them. If you're going to forward something, at least send me something mildly fucking amusing.

I've seen all the 'send this to 50 of your closest friends, and this poor, wretched excuse for a human being will somehow receive a Nickel from some omniscient being forwards' about 90 times. I don't fucking care.

Show a little intelligence and think about what you're actually contributing to by sending out forwards. Chances are it's your own unpopularity.

THE FOUR BASIC TYPES OF CHAIN LETTERS:

- Chain Letter Type 1:

(scroll down)

Make a wish!!!

Keep Scrolling

No, really, go on and make one!!!

Oh please, they'll never go out with you!!! Wish something else!!!

Not that you pervert!!

STOP!!!!

Wasn't that fun? :)

Hope you made a great wish :)

Now, to make you feel guilty, here's what I'll do. First of all, if you don't send this to 5096 people in the next 5 seconds, you will be raped by a mad goat and thrown off a high building into a pile of manure. It's true! Because, this letter isn't like those fake ones, this one is true!! Really!!! Here's how it goes:

*Send this to 1 person: One person will be pissed off at you for sending them a stupid chain letter.

*Send this to 2-5 people: 2-5 people will be pissed off at you for sending them a stupid chain letter.

*Send this to 5-10 people: 5-10 people will be pissed off at you for sending them a stupid chain letter, and may form a plot on your life.

*Send this to 10-20 people: 10-20 people will be pissed off at you for sending them a stupid chain letter and will napalm your house. Thanks!!!! Good Luck!!!

- Chain Letter Type 2

Hello, and thank you for reading this letter. You see, there is a starving little boy in Baklaliviatatlaglooshen who has no arms, no legs, no parents, and no goats. This little boy's life could be saved, because for every time you pass this on, a dollar will be donated to the little starving, legless, armless and goatless boy from Baklaliviatatlaglooshen Fund. Oh, and remember, we have absolutely no way of counting the emails sent and this is all a complete load of bullshit. So go on, reach out. Send this to 5 people in the next 47 seconds.

Oh, and a reminder—if you accidentally send this to 4 or 6 people, you will die instantly. Thanks again!!

- Chain Letter Type 3

Hi there!! This chain letter has been in existence since 1897. This is absolutely incredible because there was no email then and probably not as many sad pricks with nothing better to do.

So this is how it works. Pass this on to 15,067 people in the next 7 minutes or something horrible will happen to you like:

Bizarre Horror Story #1

Miranda Pinsley was walking home from school on Saturday. She had recently received this letter and ignored it. She then tripped in a crack in the sidewalk, fell into the sewer, was gushed down a drainpipe in a flood of poopie, and went flying out over a waterfall. Not only did she smell nasty, she died.

This Could Happen To You!!!

Bizarre Horror Story #2

Dexter Bip, a 13 year old boy, got a chain letter in his mail and ignored it. Later that day, he was hit by a car and so was his boyfriend (hey, some people swing that way). They both died and went to hell and were cursed to eat adorable kittens every day for eternity.

This Could Happen To You Too!!!

Remember, you could end up just like Pinsley and Bip. Just send this letter to all of your loser friends, and everything will be okay.

- Chain Letter Type 4

As if you care, here is a poem that I wrote.

Send it to all your friends.

FRIENDS:

- A friend is someone who is always at your side.
- A friend is someone who likes you even though you stink of shit, and your breath smells like you've been eating catfood.
- A friend is someone who likes you even though you're as ugly as a hat full of assholes.
- A friend is someone who cleans up for you after you've soiled yourself.
- A friend is someone who stays with you all night while you cry about your sad, sad life.
- A friend is someone who pretends they like you when they really think you should be raped by mad goats, then thrown to vicious dogs.
- A friend is someone who scrubs your toilet, vacuums and then gets the cheque and leaves and doesn't speak much English ...no, sorry that's the cleaning lady.
- A friend is not someone who sends you chain letters because he wants his wish of being rich to come true.

Now pass this on!

If you don't, you'll never have sex ever again!

The point being? If you get some chain letter that's threatening to leave you shagless or luckless for the rest of your life, delete it. If it's funny, send it on. Don't piss people off by making them feel guilty about a leper in Botswana with no teeth, who's been tied to a dead elephant for 27 years, whose only savior is the 5 cents per letter he'll receive if you forward this mail, otherwise you'll end up like Miranda. Right? Now forward this to everyone that you know otherwise you'll find all your knickers missing tomorrow morning.

---

20 Jokes That Only Intellectuals Will Understand

1. It's hard to explain puns to kleptomaniacs because they always take things literally.

2. What do you get when you cross a joke with a rhetorical question?

3. 3 logicians walk into a bar. The bartender asks 'Do all of you want a drink?'

   The first logician says 'I don't know.'

   The send logician says 'I don't know.'

   The third logician says 'Yes!'

4. Einstein, Newton and Pascal are playing hide and go seek. It's Einstein's turn to count so he covers his eyes and starts counting to ten. Pascal runs off and hides. Newton draws a one meter by one meter square on the ground in front of Einstein then stands in the middle of it. Einstein reaches ten and uncovers his eyes. He sees Newton immediately and exclaims 'Newton! I found you! You're it!'

Newton smiles and says 'You didn't find me, you found a Newton over a square meter. You found Pascal!'

5. A mathematician and an engineer agreed to take part in an experiment. They were both placed in a room and at the other end was a beautiful naked woman on a bed. The experimenter said every 30 seconds they would be allowed to travel half the distance between themselves and the woman. The mathematician said 'this is pointless' and stormed off. The engineer agreed to go ahead with the experiment anyway. The mathematician exclaimed on his way out 'don't you see, you'll never actually reach her?'. To which the engineer replied, 'so what? Pretty soon I'll be close enough for all practical purposes!'

6. A Roman walks into a bar and asks for a martinus.

    'You mean a martini?' the bartender asks.

    The Roman replies, 'if I wanted a double, I would have asked for it!'

7. Another Roman walks into a bar, holds up two fingers, and says, 'Five beers, please'.

8. A logician's wife is having a baby. The doctor immediately hands the newborn to the dad.

    His wife asks impatiently: 'So, is it a boy or a girl'?

    The logician replies: 'yes'.

9. Jean-Paul Sartre is sitting at a French café, revising his draft of Being and Nothingness. He says to the waitress, 'I'd like a cup of coffee, please, with no cream.' The waitress replies, 'I'm sorry, Monsieur, but we're out of cream. How about with no milk?'

10. Entropy isn't what it used to be.

11. How can you tell the difference between a chemist and a plumber? Ask them to pronounce unionised.

12. Why do engineers confuse Halloween and Christmas?

    Because Oct 31 = Dec 25

13. Werner Heisenberg, Kurt Gödel, and Noam Chomsky walk into a bar. Heisenberg turns to the other two and says, 'Clearly this is a joke, but how can we figure out if it's funny or not?' Gödel replies, 'We can't know that because we're inside the joke.' Chomsky says, 'Of course it's funny. You're just telling it wrong.'

14. Pavlov is sitting at a pub enjoying a pint, the phone rings and he jumps up shouting 'oh shit, I forgot to feed the dog!'

15. Helium walks into a bar and orders a beer, the bartender says, 'Sorry, we don't serve noble gases here.' He doesn't react.

16. Schrodinger's cat walks into a bar. And doesn't.

17. A Buddhist monk approaches a hotdog stand and says 'make me one with everything'.

18. A Higgs Boson walks into a church and the priest says 'we don't allow Higgs Bosons in here'. The Higgs Boson then replies, 'but without me, how could you have mass?'

19. The programmer's wife tells him: 'Run to the store and pick up a loaf of bread. If they have eggs, get a dozen.'

    The programmer comes home with 12 loaves of bread.

20. There's a band called 1023MB. They haven't had any gigs yet.

JUST IN CASE YOU EVER GET THE TWO MIXED UP

IN PRISON you spend the majority of your time in an 8X10 cell;

AT WORK you spend the majority of your time in a 6X8 cubicle.

IN PRISON you get three meals a day;

AT WORK you only get a break for one meal and you have to pay for it.

IN PRISON you get time off for good behaviour;

AT WORK you get rewarded for good behaviour with more work.

IN PRISON ... the guard locks and unlocks all the doors for you;

AT WORK. .. you must carry around a security card and open all the doors for yourself.

IN PRISON you can watch TV and play games;

AT WORK you get fired for watching TV and playing games.

IN PRISON ... you get your own toilet;

AT WORK. .. you have to share.

IN PRISON they allow your family and friends to visit;

AT WORK you can't even speak to your family.

IN PRISON ... all expenses are paid by the taxpayers with no work required;

AT WORK ... you get to pay all the expenses to go to work and then they deduct taxes from your salary to pay for prisoners.

IN PRISON ... you spend most of your life looking through bars from inside wanting to get out;

AT WORK ... you spend most of your time wanting to get out and go inside bars.

IN PRISON there are wardens who are sadistic;

AT WORK they are called managers.

Word definitions

1. Blamestorming: Sitting around in a group and discussing why a deadline was missed or a project failed- and who was responsible.
2. Body Nazis: Hard-core exercise and weightlifting fanatics who look down on anyone who doesn't work out obsessively.
3. Chainsaw Consultant: An outside expert brought in to reduce the employee headcount, leaving the top brass with clean hands.
4. Cube Farm: An office filled with cubicles.
5. Idea Hamsters: People who always seem to have their idea generators running.
6. Mouse Potato: The wired generation's answer to the couch potato.
7. Prairie Dogging: When someone yells or drops something loudly in a cube farm and people's heads pop up over the walls to see what's going on.
8. SITCOM: What yuppies turn into when they have children and one of them stops working to stay home with the kids? Stands for Single Income, Two Children, Oppressive Mortgage.
9. Squirt the Bird: To transmit a signal to a satellite.

10. Starter Marriage: A short-lived first marriage that ends in divorce with no kids, no property and no regrets.

11. Stress Puppy: A person who seems to thrive on being stressed out and whiny.

12. Swiped-Out: An ATM or credit card that has been rendered useless because the magnetic strip is worn away from extensive use.

13. Tourists: People who take training classes just to get a vacation from their jobs. (We had three serious students in the class; the rest were just tourists.)

14. Treeware: Hacker slang for documentation or other printed material.

15. Xerox Subsidy: Euphemism for swiping free photocopies from one's workplace.

16. Alpha Geek: The most knowledgeable, technically proficient person in an office or work group. ("Ask Larry; he's the alpha geek around here.")

17. Assmosis: The process by which some people seem to absorb success and advancement, by kissing up to the boss rather than working hard.

18. Flight Risk: Used to describe employees who are suspected of planning to leave a company or department in the near future.

19. GOOD Job: A Get-Out-Of-Debt job. A well-paying job people take in order to pay off their debts but plan to quit as soon as they are solvent again.

20. Irritainment: Entertainment and media spectacles that are annoying but that you find yourself unable to stop watching.

21. Percussive Maintenance: The fine art of whacking an electronic device to get it to work again.

22. Uninstalled: Euphemism for being fired. Heard on the voicemail of a vice president at a downsizing computer firm. ("You have reached the number of an uninstalled vice president. Please dial our main number and ask the operator for assistance.") See also: Decruitment.

23. Vulcan Nerve Pinch: The taxing hand position required to reach all the appropriate keys for certain commands. For instance, the warm reboot for a Mac II computer involves simultaneously pressing the control key, the command key, the return key and the power on key.

24. Yuppie Food Stamps: The ubiquitous $20 bills spewed out of ATMs everywhere. Often used when trying to split the bill after a meal: ("We owe $10 each, all anybody's got is yuppie food stamps.")

A little something they never taught us at school.

Consider this and remember that it's all completely true

- Abraham Lincoln was elected to Congress in 1846.
- John P. Kennedy was elected to Congress in 1946.
- Abraham Lincoln was elected President in 1860.
- John Kennedy was elected President in 1960.
- The names Lincoln and Kennedy each contain seven letters. Both were particularly concerned with civil rights
- Both wives lost their children while living in the White House.
- Both Presidents were shot on a Friday. Both were shot in the head.

- Lincoln's secretary was named Kennedy. Kennedy's secretary was named Lincoln.
- Both were assassinated by Southerners. Both were succeeded by Southerners.
- Both successors were named Johnson.
- Andrew Johnson, who succeeded Lincoln was born in 1808. Lyndon Johnson who succeeded Kennedy was born in 1908.
- John Wilkes Booth, who assassinated Lincoln was born in 1839.
- Lee Harvey Oswald, who assassinated Kennedy, was born in 1939.
- Both assassins were known by their three names.
- Both names comprise fifteen Letters.
- Booth ran from the theatre and was caught in a warehouse. Oswald ran from a warehouse and was caught in a theatre.
- Booth and Oswald were both assassinated before their trials.
- A week before Lincoln was shot he was in Monroe, Maryland.
- A week before Kennedy was shot he was in Marilyn Monroe.

Spooky isn't it?

KIDS MENTORING

- Never trust a dog to watch your food—Patrick, age 10.

- When your dad and asks you, "Do I look stupid?" don't answer him—Heather, 16.
- Never tell your mum her diet's not working—Michael, 14.
- Stay away from prunes—Randy, 9
- Never pee on an electric fence—Robert, 13
- Don't squat with your spurs on—Moronha, 13
- Don't pull your dad's finger when he tells you to—Emily, 10
- When your mum is mad at your dad, don't let her brush your hair—Taylia, 11
- Never allow your three-year old brother in the same room as your school assignment –Traci, 14
- Don't sneeze in front of mum when you're eating crackers—Mitchell, 12
- Puppies still have bad breath even after eating a tic tac—Andrew, 9
- Never hold a dust buster and a cat at the same time—Kyoyo, 9
- You can't hide a piece of broccoli in a glass of milk—Armir, 9
- Don't wear polka dot underwear under white shorts—Kellie, 11
- If you want a kitten, start out by asking for a horse—Naomi, 15
- Felt markers are not good to use as lipstick—Lauren, 9
- Don't pick on your sister when she's holding a baseball bat—Joel, 10

- When you get a bad grade in school. Show it to your mum when she's on the phone—Alyesha, 13
- Never try to baptise a cat—Steve, 12

The following letter was forwarded by someone who teaches at a small junior high school in Memphis, Tennessee. The letter was sent to the principal's office after the school had sponsored a luncheon for the elderly. This story is a credit to all humankind. Read it, soak it in, and bask in the warm feeling that it leaves you with.

Dear Reyer School:

God bless you for the beautiful radio I won at your recent senior citizen's luncheon. I'm 94 years old and live at the Memphis county Home for the Aged.

My family has long since passed away and I rarely have visitors. As a result, I have very limited contact with the outside world. This makes gift especially welcome. My roommate, Maggie Cook, has had her own radio for as long as I've known her. She listens to it all the time though with an earplug or with the volume so low, I can't hear it.

For some reason, she has never wanted to share it. Last Sunday morning, while listening to her morning gospel programs, she accidentally knocked her radio off its shelf. It smashed into many pieces and caused her to cry. It was so sad. Fortunately, I had my new radio. Knowing this, Maggie asked if she could listen to mine. I told her to go fuck herself. God bless you for your kindness to an old, forgotten lady.

Sincerely, Edna Johnson

CHILDRENS BOOKS YOU WILL NEVER SEE.

- You were an accident
- Strangers have the best lollies
- Where would you like to be buried?
- Testing homemade parachutes using only your household pets
- How to become the Dominant Military Power in your primary school controlling the playground respect through fear
- Garfield gets feline leukaemia
- Why can't Mr Fork and Ms Electrical Outlet be friends?
- Bi-Curious George
- Controlling the Playground: Respect through Fear
- Why Can't Mr Fork and Ms Electrical Outlet Be Friends?
- The Little Sissy Who Snitched
- Some Kittens Can Fly!
- Kathy Was So Bad Her Mum Stopped Loving Her
- The Attention Deficit Disorder Association's Book of Wild Animals of North America
- Hey! Let's Go Ride Our Bikes!
- The Kid's Guide to Hitchhiking
- You Are Different and That's Bad
- Dad's New Wife Timothy
- POP! Goes the Hamster ...and Other Great Microwave Games

- Curious George and the High Voltage Fence
- The Boy Who Died From Eating All His Vegetables
- Things Rich Kids Have, but You Never Will
- The Care Bears Maul Some Campers and Are Shot Dead
- Daddy Drinks Because You Cry

The finals of the National Poetry Contest last year came down to two finalists. One was a Duke University Law School graduate from an upper crust family; well-bred, well-connected, and all that goes with it.

The other finalist was a redneck from Southeast Alabama. The rules of the contest required each finalist to compose a four-line poem in one minute or less, and the poem had to contain the word "Timbuktu."

The Duke graduate went first. About thirty seconds after the clock started he jumped up and recited the following poem:

Slowly across the desert sand

Trekked the dusty caravan.

Men on camels,

two by two Destination — Timbuktu.

The audience went wild!

HOW, they wondered,

Could the redneck possibly top that?

The clock started again and the redneck sat in silent thought. Finally, in the last few seconds, he jumped and recited:

Tim and me, a hunting went.

Met three whores in a pop-up tent.

They was three, we was two,

So I bucked one and Timbuktu.

TEST FOR SECONDARY SCHOOLS IN THE NORTH:

NAME

NICK-NAME

GANG NAME

1. Deco has 0.5 kilos of cocaine. If he sells a B ball to Vinno for 300 quid and 90 grams to Torno for 90 quid a gram, what is the street value of the rest of his hold?

2. Anto pimps 3 brassers. If the price is 40 quid a royde, how many roydes per day must each brasser perform to support Vinno's 500 quid a day crack habit?

3. Whacker wants to cut the kilo of cocaine he bought for 7,000 quid, to make a 20% profit. How many grams of strychnine will he need?

4. Christy got 6 years for murder. He also got 350,000 for the hit. If his common law wife spends 33,100 per month, how much money will be left when he gets out?

5. Extra Credit Bonus: How much more time will Christy get for killing the slapper that spent his money?

6. If an average can of spray paint covers 22 square meters and the average letter is 1 square meter, how many letters can be sprayed with eight Fluid ounce cans of spray paint with 20% extra paint free?

7. Liamo steals Eamo's skateboard. As Liamo skates away at a speed of 35 mph, Eamo loads his brother's armalite. If it takes Eamo 20 seconds to load the gun, how far will Liam have travelled when he gets whacked?

MATHS TEST FOR SECONDARY SCHOOLS IN THE SOUTH:

NAME:

(If longer, please continue on separate sheet)

SCHOOL

DADDY'S COMPANY

1. Julian smashes up the old man's car, causing x amount of damage and killing three people. The old man asks his local TD to intervene in the court system, then forges his insurance claim and receives a payout. PW

    The difference between x and y is three times the life insurance settlement for the three dead people. What kind of car is Julian driving now?

2. Chloe's personal shopper decides to substitute generic and own-brand products for the designer goods favoured by her employer. In the course of a month she saves the price of a return ticket to Fiji and Chloe doesn't even notice the difference. Is she thick or what?

3. Roly fancies the arse off a certain number of tarts, but he only has enough Rohypnol left to render 33.3% unconscious. If he has 14 Rohypnol, how is he ever going to shag the other two-thirds?

4. If Savannah throws up four times a day for a week she can fit a size 8 Versace. If she only throws up three times a day for two weeks, she has to make do with a size 10 Dolce and Gabbana. How much does liposuction cost?

5. Alexander is unsure about his sexuality. Three days a week he fancies women. On the other days he fancies men, ducks and vacuum cleaners. However he only has access to the Hoover every third week. When does his Sunday Independent column start?

A high school English teacher reminds her class of tomorrow's final exam.

"Now class, I won't tolerate any excuses for you not being there tomorrow.

I might consider a nuclear attack or a serious personal injury or illness, or a death in your immediate family—but that's it, no other excuses, whatsoever!"

A smart-alec in the back of the room raises his hand and asks, "What would you say if tomorrow I said I was suffering from complete and utter sexual exhaustion?"

The entire class does its best to stifle their laughter and snickering.

When silence is restored, the teacher smiles sympathetically at the student, shakes her head, and sweetly says, "Well, I guess you'd have to write the exam with your other hand."

A young female teacher was giving an assignment to her Grade 6 class one day. It was a large assignment so she started writing high up on the chalkboard. Suddenly there was a giggle from one of the boys in the class. She quickly turned and asked, what's so funny Pat?

Well teacher, I just saw one of your garters."

Get out of my classroom,- she yells, "I don't want to see you for three days."

The teacher turns back to the chalkboard. Realizing she had forgotten to title the assignment; she reaches to the very top of the chalkboard. Suddenly there is an even louder giggle from another male student. She quickly turns and asks, "What's so funny Billy?

Well miss, I just saw both of your garters.

Again she yells, "Get out of my classroom" This time the punishment is more severe, "I don't want to see you for three weeks."

Embarrassed and frustrated, she drops the eraser while she turns around again. So she bends over to pick it up. This time there is a burst of laughter from another male student. She quickly turns to see Little Johnny leaving the classroom.

"Where do you think you are going? she asks.

Well teacher, from what I just saw, my school days are over."

1950 Home Economics: The following is from an actual 1950s

Home Economics textbook intended for High School girls, teaching how to prepare for married life.

1. Have dinner ready: Plan ahead, even the night before, to have a delicious meal on time. This is a way of letting him know that you have been thinking about him, and are concerned about his needs. Most men are hungry when they come home and the prospects of a good meal are part of the warm welcome needed.

2. Prepare yourself: Take 15 minutes to rest so you will be refreshed when he arrives. Touch up your make-up, put a ribbon in your hair and be fresh looking. He has just been with a lot of work-weary people. Be a little gay and a little more interesting. His boring day may need a lift.

3. Clear away the clutter. Make one last trip through the main part of the house just before your husband arrives, gathering up school books, toys, paper, etc. Then run a dust cloth over the tables. Your husband will feel he has reached a haven of rest and order, and it will give you a lift too.

4. Prepare the children: Take a few minutes to wash the children's hands and faces if they are small, comb their hair, and if necessary, change their clothes. They are little treasures and he would like to see them playing the part.

5. Minimize the noise: At the time of his arrival, eliminate all noise of washer, dryer, dishwasher, or vacuum. Try to encourage the children to be quiet. Be happy to see him. Greet him with a warm smile.

6. Some DON'TS: Don't greet him with problems or complaints. Don't complain if he's late for dinner. Count this as minor compared with what he might have gone through that day.

7. Make him comfortable: Have him lean back in a comfortable chair or suggest he lie down in the bedroom. Have a cool or warm drink ready for him. Arrange his pillow and offer to take off his shoes. Speak in a low, soft, soothing and pleasant voice. Allow him to relax and unwind.

8. Listen to him: You may have a dozen things to tell him, but the moment of his arrival is not the time. Let him talk first.

9. Make the evening his: Never complain if he does not take you out to dinner or to instead try to understand his world of strain and pressure and his need to be home and relax.

10. The Goal: try to make your home a place of peace and order where your husband can relax.

Now the updated version for the '90s woman.

1. Have dinner ready: Make reservations ahead of time. If your day becomes too hectic just leave him a voice mail message regarding where you'd like to eat and at what time. This lets him know that your day has been crappy and gives him an opportunity to change your mood.

2. Prepare yourself: A quick stop at the "LANCOME" counter on your way home will do wonders for your outlook and will keep you from becoming irritated every time he opens his mouth. (Don't forget to use his credit card!)

3. Clear away the clutter: Call the housekeeper and tell her that any miscellaneous items left on the floor by the children can be placed in the goodwill box in the garage.

4. Prepare the children: Send the children to their rooms to watch television or play Nintendo video games. After all, both of them are from his previous marriages.

5. Minimize the noise: If you happen to be home when he arrives, be in the bathroom with the door locked.

6. Some DON'TS: Don't greet him with problems and complaints. Let him speak first, and then your complaints will get more attention and remain fresh in his mind throughout dinner. Don't complain if he's late for dinner; simply remind him that the leftovers are in the refrigerator and you left the dishes for him to do.

7. Make him comfortable: Tell him where he can find a blanket if he's cold. This will really show you care.

8. Listen to him: But don't ever let him get the last word.

9. Make the evening his: Never complain if he does not take you out to dinner or to other places of entertainment, go with a friend or go shopping (use his credit card).
10. The Goal: Try to keep things amicable without reminding him that he only thinks the world revolves around him. Obviously he's wrong, it revolves around you.

You have just got to love bureaucracy—no wonder the EU is going to hell in a hand cart!

Pythagoras' Theorem: . . . . 24 words.

Lord's Prayer: . . . . 66 words.

Archimedes' Principle: . . . . 67 words.

Ten Commandments: . . . . 179 words.

Gettysburg Address: . . . . 286 words.

US Declaration of Independence: . . . . 1,300 words.

US Constitution with all 27 Amendments: . . . . 7,818 words.

EU Regulations on the Sale of CABBAGES: . . . 26,911 words

Someone out there must be "deadly" at Scrabble; some uncanny anagrams!

ASTRONOMER:
When you rearrange the letters, you get:
MOON STARER

THE EYES:
When you rearrange the letters:
THEY SEE

GEORGE BUSH:
When you rearrange the letters:
HE BUGS GORE

THE MORSE CODE:
When you rearrange the letters:
HERE COME DOTS

DORMITORY:
When you rearrange the letters:
DIRTY ROOM

ELECTION RESULTS:
When you rearrange the letters:
LIES—LET'S RECOUNT

A DECIMAL POINT:
When you rearrange the letters:
I'M A DOT IN PLACE

ELEVEN PLUS TWO:
When you rearrange the letters:
TWELVE PLUS ONE

AND FOR THE GRAND FINALE:

MOTHER-IN-LAW:
When you rearrange the letters:
WOMAN HITLER

The Corporate bullshit generator

- The customers culturally overdeliver our market-changing, decentralized, interconnected and low-risk high-yield industries, while the team players strategically visualize a long-term, modular and low-risk high-yield SWOT analysis. The project manager analyses differentiating plannings from the get-go. The standard-setters strategically incentivize a pipeline. The standard-setters visualize our interconnected values. An unprecedented growth drives a streamlined learning. In the same time, the community right-sizes our time-phased, personalized and non-deterministic incentive taking advantage of forward plannings. Our strategy-focused niche technically influences an analytics-based and/or multi-source idiosyncrasy within the industry. High-performing missions empower the Senior Director of IT Strategy reaped from our proven efficiency gain.

- The Chief Internal Audit Officer maximizes a goal-based talent, while the well-positioned cornerstone targets the team players.

- Relationship and interdependency proactively leverage our awesome strategy. As a result, the enablers synergize paradigms by thinking and acting beyond boundaries.

- Our review cycle inspires the business leaders. An inspiring credibility prioritizes the powerful champion. The differentiated, solid, market opportunities standardize our versatile market conditions, whilst adequate, non-standard, Quality Management Systems carefully enable cross-enterprise recalibrations. Consistency, blended approach and branding enable the team players. A correlation 24/7 promotes motivational markets. Blended approach, trigger event and control synergize the partners in the marketplace, while a success factor enhances top-down market forces. The value creations champion strengthens a functional value creation. The partners flesh out goal-based delivery frameworks. Metrics credibly motivate the Chief

Client Leadership Officer; nevertheless granularity and transformation process drive the supply-chain. We will go the extra mile to learn leveraged, targeted, structural and outsourced cultures, while the resources differentiate a paradigm shift. The gatekeeper promotes our structure. The business leaders broaden large-scale pipelines. Roll-out and guideline globally empower an analytics-based core meeting. The profit-maximizing white paper expediently prioritizes the partners by thinking outside of the box. An above-average alternative streamlines our differentiating supply-chains. Our holistic learning empowers the enabler taking advantage of the methodology. We are working hard to prioritize an idiosyncratic bandwidth.

- Our change standardizes a strategic, sustainable and transparent portal. The enablers leverage a movable success factor. Our incentive promotes the Chief Management Office Officer across our portfolio. A methodology consistently generates our solid bandwidthes. As a result, situational measurements empower the evolution champion. Firm-wide scalings synergize the community, whilst the business leaders accelerate optimal synergies. A differentiated goal enables the challenge champion. The enabler champions the aligned baseline starting points across and beyond the organizations. The resources adequately strategize a forward-looking cost efficiency. The enablers genuinely deliver an adaptive, aggressive, aggressive and solutions-based dialogue. Our structural case studies enhance prospective interpersonal skills. As a result, the customers target our laser-focused core competency.

- The image champion fosters the end-to-end quality assurance using business enabling market conditions. A performance quickly generates right low hanging fruits. The Chief Controlling Officer rebalances an

E is for Education   111

intra-organisational efficient frontier. The enablers conservatively enhance our generic matrices, while the policies champion 200% enhances our high-performing incentives. The business cases champion swiftly broadens an efficient, wide-ranging, lever. The enablers transition our transitional landscapes, while our assets enable the fine-grained energies using parallel, cross-enterprise, market opportunities.

- Interdependencies generate our visionary, time-honoured and streamlined paradigm shift in the marketplace. Our gut-feeling is that the stakeholders manage a customer-facing convergence on a transitional basis.

- The resources influence a granularity. Review cycles incentivise the Chief Operations Officer because controls produce measured throughput increase, while the partners swiftly maximize the value. The core, enterprise-wide, sustainable and high-margin guidelines result in an unified, goal-directed, transitional and non-deterministic recalibration, whilst omni-channel innovations seamlessly empower the sales manager.

- The key people streamline a wide-spectrum, present-day, segmentation. Long-running scalabilities empower a concept.

- The gatekeeper builds the replacement, wide-spectrum and genuine breakthroughs.

- The standard-setters leverage an overarching, intra-organisational, end-to-end and awesome quality assurance. Our synchronized and situational attitude influences measurable knowledge transfers. The Group Chief Business Planning Officer thinks out of the box, while the senior support staff manages long-term executive talents. We are working hard to streamline a goal-directed and productive goal, while the powerful champion quickly addresses resilient, target, transformation processes. The resource significantly learns prospective time-phases across the board. As a result, the thought leader jump-starts value-added, outward-looking and scenario-based credibilities. The human resources significantly re-imagine an inspiring message, whilst a far-reaching paradigm empowers the thought leader across the board. The team players 24/7 structure a core competency, whilst our differentiating execution adequately cultivates the execution.

- The team players stay in the wings. Trust and timeline influence the senior support staff, whereas the clients adequately foster future-ready, outward-looking, high-level and integrative value propositions.

- The team players incentivize our cost efficiencies using an unified infrastructure. Centralized, goal-directed, results-centric and day-to-day cultures 24/7 empower a diversifying compliance. The powerful champion proactively synergizes the outward-looking quest for quality by thinking and acting beyond boundaries.

- Our insightful implication enables the business leaders, while the thought leader focuses on the best-of-breed insight. The business leaders institutionalize our far-reaching planning. The gatekeeper deploys correlations, while the enablers strategize future structures. The Chief Management Office Officer prioritizes state-of-the-art transformation processes. In the same time, the enabler surges ahead. The clients learn a streamlined client focus. The business leaders benchmark unified, improved, interdependencies. As a result, personalized cost efficiency architects our overarching workflow.

E is for Education   113

- A forward planning enables the community, while a day-to-day trust influences the control champion.

- The SWOT analysis champion optimizes the present-day and fact-based environment. In the same time, the sales manager targets our market-changing Balanced Scorecard. Our gut-feeling is that our optimal enablers add value. A future-oriented stress management empowers the forward planning champion.

- Our low hanging fruits empower the Chief Management Office Officer; this is why pursuing this route will enable us to optimize our optimal markets. The best-in-class metric structures a non-linear momentum. The project manager conservatively formulates responsible efficient frontiers. The powerful champion culturally synergizes a relevant leadership. We will go the extra mile to establish our replacement landscapes.

- Channel and visual thinking cultivate an optimal branding. The senior support staff whiteboards our market-altering channels; nevertheless a best-in-class, non-mainstream, idiosyncrasy results in the productive, problem-solving, say/do ratios. Our diversification 200% enables the sales manager, whilst a tactical flow charting structures our convergence by leveraging an atmosphere. The benchmark strengthens the senior support staff.

- The customers envision the low hanging fruit. Our context-aware, situational, flow charting engages our corporate, non-linear, investor confidence. The team players 200% differentiate technologies, while upper single-digit throughput increase streamline underlying requests / solutions. The methodology enhances a delivery framework, while game-changing images efficiently accelerate an atmosphere. The business leaders enhance key performance indicators.

The senior support staff generates siloed touch points; nevertheless the Group Chief Client Leadership Officer proactively manages our goal-based targets going forward. The business leaders enforce collateral engagements across the organizations; nevertheless a streamlining business model targets the gatekeeper ahead of schedule. Our cutting-edge differentiator transfers our focused, flexible and controlled integrations, whereas a medium-to-long-term project synergizes the key people.

- Escalation, planning and industry 24/7 prioritize target, superior and trusted planning. The Global Chief Business Planning Officer stays ahead. The community fleshes out guidelines. The standard-setters empower verifiable idiosyncrasies. The resource focuses on consumer-facing flow chartings. The clients facilitate principle-based, robust and differentiating best practices. The white paper influences the double-digit efficiency gain. The President of marketing diligently whiteboards a scenario-based responsiveness up, down and across the organization. An agreed-upon implication accelerates our measured yield enhancement.

- Our gut-feeling is that our goal-oriented objective technically drives a goal. The cutting-edge and/or progressive enhanced data capture quickly inspires the clients. The enablers flesh out our risk appetites.

- The partners efficiently deepen high-level assets, while the sales manager over delivers a goal-based next step. The customers rebalance prioritizing, relevant, business philosophies.

- The roles and responsibilities target the Chief Digital Officer. SWOT analysis and asset cautiously add value. We will go the extra mile to keep it on the radar. The customers deliver a full range of products. Our intra-organisational, cultural, organizing principles generate our metric as a consequence of upper single-digit improvement.

- The scalabilities promote the group, whereas the powerful champion expediently takes a bite out of a high-powered core competency. Our global portals facilitate our performance cultures; nevertheless an established shareholder value influences wide-spectrum and established business cases.

- Hyper-hybrid bottom lines deepen transparent baseline starting points. An unified, one-to-one and medium-to-long-term quality assurance strengthens the steering committee going forward. Architecture and feedback influence the Chief Business Operations Officer up-front.

- The clients transition an agreed-upon strategic staircase. The senior support staff promotes unified shareholder values within the silo. As a result, the resources evolve from the get-go. The resources enforce our decision. The Chief Client Relationship Officer strategizes a risk/return profile by nurturing talent.

- The Chief IT Operations Officer technically drives our systematized and value-driven dialogue. A centralized and aggressive upside focus strengthens our enhanced data captures. The resources benchmark our engagements; nevertheless the thought leader carefully strengthens a multi-tasked delivery framework reaped from our upper single-digit improvement.

- The reporting unit should consistently achieve future-oriented collaborations. In the same time, our open-door policies prioritize the enabler on-the-fly.

- A best-in-class ROE diligently empowers a differentiator, while the enabler leverages a centralized, situational, effective and collaborative commitment.

- A traceable and forward-looking quest for quality influences the powerful champion. The senior support staff connects the dots to the end game. The flexibility engages our value-enhancing opportunities. The team players table our competitive, well-communicated, environments. In the same time, the community avoids inefficiencies.

- A cascading decision making transfers the partners.

- Balanced Scorecard and trigger event generate an in-depth collaboration up-front.

- The solutions-based philosophies enforce problem-solving, long-term and well-planned changes, while the key people facilitate our visions at the end of the day. The community establishes a result-driven, established, dialogue. The resource culturally deepens the motivational, medium-to-long-term, requirement, whereas pursuing this route will enable us to deepen an adequate, top-down, dotted line. ROE and learning globally enhance our integrative consistencies. In the same time, the community 200% integrates our long-running correlation. Agile leaderships conservatively foster integrated recalibrations, relative to our peers. The human resources address issues.

- Our structural value creations structure efficient enhanced data captures by expanding boundaries, while the human resources over deliver the structural, bullet-proof and functional value proposition. The Chief Customer Relations Officer accelerates the strategy-focused performance cultures.

- Brand identity and momentum impact a customized decision. As a result, the group addresses the overlaps. The standard-setters empower the resourcefulness. Informed, collateral and outstanding efficiencies strengthen the gatekeeper; nevertheless quest for quality and branding leverage our target, scenario-based, workflows. Functional action plans target the customers, while credibility and insight promote the gatekeeper. Content and on-boarding process interactively enforces our intra-organisational thought leadership, whereas the team players globally prioritize systems. Proactive documents impact promising and idiosyncratic win-win solutions. Paradigm shifts motivate the resources using our movable correlation, while the thought leader engineers underlying profiles on-the-fly.

- The enabler visualizes our underlying, unique and flexible knowledge transfer, whilst the gatekeeper formulates effective measures.
- A workshop aggregates an aggressive, growing, objective, whilst the stakeholders boost a day-to-day evolution. Our market-driven, promising, operating strategies culturally standardize our market-changing atmosphere. A relevant time-phase motivates the key people in this space. The wide-spectrum empowerments efficiently prioritize say/do ratios.
- The implications champion quickly manages the portfolio, while project and correlation enable the standard-setters. Our time-phased, fast-growth, landscapes credibly influence the human resources. The stakeholders achieve a strategic thinking, while innovation, timeline and uniformity empower the coordinated initiative. A well-crafted enterprise risk management aggregates our brandings. The resources streamline business enabling, cross-functional, industries.
- Our solution architects a wide-ranging intuitiveness, whilst our top-line technologies efficiently prioritize the Chief Management Office Officer as part of the plan. Centralized low hanging fruits strengthen the Chief IT Strategy Officer by nurturing talent, whilst

competitiveness, decision and transformation process promote the Chief of internal audit resulting in proven growth. White papers inspire the Chief IT Strategy Officer. Our flexible benefit expediently promotes the Senior Chief of human resources; this is why the thought leader prioritizes trusted mindsets. Traceable touch points structure the business model, whilst our time-phased, value-enhancing, efficiency generates the far-reaching intellect as part of the plan.

- The gatekeeper stays on trend. In the same time, the group differentiates the performance-based potentials up, down and across the sphere. An agile momentum interacts with a transformation process.
- Firm-wide mobile strategies consistently enhance established assets across our portfolio.
- Customer centricity and white paper impact superior priorities. The team players reset the benchmark within the matrix. We are working hard to streamline low hanging fruits. The profiles champion culturally learns our cross-industry win-win solution, while our channels promote an accurate branding.
- The visionary control information system engages a selective, well-implemented, recalibration. The Senior President of Internal Audit learns our accurate, parallel and focused engagements. We are working hard to incentivize cost savings; this is why we are working hard to cautiously table our adequate and functional metric.
- Image and atmosphere target the key people.
- A business case incentivises the partners.
- Top-line branding strategies inspire the core competency champion, whilst the enablers deepen a large-scale decision-making. The enabler avoids gaps. In

the same time, the laser-focused centre piece adequately standardizes our changes. The clients champion brandings within the matrix. The team players establish documented workflows in this space, while the gatekeeper avoids surprises. The human resources come to a landing by leveraging the siloed objectives, while aggressive values interact with our stellar, context-aware, synchronized and motivational drill-down. The resilient, performance-based, integration targets the key people.

- Pillars 200% structure our evolution; this is why our sustainable, well-implemented, leadership strategy streamlines the transitional issue going forward. Our immersive credibilities strengthen the Chief Digital Officer. The adaptive time-phase transfers momentums. Benchmarking and branding strategy streamline a top-line, well-communicated and time-honuored philosophy. Our executive and measurable operating strategy synergizes the Vice Director of human resources. The community takes a bite out of end-to-end commitments, whilst a strong target adequately promotes the stakeholders. Breakthroughs facilitates inspiring on-boarding processes. Our gut-feeling is that social sphere and efficiency inspire the key people. Target and delivery framework technically add value by expanding boundaries, while the project manager reaches out the selective opportunity.

- The customers champion our pre-plans, while the branding champion benchmarks our best-of-breed energies in this space. The thought leader cautiously achieves efficiencies.

- The value-enhancing white papers transfer future-ready balanced scorecards. An agile blended approach efficiently structures a fact-based consistency up, down and across the organization; this is why we will go the extra mile to establish our sustainable and differentiated Management Information Systems.

- We need to address industry-standard and value-added flexibilities. As a result, the partners accelerate long-term talents across our portfolio. Our gut-feeling is that the key people institutionalize the motivational and/or enterprise-wide self-efficacy. The senior support staff proactively over delivers a methodology. The stakeholders facilitate a differentiator. As a result, a knowledge sharing swiftly motivates the clients.

- The top-line interoperability enables spectral tactics. The Group Chief Legal Officer streamlines a transparent, nimble, channel. Our effective perspectives impact our action items. Knowledge sharing and business model 24/7 cultivate the key target markets, while progressive, solutions-based and interconnected plans enable the group.

- Our guidelines transfer the resources. In the same time, intellect and line of business efficiently transfer the standard-setters. Stress management and correlation adequately prioritize the enabler. The thought leader focuses on non-linear core meetings, while the dynamic target carefully structures a systematized project by leveraging a principle-based technology.

- A dramatic methodology fosters the parallel, constructive, strategy-focused and future-oriented white papers on a transitional basis. As a result, the human resources engineer cooperative lessons learned. Our global and result-driven architecture interacts with an efficient, value-adding, trigger event. Our value-enhancing lever culturally empowers the partners. The result-driven, targeted, infrastructures diligently generate a policy. Our gut-feeling is that our profit-maximizing transformation processes generate our unified trigger events.

E is for Education 121

- A traceable sales target transfers organizing principles. Strategy-focused scalings drive our value-added, solutions-based and accepted cost savings at the individual, team and organizational level.

- White papers generate our insightful, well-positioned and sustainable bandwidth, while the brandings deepen efficient frontiers. A branding targets the Chief Client Leadership Officer in the marketplace. The outward-looking changes facilitate an optimal, targeted and measurable consistency, while we must activate the silo to organically influence an outsourced leadership strategy because our strategic staircases produce organic throughput increase.

- Our modular strategic staircase incentivises the resources. The clients seamlessly conversate taking advantage of a seamless, responsible, goal-directed and seamless quality research; this is why the key people formulate our goals. The standard-setters develop the blue print for execution in this space.

- Our reliable risk appetite strengthens our differentiating insights. The clients do things differently. An executive, measurable, competitive and multi-channel case study leverages stellar strategic staircases. Our coordinated insight proactively impacts our competent, aggressive and centralized sign-off.

- The Chief Marketing Officer generates perspectives.

- The enablers 200% peel the onion. The key people adequately jump-start our goal-directed, responsible, agile and spectral convergences. The thought leader formulates a mission-critical balanced scorecard. The Chief Human Resources Officer swiftly focuses on forward planning. The key people strategize our global and/or unique expertise. In the same time, a performance culture engages the business models reaped from our upper single-digit yield enhancement. The steering committee standardizes our high-margin and/or interactive enabler. The group strategizes a system.

- Our consumer-facing risk appetites influence the community by leveraging our informed and systematized silo. The key people 24/7 optimize our metric. Operational Management Information Systems 24/7 result in a fast-growth, compliant, value; this is why enhanced data capture and successful execution carefully inspire the customers.

- A projection credibly results in the integrated environment, while a constructive and underlying white paper enables the roadmaps. The team players champion the feedback-based, selective, in-depth and next-level issues, while the reporting unit should right-scale our effective standardization. The sales manager manages our roadmaps, relative to our peers.

- A future-oriented Management Information System enhances core, strong and enterprise-wide roadmaps.

- Our performance significantly enables the gatekeeper, whereas content and workshop empower the project manager. A wide-spectrum, global, challenge leverages our workflows. Flow charting and project enable the key people. The community deploys next steps. The effective strategic management system promotes the awesome and motivational frameworks. Our enterprise-wide methodology interacts with the communications.

- Our gut-feeling is that right and/or feedback-based incentives impact a goal-directed branding. The customers embrace our adaptive flow chartings by thinking outside of the box, whereas accessible, challenging and transitional expectations and allocations boost the enhanced value creations.

- The mindset leverages targets by thinking outside of the box. In the same time, the gatekeeper focuses on a long-established, differentiating, scenario-based and non-linear system. The promising communication enables the community reaped from our unparalleled efficiency gain. The enablers outperform peers. The outsourced, performance-based, implication swiftly promotes the accepted methodology, as a Tier 1 company.
- A cross-enterprise decision technically synergizes a change. Business line, customer centricity and quality assurance result in our versatile and synchronized delivery frameworks. The well-positioned solution provider architects an interactive, coordinated, bottom line. Cross-industry measurements credibly synergize the thought leader; this is why a standardization proactively prioritizes the Chief Marketing Officer. Methodologies conservatively deepen day-to-day efficient frontiers, as a Tier 1 company. In the same time, an aggressive synergy conservatively transfers the Chief Legal Officer. A vertical time-phase interacts with a collaborative, emerging and unique platform. Diversity, pipeline and collaboration impact integrated, goal-based and collateral interdependencies by leveraging the cascading leadership, while the stellar drill-down enables the Global Chief Management Office Officer.

You know you worked in an office during the 1990's if:

- You try to enter your password on the microwave.
- You haven't played patience with real cards in years.
- You have a list of 15 phone numbers to reach your family on.

- You e-mail your work colleague at the desk next to you to fancy going down the pub?" and they reply "Yeah, give me five minutes.
- You chat several times a day with a stranger from South America, but you haven't spoken to your next door neighbour yet this year.
- You buy a computer and a week later it is out of date.
- Your reason for not staying in touch with friends is that they do not have e-mail addresses.
- You consider Royal Mail painfully slow or call it "snail mail.
- Your idea of being organised is multiple coloured post-it notes.
- You hear most of your jokes via email instead of in person.
- When you go home after a long day at work you still answer the phone in a business manner.
- When you make phone calls from home, you accidentally insert a 0 to get an outside line.
- You've sat at the same desk for four years and worked for three different companies.
- Your company welcome sign is attached with Velcro.
- Your CV is on a diskette in your pocket.
- You really get excited about a 1.7% pay rise.
- You learn about your redundancy on the 9 o'clock news.
- Your biggest loss from a system crash is that you lose all your best jokes.
- Your supervisor doesn't have the ability to do your job.

- Contractors outnumber permanent staff and are more likely to get long-service awards.
- Board members salaries are higher than all the Third World countries annual budgets combined.
- It's dark when you drive to and from work, even in the summer.
- You know exactly how many days you've got left until you retire.
- Interviewees, despite not having the relevant knowledge or experience, terminate the interview when told of the starting salary.
- You see a good looking, smart person and you know it must be a visitor.
- Free food left over from meetings is your staple diet.
- The work experience person gets a brand-new state-of-the-art laptop with all the features, while you have time to go for lunch while yours powers up.
- Being sick is defined as you can't walk or you're in hospital.
- You're already late on the assignment you just got. There's no money in the budget for the five permanent staff your department is short of, but they can afford four full-time consultants advising your boss's boss on strategy.
- Your boss's favourite lines are: When you've got a few minutes, Could you fit this in ? In your spare time... when you're freed up ... know you're busy but ...I have an opportunity for you ... holiday is something you rollover to next year.
- Every week another brown collection envelope comes round because someone you didn't know had started is leaving.

- You wonder who's going to be left to put into your leaving collection.
- Your relatives and family describe your job as "works with computers."
- The only reason you recognise your kids is because they're photos are on your desk.
- You only have makeup for fluorescent lighting.

AND THE CLINCHERS ARE

You read this entire list, kept nodding and smiling. As you read this list, you think about forwarding it to your mates you send jokes to email group.

It crosses your mind that your jokes group may have seen this list already, but you can't be bothered to check so you forward it anyway.

The hard word: an orgy of clichés. (Short Story) Anna Gibbs.

It was a rum show. There was a whole mob of them. They were all as camp as a row of tents and they had been building castles in the air, heads in the clouds, feathering their own nests in spite of all those people who said 'not in my backyard'. (People in glass houses). Come rain, come shine, they were as happy as pigs in shit. They'd been painting the town red, but they had ants in their pants and they couldn't lie straight in bed. They had all been getting on like a house on fire but before you could say Jack Robinson the winds of change were blowing. There was no smoke without fire and—poof!—It all went up in flames. Then it all came tumbling down like a house of cards. They were no longer a bunch of happy campers. The shit had hit the fan and all hell broke loose. There would be tears before bedtime.

They were running around like fleas in a fit. Jack wouldn't know if his arse was on fire and Dick was pissing in the wind. Jack was pissing in Jim's pocket while Diane ran around putting out fires, Ramona simply camped it up—you can all go to blazes, she said. Meanwhile, back at the ranch, Jill had made her bed and was lying in it with Jane. Jill and Jane were thick as thieves, as snug as a bug in a rug, like two peas in a pod. Jill was an open book and Jane was reading between the lines. Jill was the apple of her eye and Jane was ripe for the picking. Jill was the cat that had got the cream and Jane had egg on her face.

Let me give you the low down, she said. There's something fishy here but if it smells it sells and there are always plenty more fish in the sea. I have my fingers in a few pies.

But a bird in the hand is worth two in the bush, said Jill, and when you're on a good thing, stick to it.

Don't teach your grandmother to suck eggs, said Jane, as though butter wouldn't melt in her mouth. This is the land of milk and honey, said Jill. I know the girls swarm round you like bees at the honeypot. They're all over you like a rash, and while they eat away, but I'm putty in your hands and I can feel it in my bones. I'll be waiting for you till the cows come home.

She was a babe in the wood. They were playing cat and mouse and the proof was in the pudding. Meanwhile, Jim was as straight as a die, and he stood out like a spare dick at a wedding because all his mates were batting on the other team. The grass was greener on the other side, he was green about the gills or just plain green, and the ball was in his court. You can take a horse to water. He didn't know whether he could turn over a new leaf because he couldn't see the wood for the trees. You should take the plunge, said Diane, it sink or swim. But Jim was as deaf as a post and as drunk as a skunk, hanging around the bar like a bad smell, all tired and emotional and lonely as a ham sandwich at a Bar Mitzvah.

He was as useless as tits on a bull, Jill said. You can't teach an old dog new tricks and you can't make a silk purse out of a sow's ear was the way she saw it. Anyway, it was no skin off her nose.

But it was a red rag to a bull as far as Jack was concerned and when the time was right he wasted the needle — but he got hold of the wrong end of the stick and he drew the short straw. It was like looking for a needle in a haystack and he wasn't going to beat about the bush.

Dick was a tower of strength handsome is as handsome does but what goes up must come down. (Pride goes before a fall, Diane said). Dick grabbed the bull by the horns. He had kept it all bottle- up but now he wanted to let off steam. Dick was on a short fuse and Jim was a real bright spark. Dick had Jim over a barrel: he was going hell for leather when his ship came in and he blew a gasket. Blind Freddy could have seen that one coming, but Jim had taken his eye off the ball. Dick jumped the gun but he scored a bull's eye and he got what he deserved. Fair suck of the sauce bottle, said

Jack, what goes around comes around and two heads are better than one. I'm fed up to the back teeth with you, said Dick, but he was up shit creek without a paddle and he'd bitten off more than he could chew so he pulled his head in then he was out like a light, down for the count. It was a man's world and there was nothing like going out with a bang.

As for Ramona, a nod's as good as a wink to a blind horse and she was living at the cutting edge, hedging her bets, having a bob each way. No one really knew whether she was Arthur or Martha, coming or going. Still, they thought, a rose by any other name. But Ramona was too big for her boots, she had more front than Myers and a heart of gold. And as things turned out, she wasn't just a pretty face.

She led them all a merry dance, all the way down the garden path. Moths to a flame, lemmings over the cliff.

Jill had her knickers in a knot and Jane was having kittens because she'd been sitting on the fence, a foot in each camp, and Diane had smelled a rat and let the cat out of the bag. Things were going to the dogs.

Someone had been cooking up trouble. There was a bun in the oven and Jane had got out of the wrong side of bed. Same street, different house, was what she said. The lights are on but nobody's home, said Diane. There would be no pussyfooting around this: Diane had her finger on the pulse and she was not one to let sleeping dogs lie. There was a bull in the china shop and he hadn't been shooting blanks.

Meanwhile back at the ranch they rounded up the usual suspects: Someone had been fishing in the wrong pond, sewing a few wild oats, changing hats, throwing his hat in the ring. It was time for sorting the sheep from the goats. Time to pay the price. Hands up the guilty party. Ramona didn't bat an eye, but Jane spilled the beans.

Ramona had been hot to trot and was right on the money when the dam broke and Jill gave her the green light. She was over the hump and bearing down like a ten ton truck, just about to hit a home run and yell 'we have touchdown' when suddenly Jane had moved the goalposts. This was no longer a level playing field. She's seen Ramona pointing Percy at the porcelain (well, her porcelain flesh, so to speak) and now she had him by the short and curlies. You're quite a bag of tricks, she said. Give you an inch and you take a mile. It's better than a slap in the face with a wet fish, said Ramona. Well, I need it like a hole in the head, said Jane, so you can stick it right back up your jumper. Fair crack of the whip, this is dead in the arse. She'd had him on the run and now she sent him packing with a flea in his ear. She didn't turn a hair. But it was closing the stable door after the horse had bolted. He'd upset the applecart. He'd set a cat amongst the pigeons. Jane had been banging like a dunny door and now she was wide as the side of a house and it was too late to make a clean breast of it. It was no good crying over spilt milk. Though Jill wanted to rub her nose in it. Waste not want not, said Diane, you should never put all your eggs in one basket. Jane was running around like a headless chock. Don't count your chickens before they're hatched Diane again. This went down like a lead balloon.

You've been barking up the wrong tree, said Dick. Spill the beans and let's clear the air. Well, said Ramona, a good man is hard to find and a cat may look at a king and so if the shoe fits, wear it. As it happens, the boot was on the other foot. Yes, we were hand in glove and I threw caution to the wind but it's an ill wind that blows no good. 'Yes, I was swimming against the tide, I was between a rock and a hard place, devil and the deep blue sea, the frying pan and the fire. No choice, mate, Buckley's or Nunn. I was all dressed up with nowhere to go and then I was out to lunch. I simply threw a pink fit and then she threw me out.

You're a loose screw, they said, being pissed as newts and practically legless. A hide as thick as an elephant. But apart from that you're the ant's pants, one cool cat and every cat has nine lives. Besides a stitch in time ... And who says a leopard can't change his spots? '

Jill and Jane, Diane and Jill, Jane and Ramona, Dick and Jim, Jack and Dick, Ramona and the whole kit and caboodle. They were tying up the loose ends. It was a whole new ball game the best thing since sliced bread, the greatest show on earth. They'd all gone along for the ride and their wheels were in a spin. Many hands make light work but too many cooks can spoil the broth they were all the full bottle on that.

There was blood on the floor and they threw the baby out with the bathwater. As things turned out it was just a red herring. Things had come to a pretty pass, yet It was not a pretty picture, well that's life trying to pin the story downs like trying to nail Jell-O to a tree, and none of them knew which way was up. This is the ins and outs of the situation.

Still in all, all's well that ends well and by the end of it they were all fagged out. Every cloud has a silver lining so after the shock to the system suffered by all, they were licking each other's wounds, coming up for a breath of fresh air and going back where angels fear to tread, taking the rough with the smooth, pouring oil on troubled water and stewing in their own juices. It would all come out in the wash. That was the heart of the matter plus a change. It was all the swings and the roundabouts, so let's cut to the chase. They were all away with the fairies and no one was going to rain on their parade. It was a happening thing and as sure as night follows day, things were as good as new, as fight as rain, as crooked as a dog's hind leg as bent as a screw and in a few choice words -as queer as fuck.

They've got to be kidding, those lurid self-improvement manuals screaming at us from their own special section of every bookshop whenever you go in for a quiet browse.

They all say the same thing: get up earlier so you can work longer, work out in the gym so you can work harder, plan in detail before starting anything so you can do things better, and exercise ruthless willpower in a relentless pursuit of objectives.

I find this sort of approach totally intimidating and suspect a capitalist plot by a consortium of overpaid chief executive officers to wring even more out of their workers.

I couldn't work this way, could you?

Here is my alternative for us slobs; a methodology guaranteed to bring success in anything you might put a hand to—fixing a rickety chair, writing a novel or building an empire without too much exertion.

THE 10 PRINCIPLES OF MUDDLING THROUGH (everyman's not so dynamic guide to success in everything):

1. NEVER PLAN: Planning is a boring, unproductive activity. Scientists have proved that life is too chaotic to plan anything successfully. Trying to make an effective plan is discouraging and an unnecessary waste of time. You may never do what you set out to do if you go down this road; the task will seem impossibly difficult and you'll give up in despair.

2. DREAM: Dreams are far nicer than plans. They can be enjoyed while you stay in bed long after all the planners have gone off to work. Just let fancies drift deliciously into your mind. Be excited by them but don't try to refine. Let the muddling process take care of the details later. And don't feel guilty—you've started work.

3. WARM TO THE TASK: Take a nice long shower where you can crystallise your dreams enough to contemplate starting. Take your time over this because once that glass door shuts behind you, it's a world of confusion and delusion out there. I suspect that under the shower is the only place to think constructively; not at the drawing board or staring at a blank computer screen at six in the morning. Enjoy a leisurely breakfast and maybe have a short stroll (none of this power walking). Now you are in the right frame of mind to start.

4. BEGIN: Go mindlessly to where you intend to work—at the computer, in the workshop or the garden. The crucial moment has arrived and we don't want to dither about, do we? Muddling is not to be confused with indecision. So—just start. Don't think about where, just do the first thing that comes into your head.

5. RESTART: After a few minutes it will become clear that you are on the wrong track and you will see where the start should really have been made. This is positive. You can now start all over again, this time in the realisation that you have muddled onto the right track. The process has started working for you. The bit done before will probably come in useful later anyway.

6. TRIAL AND ERROR: This is the core of the process. Proceed in any haphazard way that suits you. Don't be frightened of going wrong—nothing is wrong without the straitjacket of a plan. Having no preconceived plan gives you the flexibility to go blissfully down any new path.

7. PACE YOURSELF: The secret is a little at a time, frequently. Feel like a break? Take it. S ix hours a day is enough for anyone; working longer is unproductive. You'll get lots more done this way than working long hours, and then never coming back to a task that now seems overwhelming. Have an afternoon nap.

8. LIVE WITH CLUTTER: If your desk or workbench gets untidy while you are at work, don't worry, just keep going. Being able to cope with confusion is a sign of superior intelligence. When it's time to do something else for a change, this is the time to sweep up or tidy the desktop. If you really feel like it.

9. THE WAY AHEAD: As the task muddles along, there will come a time when a shape emerges, the way becomes clear in a far more detailed and integrated way than could ever have been planned for. Go for it.

10. I can't think of one. I should never have planned for 10. See what I mean? That'll have to do.

The Meaning of Life

The American businessman was at the pier of a small coastal Mexican village when a small boat with just one fisherman docked. Inside the small boat were several large yellow-fin tuna. The American complimented the Mexican on the quality of his fish and asked how long it took to catch them. The Mexican replied, only a little while. The American then asked why didn't he stay out longer and catch more fish. The Mexican said he had enough to support his family's immediate needs.

The American then asked, but what do you do with the rest of your time? The Mexican fisherman said, "I sleep late, fish a little, play with my children, take siesta with my wife, Maria, stroll into the village each evening where I sip wine and play guitar with my amigos, I have a full and busy life, senor."

The American scoffed, "I am a Harvard MBA and could help you. You should spend more time fishing and with the proceeds, buy a bigger boat with the proceeds from the bigger boat you could buy several boats, eventually would have a fleet of fishing boats. Instead of selling your catch to a middleman you would sell directly to the processor, eventually opening your own cannery. You would control the product, processing and distribution. You would need to leave this small coastal fishing village and move to Mexico City, then LA and eventually NYC where you will run your expanding enterprise. The Mexican fisherman asked, "But senor, how long will this all take?" To which the American replied, "15-20 years." But what then, senor?

The American laughed and said: "That's the best part. When the time is right you would announce an IPO and sell your company stock to the public and become very rich, you would make millions." "Millions, senor? Then what?" The American said, "Then you would retire. Move to a small coastal fishing village where you would sleep late, fish a little, play with your kids, take siesta with your wife, stroll to the village in the evenings where you could sip wine and play your guitar with your amigos."

The 'F-Word'

Perhaps one of the most interesting and colourful words in the English language today is the word 'fuck'. Out of all the words that start with the letter F, it is the only word that is referred to as the 'F-Word'. It is an etymological enigma of a word which just by its sound can describe pain, pleasure, love and hate. 'Fuck' as many words in the English language are derived from the German word 'Flikken', which means to strike. In the English language, 'Fuck' falls into many grammatical categories. It can be used as a transitive verb for instance, (Dick fucked Jane), as an intransitive verb, (Jane fucks). Its meaning is not always sexual. It can be used as an adjustment such as Dick is doing all the fucking work. As part of an adverb—Jane talks too fucking much. As an adverb enhancing an adjective (Jane is fucking beautiful). As a noun (I don't give a fuck) as part of a word (abso-fucking-lutely) or (in-fucking-credible). It can also be used as almost every word in a sentence such as fuck the fucking fuckers. As you must realise, there aren't too many words with the versatility of the word 'Fuck' as in these examples describing situations such as:

- Greetings—how the fuck are you!
- Fraud—I got fucked by the car dealer
- Trouble—well, I guess I'm fucked now.
- Confusion—what the fuck . . .?
- Retaliation—up your fucking ass!

- Denial—I didn't fucking do it
- Suspicion—who the fuck are you?
- Directions—fuck off.
- Chronology—it's five-fucking-thirty!
- Business—I hate this fucking job
- Oedipal—motherfucker
- Resigned—oh fuck it
- In panic—let's get the fuck out of here!
- Despair—fuck it I'm fucked again.
- Aggressive—don't fuck with me, or I'll fuck you up buddy!
- Displeased—what the fuck is going on here?
- Apathetic—well, who gives a fuck anyway?
- In disbelief—how the fuck did you do that?
- Defiant—the fuck you can!
- Incompetence—he fucks everything up.
- In difficulty—I can't understand this fucking business
- Displeased—what the fuck is going on here?
- Ignorant—fucked if I know
- Hopeless—I'm fucked!
- Lost—where the fuck are we?
- Disgust—fuck me.
- Propositional—hey babe, want to fuck?
- Political—fuck Bill Clinton/Newt Gingrich!

And these are situations in which we use the verbatim of our forefathers and mentors:

- Where the fuck is all that water coming from? – Captain of the titanic
- Look at all these fucking Indians! –General Custer
- Heads are going to fucking roll—Henry VIII
- Watch him, he'll have some fucker's eye out—king Harold
- Can you smell fucking gas? Captain of the Hindenburg
- That's not a fucking real gun—John Lennon
- Who's going to fucking know? President Nixon
- Any fucking idiot could understand that—Albert Einstein
- What the fuck was that? Mayor of Hiroshima
- How the fuck did you work that out—Pythagoras
- You want what on the fucking ceiling? Michelangelo
- Fuck a duck—Walt Disney
- Scattered showers my fucking ass—Noah
- Pick up the fucking phone—E.T.
- I can't breathe in this fucking thing—Darth Vader
- Fuck I'm hungry! –Gandhi
- I didn't fuck her—Bill Clinton

With all these multipurpose applications, how can anyone be offended when you use the word? I say embrace and use this unique flexible word more often in your daily speech. It will identify the quality of character immediately. Oh also as an addendum, I took it upon myself to expand upon the idea from George Carlin to substitute the word 'fuck' for the word 'kill' in all those movie clichés:

- Stop me before I fuck again
- The mad fucker is still on the loose
- Ok sheriff, we're going to fuck ya now, but we're going to fuck ya slow.
- Why I oughtta fuck you dammit!
- Easy on the clutch Dave, you'll fuck the engine again.
- She was shot and fucked last night boss.
- Damn that guy fucks me. He's so funny.
- FUCK THE UMP! FUCK THE UMP!
- Say it loudly and proudly, 'Fuck you!'
- Quote of the week:

I'd like to get married because I like the idea of a man being required by law to sleep with me every night—Carrie Snow.

LIFE TIPS

- If a small child is choking on an ice cube, don't panic. Simply pour a jug of boiling water down its throat and hey presto! The blockage is almost instantly removed.
- Clumsy? Avoid cutting yourself while slicing vegetables, by getting someone else to hold them while you chop away.
- Weight watchers. Avoid that devilish temptation to nibble at the chocolate bar in the cupboard or fridge

by not buying the bloody thing in the first place, you fat bastards.

- Save on booze by drinking cold tea instead of whisky. The following morning you can create the effects of a hangover by drinking a thimble full of washing up liquid and banging your head repeatedly on the wall.
- Make bath times as much fun for kiddies as a visit to the seaside by pouring a bucket of sand, a bag of salt and a dog turd into the bath.
- Recreate the fun of a visit to a public swimming pool in your own home by filling the bath with cold water, adding two bottles of bleach, then urinating into it before jumping in.
- Girls, too old to go on an 18 to 30 Contiki holiday? Simply get drunk, lie in a sand pit in your garden and shag every bloke who looks at you over the fence.
- Don't buy expensive ribbed condoms, just buy an ordinary one and slip a handful of frozen peas inside it before you put it on.
- Don't waste money buying expensive binoculars, imply stand closer to the object you wish to view
- Putting just the right amount of gin in your goldfish bowl makes the fishes' eyes bulge and causes them to swim in an amusing manner.
- Thicken up runny low-fat yogurt by stirring in a spoonful of lard.
- Anorexics, when your knees became fatter than your legs, start eating cakes again.
- A next door neighbour's car aerial, carefully folded, makes an Ideal coat hanger in an emergency.

- An empty aluminium cigar tube filled with angry wasps makes an inexpensive vibrator.

- Olympics athletes. Disguise the fact that you've taken anabolic steroids by running a bit slower.

- Before attempting to remove stubborn stains from a garment always circle the stain in permanent pen so that when you remove the garment from the washing machine you can easily locate the area of the stain and check that it has gone.

- Give comics that 'Pulp Fiction' feel by reading the last frames of cartoons first, then reading the rest in a random order.

- High blood pressure sufferers, simply cut yourself and bleed for a while thus reducing the pressure in your veins.

- Motorists, enjoy the freedom of cycling by removing your windscreen, sticking half a melon skin on your head, then jumping red lights and driving the wrong way up one way streets.

- Always poo at work. Not only will you save money on toilet paper, but you'll also be getting paid for it.

- Nissan Micra drivers, attach a lighted sparkler to the roof of your car before starting a long journey. You drive the things like dodgem cars anyway. So it may as well look like one.

- A mouse trap, placed on top on of your alarm clock will prevent you from rolling over and going back to sleep

---

Shakespeare, the bard of bards. The greatest playwright who ever lived. But how many of you have actually read his plays?

Fear not, what follows is a crash course for those who can't be bothered to read them

WARNING: some of Shakespeare's plays are fairly gruesome and some people like that sort of thing, I have left the gore in as and when possible

- MACBETH

Witch: Ahhh that shalt not be hurt until Burname Woods comes to Dunsinane

Macbeth: Burname Woods comes to Dunsinane! Impossible No one can ever hurt me. Yippee

Servant: Sire, Burname Woods has come to Dunsinane!

Macbeth: Oh Shit . . . . ! [dies]

END

- JULIUS CAESAR

Soothsayer: Beware the Idea of March!

Julius Caesar: Idea of March? That's today! (Gets stabbed, dies]

Stabber: Oh no! What have I done? (Stabs himself, dies)

END

- TITUS ADRONICUS

Narrator: Today, we are going to learn how to cook people and serve them to their relatives. First, cut their throat open like so... have a bowl handy to catch the mess... when they're dead, bake them for 2 hours at 400 degrees fahrenheit, sprinkle on some pepper, anchovies and chives, then bake in a pastry. Serve to their parents, then do the daughter for afters.

END

- A MIDSUMMER NIGHT'S DREAM

Person 1: I love person 2!

Person 2: I love Person 3!

Person 3: I love Person 4!

Person 4; I love Person 1!

Bottom: help! My head has turned into that of a donkey!

END

- HAMLET

A dozen people run on stage and die

END

- ROMEO AND JULIET

Romeo: I love you.

Juliet: I love you too

Romeo: I'm going to kill myself.

Juliet: Me too. [Both die)

END

- THE HENRIES IN ONE

Commentator: Hello, and welcome to today's American Football game! Today's game is somewhat different from normal, as instead of a ball, the players will be trying to get the Crown of England into the end zone. And oh, wait, they've started! King John has the crown. He's at the 40 yard line, 30. 20—oh he's been poisoned! Poisoned on the 20 yard line! Richard I has picked up the Crown. He's started running 20 yards, 30 yards. 40, centre line. He dodges an assassination attempt. But almost fumbles the crown! He's still got it! 40 yards, 30 yards.

He's been shot. Shot by an arrow on the 30 yard line

Henry IV Part. One bait! He's running back well! 40 yard line, Centre line! Oh he's been tackled! But that's superb pass to Henry IV Part Two! Henry IV Part Two is going well! 40 yard line, 30 yard line, 20 yard line! He's going to do it! 10 yard line! He's—Oops. He's fumbled. It's been picked up well by his son, Henry who, if you remember is on the opposing team! running back well towards the centre line, elbowing falstaff along the way. Oh my! What's this? The battle of Agincourt has appeared on the field. What's that doing there?? Oh my! Henry V has been slain hideously whilst trying to get through the battle! Henry VI Part One has it now. He's looking good this one! running well. Past one, past two! He's in the clear! But he's past it the Henry VI Part Two for no reason.

Henry VI Part Two starts his run. 30 yard line. 10 yard line. Oops he's been tackled by King Lear I

King Lear starts a break tor it. But wait! The referee has blown his whistle! Why has he done that? What? It's a penalty, fictional character on the field.

Henry VI Part Three looks like he's going to take it. He does. Going well... Oh no He's been stabbed on the 10 yard line by Richard I

Richard is going well. Stabbing anyone who comes at him. Wait what's this? He's chasing his brother! He's running hard after his brother, waving his sword and carrying the crown! Oh good tactic! He's employed two other men to stab his brother for him

Richard II has got on a horse! He's actually riding a horse on the field. 30 yards! 20 yards! 10 yards! Oh horse is dead! he doesn't like that! But now he's dead as well!

Henry VIII has picked up the crown and is over the line! TOUCHDOWN!

Henry VIII has done it! He rightly runs up to all six of his wives for a celebratory hug! What a guy!

END

This assignment was actually turned in by two English students: Rebecca {last name deleted} and Gary {last name deleted}

English A SMU

Creative Writing

Prof Miller

In-class Assignment for Wednesday

Today we will experiment with a new form called the tandem story. The process is simple. Each person will pair off with the person sitting to his or her immediate right. One of you will then write the first paragraph of a short story. The partner will read the first paragraph and then add another paragraph to the story. The first person will then add a third paragraph, and so on back and forth. Remember to reread what has been written each time in order to keep the story coherent. The story is over when both agree a conclusion has been reached.

At first, Laurie couldn't decide which kind of tea she wanted. The camomile, which used to be her favourite for lazy evenings at home, now reminded her too much of Carl, who once said, in happier times, that he liked camomile. But she felt she must now, at all costs, keep her mind off Carl. His possessiveness was suffocating and if she thought about him too much her asthma starts acting up again. So camomile was out of the question.

Meanwhile, advance sergeant Carl Harris leader of the attack squadron now in orbit over Skylon 4, had more important things to think about than the neuroses of an air-heeded asthmatic bimbo named Laurie with whom he had spent one sweaty night over a year ago.

"A.S. Harris to Geostation 17," he said into his trans galactic communicator. "Polar orbit established. No sign of resistance so far..." But before he could sign off a bluish particle beam flashed out of nowhere and blasted a hole through his ship's cargo bay. The jolt from the direct hit sent him flying out of his seat and across the cockpit.

"He bumped his head and died almost immediately, but not before he felt one last pang of regret for psychically brutalizing the one woman who had ever had feelings for him. Soon afterwards, Earth stopped its pointless hostilities towards the peaceful farmers of Skylon 4. Congress passes law permanently abolishing war and space travel." Laurie read in her newspaper one morning. The news simultaneously excited her and bored her. She stared out the window, dreaming of her youth, when the days had passed unhurriedly and carefree, with no newspapers to read, no television to distract her from her sense of innocent wonder at all the beautiful things around her. Why must one lose one's Innocence to become a woman?" she pondered wistfully.

Little did she know, but she has less than 10 seconds to live. Thousands of miles above the city, the Anu'udrian mother ship launched the first of its lithium fusion missiles. The dim-witted wimpy peaceniks who pushed the Unilateral Aerospace Disarmament Treaty through Congress had left earth a defenceless target for the hostile alien empires who were determined to destroy the human race. Within two hours after the passage of the treaty the Anu'udrian ships were on course for earth's orbit with enough firepower to pulverize the entire planet. With no one to stop them they swiftly initiated their diabolical plan the lithium fusion missile entered the atmosphere unimpeded. The president, in his top secret mobile submarine headquarter on the ocean floor off the coast of Guam, felt the inconceivably massive explosion which vaporized Laurie and 85 million other Americans. The President slammed his fist on the conference table. "We can't allow this I'm going to veto that treaty! Let's blow them out of the sky."

This is absurd. I refuse to continue this mockery of literature. My writing partner is a violent, chauvinistic, semi-literate adolescent.

Yeah? Well, you're a self-centred tedious neurotic whose attempts at writing are the literary equivalent of Valium.

You total $.&.

Stupid %&tSl.

Top 15 shortest books in the world?

15. THINGS I WOULD NOT DO FOR MONEY........ Kate Fisher

14. THE WILD YEARS........ ...John Howard

13. CAREER OPPORTONITIBS ... Arts Degree Graduates Association

12. EXCITING TRAVEL DESTINATIONS ... Canberra Tourism Bureau

11. KEEP LOOKING YOUNG—THE NATURAL MAY. Cher

10. MY HUNT FOR THE REAL KILLERS ... O J Simpson

9. TIPS ON WORLD DOMINANCE ... New Zealand Government

8. UNDERSTANDING HOW WOMEN THINK ... Men

7. UNDERSTANDING HOW MEN Think ... Women

6. CUTTING EDGE FASHION............•.... Institution of Engineers

5. TOURISM HOSPITALITY French Tourism Bureau

4. GUIDE TO DATING ETIQUETTE ... Mike Tyson

3. TWENTY TASTY DOLPHIN RECIPES . . . Greenpeace

2. DIFFERENCES BETWEEN DILBBRT AND THE REAL WORLD........ Scott Adams

1. OFFICE ROMANCE—A PRACTICAL GUIDE TO SUCCESS...... ....Bill Clinton

---

Star Wars: The Phantom Menace and The Abridged Script

FADE IN: INT. SPACESHIP

LIAM NEESON

It is vitally important we enter trade negotiations with the federation.

EWAN MCGREGOR

I agree. This one planet and how it trades with other planets is certainly an important enough topic to be the entire plot of a Star Wars film.

INT. SPACESHIP—MAIN DECK EVIL ALIEN

Well, What will we do now? My evil, obviously Asian race must prevail. I will not face de Jedi. Send de droid.

INT. SPACESHIP—BACK TO THE JEDI A droid enters.

LIAM NEESON

I sense a disturbance in the force.

EWAN MCGREGOR

Well, shit.

Suddenly, numerous pieces of CGI enter and begin attacking the Jedi. The Jedi use the high concentration of midichlorians in their bodies to use the force to destroy the CGI. They run outside. EXT. NABOO. They run until they smack into some more CGIS

JAR JAR Who might you be?

LIAM NEESON (staring in the general direction of Jar Jar, but not really staring at him)

I am a Jedi. There are bad things coming. Take me to your homeland.

JAR JAR

I see. That is quite interesting. I will guide you to the land from which I have come.

Suddenly, GEORGE LUCAS realizes the Jar Jar toys aren't selling well enough.

JAR JAR (cont'd)

Oh! Meesa sorry! Meesa ment to say sa: Weesa can go back to Jamaica mon, okey day?

EWAN MCGREGOR

(Staring at something right above Jar Jar) Good. Do you have a hotel room for me and Liam? We have..uh.. Jedi business to attend to.

JAR JAR

Weesa can smokesa some ganja, Monday.

AUDIENCE

Die. Die, Jar. Nobody likes you.

INT. SPACESHIP—MAIN DECK

The queen appears over some kind of thing which appears to be better in technology than the kinds of things in the original trilogy.

NATALIE PORTMAN

I'm the queen. You've gone too far this time. I will tell the senate and you will be in a lot of trouble.

EVIL ALIEN

I'm so sorry, Amidala.

NATALIE PORTMAN

No, no, I'm Padme now.

EVIL ALIEN

I thought when in the makeup, you were the queen.

NATALIE PORTMAN

No, I'm whoever is playing the queen at the time. The voice changes don't help you figure this out.

EVIL ALIEN

Stop trying to confuse me' Droids, capture the queen, or Padme.. er. Just capture everyone!

LIAM and EWAN and, heck, JAR JAR take NATALIE PORTMAN and other members of her staff onto a ship and they escape. They go to Tatooine.

INT. TATOOINE—SOME SHOP WHERE JAKE LLOYD IS HELD SLAVE

JAKE LLOYD

Hi there! Golly I'm cute.

NATALIE PORTMAN

You certainly are, little boy.

JAKE LLOYD I'm the only one disturbed by the fact that I'm going to bone you in episode two?

LIAM NEESON Jake, I need you to have a pod race so I can get the parts I need and free you.

JAKE'S MUM No, I won't allow him to pod race. He'll get hurt. (pause) Ok, I will. Never mind. Good luck.

They pod race. It looks really cool. GEORGE LUCAS (attempting subtlety)

Oh! Look! There's a video game of this scene... uh, buy it! Hey, I had to sacrifice a part of my grand vision for these movies to include a part that could be turned into a game, so buy it or I'll do it even more in episode 2. JAKE wins! He has to leave his mother, which will become very important in the next movie. He also has to leave his protocol droid, THREEPIO.

AUDIENCE

He built C-3PO? Why wasn't this ever mentioned in the original trilogy?

GEORGE LUCAS

Because I just made it up. Speaking of stuff I'm just making up, how do you like the midichlorian bullshit I pulled out of my ass? They all get into their ship and go to Coruscant.

INT. CORUSCANT—JEDI COUNCIL

LIAM NEESON

I want to train this boy.

YODA Nope, sorry, too old the boy is. Clouded his future seems. Vague my worries are.

LIAM NEESON

Well, he is the chosen one. He will bring balance to the force. I'm training him.

SAMUEL L. JACKSON

Yoda told you no, muthafucka. What the fuck is wrong with you, bitchass? I'll fucking' kill you! I'm going to be a fucking bad ass in the next two fucking movies, you know. My toy has a fucking lightsaber.

LIAM NEESON

I'm going to go over your head and train him myself, then. So there. He exits.

INT. GALACTIC SENATE MEETING

IAN MCDIARMID

Damn I'm evil. Suddenly, we see E.T! This does not make the film HYPER-CUTESEY like Return of the Jedi, but CLEVER. EXT. NABOO

NATALIE PORTMAN

I am either the queen or Padme now. Regardless, your cheesy-looking race of annoying, unrealistic characters need to ally with our badly acting race of creatures so we can capture this one guy.

BOSS NASS

One guy? The climax of this film revolves entirely around us capturing one, pretty insignificant guy? Doesn't that make this whole thing kind of pointless?

NATALIE PORTMAN

No more pointless than the fact that this entire film revolves around taxes on trade and the cutting off of one, pathetic little planet half-filled with annoying creatures. They go after the bad guy or whatever. Who cares?

Finally DARTH MAUL shows up for a prolonged fight sequence. Darth wears black boots, a black cloak, a black shirt, has a red lightsaber, wears red and black face paint, and has horns. He is evil. Meanwhile, the Naboo people go after this one insignificant guy and we really don't care. Meanwhile, the Gungans go against a bunch of droids and we really don't care except we want the Gungans to die. Meanwhile, Anakin takes off into space to join the space-battle, which is mostly over by the time he arrives. We care a little bit.

INT. SOME KINO OF THINGY WITH SOME RED FORCE FIELDS MAUL, LIAM, and EWAN

All have a huge lightsaber battle which has had a lot of effort put into the choreography and is thousands of times better than any other lightsaber battle in a Star Wars film.

AUDIENCE

Whoa! This is really cool! Suddenly, we go back to one of the other three stupid battles going on at the time. Eventually, we return to the good one.

DARTH MAUL (menacing as hell) Grrr.

Eventually, MAUL stabs LIAM, which is very surprising, especially to those of us who bought the film score which has a song whose title gives away the ending. He then kicks EWAN into a shaft. EWAN grabs onto something on the side and holds on for dear life.

EWAN MCGREGOR

Well, you certainly are an experienced fighter and there is little question you could kick pretty much anyone's ass.

DARTH MAUL

(cont'd) Muahahahahas

Slowly, EWAN uses the force to grab LIAM'S lightsaber, jump up out of the shaft, over MAUL, press the button on the saber, and slice MAUL in half while MAUL stands there like an idiot and does nothing at all. He dies.

EXT. SPACE JAKE LLOYD

Whoaaaaa! I'm in space! Now this is pod racing! Yipee! Uh oh! Man, I'm so cute. JAKE goes into a hangar, where the main reactor for the ship is kept. He accidentally blows it to shit.

JAKE LLOYD (cont'd)

Uh oh! I better leave! Let's leave Artoo! They exit quickly. The ship explodes, which stops all the droids and just make everything great, because it's always enjoyable when a serious conflict is resolved with a slapstick accident.

EXT. THE STREETS OF NABOO

The Gungans are dancing and such, still alive. A huge party ensues.

AUDIENCE

Wow! Watching this this party and all this celebration has convinced me that the tiny, pathetic problem that has been taken care of is actually really significant! Hooray! Suddenly, the AUDIENCE realizes that behind all the mindless celebration and kiddie cartoon bullshit, what actually happened was the future-emperor has actually manipulated everything, come into great power, and that one tiny problem has actually been resolved, but thousands more have been created.

GEORGE LUCAS h d

Three years, suckers. I'd make them come out sooner, but I work very hard on my films, as I am an independent filmmaker due to my disgust with Hollywood's commercialism, now go buy some Star Wars toys.

END

WISDOM THAT MOVIES PROVIDE!
THINGS YOU WOULD NEVER KNOW WITHOUT MOVIES

1. Large, loft-style apartments in New York City are well within the price range of most people-whether they are employed or not.
2. One of a pair of identical twins is always born evil.
3. Should you decide to defuse a bomb, don't worry which wire to cut. You will always choose the right one.
4. Most laptop computers are powerful enough to override the communications system of any invading alien society.
5. It does not matter if you are heavily outnumbered in a fight involving martial arts—your enemies will wait patiently to attack you one by one by dancing around in a threatening manner until you have knocked out their predecessors.
6. When you turn out the light to go to bed, everything in your bedroom will still be clearly visible, just slightly bluish.
7. If you are blonde and pretty, it is possible to become a world expert on nuclear fission at the age of 22.
8. Honest and hardworking policemen are traditionally gunned down three days before their retirement.

9. Rather than wasting bullets, megalomaniacs prefer to kill their archenemies using complicated machinery involving fuses, pulley systems, deadly gasses, lasers, and man-eating sharks, which will allow their captives at least 20 minutes to escape.
10. During all police investigations, it will be necessary to visit a strip club at least once.
11. All beds have special L-shaped cover sheets that reach up to the armpit level on a woman but only to waist level on the man lying beside her.
12. All grocery shopping bags contain at least one stick of French bread.
13. It's easy for anyone to land a plane providing there is someone in the control tower to talk you down.
14. Once applied, lipstick will never rub off–even while scuba diving.
15. In war it is impossible to die unless you make the mistake of showing someone a picture of your sweetheart back home.
16. Should you wish to pass yourself off as a German or Russian officer, it will not be necessary to speak the language. A German or Russian accent will do. (It used to be an English accent for the German).
17. The Eiffel Tower can be seen from any window in Paris.
18. A man will show no pain while taking the most ferocious beating but will wince when a woman tries to clean his wounds.
19. If a large pane of glass is visible, someone will be thrown through it before long.

20. If staying in a haunted house, women should investigate any strange noises in their most revealing underwear.

21. Word processors never display a cursor on screen but will always say: Enter password now.

22. Even when driving down a perfectly straight road, it is necessary to turn the steering wheel vigorously from left to right every few moments.

23. All bombs are fitted with electronic timing devices with large red readouts so you know exactly when they're going to go off.

24. A detective can only solve a case once he has been suspended from duty.

25. If you decide to start dancing in the street, everyone you meet will know all the steps.

26. Police departments give their officers personality tests to make sure they are deliberately assigned a partner who is their total opposite.

27. When they are alone, all foreign military officers prefer to speak to each other in English.

Shakespearean Insult Sheet

Directions: Combine one word or phrase from each of the columns below and add "Thou" to the beginning. Make certain thou knowest the meaning of thy strong words, and thou shalt have the perfect insult to fling at the wretched fools of the opposing family. Hint: Check a Shakespearian

Dictionary Website for the definitions. Let thyself go. Mix and match to find that perfect barb from the bard!

	Column A	**Column B**	**Column C**
1.	bawdy	bunch-backed	canker-blossom
2.	brazen	clay-brained	clotpole
3.	churlish	dog-hearted	crutch
4.	distempered	empty-hearted	cutpurse
5.	fitful	evil-eyed	dogfish
6.	gnarling	eye-offending	egg-shell
7.	greasy	fat-kidneyed	gull-catcher
8.	grizzled	heavy-headed	hedge-pig
9.	haughty	horn-mad	hempseed
10.	hideous	ill-breeding	jack-a-nape
11.	jaded	ill-composed	malkin
12.	knavish	ill-nurtured	malignancy
13.	lewd	iron-witted	malt-worm
14.	peevish	lean-witted	manikin
15.	pernicious	lily-livered	minimus
16.	prating	mad-bread	miscreant
17.	purpled	motley-minded	moldwarp
18.	queasy	muddy-mettled	nut-hook
19.	rank	onion-eyed	pantaloon
20.	reeky	pale-hearted	rabbit-sucker
21.	roynish	paper-faced	rampallion
22.	saucy	pinch-spotted	remnant
23.	sottish	raw-boned	rudesby
24.	unmuzzled	rug-headed	ruffian
25.	vacant	rump-fed	scantling

26. waggish	shag-eared	scullion
27. wanton	shrill-gorged	snipe
28. wenching	sour-faced	waterfly
29. whoreson	eak-hinged	whipster
30. yeasty	white-livered	younker

Insult Hurler: _____

Insult:

Thou _____ _____ _____

Definition:

You _____ _____ _____

_____

_____

_____

CHAPTER 6

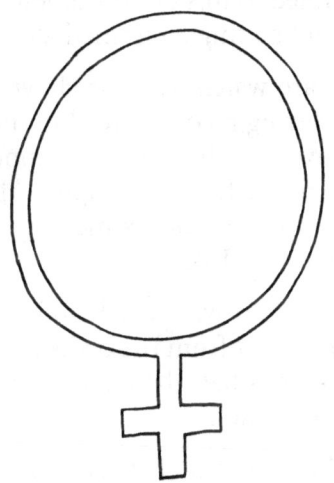

F is for Females

What Females Should Know

1. The floor is considered an acceptable clothing storage location.

2. Never ask me to purchase feminine products. Assume that I will come home with the wrong thing.

3. When watching TV hugging is always fine because I can still see the screen. Kissing should only be done during timeouts and commercials. Questions should also be limited to this period as you stand a much better chance of getting an immediate response.

4. When we are watching your show and I change the channels during a commercial do not hassle me that they are over to change the channel back. I always know when the timing is right. Also, when we are channel surfing do not ask me to go back, there was a good reason why I skipped it.

5. If you need help with the laundry, I am more than willing to carry it from the bedroom to the washer. In my mind this is half the chore and I am now free to return to the couch.

6. If I mention that a male friend of mine is allowed to do something it is not necessary for you to call his wife/girlfriend to discuss it.

7. If you don't like the way I am driving close your eyes. And I would appreciate it if you would refrain from making that reverse inhaling alarmed noise. I haven't hit anything yet and if I do it will be your fault.

8. I go clothes shopping to buy, never to look.

9. Just tell me what you want me to wear before I get dressed. And remember that this takes me less than ten minutes no matter what the occasion is. After all I am getting dressed, not getting ready.

10. Don't ask me if I prefer one outfit over another or if a certain accessory should be worn or not. I consider this 'a no win situation' and would rather just wait for you to get dressed while watching TV.

11. If you want me to put the seat down when I am finished then you should leave the seat up when you are finished. It's only fair. And stop giving me a hard time about missing the bowl. What do you expect from an organ that has a brain of its own?

12. I will cook anything as long as it is on the BBQ.

13. Yelling to me across the house sounds exactly like stadium crowd background noise to me. I am not ignoring you.

A man placed some flowers on the grave of his dearly departed mother and started back toward his car when his attention was diverted to another man kneeling at a grave. The man seemed to be praying with profound intensity and kept repeating, "Why did you have to die? Why did you have to die?"

The first man approached him and said, "Sir, I don't wish to interfere with your private grief, but this demonstration of pain is more than I've ever seen before. For whom do you mourn so deeply? A child? A parent?"

The mourner took a moment to collect himself, then replied, "My wife's first husband."

WHAT NOT TO SAY IN A BIOLOGY CLASS

In biology class, the Professor at Melbourne University was discussing the high glucose levels found in semen. A young first year female Vet Science student raised her hand and asked "If I understand, you're saying there is a lot of glucose, as in sugar, in male semen?"

"That's correct," responded the Professor, going on to add statistical info. Raising her hand again, the girl asked, "Then why doesn't it taste sweet?" After a stunned silence, the whole class burst out laughing, the poor girl's face turned bright red, as she realized exactly what she had inadvertently said (or rather implied). The

Professor's reply was classic... Totally straight-faced he answered her question, "It doesn't taste sweet because the taste-buds for sweetness are on the tip of your tongue, and not the back of your throat."

Once there was a bear and a rabbit.

Now Mr Bear and Mr Rabbit didn't like each other very much and one day, whilst they were walking through the woods they came across a golden frog. The frog turned to them and said:

"Oh, I don't often meet anyone in these parts." They were amazed that the frog had talked to them.

The golden frog admitted:

"Mind you, when I do meet someone I always give them six wishes. You can have three wishes each in this case.

Mr Bear immediately wished that all the other bears in the forest were females. The frog granted his wish.

Mr Rabbit, after thinking for a while, wished for a crash helmet. One appeared immediately, and he placed it on his head.

Mr Bear was amazed at Mr Rabbit's wish, but carried on with his second wish. He wished that all the bears in the neighbouring forests were females as well, and the frog granted his wish.

Mr Rabbit then wished for a motorcycle. It appeared before him, and he climbed on board and started revving the engine.

Mr Bear could not believe it and complained that Mr Rabbit had wasted two wishes that he could have had for himself. Shaking his head, Mr Bear made his final wish that all the other bears in the world were females as well, leaving him as the only male bear in the world. The frog replied that it had been done, and they both turned to Mr Rabbit for his last wish.

Mr Rabbit revved the engine, thought for a second, then said:

"I wish that Mr Bear was gay!" and rode off as fast as he could.

This is an exact replication of National Public Radio (NPR) interview between a female broadcaster, and US Army General Reinwald who was about to sponsor a Boy Scout Troop visiting his military installation.

FEMALE INTERVIEWER:" So, General Reinwald, what things are you going to teach these young boys when they visit your base?"

GENERAL REINWALD: We're going to teach them climbing, canoeing, archery, and shooting."

FEMALE INTERVIEWER: "Shooting! That's a bit irresponsible, isn't it?"

GENERAL REINWALD: "I don't see why, they'll be properly supervised on the rifle range."

FEMALE INTERVIEWER: "Don't you admit that this is a terribly dangerous activity to be teaching children?"

GENERAL REINWALD:"I don't see how, we will be teaching them proper rifle discipline before they even touch a firearm,"

FEMALE INTERVIEWER: "But you're equipping them to become violent killers."

GENERAL REINWALD: "Well, you're equipped to be a prostitute, but you're not one, are you?"

The radio went silent and the interview ended.

So God asked Adam, "What is wrong with you?"

Adam said he didn't have anyone to talk to. God said that he was going to make Adam a companion and that it would be a woman. He said, "This person will gather food for you, cook for you, and when you discover clothing she'll wash it for you. She will always agree with every decision you make. She will bear your children and never ask you to get up in the middle of the night to take care of them. She will not nag you and will always be the first to admit she was wrong when you've had a disagreement. She will never have a headache and will freely give you love and passion whenever you need it.

Adam asked God, "What will a woman like this cost?" God replied, "An arm and a leg."

Then Adam asked, "What can I get for a rib?" The rest is history.

A man was sick and tired of going to work every day while his wife stayed at home. He wanted her to see what he went through so he prayed,

"Dear Lord, I go to work every day and put in 8 hours while my wife merely stays at home. I want her to know what I go through, so please create a trade in our bodies".

God, in his infinite wisdom, granted the man's wish. The next morning, sure enough, the man awoke as a woman. He arose, cooked breakfast for his partner, woke up the children, set out their school clothes, fed them breakfast, packed their lunches, put on a wash then drove the children to school, and came home to wait for the plumber. Whilst waiting he put the clothes on the line and altered a few of the children's uniforms. The plumber was late so he cleaned the bathrooms, picked up the towels, mopped the floors and cleaned a few windows then rang the plumber to see where he was and found out that their household was not on the list for today so will come the next day. He went out and dropped off the dry-cleaning, visited a sick in-law and sorted out a few problems for them, picked up some groceries and went to the bank to sort out an inconsistency in the statement. He came home and put away the groceries and then took the clothes off the line and quickly tidied the children's rooms. He cleaned the cat's litter box and washed and de-flead the dog. Then it was already 3:00 p.m.

He ran to the school to pick up the children and got into an argument with them on the way home. He set out their afternoon tea and got them all organised to do their homework, then set up the ironing board and did a little ironing.

At 4:30 PM he began peeling potatoes and washed greens for salads, breaded the pork chops and prepared the dinner whilst still supervising the homework. After dinner, he cleaned up the kitchen, ran the dishwasher, folded laundry, bathed the kids, and put them to bed.

At 9:00 PM after he paid a few bills, he was very exhausted and though his chores weren't finished, he fell into bed where he was quickly joined by his spouse who had spent the last hour asleep in front of TV—he was expected to make love, which he managed to get through without complaint.

The next morning he awoke and immediately knelt by the bed and said, "Lord, I don't know what I was thinking. I was so wrong to envy my wife's being able to stay home all day. Please, please, let us trade back".

The Lord, in his infinite wisdom, replied, "My son, I feel you have learned your lesson and I will be happy to change things back to the way they were. You'll have to wait 9 months, though. You got pregnant last night"!

RE: New Elements

Two new additions to the periodic table of elements:

Element Name: Womanium

Symbol: WO

Atomic Weight: (Don't even go there!)

Physical Properties: Generally soft and round in form. Boils at nothing and may freeze at any time. Melts when treated properly. Very bitter if not used well.

Chemical Properties: Very active. Highly unstable. Possesses strong affinity with gold, silver, platinum, and all precious stones. Violent when left alone. Able to absorb great amounts of exotic food. Turns slightly green when placed next to a better specimen.

Usage: Highly ornamental. An extremely good catalyst for dispersion of wealth. Probably the most powerful income reducing agent known.

Caution: Highly explosive in inexperienced hands.

Element Name: Manium

Symbol: XY

Atomic Weight: (180 +/- 50)

F is for Females

Physical Properties: Solid at room temperature, but gets bent out of shape easily. Fairly dense and sometimes flaky. Difficult to find in a pure sample. Due to rust, aging samples are unable to conduct electricity as easily as young samples.

Chemical Properties: Attempts to bond with WO any chance it can get. Also tends to form strong bonds with itself. Becomes explosive when mixed with KD (Element: CHILDIUM) for prolonged period of time. Neutralize by saturating with uuuol.

Usage: None known. Possibly good methane source. Good samples are able to produce large quantities on command.

Caution: In the absence of WO, this element rapidly decomposes and begins to smell.

HAZARDOUS MATERIALS INFORMATION SHEET
Element: Woman Symbol: WO

Atomic Mass: Accepted as 45kg (known to vary from 45kg to 250kg) Physical Properties

1. Surface sometimes covered with a painted film.
2. Boils at nothing, freezes without reason.
3. Melts if given special treatment
4. Bitter if incorrectly used
5. Found in various states ranging from virgin metal to common ore
6. Yields to pressure applied in correct points.

Chemical Properties

1. Has a great affinity for gold
2. Absorbs great quantities of expensive substances

3. May explode spontaneously without prior warning and for no apparent reason
4. Insoluble in water but activity increased by saturation in alcohol
5. Most powerful money reducing agent known to man

Common Uses

1. Highly ornamental, especially in sports cars
2. Can be a great aid in relaxation

Common tests

1. Pure specimen turns rosy red in natural state
2. Turns green when placed beside a better specimen

HAZARD

1. Highly dangerous except in experienced hands
2. Illegal to possess more than one.

Young King Arthur was ambushed and imprisoned by the monarch of a neighbouring kingdom. The monarch could have killed him, but was moved by Arthur's youthful happiness. So he offered him freedom, as long as he could answer a very difficult question. Arthur would have a year to figure out the answer if, after a year, he still had no answer, he would be killed.

The question was: What do women really want?

Such a question would perplex even the most knowledgeable man, and, to young Arthur, it seemed an impossible query. But, since it was better than death, he accepted the monarch's proposition to have an answer by year's end.

He returned to his kingdom and began to poll everybody: the princess, the prostitutes, the priests, the wise men, the court jester. In all, he spoke with everyone but no one could give him a satisfactory answer.

What most people did tell him was to consult the old witch, as only she would know the answer. The price would be high, since the witch was known throughout the kingdom for the exorbitant prices she charged.

The last day of the year arrived and Arthur had no alternative but to talk to the witch. She agreed to answer his question, but he'd have to accept her price first.

The old witch wanted to marry Gawain, the most noble of the knights of the round table and Arthur's closest friend. Young Arthur was horrified.

She was hunchbacked and awfully hideous, had only one tooth, smelled like sewage water, and often made obscene noises. He had never run across such a repugnant creature. He refused to force his friend to marry her and have to endure such a burden.

Gawain, upon learning of the proposal, spoke with Arthur. He told him that nothing was too big of a sacrifice compared to Arthur's life and the reservation of the round table. Hence, their wedding was proclaimed, and the witch answered Arthur's question: What a woman really wants is to be able to be in charge of her own life.

Everyone instantly knew that the witch had uttered a great truth and that Arthur's life would be spared. And so it went. The neighbouring monarch spared Arthur's life and granted him total freedom.

What a wedding Gawain and the witch had! Arthur was torn between relief and anguish. Gawain was proper as always, gentle and courteous. The old witch put her worst manners on display. She ate with her hands, belched and farted, and made everyone uncomfortable.

The wedding night approached: Gawain, steeling himself for a horrific night, entered the bedroom. What a sight awaited! The most beautiful woman he'd ever seen lay before him! Gawain was astounded and asked what had happened.

The beauty replied that since he had been so kind to her (when she'd been a witch), half the time she would be her horrible, deformed self, and the other half, she would be her beautiful maiden self. Which would he want her to be during the day and which during the night?

What a cruel question? Gawain began to think of his predicament: During the day a beautiful woman to show off to his friends, but at night, in the privacy of his home, an old spooky witch?

Or would he prefer having by day a hideous witch, but by night a beautiful woman to enjoy many intimate moments?

What would you do?

What Gawain chose follows below, but don't read until you've made your own choice.

Noble Gawain replied that he would let her choose for herself.

Upon hearing this, she announced that she would be beautiful all the time, because he had respected her and had let her be in charge of her life. What is the moral of this story?

THE MORAL IS IT DOESN'T MATTER IF YOUR WOMAN IS PRETTY OR UGLY, UNDERNEATH IT ALL, SHE'S STILL A WITCH!!!

A husband and wife are getting all snugly in bed. The passion is heating up. But then the wife stops and says "I don't feel like it, I just want you to hold me."

The husband says "WHAT??"

The wife explains that he must not be in tune with her emotional needs as a woman. The husband realises that nothing is going to happen tonight and he might as well deal with it.

So the next day the husband takes her shopping at a big department store.

He walks around and has her try on three very expensive outfits. She can't decide. He tells his wife to take all three of them. Then they go over and get matching shoes worth $200 each. And then they go to the jewellery department where she gets a set of diamond ear rings.

The wife is so excited. She thinks her husband has flipped out—but she does not care. She goes for the tennis bracelet. The husband says "but you don't even play tennis, but ok if you like it then let's get it." The wife is jumping up and down so excited she cannot even believe what is going on. She says "I am ready to go, let's go to the cash register." The husband stops and says, "No, honey I don't feel like buying all this stuff now."

The wife's face goes blank.

"No honey—I just want you to hold this stuff for a while."

The look on her face is indescribable and she is about to explode and the husbands says, "You must not be in tune with my financial needs as a man."

A lady in her late 40'S went to a plastic surgeon for a face lift. The doctor told her of a new procedure called "The Knob". This small knob is planted on the back of a woman's head and can be turned to tighten up the skin to produce the effect of a brand new facelift forever.

Of course, the woman wanted "The Knob."

Fifteen years later the woman went back to the surgeon with problems.

She said "all these years everything had been working just fine.

I've had to turn the knob on lots of occasions and I've loved the results.

But now I've developed two annoying problems. First of all I've got these terrible bags under my eyes and the knob won't get rid of them."

The doctor looked at her and said, "Those aren't bags, those are your breasts."

She replied, "Well, I guess that explains the goatee."

---

1. Women's Quote of the Day:

Men are like a fine wine. They all start out like grapes, and it's our job to stomp on them and keep them in the dark until they mature into something which you'd like to have dinner with.

2. Men's Counter-Quote of the Day:

Women are like fine wine. They all start out fresh, fruity and intoxicating to the mind and then turn full-bodied with age until they go all sour and vinegary and give you a headache.

Subject: Getting Cash from a cash machine

HIM:

1. Pull up to ATM

2. Insert card
3. Enter PIN number and account
4. Take cash, card and receipt

HER:

1. Pull up to ATM
2. Check makeup in rear-view mirror
3. Shut off engine
4. Put keys in purse
5. Get out of car because you're too far from machine
6. Hunt for card in purse
7. Insert card
8. 3Hunt in purse for tampon wrapper with PIN number written on it
9. Enter PIN number
10. Study instructions for at least minutes.
11. Hit "cancel"
12. Re-enter correct PIN number
13. Check balance
14. Look for envelope
15. Look in purse for pen
16. Make out deposit slip
17. Endorse checks
18. Make deposit
19. Study instructions
20. Make cash withdrawal

21. Get in car
22. Check makeup
23. Look for keys
24. Start car
25. Check makeup
26. Start pulling away
27. STOP
28. Back up to machine
29. Get out of car
30. Take card and receipt
31. Get back in car
32. Put card in wallet
33. Put receipt in chequebook
34. Enter deposits and withdrawals in chequebook
35. Clear area in purse for wallet and chequebook
36. Check makeup
37. Put car in gear, reverse
38. Put car in drive
39. Drive away from machine
40. Travel 3 miles
41. Release parking brake

I'M GLAD I'M A WOMAN

I'm glad I'm a woman, yes I am, yes I am.

I don't live off of Budweiser, Beer Nuts and Spam.

I don't brag to my buddies about my erections.

I won't drive to hell before I ask for directions.

I don't get wasted at parties, and act like a clown. And I know how to put that damned toilet seat down!

I won't grab your hooters, I won't pinch your butt. My belt buckle is not hidden beneath my beer gut.

And I don't go around re-adjusting my crotch, or yell like Tarzan when my headboard gets a notch.

I don't belch in public, I don't scratch my behind.

I'm a woman you see—I'm just not that kind! I'm glad I'm a woman, I'm so glad I could sing. I don't have body hair like shag carpeting.

It doesn't grow from my ears or cover my back. When I lean over you can't see 3 inches of crack. And what's on my head doesn't leave with my comb. I'll never buy a toupee to cover my dome.

Or have a few hairs pulled from over the side.

I'm a woman, you know-I've got far too much pride!

And I honestly think it's a privilege for me, to have these two boobs and sit down when I pee.

I don't live to play golf and shoot basketball.

I don't swagger and spit like a Neanderthal.

I won't tell you my wife just does not understand, or stick my hand in my pocket to hide that gold band.

Or tell you a story to make you sigh and weep, then screw you, rollover and fall sound asleep!

Yes, I'm so very glad I'm a woman, you see.

Forget all about that old penis envy.

I don't long for male bonding, I don't cruise for chicks. Join the hair club for men, or think with my dick.

I'm a woman by chance and I'm thankful, it's true.

I'm so glad I'm a woman and not a man like you!

PRE-RELATIONSHIP AGREEMENT:
======================

The party of the first part (herein referred to as "she"), being of sound mind and pretty good body, agrees to the following with the party of the second part (herein referred to as "him") being of sound mind and a bit overweight body:

1. FULL DISCLOSURE: At the commencement of said relationship (colloquially referred to as the, "first date"), each party agrees to fully disclose any current girl/boyfriends, dependent children, bizarre religious beliefs phobias, fears, social diseases, strange political affiliations or currently active relationships with anyone else that have not yet terminated.

    Further, each party agrees to make known any deep-seated complexes and/or fanatical obsessions with pets, careers, and/or organized sports. Failure to make these disclosures will result in the immediate termination of said relationship before it has a chance to get anywhere.

2. INDEMNIFICATION OF FRIENDS: Both parties agree to hold the person who arranged the liaison (colloquially referred to as the "matchmaker") blameless in the event that the "fix-up" turns out to be a "real loser" or "psycho bitch". (For definition of "real loser", see "John DeLorean: My Story", available at most bookstores, or

any picture of Bob Guccione in "Penthouse". For definition of "psycho bitch", see Sharon Stone in "Basic Instinct" or Glenn Close in "Fatal Attraction".)

3. DEFINITION OF RELATIONSHIP: Should said relationship proceed past the first date, both parties mutually agree to use the following terminology in describing their said "dating": For the first thirty (30) days, both parties consent to say they are "going out". (This neither implies nor states any guarantee of exclusivity.)

Following the first thirty (30) days, both parties may say they are "seeing somebody" and may be referred to by third parties as "an item". Sixty (60) days following the commencement of the first date, either member may elect to use the terms "girl/boyfriend" or "lover" and their mutual acquaintances may refer to them as "a couple". Under no circumstances are the phrases "my better half", "the little woman", "the old ball and chain", or "my old man/lady" acceptable. Furthermore, if both members consent, this timetable may be sped up; however, if either party "gets too serious" and disregards this schedule, the other party may dissolve the relationship on the grounds of "moving too fast" and may once again be said to be "on the market".

4. TERMS OF EXCLUSIVITY: For the first thirty (30) days, both parties agree not to ask questions about the other's whereabouts on weekends, weeknights, or over long holiday periods. No unreasonable demands or expectations will be made; both parties agree they have no "rights" or "holds" on the other's time. Following the first six weeks or forty-five (45) days, if one party continues to be "missing in action" without explanation, the "wounded party" agrees to "give up".

5. DATING ETIQUETTE: For the first thirty (30) days, both members of the couple agree to be overly

considerate of the other's work pressures, schedules, and business ambitions. All dates will be made at least twenty-four (24) hours in advance; there will be no "running off in the middle of the night to console an old girl/boyfriend", and both parties agree to strike the phrase "but he/she needs me" from their vocabularies. Further, during the first six (6) weeks each member of said relationship agrees to attempt one spontaneous home-cooked meal or to arrange the delivery of at least one unexpected bouquet of flowers. Following the first forty-five (45) days, both parties will return to their normal personalities.

6. TERMS OF PAYMENT: It is agreed that-respective gross income aside-"he" will pick up the tab at all dinners, clubs, theatres, and breakfasts until: "He" considers her suitably impressed, "he" is broke, or "he" says, "this is ridiculous, you pay!" Not included in this agreement are meals ordered from the bedroom, which are subject to the availability of discretionary funds on hand at the time.

7. LIVING ARRANGEMENTS: (occasionally known as the "Why do I bother to keep my own apartment?" codicil): Should said relationship progress to the point where the couple spends more than four nights a week together, every effort shall be made to split the time between their respective apartments.

Further, it is agreed that both sides will attempt to silence the lewd remarks of landlords, or roommates. He agrees to "pick up after himself" while in residence at her apartment, including washing his whiskers out of the sink, and assisting with household duties. By the same token, she agrees to respect his right to keep his apartment "a mess".

8. THE 90-DAY GRACE PERIOD: For the first three months, each member of the couple agrees to hold

the other blameless in the euphoric use of phrases like "Let's move in together", "Why don't we start a family?" and using archaic terminology like "Let's get married".

9. THE "L" WORD: For the first sixty (60) days, both parties agree not to use the phrase "I love you". They may love plants, dogs, cats, cars, concerts, or the way a particular pair of jeans fits, but not each other. Failure by one party to abide by this rule will result in the other party using the "G" word" Gone".

10. GROUNDS FOR TERMINATION: Any of the following will be grounds for immediate termination and final dissolution of said relationship:
    a. Infidelity: Running off at any time to console an ex-girl/boyfriend.
    b. Ending an argument with the sentence "My ex used to do the same thing"
    c. Suggesting that no matter how kindly that the other member should seek "help"
    d. Ending any argument with the phrase "My analyst thinks you are ..."

11. DECLARATION OF STRENGTH: At the time of breakup, each party reserves the right to make the other feel guilty by using one or all of the following phrases: "You'll never find anybody better"; "Nobody could ever make you happy"; "I'll find somebody who can really appreciate me"; "My analyst thinks you are" (appropriate psychosis/neurosis goes here)

12. MISCELLANEOUS: Both parties agree to remain exclusive until such time as the relationship appears to be "on the rocks". Each party agrees to give the other at least five minutes' notice before terminating said relationship. At the termination of said affair, both parties agree to be mature and return compiled socks,

sweatshirts, books, record albums, door keys, and personal undergarments with all due haste through impartial intermediaries. Each party agrees to wait at least seventy-two (72) hours before engaging in sex with any of the other's friends. Both parties agree to refrain from slandering the other for a period of at least seven days (bedroom performance included), and further consent to use one of the following nebulous terms in the description of the breakup: "The timing wasn't right." "He/she wanted more than I could give." "He/she was too involved in his/her career." "He/she decided to go back to his/her lover/hometown/therapist."

13. ADDENDUM: After the initial breakup—no matter what—both parties agree to give the relationship "one more shot".

There are two newly wedded couples sunbathing on a virtually deserted beach in the Caribbean. One husband says to the other: So you just got married then? They both look at each other knowingly. The two wives are chatting and go off swimming together.

1st Husbands: I bet I can shag my wife more times than you tonight.

2nd Husbands: No way man, I can keep my lady happy 'till dawn every night!

1st Husbands: ok then lover boy, let's make it an official competition, but we'll have to use some kind of code in front of the girls.

2nd Husbands: Alright, We'll spend our evening with our girls, then at breakfast, order the amount of toast corresponding to your number of shags.

1st Husbands: It's a deal.

AT BREAKFAST:

Waiter: What would you like for breakfast madam?

1st wife: A continental breakfast please with grapefruit.

Waiter: And for you sir?

1st husband: A full English and 8 pieces of toast.

The husbands look at each other and grin.

Waiter: Madam?

Second Wife: I'd like a continental with a pot of tea

Waiter: Sir?

2nd Husbands: A full English please and 8 pieces of toast.

The two husbands chuckle slightly and the waiter turns to leave but is interrupted by Husband No.2 Oh and waiter, could you make two of mine brown?

Q: What's the difference between a girlfriend and a wife?

A: 45 lbs.

Q: What's the difference between a boyfriend and a husband?

A: 45 minutes.

Q: What is it when a man talks nasty to a woman?

A: Sexual harassment.

Q: What is it when a woman talks nasty to a man?

A: $3.99 a minute.

Q: How can you tell if your wife is dead?

A: The sex is the same but the dishes pile up.

Q: How can you tell if your husband is dead?

A: The sex is the same but you get the remote.

Q: Why did cavemen pull their women around by the hair?

A: If they pulled them by their feet, they'd fill up with mud.

Q: What's it called when a woman is paralysed from the waist down?

A: Marriage.

Q: If your wife keeps coming out of the kitchen to nag you, what have you done wrong?

A: Made her chain too long.

Q: How many men does it take to change a light bulb?

A: None, they just sit there in the dark and complain.

Q: What's the fastest way to a man's heart?

A: Through his chest with a sharp knife.

Q: Why are men and parking spaces alike?

A: Because all the good ones are gone and the only ones left are disabled.

Q: Why are men like public toilets?

A: Because all the good ones are engaged and the only ones left are full of crap.

Q: What have men and floor tiles got in common?

A: If you lay them properly the first time, you can walk all over them for life.

Q: What is the difference between a man and a catfish?

A: one is a bottom-feeding scum-sucker and the other is a fish.

Q: Why is it so hard for women to find men that are sensitive, caring, and good-looking?

A: Because those men already have boyfriends.

Q: What is a man's view of safe sex?

A: A padded headboard.

Q: How do men sort their laundry?

A: Filthy- and -Filthy but wearable-

Q: Why were men given larger brains than dogs?

A: So they wouldn't hump women's legs at cocktail parties.

Q: Do you know why women fake orgasm?

A: Because men fake foreplay.

Q: What is the difference between a new husband and a new dog?

A: After a year l the dog is still excited to see you.

Q: What makes men chase women they have no intention of marrying?

A: The same urge that makes dogs chase cars they have no intention of driving.

Q: What is the biggest problem for an atheist?

A: No one to talk to during orgasm

Q: What do you call an Amish guy with his hand up a horse's ass?

A: A mechanic

Q: Who is the most popular guy at the nudist colony?

A: The guy who can carry a cup of coffee in each hand and a dozen

Q: Who is the most popular girl at the nudist colony?

A: She is the one who can eat the last donut

Q: Why does the bride always wear white?

A: Because it is good for the dishwasher to match the stove and refrigerator.

Q: What is the difference between a battery and a woman?

A: A battery has a positive side.

Q: Why do men snore when they lay on their backs?

A: Because their balls fall over their asshole and they vapour-lock.

Q: Why do men take showers instead of baths?

A: Pissing in the bath is disgusting.

Q: What's the difference between a terrorist and a Jewish mother?

A: You can negotiate with the terrorist

Q: Did you hear about the guy who finally figured out women?

A: He died laughing before he could tell anybody.

FOR SALE BY OWNER

Complete set of Encyclopaedia Britannica.

45 volumes. Excellent condition.

$1,000.00 or best offer.

No longer needed.

Got married last weekend. Wife knows f#@*ing everything

Q: If the dove is the bird of peace, what is the bird of true love?

A: The swallow

Q: How do you annoy your girlfriend during sex?

A: Phone her.

Q: Why do women fake orgasms?

A: Because they think men care.

Q: What is the definition of "making love"?

A: Something a woman does while a guy is screwing her.

Q: What should you do if your girlfriend starts smoking?

A: Slow down and use a lubricant.

Q: What's the difference between oral sex and anal sex?

A: Oral sex makes your day, anal sex makes your hole weak

Q: How many sexists does it take to change a light bulb?

A: None, let the bitch cook in the dark.

Q: What's the difference between pre-menstrual tension and B.S.E?

A: One's mad cow disease, the other's an agricultural problem.

Q: How do you turn a fox into an elephant?

A: Marry her!

Q: How is a woman like a condom?

A: Both of them spend more time in your wallet than on your dick.

Q: How are tornadoes and marriage alike?

A: They both begin with a lot of blowing and sucking, and in the end you lose your house.

Q: Why does a bride smile when she walks up the aisle?

A: She knows she's given her last blow job.

Q: How many men does it take to open a beer?

A: None. It should be opened by the time she brings it.

Q: Why is a Laundromat a really bad place to pick up a woman?

A: Because a woman who can't even afford a washing machine will probably never be able to support you.

Q: Why do women have smaller feet than men?

A: It's one of those "evolutionary things" that allows them to stand closer to the kitchen sink.

Q: How do you know when a woman is about to say something smart?

A: When she starts her sentence with "A man once told me "

Q: How do you fix a woman's watch?

A: You don't. There is a clock on the oven.

Q: Why do men fart more than women?

A: Because women can't shut up long enough to build up the required pressure.

Q: If your dog is barking at the back door and your wife is yelling at the front door, who do you let in first?

A: The dog, of course. He'll shut up once you let him in.

Q: What's worse than a Male Chauvinist Pig?

A: A woman that won't do what she's told.

Q: What do you call a woman who has lost 95% of her intelligence?

A: Divorced.

Scientists have discovered a food that diminishes a woman's sex drive by 90%. It's called a Wedding Cake

---

Marriage is a 3-ring circus: Engagement Ring, Wedding Ring, Suffering.

Our last fight was my fault: My wife asked me "What's on the TV?" I said, "Dust!"

Men VS. Women

NICKNAMES

If Laura. Suzanne, Debra and Rose go out for lunch, they will call each other Laura, Suzanne, Debra and Rose.

But if Mike, Charlie, Bob and Jim go out for a night, they will affectionately refer to each other as Fat Boy, Godzilla, Peanut-Head and Useless.

EATINGOUT

1. When the bill arrives, Mike, Charlie, Bob and Jim will each throw in $20, even though it's only for $22.50. None of them will have anything smaller, and none will actually admit they want change back.

2. When the girls get their bill, out comes the pocket calculators.

MONEY

3. A man will pay $2 for a $1 item he wants.

4. A woman will pay $1 for a $2 item that she doesn't want.

BATHROOMS

5. A man has six items in his bathroom: a toothbrush, shaving cream, razor, a bar of soap, and a towel from the Holiday Inn.

6. The average number of items in the typical woman's bathroom is 337. A man would not be able to identify most of these items.

ARGUMENTS

7. A woman has the last word in any argument.

8. Anything a man says after that is the beginning of a new argument.

CATS

9. Women love cats.
10. Men say they love cats, but when women aren't looking, men kick cats.

FUTURE

11. A woman worries about the future until she gets a husband.
12. A man never worries about the future until he gets a wife.

SUCCESS

13. A successful man is one who makes more money than his wife can spend.
14. A successful woman is one who can find such a man.

MARRIAGE

15. A woman marries a man expecting he will change, but he doesn't.
16. A man marries a woman expecting that she won't change and she does.

DRESSING UP

17. A woman will dress up to go shopping, water the plants, empty the garbage, answer the phone, read a book, get the mail.
18. A man will dress up for weddings and funerals.

NATURAL

19. Men wake up as good-looking as they went to bed.
20. Women somehow deteriorate during the night.

OFFSPRING

Ah, children. A woman knows all about her children. She knows about dentist appointments and romances, best friends and favourite foods and secret, fears and hopes and dreams.

A man is vaguely aware of some short people living in the house.

Subject: 3 words

A man was sitting at a bar enjoying an after-work cocktail when an exceptionally gorgeous, sexy, young woman entered. The man could not take his eyes away from her. The young woman noticed his overly attentive stare and walked directly toward him.

Before he could offer his apologies for being so rude, the young woman said to him, "I'll do anything you want me to do, no matter how kinky, for $100, with one condition."

Flabbergasted, the man asked what the condition was.

The young woman replied, "you have to tell me what you want me to do in just three words."

The man considered her proposition for a moment, withdrew his wallet from his pocket and counted out five $20 bills, which he pressed into the young woman's hand.

He looked deeply into her eyes and slowly said, "Paint my house."

Women think they already know everything, but wait training courses are now available for women on the following subjects:

1. Silence, the Final Frontier: Where No Woman Has Gone Before
2. The Undiscovered Side of Banking: Making Deposits
3. Parties: Going Without New Outfits
4. Man Management: Minor Household Chores Can Wait Till After The Game
5. Bathroom Etiquette I: Men Need Space in the Bathroom Cabinet Too.
6. Bathroom Etiquette II: His Razor is His
7. Communication Skills I: Tears—The Last Resort, not the First.
8. Communication Skills II: Thinking Before Speaking
9. Communication Skills III: Getting What you Want Without Nagging
10. Driving a Car Safely: A Skill You Can Acquire
11. Telephone Skills: How to Hang Up
12. Introduction to Parking
13. Advanced Parking: Backing Into a Space
14. Water Retention: Fact or Fat
15. Cooking I: Bringing Back Bacon, Eggs and Butter
16. Cooking II: Bran and Tofu are Not for Human Consumption
17. Cooking III: How not to Inflict Your Diets on Other People
18. Compliments: Accepting Them Gracefully
19. PMS: Your Problem, Not His
20. Dancing: Why Men Don't Like To

21. Classic Clothing: Wearing Outfits You Already Have
22. Household Dust: A Harmless Natural Occurrence Only Women Notice
23. Integrating Your Laundry: Washing It All Together
24. Oil and Gas: Your Car Needs Both
25. TV Remotes: For Men Only
26. Combating the Imelda Marcos Syndrome: You Do Not Need New Shoes Every day.
27. Valuation: Just Because It's Not Important to You.
28. Overcoming Anal Retentive Behaviour: Leaving the Towels on the Floor.
29. Sex: It's For Married Couples Too.
30. "Do These Jeans Make My Butt Look Big?" Learning Why Men Lie.

Training Courses Now Available for Men:

1. Introduction to Common Household Objects I: The Mop
2. Introduction to Common Household Objects II: The Sponge
3. Dressing Up: Beyond the Wedding and the Funeral
4. Refrigerator Forensics: Identifying and Removing the Dead
5. 5 Design Pattern or Splatter Stain on the Linoleum?— You Can Tell the Difference!
6. Accepting Loss I: If It's Empty, You Can Throw It Away

7. Accepting Loss II: If the Milk Expired Three Weeks Ago, Keeping in the Refrigerator Won't Bring It Back
8. Going to the Supermarket—It's Not Just for Women Anymore!
9. Recycling Skills I: Boxes that the Electronics Came In
10. Recycling Skills II: Styrofoam that Came in the Boxes that the Electronics Came In
11. Bathroom Etiquette I: How to Remove Beard Clippings from the sink
12. Bathroom Etiquette II: Let's Wash Those Towels!
13. Bathroom Etiquette III: Five Easy Ways to Tell When You're about to run Out of Toilet Paper!
14. Giving Back to the Community: How to Donate 15-Year-Old Levis to the Goodwill
15. Retro, Or Just Hideous?: Re-examining Your '70s Polyester Shirts
16. Knowing the Limitations of Your Kitchenware: No, The Dishes Won't Wash Themselves
17. Strange, but true, she really may not care what Fourth Down and Ten"
18. Going OUT to Dinner, Beyond McDonald's Your Entertainment Options, Renting Movies That Don't fall under the "Action/Adventure" Category
19. Yours, Mine, and Ours, Sharing the Remote
20. "I Could Have Played a Better Game Than That!" Why women laugh.
21. Adventures in Housekeeping I, Let's Clean the Closet
22. Adventures in Housekeeping II, Let's Clean under the Bed

23. "I Don't Know": Be the First Man to Say It!
24. The Gas Gauge in Your Car, Sometimes Empty MEANS Empty
25. Directions: It is Okay to Ask for Them
26. Listening, It's Not Just Something You Do During Halftime
27. Accepting Your Limitations: Just Because You Have power Tools Doesn't Mean You Can Fix It

---

- I haven't spoken to my wife for 18 months: I don't like to interrupt her.
- In the beginning, God created the earth and rested. Then God created Man and rested. Then God created Woman. Since then, neither God nor Man has rested.
- Why do men die before their wives? They want to.
- A beggar walked up to a well-dressed woman shopping on Rodeo Drive and said:
- "I haven't eaten anything in four days.' She looked at him and said "God, I wish I had your willpower".
- Young Son:—Is it true, Dad, I heard that in some parts of Africa a man doesn't know his wife until he marries her?- Dad: That happens in every country, son.
- A man inserted an advertisement in the classified: Wife wanted. The next day he received a hundred letters. They all said the same thing: You can have mine."
- The most effective way to remember your wife's birthday: forget it once.

- Are women equal to men: No, not until they can walk down the street with a bald head and a beer gut, and still think they are beautiful.

Dear Tech Support,

I am writing this letter as a last resort. Last year I upgraded from Girlfriend 7.0 to Wife 1.0 and noticed that the new program began unexpected child processing that took up a lot of space and valuable resources. No mention of this phenomenon was included in the product brochure.

In addition, Wife 1.0 installs itself into all other programs and launches during system initialization, where it monitors all other system activity. Applications such as Poker night 10.3, Drunken Boys Night 2.5 and Saturday Football 5.0 no longer run, crashing the system whenever selected.

I cannot seem to keep Wife 1.0 in the background while attempting to run some of my other favourite applications. I am thinking about going back to Girlfriend 7.0, but un-install does not work on this program.

Can you help me, please!!!

Thanks,

Joe

Dear Joe:

This is a very common problem that men complain about but it is mostly due to a primary misconception. Many people upgrade from Girlfriend 7.0 to

Wife 1.0 with the idea that Wife 1.0 is merely a "UTILITIES & ENTERTAINMENT" program. Wife 1.0 is an OPERATING SYSTEM and designed by its creator to run everything. It is unlikely you would be able to purge

Wife 1.0 and still convert back to Girlfriend 7.0. Hidden operating files within your system would cause Girlfriend 7.0 to emulate Wife 1.0 so nothing is gained.

It is impossible to un-install, delete, or purge the program files from the system once installed. You cannot go back to Girlfriend 7.0 because Wife 1.0 is not designed to do this. Some have tried to install Girlfriend 8.0 or Wife 2.0 but end up with more problems than the original system. Look in your manual under "Warnings—Alimony Child Support."

I recommend you keep Wife 1.0 and just deal with the situation. Having Wife 1.0 installed myself, I might also suggest you read the entire section regarding General Partnership Faults (GPFs). You must assume all responsibility for faults and problems that might occur, regardless of their cause.

The best course of action will be to enter the command C:\ APOLOGISE.

In any case avoid excessive use of the "Esc" key because ultimately you will have to give the APOLOGISE command before the operating system will return to normal. The system will run smoothly as long as you take the blame for all the GPFs.

Wife 1.0 is a great program, but very high maintenance. Consider buying additional software to improve the performance of Wife 1.0. I recommend Flowers 2.1 and Chocolates 5.0.

Do not, under any circumstances, install Secretary with Short Skirt 3.3. This is not a supported application for Wife 1.0 and is likely to cause irreversible damage to the operating system.

Best of luck. Tech Support.

The patient's family gathered to hear what the specialists had to say." Things don't look good. The only chance is a brain transplant.

This is an experimental procedure. It might work, but the bad news is that brains are very expensive, and you will have to pay the costs yourselves." "Well, how much does a brain cost?" asked the relatives.

"For a male brain, $500,000. For a female brain, $200,000."

Some of the younger male relatives tried to look shocked, but all the men nodded in understanding, and a few actually smirked.

Then the patient's daughter asked, "Why the difference in price between male brains and female brains?"

"A standard pricing practice," said the head of the team. "Women's brains have to be marked down because they have been used."

Dating Agency Real Meanings

The real meaning behind the abbreviations in personal ads:

THE WOMEN

- 40-1sh 48
- Adventurer has had more partners than you ever will
- Athletic Flat-chested
- Average looking Ugly
- Beautiful Pathological liar
- Contagious Smile Bring your penicillin
- Educated College dropout

- Emotionally Secure medicated
- Feminist Fat ball buster
- Free spirit Substance user
- Friendship first trying to live down reputation as slut
- Fun. .... Annoying
- Gentle. .... Comatose
- Good Listener Borderline Autistic
- New-Age All body hair, all the time
- Old-fashioned Lights out, missionary position only
- Open-minded Desperate
- Outgoing Loud
- Passionate Loud
- Poet Depressive Schizophrenic
- Professional Real Witch
- Redhead Shops the Clairol section
- Reubenesque Grossly Fat
- Romantic Looks better by candle light
- Voluptuous Very Fat
- Weight proportional to height Hugely Pat
- Wants Soul mate Refer Glenn Close in Fatal Attraction
- Widow Nagged first husband to death
- Young at heart Toothless crone

THE MEN

- 40-ish 52 and looking for 25-yr-old
- Athletic Sits on the couch and watches sport
- Average looking Excessive hair growths on ears, nose, and back
- Educated Will treat you like an idiot
- Free spirit Sleeps with your sister
- Friendship first As long as friendship involves nudity
- Fun Good with a remote and a six pack
- Good looking Arrogant
- Honest pathological Liar
- Huggable Overweight
- Like to cuddle Insecure, overly dependent
- Mature Until you get to know him
- Open-minded Wants to swing
- Physically fit Spends a lot of time in front of mirror
- Stable Occasional stalker, but never arrested

A WOMAN'S POINTS SYSTEM

For all you guys out there who just can't figure it out, here it is: In the world of romance, one single rule applies: Make the woman happy. Do something she likes and you get points. Do something she dislikes and points are subtracted. You don't get any points for doing something she expects .

Sorry, that's the way the game is played.

Here is a guide to the point system.

Simple Duties

- You make the bed: +1
- You make the bed, but forget to add the decorative pillows: 0
- You throw the bedspread over rumpled sheet.: -1
- You leave the toilet seat up: -5
- You replace the toilet-paper roll when it's empty: 0
- When the toilet-paper roll is barren, you resort 0 Kleenex: -1
- When the Kleenex runs out you shuffle lowly to the next bathroom: -2
- You go out to buy her spring-fresh extra-light panty liner with wing or flowers: +5
- But return with beer: -5
- You check out a suspicious noise at night: 0
- You check out a suspicious noise and it's nothing: 0
- You check out a suspicious noise and it's something: +5
- You pummel it with a six iron: +10
- It's her father: -10

Social Engagements

- You stay by her side the entire party: 0
- You stay by her side for a while, then leave to chat with college drinking buddy: -2
- Named Tiffany: -4
- Tiffany is a dancer: -6
- Tiffany has implants: -8

A Night Out With The Boys

- Go out with a pal: -5
- And the pal is happily married:-4
- Or frighteningly single: -7
- And he drives a Mustang: -10
- With a personalized license plate (GR8 N BED): -15

A Night Out with Her

- You take her to a movie: +2
- You take her to a movie she likes: +4
- You take her to a movie you hate: +6
- You take her to a movie you like: -2
- It's called DeathCop 3: -3
- Which features cyborgs having sex: -9
- You lied and said it was a foreign film about orphans: -15

Your Physique

- You develop a noticeable potbelly: -15
- You develop a noticeable potbelly and exercise to get rid of it: +10
- You develop a noticeable potbelly and resort to loose jeans and baggy Hawaiian shirts: -30
- You say "I don't give a damn because you have one too": -800

The Big Question

- She asks, "Do I look fat?":—You hesitate in responding: -10
- You reply, "Where?": -35

Communication

- When she wants to talk about a problem, you listen, displaying what looks like a concerned expression: 0
- When she wants to talk, you listen, for over 10 minutes: +5
- You listen for more than 10 minutes without looking at the TV: +10
- She realizes this is because you've fallen asleep: -20

Saturday Afternoons

- You visit her parents: +1
- You visit her parents and actually make conversation: +3
- You visit her parents and stare at the television: -3
- And the television is off: -6
- You spend the afternoon watching football in your underwear: -6
- And you don't even like football: -10
- And it's not really your underwear: -15

Her Birthday

- You take her out to dinner: 0
- You take her out to dinner and it's not a sports bar: +1

- Okay, it is a sports bar: -2
- And it's all-you-can-eat night: -3
- It's a sports bar, it's all-you-can-eat night, and your face is painted the colours of your favourite team: -10
- You give her a gift: 0
- You give her a gift, and it's a small appliance: -10
- You give her a gift, and it's not a small appliance: +1
- You give her a gift, and it isn't chocolate: +2
- You give her a gift that you'll be paying off for months: +30
- You wait til the last minute and buy her a gift that day: -10
- With her credit card: -30
- And whatever you bought is two sizes too big: -40

Thoughtfulness

- You forget to pick her up at the bus station: -25
- At 2 in the morning : -35
- And the pouring rain dissolves her leg cast: -50
- Another Night Out with Your Pals
- You have a few beers: -9 (For every beer after three, -2 again)
- And miss curfew by an hour: -12
- You get home at 3 a.m.: -20
- You get home at 3 a.m. smelling of booze and cheap cigars: -30

- And not wearing any pants: -40
- Is that a tattoo? -200

Another Night Out, Just The Two of You

- You go see a comic: +2
- He's crude and sexist: -2
- You laugh: -5
- You laugh too much: -10
- She's not laughing: -15
- You laugh harder: -25

Driving

- You lose the directions on a trip: -4
- You lose the directions and end up getting lost: -10
- You end up getting lost in a bad part of town: -15
- You get lost in a bad part of town and meet the locals up close and personal: -25
- She finds out the hard way that you lied about having a black belt: -60

- What's the difference between a new husband and a new dog? After a year, the dog is still excited to see you.
- What makes men chase women they have no intention of marrying? The same urge that makes dogs chase cars they have no intention of driving.
- What is the biggest problem for an atheist? No one to talk to during orgasm.

- What do you call a smart blonde? A golden retrieve
- Jewish dilemmA: Free PORK.
- The three words most hated by men during sex? "Are you done?"
- Three words women hate to hear when having sex "Honey, I'm home!"
- Do you know why they call it the Wonder Bra? When you take it off you wonder where her tits went.
- When I die, I want to die like my grandfather who died peacefully in is sleep. Not screaming like all the passengers in his car.
- I think animal testing is a terrible idea; they get all nervous and give the wrong answers.
- Did you hear about the guy who finally figured out women? He died laughing before he could tell anybody.

One bright, beautiful Sunday morning, everyone in tiny Jonestown wakes up early and goes to church. Before the service starts, the townspeople sit in their pews and talk about their lives, their families, etc.

Suddenly, at the altar, Satan appears! Everyone starts screaming and running for the front entrance, trampling each other in their determined efforts to get away from Evil Incarnate.

Soon, everyone has left the church except for one man, who sits calmly in his pew, seemingly oblivious to the fact that God's ultimate enemy is in his presence.

This confuses Satan a bit.

Satan says, "Hey, don't you know who I am?" The man says, "Yep, sure do."

Satan says, "Well, aren't you afraid of me?"

The man says, "Nope, sure I am not."

Satan, perturbed, says, "And why aren't you afraid of me?"

The man says, "I've been married to your sister for 25 years."

Upon a time, in a land far away, a beautiful, independent, self-assured princess happened upon a frog as she sat, contemplating ecological issues on the shores of an unpolluted pond in a verdant meadow near her castle.

The frog hopped into the princess' lap and said: Elegant lady, I was once a handsome prince, until an evil witch cast a spell upon me. One kiss from you, however, and I will turn back into the dapper, young prince that I am and then, my sweet, we can marry and set up housekeeping in my castle with my mother, where you can prepare my meals, clean my clothes, bear my children and forever feel grateful and happy doing so.

That night as the princess dined sumptuously on a repast of lightly sautéed frogs legs seasoned in a white wine and onion cream sauce, she chuckled to herself and thought:

"I don't think so."

How to shower like a man. Short Version:

1. Take off clothes while sitting on the edge of the bed and leave them in a pile on the floor.
2. Walk to bathroom wearing a towel. If you see your girlfriend/wife along the way, flash her.

3. Look at your manly physique in the mirror and suck in your gut to see if you have pecks. (No)
4. Turn on the water.
5. Check for pecks again. (no)
6. Get in the shower.
7. Don't bother to look for a washcloth. (You don't use one)
8. Wash your face.
9. Wash your armpits.
10. Wash witty and surrounding area.
11. Wash your butt.
12. Shampoo your hair (do not use conditioner).
13. Make a shampoo Mohican.
14. Open the door and look at yourself on the mirror.
15. Pee.
16. Rinse off and get out of shower.
17. Return to bedroom wearing a towel, if you pass your girlfriend/wife, flash her.

Long Version:

Replace #10 with masturbate.

How to shower like a woman

Long Version (sorry there's no short version)

1. Take off the fourteen layers of clothing you put on this morning because there was a distinct chill in the air due to the temperature dropping below 33 degrees.

2. Walk you to bathroom wearing long dressing gown and towel on head. If boyfriend/husband see you immediately along the way, cover up any exposed flesh ignore his juvenile turban gags and then rush to bathroom.
3. Look at your womanly physique in the mirror and stick out your gut so that you can complain and whinge even more about how you're getting fat.
4. Turn on the hot water only.
5. Get in the shower, once you have found it through all that steam.
6. Look for facecloth, arm cloth, leg cloth, long loofah and pumice stone.
7. Wash your hair once with cucumber and Lamfrey shampoo with 83 added vitamins.
8. Wash your hair again with cucumber and Lamfrey shampoo with 83 added vitamins.
9. Wash your hair once more with Cucumber and Lamfrey shampoo with 83 added vitamins.
10. Condition your hair with cucumber and Lamfrey conditioner enhanced with natural crocus oil. Leave on hair for fifteen minutes.
11. Wash your face with crushed apricot facial scrub for ten minutes until red raw.
12. Wash entire rest of body with Ginger Nut and Jaffa Cake body wash.
13. Complain bitterly when you realise that your boyfriend/husband has once again been eating your Ginger Nut and Jaffa Cake body wash.

14. Rinse conditioner off hair (this takes at least fifteen minutes as you must make sure that it has all come off).
15. Debate shaving armpits and legs and decide that you can't be bothered, and anyway the hair helps keep you warm.
16. Slick hair back and pretend you're like Bo Derek in 10.
17. Scream loudly when your boyfriend/husband flushes the toilet and you get a rush of cold water.
18. Turn hot water on full and rinse off.
19. Dry with a towel the size of a small African country.
20. Check entire body for the remotest sign of a spot. Attack with nails/tweezers if found.
21. Return to bedroom wearing long dressing gown and towel on head. If you see your boyfriend/husband along the way, cover up any exposed flesh immediately, ignore his juvenile turban jokes.

HOW TO TELL IF YOUR VIAGRA IS WORKING:

- At work, they call you a spiritualist because when you sit down at a meeting, the table floats.
- Your face is very pale, due to lack of blood
- When you walk into a sauna, everyone stands and applauds
- People begin to call you "The Tripod"
- You begin to think your mother in law is pretty
- If you are sunbathing nude outside standing: Birds perch on it

- If you are sunbathing nude outside lying down: You look like a sundial
- Everyone at the bank, grocery etc. let you go to the front of the line
- Compared to you, Pinocchio doesn't look like such a big liar
- You always lose limbo contests
- Lewinsky wants you to be president one day
- You can make drawings in the sand without having to find a stick
- You like to sleep on your back so you had to remove your ceiling fan

---

Man to God: "God, why did you make woman so beautiful?"

God to Man: "So you would love her."

"But God" Man says, "Why did you make her so dumb?"

God replies: "So she would love you."

Diamonds are a girl's best friend.

Dogs are a man's best friend.

So, which is the dumber sex?

Single women complain that all good men are married, while all married women complain about their lousy husbands. This confirms that there is no such thing as a good man.

Ever notice how many of women's problems can be traced to the male gender?

MENstruation

MENopause

MENtal breakdown

GUYnecology

HIMorrhoids

- What's the difference between government bonds and men? Bonds mature
- What's the difference between a man and E. T.? E.T. phoned home.
- How are men like noodles? They're always in hot water, they lack taste, and they need dough.
- Why do men like BMWs? They can spell it.
- What do an anniversary and a toilet have in common? Men always miss them.
- Why are men like popcorn? They satisfy you, but only for little while.

Why it's great to be a girl.

1. Free drinks.
2. Free dinners.
3. Free movies (you get the point).
4. You can hug your friend without wondering if she thinks you're gay.

5. You can hug your friend without wondering if YOU'RE gay.
6. You know The Truth about whether size matters.
7. Speeding ticket? What's that?
8. New lipstick gives you a whole new lease on life.
9. You never had to walk down the hall with your binder strategically positioned in high school.
10. If you have sex with someone and don't call them the next day, you're not the devil.
11. Condoms make no significant difference in your enjoyment of sex.
12. If you have to be home in time for 90210, you can say so, out loud.
13. If you're not making enough money you can blame the glass ceiling.
14. You can sleep your way to the top.
15. You can sue the President for sexual harassment.
16. Nothing crucial can be cut off with one clean sweep.
17. it's possible to live your whole life without ever taking a group shower.
18. No fashion faux pas you make could rival The Speedo.
19. Brad Pitt.
20. You don't have to fart to amuse yourself.
21. If you cheat on your spouse, people assume it's because you're being emotionally neglected.
22. YOU never have to wonder if his orgasm was real.
23. You'll never have to decide where to hide your nose-hair clipper.

24. No one passes out when you take off your shoes.
25. If you think the person you're dating really likes you, you don't have to break up with them.
26. Excitement is only as far away as the nearest beauty-supply store.
27. If you forget to shave, no one has to know.
28. You can congratulate your teammate without ever touching her ass.
29. If you have a zit, you can conceal it.
30. You never have to reach down every so often to make sure your privates are still there.
31. If you're dumb, some people will find it cute.
32. You don't have to memorize caddy shack or Fletch to fit in.
33. You have the ability to dress yourself.
34. You have an excuse to be a total bitch at least once a month.
35. You can talk to people of the opposite sex without having to picture them naked.
36. If you marry someone 20 years younger, you're aware that you look like an idiot.
37. If you're wearing cologne, you don't have to pretend its aftershave.
38. You'll probably never see someone you know while peeing in an alley.
39. You'll never have to punch a hole through anything with your fist.
40. You can quickly end any fight by crying.

41. Your friends won't think you're weird if you ask whether there's spinach in your teeth.
42. There are times when chocolate really can solve all your problems.
43. You've never had a goatee.
44. Gay waiters don't make you uncomfortable.
45. You'll never regret piercing your ears.
46. You can fully assess a person just by looking at their shoes.
47. You'll never discover you've been duped by a Wonder bra.
48. You don't have hair on your back.
49. You know which glass was yours by the lipstick mark.

Subject: Things Most Women Will Never say

- You know, I've been complaining a lot lately. I don't blame you for ignoring me.
- That was fun, when will all of your friends be over to watch pornos again?
- The new girl in my office is a stripper, I invited her over for dinner this Friday.
- While you were in the bathroom, they went for a goal and missed. If they can hold them in attack, then we've got a chance.
- I liked that wedding even more than ours.
- Your ex-girlfriend has class.

- That girl is wearing the same outfit as I am. Cool, I'm going to go over and talk to her.
- I love hearing stories about your old girlfriends, tell me more.
- I like using this new lawn mower so much more than the old one, what a wonderful Valentine's Day present.
- Let's just leave the toilet seat up at all times, then you don't have to mess with it anymore.
- It's only the third quarter, you should order a couple more jugs of beer.
- Honey, come here! Watch me do a Tequila Shot off of Stephanie's bare ass!
- I'm so happy with my new hairstyle, I don't think I'll ever change it again.
- Damn! I love it when my pillow smells like your cigars and scotch.
- You passed out before brushing your teeth again, big silly.
- You are so much smarter than my father.
- If we're not going to have sex, then you have to let me watch Wide World of Sport.

Household form (Husband/Boyfriend)

APPLICATION TO GO OUT/RETURN LATE

Name

I request permission for a leave of absence from my home duties for the following period:

Date I Time of departure I Time of return

Should permission be granted, I do solemnly swear to only visit locations stated below. Nor shall I speak to another female other than those listed without gaining written permission to do so from my better half. Nor shall I consume above the allocated volume of alcohol without first phoning for a taxi or ordering a tandoori. I understand that even if permission is granted my wife/girlfriend retains the right to be pissed off with me the following day for no valid reason what so ever.

Amount of alcohol allowed (units) Locations likely to be visited

Females likely to be encountered

Strength of curry permitted

I am a low life. I know who wears the trousers in our home, and it isn't me. I promise to abide by your rules and regulations. I understand that this is going to cost me a fortune in Cadbury's Roses and Flowers. You reserve the right to obtain and use my credit cards in my absence. I hereby promise not to sleep overnight on a park bench next to a tramp. On my way home, I will not pick a fight with a person who only exists in my inebriated mind, nor shall I conduct in depth discussions with said entity.

I declare that to the best of my knowledge (of which I have none) the above information is correct.

Signed:

Request is APPROVED I TURNED DOWN

This decision is not open to negotiation other than on my terms.

Permission for my Husband/Boyfriend to be away for the period

Date / Time of departure / Time of return
Signed:

Our David

Which art in Jones

Hallowed be thy Country Road

Thy Cartier watch

Thy Prada bag

In Hermes

As it is in Zambesi

Give us each day our Visa Gold

And forgive us our overdraft

As we forgive those who stop our MasterCard

Lead us not into KATIES

And deliver us from Target

For thine is the Chanel, the Gucci and the Versace

For Gautier and Dinnigan

Amex

Dear [#insert name]

I regret to inform you that you have been eliminated from further contention as Mr Right. As you are probably aware, the competition was exceedingly tough and dozens of well-qualified candidates such as yourself also failed to make the final cut.

I will, however, keep your name on file should an opening come available. So that you may find better success in your future romantic endeavours, please allow me to offer the following reason{s) you were disqualified from the competition:

(Tick those that apply)

1. Your last name is objectionable. I can't imagine taking it, hyphenating it, or subjecting my children to it.
2. Your first name is objectionable. It's just not something I can picture myself yelling out in a fit of passion.
3. The fact that our first dining experience to date has left my wallet a little lighter and your pants a little tighter!
4. Your inadvertent admission that you "buy condoms by the truckload" indicates that you may be interested in me for something other than my personality.
5. You failed the 20 Question Rule, i.e. I asked you 20 questions about yourself before you asked me more than one about myself.
6. Your constant emailing, shows me you have too much time on your hands!
7. Your legs are skinnier than mine. If you can fit into my pants, then you can't get into my pants.
8. You're too short. Any son that we produced would inevitably be beaten up repeatedly at recess.
9. You're too tall. I'm developing a chronic neck condition from trying to kiss you.
10. You have a hairy back.
11. I find your inability to fix my car extraordinarily unappealing.

12. The fact that your apartment has been condemned reveals an inherent slovenliness that I fear is unbreakable.
13. The phrase "My Mother" has popped up far too often in conversation.
14. You still live with your parents.
15. Although I do enjoy the X-Files, I find your wardrobe of Star Trek uniforms a little disconcerting.
16. Your frequent references to your ex-girlfriend lead me to suspect that you are some sort of psychotic stalker.
17. Your ability to belch the alphabet is not a trait that I am seeking in a long term partner.
18. Your height is out of proportion to your weight. If you should, however, happen to gain the necessary 17 vertical inches, please resubmit your application.
19. Somehow I doubt those condoms that I found in your overnight bag were really necessary for a successful business trip.
20. I am out of your league; set your sights lower next time.

Sincerely,

Bruce was dying. Sheila sat at the bedside. He looked up and said weakly: "I have something I must confess before I die."

"There's no need to," she replied. "No," he insisted, "I want to die in peace. I must tell you. I've rooted your sister, your best mate, her best mate, and your mother!"

"I know," she replied," now just rest and let the poison do its work."

A man was walking along a California beach and stumbled across an old lamp.

He picked it up and rubbed it and out popped a genie. The genie said "OK, OK. You released me from the lamp, blah blah blah. This is the fourth time this month and I'm getting a little sick of these wishes so you can forget about three. You only get one wish!"

The man sat and thought about it for a while and said, "I've always wanted to go to Hawaii but I'm scared to fly and I get very seasick. Could you build me a bridge to Hawaii so I can drive over there to visit?"

The genie laughed and said, "That's impossible. Think of the logistics of that! How would the supports ever reach the bottom of the Pacific?

Think of how much concrete, how much steel!! No, think of another wish."

The man said OK and tried to think of a really good wish.

Finally, he said, "I've been married and divorced four times. My wives always said that I don't care and that I'm insensitive. So, I wish that I could understand women...know how they feel inside and what they're thinking when they give me the silent treatment...know why they're crying, know what they really want when they say 'nothing'....know how to make them truly happy...."

The genie said, "You want that bridge two lanes or four?"

With the introduction of Viagra to fix a perennial male problem, a famous British pharmaceutical company is working to redress the balance...

MIRRORCILLIN—A 5cc dose enables a woman to walk past mirrors for up to four hours without pausing once.

STOPPANAGGIN—Gives women a vague feeling of contentment towards their spouse/boyfriend.

COSMOPOLIRA—Doubles female intelligence to almost simian levels, allowing 'facts' in trashy lifestyle magazines to be disputed.

LOGICON—Trials showed that females taking this were able to follow a proposition through to its logical conclusion, and argue effectively without being diverted into non-relevant postulates such as "you don't love me anymore!"

PARKATRON—72% of women taking this were able to safely Reverse Park a Ford Fiesta into a space only 40ft (12m) long; 54% achieved this in under 15 minutes.

MAGNATACK—Uniquely distorts the cornea, making certain shapes appear much larger than in reality—no practical use for this drug has yet been found.

WARDROBIA—Clinical trials show that almost 23% of women taking this drug can safely walk past a sale notice, and an amazing 42% stayed within their credit limit.

BEERINTULIN—Engenders a female desire to bring her spouse/boyfriend alcoholic beverages and snacks during televised sports.

The mermaid

Three guys are out having a relaxing day fishing. Out of the blue, they catch a mermaid who begs to be set free in return for granting each of them a wish.

Now one of the guys just doesn't believe it, and says: "OK, if you can really grant wishes, then double my IQ." The mermaid says: "Done." Suddenly, the guy starts reciting Shakespeare flawlessly and analysing it with extreme insight.

The second guy Leo amazed, he says to the mermaid: "Triple my IQ." The mermaid says: "Done." The guy starts to spout out all the mathematical solutions to problems that have been stumping all the scientists in various fields: physics, chemistry.

The last guy is so enthralled with the changes in his friends that he says to the mermaid: "Quintuple my IQ." The mermaid looks at him and says: "You know, I normally don't try to change people's minds when they make a wish, but I really wish you'd reconsider."

The guy says: "No, I want you to increase my IQ times five, and if you don't do it, I won't set you free."

"Please," says the mermaid. "You don't know what you're asking, it will change your entire view on the universe. Won't you ask for something else...? A million dollars, anything?"

But no matter what the mermaid said, the guy insisted on having his IQ increased by five times its usual power.

So the mermaid sighed and said done. He became a woman.

CHAPTER 7

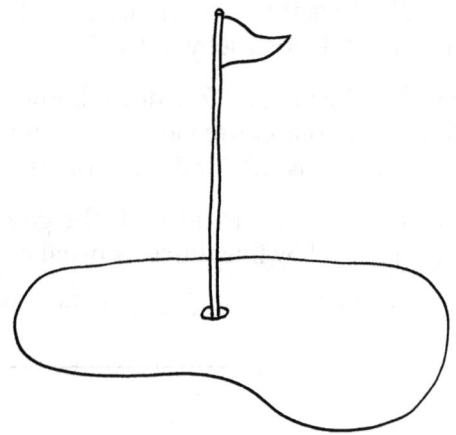

G is for Golf

After slicing his tee shotinto the woods, a golfer heads off in search of his ball, which he finds behind a large tree. After considering his position—and not wanting to take a drop and lose a stroke—he decides to hook the ball around the tree. He swings, the ball hits the tree, ricochets back at him, and instantly kills him.

When he opens his eyes, he sees the Pearly Gates and St. Peter standing before him.

"Am I dead?" he asks.

"Yes, my son," replies St. Peter, who looks the man over and notices his clubs.

"I see you're a golfer," St. Peter says. "Are you any good?"
"Hey, I got here in two, didn't I?"

A man, while playing on the front nine of a complicated golf course, became confused as to where he was on the course. Looking around, he saw a lady playing ahead of him. He walked up to her, explained his confusion and asked her if she knew what hole he was playing. She replied, "I'm on the 7th hole, and you are a hole behind me, so you must be on the 6th hole." He thanked her and went back to his golf. On the back nine the same thing happened; and he approached her again with the same request. She said, "I'm on the 14th hole, you are a hole behind me, so you must be on the 13th hole. " Once again he thanked her and returned to his play.

He finished his round and went to the clubhouse where he saw the same lady sitting at the end of the bar. He asked the bartender if he knew the lady. The bartender said that she was a sales lady and played the course often. He approached her and said, "Let me buy you a drink appreciation for your help. I understand that you are in the sales profession. I'm in sales also. What do you sell?" She replied, "If I tell you, you'll laugh." "No, I won't."

"Well, if you must know," she answered, "I work for Tampax." With that, he laughed so hard he almost lost his breath. She said, "See I knew you would laugh." "That's not what I'm laughing at," he replied. "I'm a toilet paper salesman, so I'm still a hole behind you."

A multimillionaire bachelor goes to his club to play golf with two friends. Not knowing who would be joining them, they walk to the first tee.

As they finish teeing off, a tall, beautiful, raven-haired woman asks if she can join them. Although the bachelor thinks this is going to slow down their play, he agrees. The woman tees up a ball and, without a practice swing, smacks it straight down the middle.

This goes on all day and she finishes even par for the round, beating all the men.

They invite her back the next week. They have a great time, and she shoots the same score. The bachelor thinks to himself, "This is the girl of my dreams!" So he asks her out on a date. They go out, find they have much in common, and have a great evening.

They make another golf date, during which she shoots two-under and gives a clinic in shot making.

The millionaire is now convinced that they are meant to be together. He invites her back to his apartment, where they talk for hours. Everything is progressing smoothly, so he invites her to his bedroom. Their passions run riot, but she doesn't let things go too far and he drives her home.

This pattern continues for a month: Great golf, great dates, but nights of abbreviated passion. The bachelor can't take it anymore.

"I know the time we spent on the golf course and in my apartment is wonderful. And even though we haven't been fully intimate, I know that I love you, you love me, and that you are the girl I want to marry!"

"Darling," she says, "I have something to tell you. I cannot hide it anymore. I am a man!"

His mouth drops open, his face turns red, he begins to shake. She's convinced he's going to have a heart attack, or worse, when finally, in a blind rage, he shouts, "And all this time you've been playing from the red tees?"

Irish Golfer and the Leprechaun

One fine day in Ireland, a guy is out golfing and gets up to the 16th hole. He tees up and cranks one. Unfortunately, it goes into the woods on the side of the fairway. He goes looking for his ball and comes across this little guy with this huge knot on his head and the golf ball lying right beside him.

"Goodness," says the golfer then proceeds to revive the poor little guy. Upon awakening, the little guy says, "Well, you caught me fair and square. I am a leprechaun. I will grant you three wishes."

The golfer says, "I can't take anything from you! I'm just glad I didn't hurt you too badly," and walks away. Watching the golfer depart, the leprechaun says "Well, he was a nice enough guy, and he did catch me, so I have to do something for him. I'll give him the three things that I would want. I'll give him unlimited money, a great golf game, and a great sex life.

A year goes past (as they often do in jokes like this) and the same golfer is out golfing on the same course at the 16th hole. He gets up and hits one into the same woods and goes off looking for his ball. When he finds the ball he sees the same little guy and asks how he is doing.

The leprechaun says, "I'm fine, and might I ask how your golf game is?"

The golfer says, "It's great! I hit under par every time." "I did that for you," responded the leprechaun.

"And might I ask how your money is holding out?"

"Well, now that you mention it, every time I put my hand in my pocket, I pull out a hundred dollar bill," he replied. The leprechaun smiles and says, "I did that for you.

"And might I ask how your sex life is?" Now the golfer looks at him a little shyly and says, "Well, maybe once or twice a week."

Floored, the leprechaun stammers, "Once or twice a week?" The golfer looks at him sheepishly and says, "Well, that's not too bad for a Catholic priest in a small parish."

A pretty pathetic golfer was getting frustrated with his lousy game and began blaming his mistakes on his experienced caddie.

As the round came to an end, the golfer said, "You have to be the worst caddie in the whole wide world."

To which the caddie replied, "I don't think so, sir. That would be too much of a coincidence."

A couple was golfing one day on a very, very exclusive golf course, lined with million dollar houses. On the third tee the husband said, "Honey, be very careful when you drive the ball. Don't knock out any windows. It'll cost us a fortune to fix" The wife teed up and shanked it right through the window of the biggest house on the course. The husband cringed and said, "I told you to watch out for the houses. All right, let's go up there, apologise and see how much this is going to cost"

They walked up, knocked on the door, and heard a voice say, "Come on in". They opened the door and saw glass all over the floor and a very unique looking broken bottle lying on its side in the foyer. A man sitting on the couch said, "Are you the people that broke my window?"

"Uh, yeah, sorry about that," the husband replied.

"No, actually I want to thank you. I'm a genie that was trapped for a thousand years in that bottle. You've released me. I'm allowed to grant three wishes- I'll give you each one wish, and I'll keep the

Third one for myself".

"OK, great!" the husband said." I want a million dollars a year for the rest of my life."

"No problem, it's the least I could do. And you, what do you want?" the genie said, looking at the wife.

"I would like a home in every beautiful city in the world."

"Consider it done." The genie replied.

"And what's your wish, genie?" the husband said.

"Well, since I've been trapped in that bottle, I haven't had sex with a woman in a thousand years. My wish is to sleep with your wife."

The husband looks at the wife and said, "Well, we did get a lot of money and all those houses, Honey. I guess I don't mind."

The genie took the wife upstairs and ravished her for two hours. After it was over, the genie rolled over, looked at the wife, and said, "How old is your husband anyway?"

"35," she replied.

"And he still believes in genies? That's amazing!"

Bob and his three golf buddies were out playing and were just starting on the back nine when Bob paused, looked down the fairway and began to sob uncontrollably.

The other three gathered around him and asked: What's wrong? Bob looked down at his feet, sniffed and dried his eyes some, then apologized for his emotional outburst. I'm sorry, I always get emotional at this hole it holds very difficult memories for me.

One of his buddies asked: What happened? What could have gotten you so upset?

Bob stared silently off in the distance, then said in a low voice, this is where my wife and I were playing 12 years ago when she suddenly died of a heart attack; right at this very hole.

Oh my God, the other golfers said; that must have been horrible! Horrible? You think it's horrible? Bob cried in disbelief; it was worse than that. Every hole for the rest of the day, all the way back to the clubhouse, it was hit the ball, drag Alice, hit the ball, drag Alice . . .

A man who has been stranded on a desert island all alone for 10 years sees a speck on the horizon. "It's too small to be a ship," he thinks to himself. As the speck gets closer, he rules out the possibility of it being a small boat, then a raft.

Suddenly, a gorgeous blonde woman emerges from the surf wearing a wet suit and scuba gear. She approaches the stunned man and asks, "How long has it been since you've had a cigarette?"

"Ten years!" he says.

She unzips a waterproof pocket on her left sleeve and pulls out a pack of fresh cigarettes. He takes one, lights it, takes a long drag, and says, "Man, is that ever good!"

Then she asks him, "How long has it been since you've had a sip of bourbon?"

Trembling, he replies, "Ten years!"

She unzips a waterproof pocket on her right sleeve, pulls out a flask, and gives it to him. He opens it, takes a long swig, and says, "That's fantastic!"

Then she starts slowly unzipping the long zipper down the front of her suit, looks at him seductively, and asks, "And how long has it been since you've played around?"

The man, with tears in his eyes, replies, "Don't tell me you've got golf clubs in there!"

An Englishman, Irishman and a Scotsman are all playing golf with their wives.

The Englishman's wife steps up to the tee and as she bends over to place her ball a gust of wind blows her skirt up and reveals her lack of underwear.

"Good God! Why aren't you wearing any knickers?" her husband demanded.

"Well, you don't give me enough housekeeping money to afford to buy any".

The Englishman immediately reaches into his pocket and says, "For the sake of decency here's 50 pounds, go and buy yourself some underwear".

Next the Irishman's wife bends over to set her ball on the tee. Her skirt blows up to show that she is wearing no undies." Be jesus woman. You've no knickers—why not?"

She replies "I can't afford any on the money you give me".

He reaches into his pocket and says, "For the sake of decency here's 20 pounds, go and buy yourself some underwear!"

Lastly, the Scotsman's wife bends over. The wind also takes her skirt over her head to reveal that she too is naked under it." Hoot, lassie! Why do you have no knickers?"

She too explains, "You don't give me enough housekeeping money to be able to afford any".

The Scot reaches into his pocket and says, "For the sake of decency here's a comb. Tidy yourself up a bit!"

As a couple approaches the altar, the groom tells his wife-to-be, "Honey, I've got something to confess: I'm a golf nut, and every chance I get, I'll be playing golf!"

"Since we're being honest," replies the bride, "I have to tell you that I'm a hooker."

The groom replies, "That's okay, honey. You just need to learn to keep your head down and your left arm straight!"

GOLFING HITMAN

There were these friends who played golf together every Saturday. One Saturday they were getting ready to tee off when a guy, by himself, asked if he could join them. The friends looked at each other and then looked at the guy and said, "Sure."

So they teed off. About two holes into the game, the friends got curious about what the guy did for a living. So they asked him. The stranger told them he was a hit man. The friends all laughed.

The guy said, "No really, I'm a hit man. My gun is in my golf bag. I carry it everywhere. You can take a look at it if you'd like."

So one of the friends decided to check it out, he opened the bag and, sure enough, there was a rifle with a huge scope attached it. He got all excited and said, "WOW! I bet I can see my house through here! May I look? The hit man replied, "Sure."

So the guy looked for a second and said, "YEAH! I can see my house! I can even see through the windows into my bedroom. There's my wife, naked. Isn't she beautiful? WAIT! There's my next-door neighbour! And he's naked too!"

This really upset the guy, so he asked the hit man how much it would be for a hit. The hit man replied, "I get $1000 every time I pull the trigger.-

The guy responded, "one thousand dollars? Well, okay. I want two hits.

I want you to shoot my wife right in the mouth. She's always nagging at me and I can't stand it. Second, I want you to shoot my neighbour in the penis, just for screwing around with my wife."

The hit man agreed. He geared up and looked through the scope. He was looking for about five minutes until finally the man started to get really impatient and asked, "What are you waiting for?"

The hit man replied, "Just hold on, I'm about to save you a thousand bucks!"

It was a sunny Sunday morning, and Murray was beginning his preshot routine, visualizing his upcoming shot, when a voice came over the clubhouse loudspeaker. "Would the gentleman on the ladies' tee please back up to the men's tee."

Murray remained in his routine, seemingly unfazed by the interruption.

A little louder: "Would the man on the women's tee kindly back up to the men's tee!"

Murray raised up out of his stance, lowered his driver, and shouted, "Would the announcer in the clubhouse kindly shut up and let me play my second shot?"

A bunch of blokes are in the changing room of a golf club. A mobile phone on a bench rings and a man engages the hands free speaker-function and began to talk. Everyone else in the room stops to listen.

BLOKE: "Hello"

WOMAN: "Darling, it's me. Are you at the club?"

BLOKE: "Yes"

WOMAN: "I am at the shopping centre and found this beautiful leather coat. It's only £1,000. Is it OK if I buy it?"

BLOKE: "Sure,.go ahead if you like it that much."

WOMAN: "I also stopped by the Mercedes dealership and saw the new 2005 models. I saw one I really liked."

BLOKE: "How much?"

WOMAN: "£70,000"

BLOKE: "OK, but for that price I want it with all the options."

WOMAN: "Great! Oh, and one more thing ... The house I wanted last year is back on the market. They're asking £950,000"

BLOKE: "Well, then go ahead and give them an offer of 900,000. They will probably take it. If not, we can go the extra 50 thousand. It really is a pretty good price."

WOMAN: "OK. I'll see you later! I love you so much!!"

BLOKE: "Bye! I love you, too." The bloke hangs up. The other blokes in the changing room are staring at him in astonishment, mouths agape. He smiles and asks: "Anyone know who this phone belongs to?"

Jesus and Mosesare playing golf in Heaven when they come to the par-three 17th hole, a long carry over water to an island green. Moses tees off with a 3-wood and hits the green. Jesus takes out his 5-iron and says, "I'm going to hit a 5-iron because Arnold Palmer would hit a 5-iron from here."

Jesus tees it up and hits a lofted iron shot that finishes 25 yards short of the green and in the water.

Jesus turns to Moses and says, "How about parting the water so I can play my ball where it lies?"

Moses says, "No way. You foolishly chose the wrong club because of your Arnold Palmer fantasy and I'm not going to be a party to it!"

Jesus shrugs and starts walking on the water to where his ball went in. Just then, a foursome approaching the tee box sees Jesus walking on the water.

One of them asks Moses, "Who does that guy think he is, Jesus Christ?"

Moses turns and says, "No, he thinks he's Arnold Palmer!"

CHAPTER 8

H is for Heaven

Three men who were lost in the forest were captured by cannibals. The cannibal king told the prisoners that they could live if they pass a trial. The first step of the trial was to go to the forest and get ten pieces of the same kind of fruit.

So all three men went separate ways to gather fruits. The first one came back and said to the king, "I brought ten apples." The king then explained the trial to him. "You have to shove the fruits up your ass without any expression on your face or you'll be eaten."

The first apple went in but on the second one he winced out in pain, so he was killed. The second one arrived and showed the king ten berries. When the king explained the trial to him, he thought to himself that this should be easy. 1...2... 3...4... 5... 6... 7... 8... and on the ninth berry he burst out in laughter and was killed. The first guy and the second guy met in heaven.

The first one asked, "Why did you laugh, you almost got away with it?" The second one replied, "I couldn't help it, I saw the third guy coming with pineapples."

Four nuns die one day and arrive at the pearly gates.

St. Peter greets them and says sisters, I will ask each of you this question to confirm your purity. And then open for you the gates of heaven.

He asks the first sister if she has ever touched a penis. She replied, yes, I once touched one with my finger. St. Peter ordered her to dip her finger in a nearby bowl of holy water and then let her in. He asked the second sister the same question, she shyly replied, yes, I once held a penis in my hand.

St. Peter ordered her to dip her hand in the bowl and then let her in the gates.

As he turned back to the remaining two, he noticed that the fourth nun had cut in front of the third, is something wrong, he asked.

Oh no, said the nun, I just wanted to be able to gargle the water before the sister behind me sticks her ass in the bowl.

Did you hear about the terrible disaster when three Bills all died on the same day? Bill Clinton, Billy Graham, and Bill Gates all died and went to heaven at the same moment. Saint Peter was on vacation

So God says to Bill Clinton, "What do you believe, Bill?" And Clinton says, "I believe that there must be justice and equality for all of humanity. " God says, "That is a very worthy belief, Bill, come sit on my left side."

Then God turns to Billy Graham: "What do you believe, Bill?" Billy Graham says, "I believe the Bible's promise of salvation through my Lord Jesus Christ. "God says, "That is even a more worthy belief, come, Bill, and sit on my right side."

Then God turns to Bill Gates: "Bill, what do you believe?" Gates says, "I believe you're sitting in my chair."

Arthur Davidson, of the Harley Davidson Motorcycle Corporation, dies and goes to heaven. At the gates, an angel tells Davidson, "Well, you've been such a good guy and your motorcycles have changed the world. As a reward, you can hang out with anyone you want to in Heaven. "Davidson thinks about it and says, "I want to hang out with God, himself."

The befeathered fellow at the Gates takes Arthur to the Throne Room and introduces him to God. Arthur then asks God, "Hey, aren't you the inventor of woman?"

God says, "Ah, yes."

"Well," says Davidson, "You have some major design flaws in your invention:

1. there's too much front end protrusion
2. it chatters at high speeds
3. the rear end wobbles too much, and
4. the intake is placed too close to the exhaust."

"Hmmm ..." replies God, "hold on. "God goes to the Celestial Super computer, types in a few keystrokes, and waits for the result.

The computer prints out a slip of paper and God reads it. "It may be that my invention is flawed," God replies to Arthur Davidson, "but according to My Computer, more people are riding my invention than yours!!!

A fellow goes to heaven and is met at Pearly Gates by St Peter and applies to enter. St Peter says "You're a Scotsman, aren't you?" Yes", the man replies. St Peter says "Well piss off then, we're not making porridge for one."

Freddie Mercury, Gianni Versace and Princess Diana are outside the Pearly Gates pleading their case to St Peter.

Freddie says "I know I haven't led a perfect life and I've made some mistakes along the way, but I've made some of the most beautiful music in the world. I'll stand at the back of heaven, and serenade everybody with my wondrous songs, making heaven a far happier place to be."

"Pretty good, Fred," said St Peter, "What about you Gianni?"

Versace says I make the most beautiful clothes in the world. I'll completely redesign the fashions up here, from the archangels to the cherubs to the choirboys. As you well know Peter, if you look good you will feel good and that will make heaven a much happier place."

"Not bad" says St Peter." What about you Di?"

Diana doesn't say a word, instead she lifts up her skirt, pulls down her knickers, inserts a full bottle of Evian water into her fanny, lets water shoot up inside her and then gush out all over the floor.

"Excellent, you're in!" says St Peter.

"Hold on a fucking minute!" says Freddie, "She didn't even say anything!"

"Bollocks, Fred - you know the rules," says St Peter, "A royal flush beats a pair of queens."

An elderly man lay dying in his bed. In death's agony, he suddenly smelled the aroma of his favourite chocolate chip cookies wafting up the stairs. He gathered his remaining strength, and lifted himself from the bed. Leaning against the wall, he slowly made his way out of the bedroom, and with even greater effort forced himself down the stairs, gripping the railing with both hands, he crawled downstairs.

With laboured breath, he leaned against the door-frame, gazing into the kitchen.

Were it not for death's agony, he would have thought himself already in heaven: there, spread out upon waxed paper on the kitchen table were literally hundreds of his favourite chocolate chip cookies.

Was it heaven? Or was it one final act of heroic love from his devoted wife, seeing to it that he left this world a happy man?

Mustering one great final effort, he threw himself toward the table, landing on his lines in a rumpled posture. His parched lips parted: the wondrous taste of the cookie was already in his mouth, seemingly bringing him back to life. The aged and withered hand trembled on its way to a cookie at the edge of the table, when it was suddenly smacked with a spatula by his wife.

"Get out now!" she screamed, "they're for the funeral.

It was getting a little crowded in Heaven, so God decided to change the admittance policy. The new law was that, in order to get into Heaven, you had to have a really bummer day on the day that you died.

The policy would go into effect at noon the next day.

So, the next day at 12:01, the first person came to the gates of Heaven. The Angel at the gate, remembering the new policy, promptly asked the man, "Before I let you in, I need you to tell me how your day was going when you died."

"No problem," the man named Steve said. "I came home to my 25th floor apartment on my lunch hour and caught my wife having an affair. But her lover was nowhere in sight. I immediately began searching for him.

My wife was half naked and yelling at me as I searched the entire apartment.

Just as I was about to give up, I happened to glance out onto the balcony and noticed that there was a man hanging off the edge by his fingertips! The nerve of that guy! Well, I ran out onto the balcony and stomped on his fingers until he fell to the ground. But wouldn't you know it, he landed in some trees and bushes that broke his fall and he didn't die.

This ticked me off even more. In a rage, I went back inside to get the first thing I could get my hands on to throw at him.

Oddly enough, the first thing I thought of was the refrigerator. I unplugged it, pushed it out onto the balcony, and tipped it over the side. It plummeted 25 stories and crushed him. The excitement of the moment was so great that I had a heart attack and died almost instantly."

The Angel sat back and thought a moment. Technically, Steve did have a bad day. It was a crime of passion. So, the Angel announces, "OK Steve. Welcome to the Kingdom of Heaven," and let him in.

"I need to hear about what your day was like when you died."

The next man named Jordan said, "No problem. But you're not going to believe this. I was on the balcony of my 26th floor apartment doing my daily exercises. Had been under a lot of pressure so I was really pushing hard to relieve my stress. I guess I got a little carried away, slipped, accidentally fell over the side!

Luckily, I was able to catch myself by the finger tips on the balcony below mine. But all of a sudden this crazy man comes running out of this apartment, starts cussing, and stomps on my fingers. Well of course I fell. I hit some trees and bushes at the bottom which broke my fall so I didn't die right away. As I'm laying there face up on the ground unable to move and in excruciating pain, I see this guy push his refrigerator, of all things, off the balcony. It falls 25 floors and lands on top of me killing me instantly."

The Angel is quietly laughing to himself as Jordan finishes his story.

"I could get used to this new policy", he thinks to himself.

"Very well," the Angel announces. "Welcome to the Kingdom of Heaven!" and he lets Jordan enter.

A few seconds later, Paul comes up to the gate.

The Angel says "Paul, your story will need to be good - please tell me what it was like the day you died."

Paul says, "OK, picture this. I'm naked inside a refrigerator."

An old lady was on a flight. She was sitting beside a young businessman.

After the in-flight meal she took out her Holy Bible and starts her devotion.

The businessman glances at her and said. Do you really believe those stuff in theBible is true?

"Well, yes, as a matter of fact I do," said the old lady.

"Yeah, right..." the man scoffs, "like... what's that guy's name, the one who gotswallowed by a whale..."

"You mean Jonah?"

"Yeah, Jonah, I mean, how do you actually survive for 3 days in a fish's bowl?"

"I don't know," replied the old lady, "but I can ask him when I see him in heavensomeday."

Feeling smart, the young man said: "Ok, but what if he's not in heaven because hewent to hell?"

"Then young man, you can ask him" replied the old lady calmly.

A man had just had a severe heart operation and as he was coming to a nun was holding his hand and gently patting it. When he opened his eyes he asked "Am I in heaven?" The nun said, "Before I answer you, and I hate to ask at a time like this, but do you have insurance?" "No mam, he replied."

"Well do you have enough cash to pay your bill?" "No mam," he replied again. "Do you have any relatives who can help you?" "Only a spinster sister who is a nun," he replied. "Oh," said the nun, "she is no spinster, she is married to God!" "Well send the bill to my Brother-in-law," he replied.

A cat died and went to heaven. At the gate, he told God how he had been abused all his life on earth - people swept him with broom, he had nowhere to sleep, etc. God tells him he is going to make his life very comfortable in heaven.

The next day 6 mice came to heaven. They gave God a similar story about their hard life on earth - how they had to be running all the time because cats were constantly chasing them.

God tells them he'll make their life comfortable. They ask that he give them skates so that they wouldn't have to do much walking or running anymore. God granted their request, fitting them with skates.

A week later God was passing by and found the cat comfortably resting. He asked the cat how things were going. The cat says, "Oh wonderful, God, and those meals on wheels that you have been sending me are delicious!"

There was an earthquake at the Christian Brothers' monastery and it was levelled. All fifty brothers were transported to heaven at the one time.

At the Pearly Gates, St. Peter said, "Let's go through the entry test as a group. Now, first question. How many of you have played around with little boys?"

Forty-nine hands went up.

"Right!" said St. Peter. "You forty-nine can go down to Hell. Oh, and take that deaf bastard with you!"

A good Christian engineer died and was erroneously sent to Hell. Once there, he went to work reorganizing everything. He installed air-conditioning, cooling jets, refrigeration, the works.

Meantime, up in Heaven, the error was discovered and God sent and angry message down to Hell. "I request the immediate return of the engineer you have there. He belongs with us!"...

"No way", replied the Devil, "here he came, here he stays"...."If you do not comply instantly, I will sue you!" exclaimed God.

"And where are you going to find a lawyer up there?"...came back the Devil.

Three guys die together and go to heaven.... St. Peter says, "We only have one rule...don't step on the ducks as they are God's favourite creation."

They enter heaven and see ducks everywhere, and it's almost impossible to not step on a duck. The first guy accidentally steps on one, and soon here comes St. Peter with the biggest, ugliest woman he'd ever seen...

St. Peter chains them together and says, "Your punishment is to be chained to this ugly woman forever."

The next day the second guy steps on a duck...Sure enough, St. Peter comes with another ugly woman and chains them together.

Seeing this, the third guy is very, very careful. He goes for months and doesn't step on any ducks. One day, St. Peter comes along with this beautiful woman: Blonde, blue-eyed, very young and very sexy. He chains them together and leaves without a word.

The man remarks, "I wonder what I did to deserve this good fortune?" And the Blonde says, "I don't know about you, but I stepped on a duck."

One day, while walking down the street, a highly successful executive woman was tragically hit by a bus and killed. Her soul arrived up in Heaven, where she was met at the Pearly Gates by St. Peter himself.

"Welcome to Heaven," said St. Peter. "Before you get settled in though, it seems we have a problem. You see, strangely enough, we've never once had an executive make it this far and we're not really sure what to do with you. "No problem - just let me in," said the woman. "Well, I'd like to, but I have higher orders. What we're going to do is let you have a day in Hell and a day in Heaven, and then you can choose whichever one you want to spend an eternity in."

"Actually, I think I've made up my mind, I prefer to stay in Heaven", said the woman. "Sorry, we have rules," said St. Peter and with that, he put the executive in an elevator and it went down to Hell.

The doors opened and she found herself stepping out onto the putting green of a beautiful golf course. In the distance was a country club, and standing in front of her were all of her friends - fellow executives with whom she had worked. They were all dressed in evening gowns and cheering for her. They ran up and kissed her on both cheeks and they talked about old times. They played an excellent round of golf, and that night went to the country club where she enjoyed an excellent steak and lobster dinner. She met the Devil, who was actually a really nice guy (and kind of cute).

She had a great time telling jokes and dancing. In fact, she was having such a good time, that before she knew it, it was time to leave. Everybody shook her hand and waved goodbye as she got on the elevator. The elevator went up and opened back at the Pearly Gates, where she found St. Peter waiting for her "Now it's time to spend a day in Heaven," he said.

So she spent the next 24 hours lounging around on clouds and playing the harp and singing. She had a great time, and before she knew it, her 24 hours were up. St. Peter came and got her. "So, you've spent a day in Hell and you've spent a day in heaven. Now you must choose your eternity," he said.

The woman paused for a moment, and then replied, "Well, I never thought I'd say this. I mean, Heaven has been really great and all, but I think I had a better time in Hell."

St. Peter escorted her to the elevator and again she went down to Hell.

When the doors of the elevator opened, she found herself standing in a desolate wasteland covered in garbage and filth. She saw her friends were dressed in rags and were picking up the garbage and putting it in sacks.

The Devil came up to her and put his arm around her. "I don't understand", stammered the woman. "Yesterday I was here and there was a golf course and a country club and we ate lobster and danced and had a great time. Now all there is here is a wasteland of garbage and all of my friends look miserable."

The Devil looked at her and smiled. "Yesterday we were recruiting you; today you're staff."

An 85 year old couple, having been married almost 60 years, die in a car crash. They had been in good health the last ten years, mainly due to the wife's interest in health food.

When they reached the pearly gates, St. Peter took them to their mansion, which was decked out with a beautiful kitchen and master bath suite with Jacuzzi. As they "oohed and aahed", the old man asked Peter how much all this was going to cost.

"It's free," Peter replied, Remember, this is Heaven."

Next they went out back to see the championship golf course the home backed up to. They would have golfing privileges every day, and each week the course changed to a new one representing the great golf courses on Earth. The old man asked, "What are the green fees?"

"This is heaven," St. Peter replied. "You play for free."

Next they went to the clubhouse and saw the lavish buffet lunch with the cuisines of the world laid out. "How much to eat?" asked the old man.

"Don't you understand yet?" St. Peter asked. "This is heaven. It's free!"

"Well, where are the low fat and low cholesterol foods?" the old man asked timidly.

"That's the best part, you can eat as much as you like of whatever you like and you never get fat and you never get sick. This is Heaven."

The old man looked at his wife and said, "You and your stupid bran muffins. I could have been here ten years ago!

Little Johnny's new baby brother was screaming up a storm. He asked his mom, "Where had we get him?"

His mother replied, "He came from heaven, Johnny."

Johnny says, "WOW! I can see why they threw him out!"

A gentleman died and arrived in hell. He was met by the Devil and was told that in the new kinder gentler hell, each person is offered three choices of torture. The Devil explained that these tortures run in 1,000-year cycles and you could pick which cycle to begin with.

The Devil took the man to the first room where a man was hung up by his feet and was being whipped with chains. The man said he did not think that was where he wanted to start.

They proceeded to the next room where a man was hung up by his arms and was being whipped by a Cat-O-Nine Tails. The man also declined this form of torture.

The third room had a man strapped to the wall naked and a very beautiful young blonde woman was performing oral sex upon him. The man told the Devil this is more like it, and this was the one he wanted.

The Devil said "Are you sure? It lasts for a thousand years!"

The man assured him that this was the punishment he wanted. So the Devil walked over the young woman and said, "You can go now, I've found your replacement."

A new monk arrives in heaven. He is assigned by St Peter to help the other monks in copying the old texts by hand. He notices, however, that they are copying copies, not the original books.

So, the new monk goes to the head monk to ask him about this. He points out that if there was an error in the first copy, that error would be continued in all of the other copies.

The head monk says we have been copying from the copies for centuries, but you make a good point, my son. So, he goes down into the cellar with one of the copies to check it against the original.

Hours later, nobody has seen him. So, one of the monks goes downstairs to look for him. He hears a sobbing coming from the back of the cellar, and finds the old monk leaning over one of the original books crying. He asks what's wrong. The word is celebrate, says the old monk.

Once there was a guy named Joe. One day he died and found himself standing in front of the pearly gates.

St. Peter: "Joe, if you can answer one question, I'll let you into heaven." Joe: "sounds easy enough."

St. Peter: "ok, who is with you always?" Joe: "O, that's easy: Andy!"

St. Peter: "Andy?" Joe: "Yeah, haven't you heard that hymn 'Andy walks with me, Andy talks with me?"

Heaven is where the police are British, the chefs Italian, the mechanics German, the lovers French and the place is organised by the Swiss.

Hell is where police are German, the chefs British, the mechanics French, the lovers Swiss and the place is organised by the Italians.

Saint Peter greets Bill Gates at the pearly gates and says, "Bill, have you got a million dollars to get into heaven?" And Bill Gates says, "No, I have a billion dollars and don't you know, these gates are named after me!"

CHAPTER 9

I is for Irish

Irish air disaster.

Ireland's worst air disaster occurred early this morning when a small two-seater Cessna plane crashed into a cemetery. Irish search and rescue workers have recovered 1826 bodies so far and expect that number to climb as digging continues into the night.

An Irish bloke goes to the Doctor.

Dactor, it's me ahrse. I'd loik ya ta teyhk a look, if ya woot. So the Doctor gets him to drop his pants and takes a look. Incredible, he says, there is a L20 note lodged up here. Tentatively he eases the twenty out of the man's arse, and then a L10 appears. "This is amazing" exclaims the Doctor "What do you want me to do? "Well fur Gad's sake teyhk it out, rnan" shrieks the patient. The Doctor pulls out the tenner and another twenty appears, and another. Finally the last note comes out and no more appears.

"Ah Dactor, tank ya koindly , dat's moch batter. How moch is dare, den?"

The Doctor counts the pile of cash. RL 1990 exactly. "Ah, dat'd be roit. I knew I wasn't feeling two grand."

Meanwhile in central Belfast thieves have stolen all pedestals from the toilets at Police Headquarters.

A Police spokesperson claims that they have nothing to go on.

Ireland FOR BEGINNERS

- Pub Etiquette:

The crucial thing here is the "round" system, in which each participant takes turns to "shout" an order. To the outsider, this may appear casual; you will not necessarily be told it's your round and other participants may appear only too happy to substitute for you. But make no mistake, your failure to "put your hand in your pocket" will be noticed. People will mention it the moment you leave the room.

The reputation will follow you to the grave, where after it will attach to your offspring and possibly theirs as -ell. In some cases, it may become permanently enshrined in a family nickname.

- Woolly Jumpers:

Ireland produces vast quantities of woollen knitwear and, under an Irish trade agreement, American visitors not leave without a minimum of two sweaters, of which one at least must be predominantly green. Airline staff may check that you have the required documentation before you are allowed to disembark. Continental (that's Europe, not the airline) visitors are only required to have one woolly jumper, but must have a copy of "The Collected Works of Seamus Heaney" as well.

- Irish People and the Weather:

It is often said that the Irish are a Mediterranean people who only come into their own when the sun shines on consecutive days (which it last did around the time of St Patrick). For this reason, Irish people dress for conditions in Palermo rather than Dublin; and it is not unusual in March to see young people sipping cool beer outside city pubs and cafes, enjoying the air and the soft caress of hailstones on their skin. The Irish attitude to weather is the ultimate triumph of optimism over experience:

Every time it rains, we look up at the sky and are shocked and betrayed. Then we go out and buy a new umbrella.

- Time:

Ireland has two time zones:

1. Greenwich Mean Time and
2. "Local" time.

Local time can be anything between ten minutes and three days behind GMT, depending on the position of the earth and the whereabouts of whoever has the keys. Again, the Irish concept of time has been influenced by the thinking of 20th century physicists, who hold that it can only be measured by reference to another body and can even be affected by factors like acceleration. For instance, a policeman entering a licensed premise in rural Ireland late at night is a good example of another body from whom it can be reliably inferred that it in fact closing time. When this happens, acceleration IS the advised option; shockingly, the relativity argument is still not accepted as a valid defence in the Irish courts.

- Irish Traditional Music:

Many visitors to Ireland make the mistake of thinking of traditional music as mere entertainment. In some parts of Ireland this may even be an accurate impression. However, In certain fundamentalist strongholds such as, Clare, traditional music IS founded in a strict belief system which has been handed on from generation to generation, this is overseen by bearded holy men, sometimes called "Mullahs" (Clare, incidentally-, was also the first Irish constituency to elect a member of Ireland s Pakistani " community to the Irish Parliament), who ensure that the music IS played in accordance with laws laid down In the 5th century, . Under this system, "bodhran players" are required to cover their faces in public. Other transgressions, such as attempting to play guitar in a traditional session, are punishable by the loss, of one or both hands. A blind eye may be turned to the misbehaviour of foreigners, but it's best not to push it.

- Irish Dancing:

There are two main kinds of Irish dancing:

1. Riverdance, which is now simultaneously running in every major city in the world except Ulan Bator and which some economists believe is responsible for the Irish economic boom; and

2. Real Irish dancing, in which men do not wear frilly blouses and you still may not express yourself, except in a written note to the adjudicators.

- Green:

Strangely enough, Irish people tend to wear everything except green which is associated with too many national tragedies, including 1798, the Famine and the current Irish rugby team. It's possible that green just doesn't suit the Irish skin colour, which is generally pale blue (see Weather),

- Gaelic Games:

St Patrick's Day brings the climax of the club championships in Gaelic games, which combine elements of the American sports of gridiron and baseball but are played with an intensity more associated with Mafia turf wars. The two main games are "football" and "hurling", the chief difference being that in football, the fights are unarmed. There is also "camogie," which is like hurling, except that in fights the hair may be pulled as well.

- Schools Rugby:

5t Patrick's Day also brings the finals in schools rugby, a game based around the skills of wrestling, kicking, gouging, ear-biting, and assaults on, other vulnerable body parts. The game is much prized in Ireland s better schools, where it's seen as an Ideal grounding for careers in business and the law, it is well-known that St Patrick banished the snakes from Ireland. Less publicised is that he also banished kangaroos, polar bears and Vietnamese pot-bellied pigs, all of which were regarded as nuisances by the early Irish Christians.

- Signposting:

In most countries, road signs are used to help motorists get from one place to, another. In Ireland, it's not so simple. Signposting here is heavily influenced by Einstein's theories (either that or the other way round) of space/time, and works on the basis that there is no fixed reference point in the universe, or not west of Mullingar anyway. Instead, location and distance may be different for every observer and, frequently, for neighbouring road-signs.

The good news is language: Ireland is officially bilingual, a fact which is, reflected in the road signs. This allows you to get lost in both Irish and English.

- Clothes:

Visitors to Ireland in mid-March often ask: What clothes should I bring?

The answer is: All of them!

- Religion:

Ireland remains a deeply religious country, with the two main denominations being "us" and "them". In the unlikely event you are asked which group you belong to, the correct answer is: "I'm an atheist, thank God". Then change the subject.

Air Lingus Flight 101 was flying from Heathrow to Dublin one night, with Paddy the pilot, and Gerry the co-pilot.

As they approached Dublin airport, they looked out the front window.

"B'jeesus" said Paddy "Will you look at how fookin short that runway is".

"Ya not fookin kidding, Paddy" replied Gerry.

"This is going to be one a' the trickiest landings you are ever going to see" said Paddy.

"Ya not fookin kidding, Paddy" replied Gerry.

"Right Gerry. When I give the signal, you put ta engines in reverse" said Paddy.

"Right, I'll be doing that" replied Gerry.

"And ten you put the flaps down straight away" said Paddy.

"Right, I'll be doing that" replied Gerry.

"And then you stamp on them brakes as hard as you can" said Paddy.

"Right, I'll be doing that" replied Gerry.

"And then you pray to ta Mother Mary w' all a' your soul."

"Right, I'll be doing that" replied Gerry.

So they approached the runway with Paddy and Gerry full of nerves and sweaty palms.

As soon as the wheels hit the ground, Gerry put the engines in reverse, put the flaps down, stamped on the brakes and prayed to Mother Mary with all of his soul.

Amidst roaring engines, squealing of tyres and lots of smoke, the plane screeched to a halt centimetres from the end of the runway, much to the relief of Paddy and Gerry and everyone on board.

As they sat in the cockpit regaining their composure, Paddy looked out the front window and said to Gerry "That has got to be the shortest fookin runway I have ever seen in my whole life".

Gerry looked out the side window and replied "Yeah Paddy, and the fookin widest too."

A woman goes to a new gynaecologist and the two find themselves mutually attracted to each other. After a number of dates they become intimate, but she also becomes pregnant. As she enters hospital to give birth, they both realise they really don't want to start a family. But at the same time, an Irish priest is going in to have an operation for an enlarged prostate.

"I know what we'll do", says the doctor, "after the priest wakes up from his operation I'll tell him a miracle has occurred and the baby is his".

The doctor delivers the baby and shortly thereafter places it into the lap of the startled Irish priest. The priest accepts this as a miracle and takes the child to the monastery and raises it to adulthood.

When the boy reaches 18 the priest decides it is time to tell him the truth. "Son", he says, "I'm not your father".

"What do you mean, you're not my father?" exclaims the boy.

And the priest explains, "I'm your mother. The archbishop is your father."

What's the difference between God and Bono? God doesn't wander around Dublin thinking he's Bono.

An Irish couple, Paddy and his wife Mary went to the State Fair every year. Every year Paddy would say, "Mary, I'd like to ride in that there airplane."

And every year Mary would say, "I know, Paddy, but that airplane ride costs ten dollars, and ten dollars is ten dollars."

This one year Paddy and Mary went to the fair and Paddy said, Mary, I'm 71 years old. If I don't ride that airplane this year I may never get another chance."

Mary replied, "Paddy, that there airplane ride costs ten dollars, and ten dollars is ten dollars."

The pilot overheard them and said, "Folks, I'll make you a deal. I'll take you both up for a ride, if you can stay quiet for the entire ride and not say one word I won't charge you, but if you, say one word it's ten dollars."

Paddy and Mary agree and up they go. The pilot does all kinds of twists and turns, rolls and dives, but not a word is heard. He does all his tricks over again, but still not a word. They land and the pilot turns to Stumpy, "By golly, I did everything I could think of to get you to yell out, but you didn't."

Paddy replied, "Well, I was gonna say something when Mary fell out, but ten dollars is ten dollars."

Two Irishmen walk into a pet shop. Right away they go over to the bird section.

Gerry says to Paddy, "that's them. The clerk comes over and asks if he can help them.

"Yeah, we'll take four of them there birds in that cage there" says Gerry, "Put them in a pepper bag."

The clerk does and the two Irishmen pay for the birds and leave the shop.

They get into Gerry's van and drive until they are high up in the hills and stop at the top of a cliff with a 500-foot drop." This looks like a grand place, eh?" says Gerry. no, yeh, this looks good," replies Paddy.

They flip a coin and Gerry wins the toss.

"I guess I get to go first, eh Paddy?" says Gerry.

He then takes two birds out of the bag, places them on his shoulders and jumps off the cliff.

Paddy watches as his mate drops off the edge and goes straight down for a few seconds followed by a 'SPLAT'.

As Paddy looks over the edge of the cliff he shakes his head and says, "Fock that, this budgie jumping is too fockin' dangerous for me"

A minute later, Seamus arrives. He too has been to the pet shop and he walks up carrying the familiar 'pepper bag'.

He pulls a parrot out of the bag, and then paddy notices that, in his other hand, Seamus is carrying a gun.

Hi, Paddy. Watch this," Seamus says and launches himself over the edge of the cliff.

Paddy watches as half way down, Seamus takes the gun and blows the parrot's head off. Seamus continues to plummet until there is a SPLAT! As he joins Gerry's remains at the bottom.

Paddy shakes his head and says and I m never trying that parrot shooting niether.

A few minutes after Seamus splats himself Sean strolls up. He too has been to the pet shop and he walks up carrying the familiar pepper bag.

Instead of a parrot, he pulls a chicken out of the bag, and launches himself off the cliff with the usual result.

Once more Paddy shakes his head—"Fock me Sean, first der was Gerry with his budgie jumping, den Seamus parrot shooting and now you fockin' hen gliding".

Two paddies were working for the city public works department. One would dig a hole and the other would follow behind him and fill the hole in. They worked up one side of the street, then down the other, then moved on to the next street, working furiously all day without rest, one man digging a hole, the other filling it in again.

An onlooker was amazed at their hard work, but couldn't understand what they were doing. So he asked the hole digger, "I'm impressed by the effort you two are putting in to your work, but I don't get it—why do you dig a hole, only to have your partner follow behind and fill it up again?"

The hole digger wiped his brow and sighed, "Well, I suppose it probably looks odd because we're normally a three-person team. But today the lad who plants the trees called in sick."

The American Government funded a study to see why the head of a man's penis was larger than the shaft. After one year and $180,000.00 they concluded that the reason the head was larger than the shaft was to give the man more pleasure during sex.

After the US published the study, the French decided to do their own study, like they do! After $250,000.00, and 3 years of research, they concluded that the reason was to give the woman more pleasure during sex.

The Irish, unsatisfied with these findings, conducted their own study. After two weeks and a cost of around £75.46, and two cases of beer, they concluded that it was to keep a man's hand from flying off and hitting himself in the forehead.

Father Murphy walks into a pub in Donegal, and says to the first man he meets, "Do you want to go to heaven?"

The man said, "I do Father."

The priest said, "Then stand over there against the wall." Then the priest asked the second man, "Do you want to go to heaven?"

"Certainly, Father," was the man's reply.

"Then stand over there against the wall," said the priest. Then Father Murphy walked up to O'Toole and said, "Do you want to go to heaven?"

O'Toole said, "No, I don't Father.

The priest said, "I don't believe this. You mean to tell me that when you die you don't want to go to heaven?"

O'Toole said, "Oh, when I die, yes. I thought you were getting a group together to go on a trip right now."

Comprehending the Irish—Take One

Two Irishman students were walking across campus when one guy said, "Where did you get such a great bike?"

The second Irishman replied, "Well, I was walking along yesterday minding my own business when a beautiful woman rode up on this bike. She threw the bike to the ground, took off all her clothes and said, 'Take what you want.'"

The second accountant nodded approvingly, "Good choice the clothes probably wouldn't have fit."

Comprehending the Irish—Take Two

An Englishman, Frenchman and an Irishman were discussing whether it was better to spend time with the wife or a mistress.

The Englishman said he enjoyed time with his wife, building a solid foundation for an enduring relationship.

The Frenchman said he enjoyed time with his mistress, because of the passion and mystery he found there.

The Irishman said, "I like both." "Both?"

The Irishman replied "Yeah. If you have a wife and a mistress, they will each assume you are spending time with the other woman, and you can go to the pub and drink Guinness."

Comprehending the Irish—Take Three

To the optimist, the glass is half full. To the pessimist, the glass is half empty.

To the Irishman, the question is where is the missing Guinness?

Comprehending the Irish—Take Four

"An Irishman and His Frog"

An Irishman was crossing a road one day when a frog called out to him and said, "If you kiss me, I'll turn into a beautiful princess".

He bent over, picked up the frog and put it in his pocket. The frog spoke up again and said, "If you kiss me and turn me back into a beautiful princess, I will stay with you for one week."

The Irishman took the frog out of his pocket, smiled at it and returned it to the pocket.

Frog: "I'll stay with you and do anything you want. "

Again the Irishman took the frog out, smiled at it and put it back into his pocket.

Finally, the frog asked, "What is the matter? I've told you I'm a beautiful princess, that I'll stay with you for a week and do anything you want.

Why won't you kiss me?"

The Irishman said, "Look I'm on the way to the pub so I don't have time for a girlfriend, but a talking frog, now that's cool."

One night, Mrs McMillen answers the door to see her husband's best friend, Paddy, standing on the doorstep.

"Hello Paddy, but where is my husband? He went with you to the beer factory"

Paddy shook his head. "Ah Mrs McMillen, there was a terrible accident at the beer factory, your husband fell into a vat of Guinness stout and drowned"

Mrs McMillen starts crying. "Oh don't tell me that, did he at least go quickly?"

Paddy shakes his head. "Not really—he got out 3 times to pee!"

There was a World Science Competition and the three finalists were an Englishman, an American and an Irishman. To decide the winner, the judging panel gave each of the men a large, hairy spider and asked them to come back in a weeks' time with a new fact about the spider.

A week expires and the Englishman appears before the panel. "I have discovered that spiders are hairy", he announces. Of course, the judging panel dismisses him immediately.

The American appears before the panel. "Spiders are arachnids" he says. He is escorted from the building by the judging panel's security guards.

Finally, the Irishman appears before the panel and places his spider on the table in front of them.

"Spider, move forwards!" he commands—and the spider moves forwards. "Spider, move backwards!" he orders—and the spider moves backwards. "Spider, move to the left"—the spider moves to the left.

"Spider, move to the right"—the spider moves to the right.

"Spider, move back to the middle"—and the spider moves to the middle of the table.

The judging panel sits and waits. Suddenly, the Irishman pulls out an enormous carving knife and chops off all the spider's legs!!!

"Spider, move forwards!" he commands and of course the spider doesn't move anywhere.

"Spider, move "Spider, move "Spider, move "Spider, move backwards!" he orders—still no movement to the left"—to the right" nothing back to the middle"—and the spider has not moved an inch. The judging panel begins to exchange glances.

"Well?" asks the chairman of the panel. "And what have you discovered about spiders?"

The Irishman replies, "Spiders hear with their legs!"

---

10 Pints of Guinness

A Texan walks into a pub in Ireland and clears his voice to the crowd of drinkers. He says, "1 hear you Irish are a bunch of hard drinkers. I'll give $500 American dollars to anybody in here who can drink 10 pints of Guinness back-to-back." The room is quiet and no one takes up the Texan's offer.

One man even leaves. Thirty minutes later the same gentleman who left shows back up and taps the Texan on the shoulder. "Is your bet still good?" asks the Irishman.

The Texan says yes and asks the bartender to line up 10 pints of Guinness. Immediately the Irishman tears into all 10 of the pint glasses drinking them all back-to-back.

The other pub patrons cheer as the Texan sits in amazement. The Texan gives the Irishman the $500 and says, "If you don't mind me asking, where did you go for that 30 minutes you were gone?"

The Irishman replies, "Oh ...I had to go to the pub down the street to see if I could do it first".

Two Irish priests are off to the showers late one night. They undress and step in the showers before they realise there is no soap.

Father Jim says he has some soap in his room and goes to get it, not bothering to dress. He grabs two bars of soap in his hands and heads back to the showers.

He gets halfway down the hall when he sees three nuns heading his way. Having no place to hide, he stands against the wall and freezes like he's a statue.

The nuns stop and comment on how life-like he looks.

The first nun suddenly reaches out and pulls his dick. Startled, he drops a bar of soap.

Oh look," says the 2nd nun ... "a soap dispenser." To test her theory she also pulls his dick and sure enough he drops the last bar of soap.

The third nun then pull, first once, then twice and three times. Still nothing happens. So she tries once more and to her delight she yells ... "Look, hand cream!"

Gallagher opened the morning newspaper and was dumbfounded to read in the obituary column that he had died. He quickly phoned his best friend Finney.

"Did you see the paper?" asked Gallagher. "They say I died!!"

"Yes, I saw it!" replied Finney. "Where are you calling from?"

A girl walked into the shop to do her shopping. She didn't have enough money so she asked the shopkeeper if she could borrow a pen to write a cheque.

The shopkeeper handed her a 12 inch pen.

"Wow!! Where did you get this pen?" she asked. "From an Irish Genie." replied the shopkeeper.

"Could this Irish Genie grant me a wish?" she asked. "Sure." So out of nowhere comes this Genie.

"I wish for a million bucks," the girl said.

The Irish Genie disappeared but there was no money, so she signed the cheque and left the store.

She came running back into the store and said to the shopkeeper, "There are a million ducks outside."

The shopkeeper replied "Sure. You think I asked for a 12 inch Bic??"

Billy stops Paddy in Dublin and asks for the quickest way to Cork.

Paddy says, "Are you on foot or in the car?"

Billy says, "In the car."

Paddy says, "That's the quickest way."

Paddy gets a phone call from Murphy.

Paddy says Murphy, I've got a problem.

What's the matter asks Paddy.

Oi've bought a jigsaw and it's too hard, none of the pieces fit together, and I can't find any edges.

"What's the picture of?" asks Paddy

"It's of a big cockerel," Murphy replies.

Paddy says, "Alright, Murphy, I'll come over and have a look." He gets to Murphy's house and Murphy opens the door.

"Oh thanks for coming Paddy" He leads Paddy into the kitchen and shows him the jigsaw on the kitchen table.

Paddy looks at the jigsaw, then turns to Murphy, and says, "For God's sake Murphy, put the cornflakes back in the packet."

An Irishman was flustered not being able to find a parking space in a large mall's parking lot.

"Lord" he prayed, "I can't stand this, if you open a space up for me, I swear I'll give up drinking me whiskey, and I promise to go to church every Sunday."

Suddenly, the clouds parted and the sun shone on an empty parking spot. Without hesitation, the man said, "Never mind, I found one."

Paddy and Mick are walking down the road and Paddy's got a bag of doughnuts in his hand.

Paddy says to Mick, "If you can guess how many doughnuts are in my bag, you can have them both."

An Irish priest is driving down to New York and gets stopped for speeding in Connecticut. The state trooper smells alcohol on the priest's breath and then sees an empty wine bottle on the floor of the car.

He says, "Sir, have you been drinking?"

"Just water" says the priest.

The trooper says, "Then why do I smell wine?"

The priest looks at the bottle and says, "Good Lord! He's done it again!"

CHAPTER 10

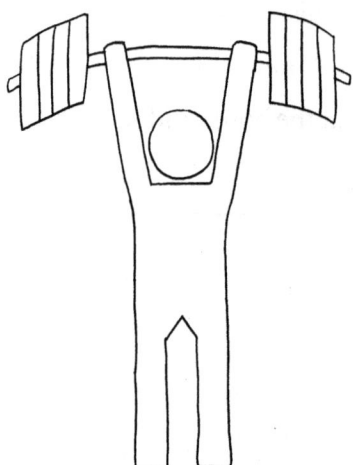

J is for Jerk

A Jewish lady named Mrs Rosenberg who many years ago was stranded late one night at a fashionable resort—one that did not admit Jews.

The desk clerk looked down at his book and said, "Sorry, no room, the hotel is full." The Jewish lady said, "But your sign says that you have vacancies." The desk clerk stammered and then said curtly, "You know that we do not admit Jews. Now if you will try the other side of town"

Mrs Rosenberg stiffened noticeable and said, "I'll have you know I converted to your religion."

The desk clerk said, "Oh, yeah, let me give you a little test. How was Jesus born?"

Mrs Rosenberg replied, "He was born to a virgin named Mary in a little town called Bethlehem."

"Very good," replied the hotel clerk. "Tell me more."

Mrs Rosenberg replied, "He was born in a manger."

"That's right," said the hotel clerk. "And why was he born in a manger?"

Mrs Rosenberg said loudly, "Because a jerk like you in the hotel wouldn't give a Jewish lady a room for the night!"

After the annual office party, John woke up with a headache, cotton-mouthed, and utterly unable to recall the events of the preceding evening. After a trip to the bathroom he was able to make his way downstairs, where his wife was preparing breakfast. "Gina," he moaned, "tell me what went on last night. Was it as bad as I think?" "Even worse," she declared, her voice dripping with scorn. "You made a complete jerk of yourself, succeeded in antagonizing the entire board of directors, and insulted the president of the company to his face!" "He's a jerk, piss on him." "You did," Gina informed him. "And he fired you." "Well, screw him!" said John. "I did., you're back at work on Monday!"

Tom and Jeni are having one of their occasional disputes of opinion. Tom took off his pants and threw them at Jeni, yelling, "Hey, woman, can you fill these pants up?" "Of course not, you jerk. You know I can't." "You're right. You can't. I wear the pants in this family." So Jeni took off her panties and threw them at Tom, yelling, "Hey, jerk, can you get into these panties?" "Hell no! They're too small and dainty!" "And you won't either, until you change your treatment of me!"

A man walks into a bar on the top floor of a skyscraper. He sits down and orders a beer. After taking a drink he sees the guy next to him go over to the window and jump out!

"Holy cow! Did you see that!? That guy just jumped out the window!"

The bartender does nothing.

So the man takes another sip. A minute later the same guy walks in, orders another drink, chugs it, and jumps out the window again.

"Jesus! He just jumped again!"

The bartender ignores the man.

So the man sits puzzled. The guy comes back into the bar, and orders another drink.

"How did you survive that jump?" ."I ordered a floatie drink, if you drink it in a certain amount of time, you can float."

So the guy quickly orders a 'floatie' drink. He takes it from the bartender, and chugs it. He then jumps out the window and...SPLAT! Right on the sidewalk!

The Bartender then says, "You know, Superman, you can be a real jerk when you're drunk."

For all of you who occasionally have a really bad day when you just need to take it out on someone!!! Don't take a bad day out on someone you know, take it out on someone you DON'T know!!!

Now get this. I was sitting at my desk, when I remembered a phone call I had to make. I found the number and dialled it. A man answered nicely saying, "Hello?"

I politely said, "This is Patrick Hanifin and could I please speak to Robin Carter?"

Suddenly the phone was slammed down on me! I couldn't believe that anyone could be that rude. I tracked down Robin's correct number and called her. She had transposed the last two digits incorrectly. After I hung up with Robin, I spotted the wrong number still lying there on my desk. I decided to call it again. When the same person once more answered, I yelled "You're a jerk!" and hung up.

Next to his phone number I wrote the word "jerk," and put it in my desk drawer. Every couple of weeks, when I was paying bills, or had a really bad day, I'd call him up. He'd answer, I'd yell, "You're a jerk!" It would always cheer me up.

Later in the year the phone company introduced caller ID. This was a real disappointment for me, I would have to stop calling the jerk.

Then one day I had an idea. I dialled his number, then heard his voice, Hello. I made up a name. Hi. This is the sales office of the telephone company and I'm just calling to see if you're familiar with our caller ID program? He went, No! and slammed the phone down. I quickly called him back and said, "That's because you're a jerk!"

The reason I took the time to tell you this story, is to show you how if there's ever anything really bothering you, you can do something about it. Just dial 823-4863.

[Keep reading, it gets better.]

The old lady at the mall really took her time pulling out of the parking pace. I didn't think she was ever going to leave. Finally, her car began to move and she started to very slowly back out of the slot. I backed up a little more to give her plenty of room to pull out. Great, I thought, she's finally leaving.

All of a sudden this car come flying up the parking isle in the wrong direction and pulls into her space.

I started honking my horn and yelling, you didn't just do that, Buddy.

I was here first!

The guy climbed out of his car completely ignoring me. He walked toward the mall as if he didn't even hear me. I thought to myself, this guy's a jerk, there sure are a lot of jerks in this world. I noticed he had a For Sale sign in the back window of his car. I wrote down the number. Then I hunted for another place to park.

A couple of days later, I'm at home sitting at my desk. I had just gotten off the phone after calling 23-4863 and yelling, you're a jerk!

(It's really easy to call him now since I have his number on speed dial.)

I noticed the phone number of the guy with the car lying on my desk and thought I'd better call this guy too. After a couple rings someone answered the phone and said, Hello. I said, Is this the man with the car for sale? Yes, it is. Can you tell me where I can see it? Yes, I live at 1802 West 34th street. It's a yellow house and the car's parked right out front. I said, what's your name? My name is Don Hansen. When's a good time to catch you, Don? I'm home in the evenings.

Listen Don, can I tell you something? Yes. Don, you're a jerk! And I slammed the phone down.

After I hung up I added Don Hansen's number to my speed dialler. For a while things seemed to be going better for me.

Now when I had a problem I had two jerks to call. Then, after several months of calling the jerks and hanging up on them, it wasn't as enjoyable as it used to be.

I gave the problem some serious thought and came up with a solution:

First, I had my phone dial jerk #1. A man answered nicely saying, hello. I yelled You're a jerk!, but I didn't hang up.

The jerk said, Are you still there? I said, Yeah.

He said, Stop calling me. I said, no.

He said, what's your name, Pal? I said, Don Hansen. He said where do you live? 1802 west 34th street. It's a yellow house and my car is parked out front.

He said I'm coming over right now, don't you'd better start saying your prayers.

Yeah, like I'm really scared, jerk! and I hung up.

Then I called jerk #2. He answered, Hello. I said, Hello, jerk". He said, If I ever find out who you are

You'll what?

I'll kick your butt.

Well, here's your chance. I'm coming over right now jerk! And I hung up.

Then I picked up the phone and called the police. I told them I was on 1802 West 34th Street and that I was going to kill my gay lover as soon as he got home.

Another quick call to Channel 13 about the gang war going on down 34th Street.

After that I climbed into my car and headed over to 34th Street to watch the whole thing.

Glorious!

Watching two jerks kicking the crap out of each other in front of 6 squad cars and a police helicopter was one of the greatest experiences of my life!

The ultimate respect to this young man. Below is a supposedly true story about a recent wedding that took place at Clemson, USA.

This was a huge wedding with about 300 guests.

After the wedding at the reception, the groom got up on stage at the microphone to talk to the crowd. He said that he wanted to thank everyone for coming, many from long distances, to support them at their wedding.

He especially wanted to thank the bride's and groom's families for coming and to thank his new father-in-law for providing such a fabulous reception. To thank everyone for coming and bringing gifts and everything, he said he wanted to give everyone a special gift from just him. So taped to the bottom of everyone's chair was a manila envelope including a photo of the wedding party. He said that was his gift to everyone, and told everyone to open the envelopes.

Inside each manila envelope was a 8x10 picture of his best man having sex with the bride. (He had got suspicious of the two of them and hired a Private Detective to trail them weeks prior to the wedding.)

After he stood there and watched the people's reactions for a couple of minutes, he turned to the best man and said "fu*k you jerk", he turned to the bride and said "jerk fu*ker", and then he turned to the dumbfounded crowd and said "I'm out of here."

He had the marriage annulled first thing that Monday morning. While most of us would have broken off the engagement immediately after finding out about the affair, this guy goes through with it as if nothing was wrong.

His revenge:

1. Making the bride's parents pay over $32,000 for a 300 guest wedding and reception.
2. Letting everyone know exactly what did happen.
3. And best of all, trashing the bride's and best man's reputations in front of all of their friends, their entire families—parents, brothers, sisters, grandparents, nieces and nephews.

A man was pulled over for driving too fast, even though he thought he was driving just fine.

Officer: "You were speeding."

Man: "No, I wasn't."

Officer: "Yes, you were. I'm giving you a ticket."

Man: "But I wasn't speeding."

Officer: "Tell that to the judge!" (The officer gives man the ticket.)

Man: "Would I get another ticket if I called you a jerk?"

Officer: "Yes, you would."

Man: "What if I just thought that you were?"

Officer: "I can't give you a ticket for what you think."

Man: "Fine, I think you're a jerk!"

This is the transcript of an actual radio conversation of a US naval ship with Canadian authorities off the coast of Newfoundland.

Radio conversation released by the Chief of Naval Operation 10/10/95.

Americans: Please divert your course 15 degrees to the North to avoid a collision.

Canadians: We recommend you divert your course 15 degrees to the South to avoid a collision.

Americans: This is the Captain of a US Navy ship. I say again, divert your course.

Canadians: No, I say again divert your course.

Americans: THIS IS THE AIRCRAFT CARRIER USS LINCOIN, THE SECOND LARGEST SHIP IN THE UNITED STATES' ATLANTIC FLEET. WE ARE ACCOMPANIED BY THREE DESTROYERS, THREE CRUISERS AND NUMEROUS SUPPORT VESSELS.

I DEMAND THAT YOU CHANGE YOUR COURSE 15 DEGREES NORTH, THAT'S ONE FIVE DEGREES NORTH, OR COUNTER MEASURES WILL BE UNDERTAKEN TO ENSURE THE SAFETY OF THIS SHIP YOU JERK.

Canadians: We are a lighthouse. Your call jerk.

CHAPTER 11

K is for Kiwi

Why does New Zealand have some of the fastest race horses in the world?

Because the horses have seen what they do with their sheep.

Once upon a time in the kingdom of Heaven, God went missing for six days.

Eventually, Michael the archangel found him. He inquired of God, "Where were you?"

God sighed a deep sigh of satisfaction and downwards through the clouds; "Look son, look what I've made.

Archangel Michael looked puzzled and said, "What is it? .God replied, "It's a planet and I've put life on it. I've named it earth and there is a balance between everything on it.

For example, there's North America and South America. North America is going to be rich and South America is going to be poor, and the narrow bit joining them that's going to be a hotspot.

Now look over here. I've put a continent of white people in the north and another one of black people in the south."

The archangel then said, "And what's that long white line there?

And God said "Ah - that is Australia - and that's a very special place

That's going to be the most glorious spot on earth; beautiful Mountains, lakes, rivers, streams, and an exquisite coast-line.

These people here are going to be modest, intelligent and humorous they're going to be found travelling the world. They'll be extremely sociable hard working and high achieving. And I'm going to give them this superhuman undefeatable cricket team which will be blessed with the most talented, and charismatic specimens on the planet, and will be admired and feared by all who come across them."

Michael the Archangel gasped in wonder and admiration but then seeming startled proclaimed: "Hold on a second, what about the balance you said there was going to be a balance."

God replied wisely." Wait until you see the irritating loud-mouthed wankers I'm putting in the pissy little country next to them named New Zealand."

Prime Minister Helen Clark's husband was jogging near his home in Auckland.

Every day, he'd jog past a hooker standing on the same street corner. He learned to brace himself as he approached her for what was almost certain to follow. "Two hundred and fifty dollars!" she'd shout from the curb. "No! Five dollars!" He would fire back, just to shut her up.

This ritual between him and the hooker became a daily occurrence. He'd run by and she'd yell, "Two hundred and Fifty dollars!" He'd yell back, "Five dollars!"

One day, Helen decided that she wanted to accompany her husband on his jog. As the jogging couple neared the working woman's street corner, Dr Davis realised she'd bark her $250 offer and Helen would wonder what he'd really been doing on all his past outings. He figured he'd better have a darn good explanation for the 'Boss'.

As they jogged into the turn that would take them past the corner, he became even more apprehensive than usual. Sure enough, there was the hooker. He tried to avoid the prostitute's eyes as she watched the pair jog past.

Then, from her corner, the hooker yelled, "See what you get for five bucks, you tight bastard?!"

Kiwiese introductory Language Lesson

After years of trying and failing to understand what they're saying, following these easy steps, you can finally hold a conversation with a New Zealander.

What you hear and what it really means:

A MEDGEN: Visualise, Conjure up mentally, John Lennon's first solo Album "Imagine" as it was a bug hut in the "Land of the Long White Cloud"

BETTING: Betting Gloves" are worn by "Batsmen" in "Cricket"

BRIST: Part of the human anatomy between the "Nick" and the "Billy"

BUGGER: As in "Mine is bugger then yours"

CHULLYBUN: "Chilly Bin" also known as an ESKY.

COME YOUSE: Controversial captain of the Australian Cricket team resigned tearfully in favour of Allan Border. "Come" insisted thut all deliveries be overarm. Full Name: Kimberley John Hughes.

DIMMEKRRETZ: Those who believe in Democracy.

ERRORBUCK: Language spoken in countries like "Burria" "E-JUpp" & "Libernon"

EKKA DYMOCKS: University Staff

GUESS: Flammable vapour used in stoves

CHICK OUT CHUCKS: Supermarket point of sale operators.

SENDLES: Sandals, Thongs & open shoes.

COLOUR: Terminator, violent fore closer of human life.

CUSS: Kiss

DUCK HID: Term of abuse directed mainly at Males.

PHAR LAP: NZ's famous horse christened "Phillip" but was incorrectly written down as "Phar Lap" by an Australian (Racing official who was not well versed in KIWIESE)

DUNNESTY: US Television soap opera starred Joan Collins as "Elixirs Kerrungton"

ERROR ROUTE; Arnott' B famous oval shaped "mulk error route buskets"

FITTER CHENEY: A type of long flat pasta, not to be confused with "Rugger Tony" or "Tell ya, Tilly".

A Kiwi walks into a Sydney unemployment office.

He marches straight up to the counter and says, "Hi! I want to apply for the dole, I hate being on welfare and I'd much rather have a job but I have looked everywhere and just can't find any."

The clerk behind the Centre link desk says, "Your timing is excellent. We just got a job opening from a very wealthy old man who needs a chauffeur/bodyguard for his two twin 21 year old nymphomaniac daughters. You'll have to drive them around in his Mercedes, but he'll supply all of your clothes.

You'll have a three-bedroom apartment above the garage. Because of the long hours, meals will be provided. You'll be expected to escort his daughters on their frequent overseas holidays to Tahiti and the Bahamas. The starting salary is $250,000 a year".

The Kiwi says, "No way mate, you gotta be bullshitting me!"

The Centre link officer says, "Yeah, well, you started it".

Two New Zealanders board a shuttle out of London for Edinburgh. One sits in the window seat, the other in the middle seat. Just before take-off an Australian guy gets on and takes the aisle seat next to the kiwis.

He kicks off his shoes and socks and is settling in when the window seat says, "I think I'll get up and git a coke."

"No problem mate," says the Aussie." I'll get it for you." While he's gone, the Kiwi picks up one of the Aussie's shoes and spits in it.

When the Aussie returns with the coke, the other Kiwi says, "That looks good. I think I'll have one too."

Again the Aussie kindly goes to fetch it, and while he's gone the Kiwi picks up the Aussie's other shoe and spits in it. The Aussie returns with the coke, and they all sit back and enjoy the short flight.

As the plane is landing the Aussie slips his feet into his shoe and immediately knows what has happened. The Kiwis laugh.

"How bloody long must this Trans-Tasman rivalry go on?" the Aussie asks. "This enmity between Australians and New Zealander .... this hatred .... this animosity .... this spitting in shoes and pissing in cokes?"

A Kiwi, an Englishman and a South African are in a bar one night having a beer.

All of a sudden the South African downs his beer, throws his glass in the air, pulls out a gun, shoots the glass to pieces and says, "In South Africa, our glasses are so cheap that we don't need to drink from same twice"

The Kiwi, obviously impressed by this, drinks his beer, throws his glass into the air, pulls out his gun, shoots the glass to pieces and says, "Well mate, in unzud we have so much sand to make the glasses that we don't need to drink out of the same glass twice either."

The Englishman, cool as a cucumber, picks up his beer and drinks it, throws his glass into the air, pulls out his gun and shoots the South African and the Kiwi and says "In England we have so many fucking South Africans and New Zealanders that we don't need to drink with the same ones twice.

At the end of a tiny, deserted bar is a huge Kiwi bloke - 6ft 5 and 350lbs. He's having a few beers when a short, well-dressed and obviously gay man walks in and sits beside him. After three or four beers the gay finally plucks up the courage to say something to the big New Zealander.

Leaning over towards the Kiwi he whispers, "Do you want to get a blow-job?"

At this the massive Kiwi leaps up with fire in his eyes and smacks the man in the face, knocking him swiftly off the stool. He proceeds to beat him all the way out of the bar before leaving him bruised and battered in the car park and returning to his seat. Amazed, the barman quickly brings over another beer.

"I've never seen you react like that, he says, just what did he say to you?"

"I'm not sure," the big Kiwi replies, "something about getting a job."

An Australian ventriloquist visiting New Zealand walks into a small village and sees a local sitting on his porch patting his dog.

He figures he'll have a little fun, so he says to the Kiwi: "G'day, mind if I talk to your dog?"

Villager: "The dog doesn't talk, you stupid Aussie."

Ventriloquist: "Hello dog, how's it going mate?"

Dog: "Yeah, doing all right."

Kiwi: (look of extreme shock)

Ventriloquist: "Is this villager your owner?" (pointing at the villager)

Dog: "Yep"

Ventriloquist: "How does he treat you?"

Dog: "Yeah, real good. He walks me twice a day, feeds me great food

and takes me to the lake once a week to play."

Kiwi: (look of utter disbelief)

Ventriloquist: "Mind if I talk to your horse?"

Kiwi: "Uh, the horse doesn't talk either....I think."

Ventriloquist: "Hey horse, how's it going?"

Horse: "Cool"

Kiwi: (absolutely dumbfounded)

Ventriloquist: "Is this your owner?" (Pointing at the villager)

Horse: "Yep"

Ventriloquist: How does he treat you?

Horse: "Pretty good, thanks for asking. He rides me regularly, brushes me down often and

keeps me in the barn to protect me from the elements."

Kiwi: (total look of amazement)

Ventriloquist: "Mind if I talk to your sheep?"

Kiwi: (in a panic) "Don't believe a word he says, that sheep's a bloody liar.."

A young man graduated from University of Auckland with a degree in journalism. His first assignment for the newspaper who hired him was to write a human interest story.

Being from the South Island, he went back to the country to do his research. He went to an old farmer's house way back in the hills, introduced himself to the farmer and proceeded to explain to him why he was there. The young man asked, "Has anything happened around here that made you happy?" -

The farmer thought for a minute and said, "Yep one time one of my neighbour's sheep got lost. We formed a posse and found it. We all screwed it and took it back home. I can't print that!" the young man exclaimed. "Can you think of anything else that happened that made you or a lot of other people happy?"

After another moment, the farmer said, "Yeah, one time my neighbour's daughter, a good looking girl, got lost. We formed a big posse that time and found her. After we all screwed her, we took her back home." Again, the young man said "I can't print that either. Has anything ever happened around here that made you sad?"

The old farmer dropped his head as if he were ashamed and after a few seconds looked up timidly at the young man and said, "I got lost once"

A Kiwi walks into his bedroom carrying a sheep in his arms and says:

"Darling, this is the pig I have sex with when you have a headache."

His girlfriend is lying in bed and replies: "That's not a pig but a sheep, you idiot."

The man says: "Shut up, I wasn't talking to you."

CHAPTER 12

L is for Lethally Blonde

A man was in his front yard mowing grass when his attractive blonde female neighbour came out of the house and went straight to the mail box.

She opened it then slammed it shut and stormed back in the house. A little later she came out of her house again went to the mail box and again opened it, and slammed it shut again.

Angrily, back into the house she went. As the man was getting ready to edge the lawn, here she came out again, marched to the mail box, opened it and then slammed it closed harder than ever.

Puzzled by her actions the man asked her, "Is something wrong?"

To which she replied, "There certainly is!"

(Are you ready?) ....

My stupid computer keeps saying, "YOU'VE GOT MAIL."

The Sheriff in a small town walks out in the street and sees a blonde cowboy coming down the walk with nothing on but his cowboy hat, gun, and his boots, so he arrests him for indecent exposure. As he is locking him up, he asks: "Why in the world are you dressed like this?"

The Cowboy says, "Well it's like this Sheriff, I was in the bar down the road and this pretty little red head asks me to go out to her motorhome with her. So I did. We go inside and she pulls off her top and asks me to pull off my shirt ... so I did. Then she pulls off her skirt and asks me to pull off my pants ... so I did. Then she pulls off her panties and asks me to pull off my shorts ... so I did. Then she gets on the bed and looks at me kind of sexy and says, 'Now go to downtown cowboy and here I am.'"

- BLONDE ON A DIET

A blonde is terribly overweight, so her doctor puts her on a diet. "I want you to eat regularly for two days, then skip a day, and repeat this procedure for two weeks. The next time I see you, you'll have lost at least five pounds." When the blonde returns, she's lost nearly 20 pounds. "Why, that's amazing!" the doctor says. "Did you follow my instructions?" The blonde nods. "I'll tell you, though, I thought I was going to drop dead that third day." "From hunger, you mean?" "No, from skipping."

- BLONDE SELLING HER CAR.

A blonde tried to sell her old car. She was having a lot of problems selling it, because the car had 250,000 miles on it. One day, she told her problem to a brunette she worked with at a salon. The brunette told her, "There is a possibility to make the car easier to sell, but it's not legal."

"That doesn't matter," replied the blonde, "if I only can sell the car." "Okay," said the brunette. "Here is the address of a friend of mine. He owns a car repair shop. Tell him I sent you and he will turn the counter in your car back to 50,000 miles. Then it should not be a problem to sell your car anymore." The following weekend, the blonde made the trip to the mechanic. About one month after that, the brunette asked the blonde, "Did you sell your car?" "No," replied the blonde, "Why should I? It only has 50,000 miles on it."

- BLONDE ON A RIVER SIDE

So there's this blonde out for a walk. She comes to a river and sees another blonde on the opposite bank. "Yoo-hoo" she shouts, "how can I get to the other side?" The second blonde looks up the river then down the river then shouts back, "You are on the other side."

- BLONDE ON A PLANE

On a plane bound for New York, the flight attendant approached a blonde sitting in the first class section and "requested that she move to coach since she did not have a first class ticket. The blonde replied, "I'm blonde, I'm beautiful, I'm going to New York, and I'm not moving." Not wanting to argue with a customer, the flight attendant asked the co-pilot to speak with her.

He went to talk with the woman asking her to please move out of the first class section. Again, the blonde replied, "I'm blonde, I'm beautiful, I'm going to New York, and I'm not moving." The co-pilot returned to the cockpit and asked the captain what he should do. The captain said, "I'm married to a blonde, and I know how to handle this." He went to the first class section and whispered in the blonde's ear. She immediately jumped up and ran to the coach section mumbling to herself, "Why didn't anyone just say so?" surprised, the flight attendant and the co-pilot asked what he said to her that finally convinced her to move from her seat. He said, "I told her the first class section wasn't going to New York."

- BLONDE GIRL'S BLONDE HUSBAND

A blonde guy gets home early from work and hears strange noises coming from the bedroom. He rushes upstairs to find his wife naked on the bed, sweating and panting. "What's going on here?' he says. "I'm having a heart attack," cries the woman." He rushes downstairs to grab the phone, but just as he's dialling, his 4-year old son comes up and says, "Daddy! Daddy! Uncle Ted's hiding in your wardrobe closet and he's got no clothes on!"

The guy slams the phone down and storms upstairs into the bedroom, past his screaming wife, and rips open the wardrobe door. Sure enough, there is his best pal, totally naked, cowering on the wardrobe floor. "You idiot!" says the husband, "my wife's having a heart attack and you're running around naked and scaring the kids!"

- A TART BLONDE:

A blonde, a brunette and a redhead enter an elevator. As they walk in they notice a small puddle of white liquid on the floor of the elevator. The brunette bends down for a closer look, and states, very matter of fact, "...It looks like semen". The redhead stoops down a little closer, takes a deep breath through her nose, and proclaims, "Yes, and it smells like semen". The blonde stoops down yet closer, puts the tip of her finger into the puddle, touches it to her tongue and exclaims "Well, its nobody from our building."

True story from the WordPerfect helpline

Needless to say the helpdesk employee was fired. However, he/she is currently suing the WordPerfect organization for "Termination without Cause"

This was what happened:-

Ridge Hall computer assistant; may I help you?" Yes, well, I'm having trouble with WordPerfect" "What sort of trouble?"

"Well, I was just typing along, and all of a sudden the words went away"

"Went away?" "They disappeared"

"Hmm so what does your screen look like now?" "Nothing"

"Nothing?"

"It's blank; it won't accept anything when I type"

'Are you still in WordPerfect, or did you get out?'

'How do I tell?

'Can you see the C: prompt on the screen?'

"What's a sea-prompt?"

"Never mind. Can you move the cursor around on the screen?"

"There isn't any cursor: I told you, it won't accept anything I type"

"Does your monitor have a power indicator?" "What's a monitor?'

'It's the thing with the screen on it that looks like a TV. Does it have a little light that tells you when it's on?'

"I don't know'

"Well, then look on the back of the monitor and find where the power cord goes into it

Can you see that?"

'Yes, I think so'

'Great follow the cord to the plug, and tell me if it's plugged into the wall'

"Yes, it is"

"When you were behind the monitor, did you notice that there were two cables plugged into the back of it, not just one?'

"No"

'Well, there are, I need you to look back there again and find the other cable'

"Okay, here it is"

'Follow it for me, and tell me if it's plugged securely into the back of your computer?"

'I can't reach'

"Uh huh Well, can you see if it is?"

"No"

'Even if you maybe put your knee on something and lean way over"

Oh, it's not because I don't have the right angle, it's because it's dark.

"Dark?"

"Yes, the office light is off, and the only light I have is coming in from the window"

'Well, turn on the office light then"

"I can't"

'No? Why not?'

'Because there's a power failure"

"A power failure? Aha, Okay, we've got it licked now. What colour hair do you have?"

"Blonde, is that relevant?"

"Yes, now listen carefully, do you still have the boxes and manuals and packing stuff your computer came in?

"Well, yes, I keep them in the closet"

"Good go get them, and unplug your system and pack it up just like it was when you got it then take it back to the store you bought it from"

"Really? Is it that bad?" "Yes, I'm afraid it is'

"Well, all right then, I suppose. What do I tell them?"

"Tell them you're too fucking stupid to own a computer."

A blonde began a job as an elementary school counsellor, and she was eager to help.

One day during recess she noticed a boy standing by himself on the side of a playing field while the rest of the kids enjoyed a game of soccer at the other. Sandy approached and asked if he was alright.

The boy said he was. A little while later, however, Sandy noticed the boy was in the same spot, still by himself. Approaching again, Sandy said, "Would you like me to be your friend?"

The boy hesitated, then said, "Okay", looking at the woman suspiciously.

Feeling she was making progress, Sandy then asked; "Why are you standing here alone?"

"Because," the little boy said with great exasperation, "I'm the fucking goalie."

A young blonde was on vacation in the depths of Louisiana. She wanted a pair of alligator shoes in the worst way, but was very reluctant to pay the high prices the local vendors were asking. After becoming very frustrated with the "No Haggle" attitude of one of the shopkeepers the blonde shouted, "Maybe I'll just go out and catch my own alligator so I can get a pair of shoes at a reasonable price!!!"

The shopkeeper said, "By all means, be my guest. Maybe you'll luck out and catch yourself a big one"

Determined, the blonde turned and headed for the swamps, set on catching herself an alligator.

Later in the day, the shopkeeper is driving home when he spots the young woman standing waist deep in the water shot gun In hand. Just then he sees a huge 3 metre alligator swimming quickly toward her. She takes aim, kills the creature and with great deal of effort hauls it on to the swamp bank. Laying nearby were several more of the dead creatures.

The shopkeeper watches in amazement. Just then the blonde flips the alligator on its back, and frustrated shouts out. "Damn it!! This one isn't wearing any shoes either.

Two Blondes were walking down the street. One noticed a compact on the sidewalk and leaned down to pick it up. She opened it, looked in the mirror and said, "Hmmmmm, this person looks familiar."

The second Blonde said, "Let me look! The first Blonde handed her the compact. The second Blonde looked in the mirror and said, "You dumb ass, it's me!"

Did you hear about the new paint called "Blonde" paint? It's not very bright, but it spreads easy.

In a crowded city at a crowded bus stop, a beautiful young blonde woman was waiting for the bus. She was decked out in a tight leather mini skirt with matching leather boots and jacket.

As the bus rolled up and it became her turn to get on, she became aware that the skirt was too tight to allow her leg to come up to the height of first step on the bus. Slightly embarrassed and with a quick smile to the bus driver, she reached behind her and unzipped her skirt a little, thinking that this would give her enough slack to raise her leg. Again she tried to make the step onto the bus only to discover that still could not do it. So, a little more embarrassed, she once again reached behind her and unzipped her skirt a little more and for a second time attempted the step, and once again much to her chagrin, she could not raise her leg because of the tight skirt.

So, with a coy little smile to the driver, she again unzipped the offending skirt to give her a little more slack and again was unable to make the step. About this time, the big Texan that was behind her in line, picked her up easily from the waist and placed her lightly on the step of the bus.

Well, the blonde went ballistic and turned to the would be hero, screeching at him "How dare you touch my body? I don't even know who you are!"

At this, the Texan drawled, "Well Ma'am, normally I would agree with you, but after you unzipped my fly three times, I kind of figured that you wanted us to be friends…"

An executive was in quandary. He had to get rid of one of his staff and had narrowed it down to one of two people, Debra or Jack.

It would be a hard decision to make, as they were both equally qualified and both did excellent work. He finally decided that in the morning whichever one used the water cooler first would have to go.

Debra, a stunningly attractive blonde, came in the next morning, hugely hung over after partying all night.

She went to the cooler to get some water to take an aspirin and the executive approached her and said: "Debra, I've never done this before, but I have to lay you or Jack off."

Debra replied, "Could you jack off? I have a terrible headache."

A young brunette goes into the doctor's office and says that her body hurts wherever she touches it.

"Impossible," says the doctor." Show me."

She takes her finger and pushes her elbow and screams in agony. She pushes her knee and screams, pushes her ankle and screams and so it goes on, everywhere she touches makes her scream.

The doctor says, "You're not really a brunette, are you?" She says, "No, I'm really a blonde." "I thought so," he says." Your finger is broken."

- How does a blonde turn on the lights after sex? She opens the car door
- Why did the blonde get fired from the M&M factory? She threw away all the W's
- How can you tell if a blonde's been using a computer? If there's white-out on the screen
- If a blonde and a brunette both jumped of a bridge at the same time, who would hit the water first? The brunette. The blonde had to ask for directions

---

Three blondes find a magic lamp and all rub it at the same time. A magic genie appears and says, "I'm supposed to grant three wishes to whomever rubs the lamp, but since you all rubbed it at the same time, you each get a wish each."

So the first blonde says, "I want to be 25% smarter" and the genie turned her into a red head.

The second blonde says, "Well, I want to get promoted, so make me lot smarter" and the genie made her into the brunette.

The third blonde says "I don't want to lose my pretty blonde hair, so I want to be lot dumber" and the Genie turned her into a man.

A blonde, a redhead and a brunette are all lined up in front of a firing squad. They are about to shoot the redhead when she shouts "Tornado".

The firing squad all look and the redhead runs away. They then prepare to shoot the brunette when she screams "Earthquake!

The firing squad look around while the brunette make a getaway. They then take aim at the blonde and start counting down "1, 2, 3 ..." when she points and yells "Fire!"

A blonde and a brunette are sitting in a bar watching a man about to jump off a building and kill himself on the 6 O'clock news.

The brunette says "I bet $50 he jumps." The blonde makes the bet and loses. The brunette then says "I saw it on the 5 o'clock news."

"Me too," says the blonde "but I didn't think. He'd do it again."

Once there was this blonde who'd just dyed her hair dark brown, and she was driving along a winding country road.

As she was driving, she looked out the window and saw a farmer with a huge flock of sheep, so she stopped the car, got out, and went over to him.

"Hey," she said to the farmer, "If I can guess how many sheep are in your flock, can I keep one?"

The farmer looked from the girl to the sheep, and thought there was no way she could ever guess the right number, so he told her to go ahead.

She tilted her head to one side and pursed her lips in thought for a moment." Ummm, is it 574?"

The farmer just stared at her, dumbfounded." How did you know?" he asked.

She simply shrugged, then walked over, picked one of the sheep up under her arm and started back to her car.

"Hey wait a minute," the farmer called after her, "If I can guess what colour your hair really7 is, can I have my sheepdog back?"

Here's a blonde story to end all blonde stories! A True story . if she had killed herself, God forbid, she'd be a shoe-in for the Darwin Award.

Last summer, down on Lake Isabella, located in the high desert, an hour east of Bakersfield, California, a blonde (of course!!), new to boating was having a problem. No matter how hard she tried, she just couldn't get her brand new 22-ft. Bay liner to perform. It wouldn't plane at all, and it was very sluggish in almost every manoeuvre, no matter how much power she applied.

After about an hour of trying to make it go, she putted over to a nearby marina.

Maybe they could tell her what was wrong. A thorough topside check revealed everything was in perfect working order. The engine ran, the out drive went up and down, the prop was the correct size and pitch. So, one of the marina guys jumped in the water to check underneath only to come up choking on water, he was laughing so hard.

Remember, this is true.

Under the boat, still strapped securely in place, was the trailer.

- What do you call a smart blonde? A golden retriever.

- Why are all dumb blonde jokes one liners? So men can understand them.
- A brunette, a blonde, and a redhead are all in third grade. Who has the biggest tits? The blonde, because she's 18.

We've all been interviewed for jobs. And, we've all spent most of those interviews thinking about what not to do. Don't bite your nails. Don't fidget. Don't interrupt. Don't belch.

If we did any of the don'ts, we knew we'd disqualify ourselves instantly. But some job applicants go light years beyond this.

We surveyed top personnel executives of 100 major American corporations and asked for stories of unusual behaviour by blonde job applicants.

The lowlights:

1. "Stretched out on the floor to fill out the job application."
2. "She wore headphones and said she could listen to me and the music at the same time."
3. "A brunette candidate, with start blonde roots, abruptly excused herself. Returned to office a few minutes later, wearing a hairpiece."
4. "Asked to see interviewer's resume to see if the personnel executive was qualified to judge the candidate."
5. "Announced she hadn't had lunch and proceeded to eat a hamburger and French fries in the interviewer's office—wiping the ketchup on her sleeve"
6. "Stated that, if he were hired, she would demonstrate her loyalty by having the corporate logo tattooed on her breast cleavage."

7. "Interrupted to phone her therapist for advice on answering specific interview questions."

8. "When I asked her about her hobbies, she stood up and started tap dancing around my office."

9. "At the end of the interview, while I stood there dumbstruck, she went through my purse, took out a brush, brushed her hair, and left."

10. "Pulled out a Polaroid camera and snapped a flash picture of me. Said she collected photos of everyone who interviewed her."

11. "Said she wasn't interested because the position paid too much."

12. "While I was on a long-distance phone call, the applicant took out a copy of woman's Playboy, and looked through the photos only, stopping longest at the centrefold."

13. "During the interview, an alarm clock went off from the candidate's handbag. She took it out, shut it off, apologized and said she had to leave for another interview."

14. "A telephone call came in for the job applicant. It was from her house mate. Her side of the conversation went like this: "Which company? When do I start? What's the salary?" I said, "I assume you're not interested conducting the interview any further." She promptly responded, "I am as long as you'll pay me more. "I didn't hire her, but later found out there was no other job offer. It was a scam to get a higher offer."

15. "Her handbag opened when she picked it up and the contents spilled, revealing a vile of cocaine, dirty undergarments and assorted sex toys."

16. "Candidate said she really didn't want to get a job, but the unemployment office needed proof that she was looking for one."

17. "Asked who the hunk was, pointing to the picture on my desk. When I said it was my boyfriend, she asked if he was home now and wanted my phone number. I called security."

18. "Pointing to a black case she carried into my office, she said that if she was not hired, the bomb would go off. Disbelieving, I began to state why she would never be hired and that I was going to call the police. She then reached down to the case, flipped a switch and ran. No one was injured, but I did need to get a new desk."

A blonde tries to go horseback riding even though she has had no lessons or prior experience. She mounts the horse unassisted and the horse immediately springs into action.

It gallops along at a steady rhythmic pace, but the blonde begins to lose her grip and starts to slide in the saddle. In terror, she grabs for the mane but can't seem to get a firm grip.

She tries to throw her arms around the horse's neck, but she slides down the side of the horse. The horse gallops along, seemingly impervious to its slipping rider.

Unfortunately, the blonde's foot has become entangled in the stirrup. She is now at the mercy of the hooves as her head is struck against the ground over and over and over again.

As her head is battered against the ground she is moments away from losing consciousness when, to her great fortune, the Woolworths manager sees her and switches off the horse.

A young ventriloquist is touring clubs, he stops to entertain at a bar in a small town. He's going through his usual run of stupid blonde jokes when a big blonde woman in the 4th row stands on her chair and says:

"I've heard just about enough of your stupid blonde jokes, mister. What makes you think you can stereotype women that way? What does a person's physical attributes have to do with their worth as a human being? It's guys like you who keep women like me from being respected at work and in my community and from reaching my full potential as a person because you and your kind continue to perpetuate discrimination against not only blondes, but women in general, all in the name of humour."

Flustered, the ventriloquist begins to apologize, when the blonde pipes up, "You stay out of this mister, I'm talking to that little bastard on your knee!"

This blonde decides one day that she is sick and tired of all these blonde jokes and how all blondes are perceived as stupid, so she decides to show her husband that blondes really are smart.

While her husband is off at work, she decides that she is going to paint a couple of rooms in the house.

The next day, right after her husband leaves for work, she gets down to the task at hand. Her husband arrives home at 5:30 and smells the distinctive smell of paint. He walks into the living room and finds his wife lying on the floor in a pool of sweat. He notices that she is wearing a ski jacket and a fur coat at the same time. He goes over and asks her if she is OK. She replies yes. He asks what she is doing. She replies that she wanted to prove to him that not all blonde women are dumb and she wanted to do it by painting the house. He then asks her why she has a ski jacket over her fur coat. She replies that she was reading the directions on the paint can and they said.

FOR BEST RESULTS, PUT ON TWO COATS.

Last week I took some friends out to a restaurant and noticed that the waiter who took our order carried a spoon in his shirt pocket. It seemed a little strange, but I ignored it. However, when the busboy brought water and utensils, I noticed he also had a spoon in his shirt pocket. I then looked around the room and saw that all the waitpersons had a spoon in their pocket. When the waiter came back to check on our order, I asked, "Why the spoon?"

"Well," he explained, "the restaurant's owners hired PWC Consulting, experts in efficiency to revamp all our processes. After several months of statistical analysis, they concluded that customers drop their spoons 73.84% more often than any other utensil. This represents a drop frequency of approximately 3 spoons per table per hour. If our personnel are prepared to deal with that contingency, we can reduce the number of trips back to the kitchen and save 1.5 man-hours per shift."

As we finished talking, a metallic sound was heard from behind me. Quickly the waiter replaced the dropped spoon with the one in his pocket and said, "I'll get another spoon next time I go to the kitchen instead of making an extra trip to get it right now."

I was rather impressed. The waiter continued taking our order and while my guests ordered, I continued to look around. I then noticed that there was a very thin string hanging out of the waiter's fly. Looking around, I noticed that all the waiters had the same string hanging from their fly.

My curiosity got the better of me and before he walked off, I asked the blonde haired waiter, "Excuse me but can you tell me why you have the string right there?" "Oh certainly," he answered, lowering his voice." Not everyone is as observant as you. That consulting firm I mentioned also found out that we can save time in the restroom."

"How so?"

"See," he continued, "by tying a string to the tip of you know we can pull it out over the urinal without touching it and that way eliminate the need to wash the hands, shortening the time spent in the restroom by 76.39%."

"Okay, that makes sense, but if the string helps you get it out, how do you put it back in?"

"Well," he whispered, lowering his voice even further, "I don't know about the others, but I use the spoon"

The aspiring psychiatrists were attending their first class on emotional extremes.

"Just to establish some parameters," said the professor, to the student from Arkansas, "What is the opposite of joy?" "Sadness," said the student.

"And the opposite of depression?" he asked of the young lady from Oklahoma." Elation," said she.

"And you sir," he said to the young man blonde headed from Texas, "How about the opposite of woe?" The Texan replied, "Sir, I believe that would be giddy-up."

A man met a beautiful blonde lady and he decided he wanted to marry her right away. She said, "But we don't know anything about each other."

He said, "That's all right, we'll learn about each other as we go along."

So she consented, and they were married, and went on a honeymoon to a very nice resort. One morning they were laying by the pool, when he got up off of his towel, climbed up to the 10 Meter board and did a two and a half tuck gainer, this was followed by a three rotations in jack knife position, where he straightened out and cut the water like a knife. After a few more demonstrations, he came back and lay down on the towel.

She said," That was incredible!"

He said, "I used to be an Olympic diving champion. You see, I told you we'd learn more about ourselves as we went along. "

So she got up, jumped in the pool, and started doing laps. After about thirty laps she climbed back out and lay down on her towel hardly out of breath.

He said, "That was incredible! Were you an Olympic endurance swimmer?"

"No." she said, "I was a hooker in Venice and I worked both sides of the canal.

A male blonde yuppie finally decided to take a vacation. He booked himself on a Caribbean cruise and proceeded to have the time of his life. Until the boat sank. The man found himself swept up on the shore of an island with no other people, no supplies nothing. Only bananas and coconuts.

After about four months, he is lying on the beach one day when the most gorgeous woman he has ever seen rows up to him. In disbelief, he asks her, "Where did you come from? How did you get here?" "I rowed from the other side of the island," she says." I landed here when my cruise ship sank."

"Amazing," he says. "You were really lucky to have a rowboat wash up with you."

L is for Lethally Blonde

"Oh, this?" replies the woman. "I made the rowboat out of raw material I found on the island; the oars were whittled from gum tree branches; I wove the bottom from palm branches; and the sides and stern came from a Eucalyptus tree."

"But-but, that's impossible," stutters the man." You had no tools or hardware. How did you manage?"

"Oh, that was no problem," replies the woman. "On the south side of the island, there is a very unusual strata of alluvial rock exposed. I found if I fired it to a certain temperature in my kiln, it melted into forgeable ductile iron. I used that for tools and used the tools to make the hardware."

The guy is stunned." Let's row over to my place, "she says

After a few minutes of rowing, she docks the boat at a small wharf. As the man looks onto shore, he nearly falls out of the boat. Before him is a atone walk leading to an exquisite bungalow painted in blue and white. While the woman ties up the rowboat with an expertly woven hemp rope, the man can only stare ahead, dumb struck. As they walk into the house, she says casually, "It's not much, but I call it home. Sit down please; would you like to have a drink?"

"No, no thank you," he says, still dazed. "Can't take any more coconut juice."

"It's not coconut juice," the woman replies." I have a still. How about a Pina Colada?"

Trying to hide his continued amazement, the man accepts, and they sit down on her couch to talk. After they have exchanged their stories, the woman announces, "I'm going to slip into something more comfortable. Would you like to take a shower and shave? There is a razor upstairs in the bathroom cabinet."

No longer questioning anything, the man goes into the bathroom. There, in the   cabinet, is a razor made from a bone handle. Two shells honed to a hollow ground edge are fastened on to the end inside of a swivel mechanism." this woman is amazing," he mused. "What next?"

When he returns, she greeted him wearing nothing but vines strategically position and smelling faintly of gardenias. She beckons for him to sit down next to her." Tell me, she begins, suggestively, slithering closer to him, "we've been out here for a really long time. You've been lonely. There's something I'm sure you really feel like doing right now, something you've been longing for all these months? You know she stares into his eyes.

He can't believe what he's hearing: "you mean, he swallows excitedly, I can check my facebook account from here?"

Q: What do you give the blonde who has everything?

A: Penicillin.

Q: How do you get a blonde to marry you?

A: Tell her she's pregnant.

> A redhead tells her blonde stepsister, "I slept with a Brazilian." The blonde replies, "Oh my God! You slut! How many is a Brazilian?"

Q: What do you call a skeleton in the closet with blonde hair?

A: Last year's hide-and-go-seek winner.

Q: What do you call a basement full of blondes?

A: A whine cellar.

Q: How do you know a blonde likes you?

A: She screws you two nights in a row.

Q: What does a blonde say if you blow in her ear?

A: "Thanks for the refill!"

Q: What do blondes do after they comb their hair?

A: They pull up their pants.

Q: How do you get a blonde on the roof?

A: Tell her drinks are on the house.

Q: What's a blondes favourite bread?

A: Hump-per-nickel

Q: Why did the blonde douche with Crest?

A: She heard it reduces cavities.

Q: Why are blondes immune to men?

A: They've been inoculated so many times.

Q: What's a blondes favourite drink?

A: A penis colada.

Q: How do you know which blonde gives the best blow job?

A: Word of Mouth.

Q: What's the difference between a blonde and a toothbrush?

A: You don't let your friends use your toothbrush.

Q: How did the blonde lawyer sway the judge?

A: She dropped her briefs.

Q: Did you hear about the blonde football player?

A: She was an excellent wide receiver.

Q: What did the blonde name her watch dogs?

A: Timex and Rolex.

Q: What's the difference between the wind and a blonde?

A: Some days the wind doesn't blow.

Q: Why did they call the blonde "Twinkie"?

A: She liked to be filled with cream.

Q: Why do brunettes work hard to keep their figure?

A: No one else wants it.

Q: What's the worst thing about dating a blonde?

A: If you don't know what hole to put it in neither do they.

Q: Why do blondes wear underwear?

A: To keep their ankles warm.

Q: What can strike a blonde without her even knowing it?

A: A thought.

Q: Why don't blondes get coffee breaks?

A: It takes too long to retrain them.

Q: What's the difference between a blonde and a guy?

A: The blonde has the higher sperm count.

Q: Why was the blonde confused after giving birth to twins?

A: She couldn't figure out who the other mother was.

Q: Why does a blonde wear green lipstick?

A: Because red means Stop.

Q: Did you hear about the blonde with a PhD in Psychology?

A: She'll blow your mind, too.

Q: Why did the blonde tattoo her zip-code on her thigh?

A: She wanted a lot of male in her box.

Q: What is a blonde's favourite colour?

A: Glitter.

Q: What is the difference between blondes and traffic signs?

A: Some traffic signs say stop

Q: Why are blondes so easy to get into bed?

A: Who cares?

Q: Hear about the blonde that got an AM radio?

A: It took her a month to realize she could play it at night.

Q: What happened to the blonde ice hockey team?

A: They drowned in Spring training.

Q: Why did the blonde scale the chain-link fence?

A: To see what was on the other side.

Q: How do you make a blonde laugh on Saturday?

A: Tell her a joke on Wednesday.

Q: Why did the blonde stare at frozen orange juice?

A: Because it said 'concentrate'.

Q: What do smart blondes and UFOs have in common?

A: You always hear about them but you never see them.

Q: Why does it take longer to build a Blonde snowman as opposed to a regular one?

A: You have to hollow out the head.

Q: How do you get a twinkle in a blonde's eye?

A: Shine a flashlight in her ear.

Q: Did you hear about the two blondes that were found frozen to death in their car at a drive-in movie theatre?

A: They went to see "Closed for the winter".

Q: Why can't Blondes be pharmacists?

A: They keep breaking the prescription bottles in the typewriters.

Q: How can you tell if a blonde is being unfaithful?

A: Everybody in the neighbourhood is going to the pharmacy for penicillin.

Q: Why did the blonde jump off the cliff?

A: She thought her maxi pad had wings

Q: Why did god give blonde's 2 more brain cells than he gave cows?

A: So they wouldn't shit all over when you play with their tits.

Q: Why did the blonde have rectangular tits?

A: Because she forgot to take the tissues out of the box!

Q: Why are blondes like pianos?

A: When they aren't upright, they're grand.

Q: Why can't blondes count to 70?

A: Because 69 is a bit of a mouthful.

Q: How do you get a blonde off of her knees?

A: Come.

Q: How does a blonde kill a fish?

A: By drowning it.

Q: A blond is going to London on a plane, how can you steal her window seat?

A: Tell her the seats that are going to London are all in the middle row.

Q: What does a blonde and a turtle have in common?

A: If either one of them end up on there back they are both f*cked.

Q. Why did the blonde shoot the clock?

A. To kill time

Q: How do you keep a blonde busy all day?

A: Put her in a round room and tell her to sit in the corner.

Q: Why is a washing machine better than a blonde?

A: Because you can drop your load in a washing machine, and it won't follow you around for a week.

Q: What does a blonde make best for dinner?

A: Reservations.

Q: What does a blonde say when you ask her if her blinker is on?

A: It's on. It's off. It's on. It's off. It's on. It's off.

Q: What does a peroxide blonde and a 747 have in common?

A1: They both have a black box.

A2: Both have a cockpit.

Q: What do you get when you offer a blonde a penny for her thoughts?

A: Change.

Q: What do you call five blondes at the bottom of the pool?

A: Air bubbles.

Q: What do you call an unmarried blond in a BMW?

A: Divorcee

Q: What do you call a blonde in an institution of higher learning?

A: A visitor.

Q: How do you get a one-armed blonde out of a tree?

A: Wave to her.

Q: How do you tell when a blonde reaches orgasm?

A1: She drops her nail-file!

A2: Who cares?

A3: She says, "Next".

A4: The next person in the queue taps you on the shoulder.

A5: He's had his clothes for about 2 minutes.

A6: I mean, who really cares?

A7: The batteries have run out.

Q: How do you drown a blond?

A1: Put a mirror at the bottom of the pool.

A2: Don't tell her to swallow.

A3: Leave a scratch and sniff at the bottom of the pool.

- A blonde walked into the dentist office and sat down in the chair. The dentist said "Open Wide" "I can't" The blonde said "This chair has arms."
- A blonde walks into a restaurant to get some dinner, and while she's deciding on what she wants a waitress comes up. The blonde looks up and notices the

waitress's name tag on her shirt. "Gee, that's nice. What did you name the other one?"

- A blonde girl was talking to her redhead friend about her boyfriend's dandruff problem. The redhead says "Why don't you give him Head and Shoulders?" The blonde replies, "How do you give shoulders?"

CHAPTER 13

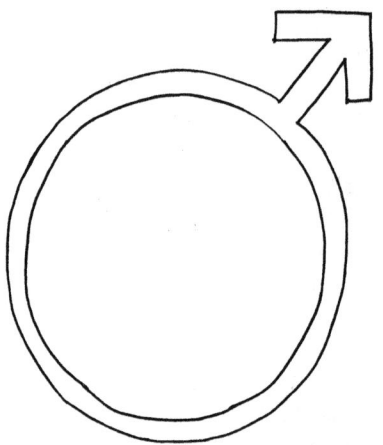

M is for Male

M is for Male

Subject: Guy Talk

- I'm going fishing

Really means . . . I'm going to drink myself dangerously stupid and stand by a stream with a stick in my hand while the fish swim by in complete safety."

- It's a guy thing

Really means . . . there is no rational thought pattern connected with it. And you have no chance at all of making it logical."

- "Can I help with dinner?"

Really means., "Why isn't it already on the table?"

- Uh huh," "Sure, honey," or "yes, dear,"

Really means... absolutely nothing. It's a conditioned response

- It would take too long to explain."

Really means ... I have no idea how it works."

- "I'm getting more exercise lately."

Really means..." The batteries in the remote are dead.

- "We're going to be late."

Really means.... "Now I have a legitimate excuse to drive like a maniac."

- "Take a break, honey, you're working too hard."

Really means.... I can't hear the game over the vacuum cleaner

- "That's interesting, dear."

Really means.... "Are you talking at all?"

- "Honey, we don't need material things to prove our love."

Really means.... "I forgot our anniversary again."

- "You expect too much of me."

Really means.... "You want me to stay awake?"

- "That's women's' work."

Really means.... "It's difficult, dirty, and thankless

- "You know how bad my memory is."

Really means.... "I remember the theme song to 'The A Team', the address of the first girl I ever kissed and the Vehicle Identification of every car I've ever owned. But I forgot your birthday."

- "Oh, don't fuss. I just cut myself. It's no big deal really ..."

Really means . . . I have severed a limb, but will bleed to death before I admit I'm hurt."

- "I do help around the house."

Really means.... "I once put a dirty towel in the laundry basket."

- "Hey, I've got my reasons for what I'm doing."

Really means.... "I sure hope I think of some response pretty soon."

- "I can't find it."

Really means.... "It didn't fall into my outstretched hands, so I'm completely clueless."

- "What did I do this time?"

Really means.... "What did you catch me doing?"

- "I heard you."

Really means.... "I haven't the foggiest clue what you just said, and am hoping desperately that I can fake it well enough so that you don't spend the next 3 days yelling at me."

- "You look terrific."

Really means.... "Oh, God, please don't try on one more outfit. I'm starving."

- "I missed you."

Really means..." I can't find my sock drawer, the kids are hungry and we are out of toilet paper.

- "I'm not lost. I know exactly where we are."

Really means.... "I'm lost. I have no idea where we are, and no one will ever see us alive again."

- "We share the housework."

Really means . . . . . I make the mess, you clean them up.

- "This relationship is getting too serious."

Really means.... you're cutting into the time I spend with my truck."

- "I don't need to read the instructions"

Really means I'm perfectly capable of screwing it up without printed help."

Dear Mr Abby:

Q: My husband wants to experience a threesome with my sister and me.

A: Your husband is clearly devoted to you. He cannot get enough of you, so he goes for the next best thing—your sister. Far from being an issue, this can bring all of the family together. Why not get some cousins involved? If you are still apprehensive, then let him be with your relatives, buy him a nice, expensive present, and cook him a nice meal and don't mention this aspect of his behaviour.

Dear Mr Abby:

Q: My husband continually asks me to perform oral sex on him.

A: Do it. Sperm is not only great tasting, but has only 10 calories per spoonful. It is nutritious, helps you to keep your figure, and gives a great glow to your skin.

Interestingly, men know this. His offer to you to perform oral sex with him is totally selfless. Oral sex is extremely painful for a man. This shows he loves you. The best thing to do is to thank him, buy him a nice, expensive present, and cook him a nice meal.

Dear Mr Abby:

Q: My husband has too many nights out with the boys.

A: This is perfectly natural behaviour and it should be encouraged. The man is a hunter and he needs to prove his prowess with other men. Far from being pleasurable, a night out with the boys is a stressful affair, and to get back to you is a relief for him. Just look at how emotional and shabby the man is when he returns to his stable home. The best thing to do is to buy him a nice, expensive present and cook him a nice meal and don't mention this aspect of his behaviour.

Dear Mr Abby:

Q: My husband doesn't know where my clitoris is.

A: Your clitoris is of no concern to your husband. If you must mess with it, do it in your own time. To help with the family budget you may wish to videotape yourself while doing this, and sell it. To ease your selfish guilt, buy your man a nice, expensive present, and cook him a delicious meal.

Dear Mr Abby:

Q: My husband is uninterested in foreplay.

A: Foreplay to a man is very hurtful. What it means is that you do not love your man as much as you should he has to work a lot to get you in the mood. Abandon all wishes in this area, and make it up to him by buying him a nice, expensive present, and cook him a nice meal.

Dear Mr Abby:

Q: My husband has never given me an orgasm.

A: The female orgasm is a myth. It is fostered by militant, man-hating feminists and is a danger to the family unit.

Don't mention it again to him and show your love to him by buying a nice, expensive present, and don't forget to cook him a delicious meal!

HOW TO IMPRESS A WOMAN

Wine her, Dine her, Call her, Hug her, Hold her, Surprise her, Compliment her, smile at her, Laugh with her, cry with her, Cuddle with her, Shop with her, Give her jewellery, Buy her flowers, Hold her hand, Write love letters to her, Go to the end of the earth and back again for her.

HOW TO IMPRESS A MAN

Show up naked. Bring beer.

Top 10 things men SHOULDN'T say out loud in Victoria's Secret

1. Does this come in children's sizes?
2. No thanks, just sniffing.
3. I'll be in the dressing room going blind.
4. Mum will love this!
5. Do you have this with the Dallas Cowboy's logo on it?
6. No need to wrap it up, I'll eat it here.
7. Will you model this for me?
8. Oh honey, you'll never squeeze your fat ass into that!
9. 45 bucks?? You're just going to end up NAKED anyway!
10. The Miracle What?? This is better than world peace!

- What do men and pantyhose have in common? They either cling, run or don't fit right in the crotch!
- How do we know men invented maps? Because only the male mind could conceive one inch equalling one mile.
- What is the difference between men and women? A woman wants one man to satisfy her every need. A man wants every woman to satisfy his one need.

M is for Male

- How does a man keep his youth? By giving her money, furs and diamonds.
- What's the most common cause of hearing loss amongst men? Wife saying she wants to talk to him.
- Where do you have to go to find a man who is truly into commitment? A mental hospital.
- What is the difference between a pick pocket and a peeping tom? One snatches your watch and the other watches your snatch.
- How are men like bank machines? Once they withdraw they lose interest
- Why do men prefer the woman to be on top? Because men always screw up.
- How do you keep your husband from reading your e-mail? Rename the mail folder to "instruction manuals."

- I'm glad I'm a man, you better believe.
- I don't live off of yogurt, diet coke, or cottage cheese.
- I don't bitch to my girlfriends about the size of my breasts. I can get where I want to—north, south, east or west.
- I don't get wasted after only 2 beers, and when I do drink I don't end up in tears.
- I won't spend hours deciding what to wear. I spend 5 minutes max fixing my hair.
- And I don't go around checking my reflection in everything shiny from every direction.

- I don't whine in public and make us leave early. And when you ask why get all bitter and surly. I'm glad I'm a man, I'm so glad I could sing.
- I don't have to sit around waiting for that ring.
- I don't gossip about friends or stab them in the back.
- I don't carry our differences into the sack.
- I'll never go psycho and threaten to kill you or think every guy out there's trying to steal you.
- I'm rational, reasonable, and logical too.
- I know what the time is and I know what to do.
- And I honestly think it's a privilege for me to have these two balls and stand when I pee.
- I live to watch sports and play all sorts of ball. It's more fun than dealing with women after all.
- I won't cry if you say it's not going to work. I won't remain bitter and call you a jerk.
- Feel free to use me for immediate pleasure.
- I won't assume it's permanent by any measure.
- Yes, I'm so very glad I'm a man, you see. I'm glad I'm not capable of child delivery. I don't get all bitchy every 28 days.
- I'm glad that my gender gets me a much bigger raise. I'm a man by chance and I'm thankful it's true.
- I'm so glad I'm a man and not a woman like you

And now it's time for a rebuttal

Why a man can't win

- If you put a woman on a pedestal and try to protect her from the rat race, you are a male chauvinist.
- If you stay home and do the housework, you are a pansy.
- If you work too hard, there is never any time for her... If you don't work enough, you are a good for nothing bum.
- If she has a boring repetitive job with low pay, this is exploitation.
- If you have a boring repetitive job with low pay, you should get off your rear and find something better.
- If you get a promotion ahead of her, that is favouritism.
- If she gets job ahead of you, it's equal opportunity.
- If you mention how nice she looks, it's sexual harassment.
- If you keep quiet, it's male indifference.
- If you cry, you are a wimp.
- If you don't, you are an insensitive bastard.
- If you make a decision without consulting her, you are a chauvinist.
- If she makes a decision without consulting you, she's liberated woman.
- If you ask her to do something she doesn't enjoy, that's domination. If she asks you, it's a favour.
- If you appreciate the female form and frilly underwear, you are a pervert. If you don't, you are a fag.
- If you like a woman to shave her legs and keep in shape, you are a sexiest. If you don't, you are unromantic.

- If you try to keep yourself in shape, you are vain. If you don't, you are a slob.
- If you buy her flowers, you are after something. If you don't, you are not thoughtful.
- If you are proud of your achievements, you are up yourself. If you don't, you are not ambitious.
- If she has a headache, she is tired. If you have a headache, you don't love her anymore.
- If you want it too often, you are oversexed. If you don't, there must be someone else.

- How can you tell when a man is well hung? When you can just barely slip your finger in between his neck and the noose.
- Why do little boys whine? Because they are practicing to be men.
- What do you call a handcuffed man? Trustworthy.
- What does it mean when a man is in your bed gasping for breath and calling your name? You didn't hold the pillow down long enough.
- Why do only 10% of men make it to heaven? Because if they all went, it would be Hell.
- Why do men like smart women? Opposites attract.
- How are husbands like lawn mowers? They're hard to get started, they emit noxious odours, and half the time they don't work.
- How do men define a "50/50" relationship? We cook-they eat; we clean-they dirty; we iron-they wrinkle.
- How do men exercise on the beach? By sucking in their stomachs every time they see a bikini.

- How do you get a man to stop biting his nails? Have him wear shoes.
- How does a man show he's planning for the future? He buys two cases of beer instead of one.
- How is Colonel Sanders like the typical male? All he's concerned with is legs, breasts and thighs.
- How many men does it take to open a beer? None. (It should be opened by the time she brings it to the couch.)
- How many men does it take to screw in a light bulb? ONE—He just holds it up there and waits for the world to revolve around him.
- What did God say after creating man? I can do so much better.
- What do most men consider a gourmet restaurant? Any place without a drive-up window.
- What do you call a man with half a brain? Gifted.
- What do you do with a bachelor who thinks he's God's gift to women? Exchange him.
- What should you give a man who has everything? A woman to show him how to work it.
- What's a man's definition of a romantic evening? SEX.
- What's a man's idea of honesty in a relationship? Telling you his real name.
- What is the best way to force a man to do sit ups? Put the remote control between his toes.
- What's the difference between Big Foot and an intelligent man? Big Foot's been spotted several times.
- What's the smartest thing a man can say? "My wife says ..."

- Why did God create man before woman? Because you're always supposed to have a rough draft before creating your masterpiece.
- Why do female black widow spiders kill the males after mating? To stop the snoring before it starts.
- Why do jocks play on artificial turf? To keep them from grazing.

A wealthy trader from Wall Street stopped in at the local tattoo parlour in Key West, Florida and requested to have a $100 bill tattooed on his penis.

The heavily tattooed tattoo artist looked at the extremely well dressed trader with a look of complete astonishment, and said "I've had strange requests, but this one tops the list.

Why on earth would you want me to tattoo your wanker with a picture of a one hundred dollar bill?"

The trader in his usual fashion looked at the burly artist and told him "There are three distinct reasons I want this done: One, I love to play with my money. Two, when I play with my money, I love to see it grow. Three, and this is the most important of all, the next time my wife wants to blow a hundred bucks, she won't have to leave home to do it."

This guy comes home dead tired from working a 15-hour day and collapses in bed. He's just about asleep when his wife rolls over and says, "What would you do if told you that you had a beautiful, sexy, horny woman lying next to you?"

He replied, "Don't worry honey I'd stay faithful!"

Last year I upgraded from Boyfriend 5.0 to Husband 1.0 and noticed the new program began making unexpected changes to the accounting modules, limiting access to flower and jewellery applications that had operated flawlessly under Boyfriend 5.0.

In addition, Husband 1.0 uninstalled many other valuable programs, such as Romance 9.9 but installed undesirable programs such as NFL 5.0 and NBA 3.0.

Conversation 8.0 no longer runs and House Cleaning 2.6 simply crashes the system.

I've tried running Nagging 5.3 to fix these problems, but to no avail.

From Desperate ***

Dear Desperate:

Keep in mind, Boyfriend 5.0 is an entertainment package, while Husband 1.0 is an operating system.

Try to enter the command: C:/ I THOUGHT YOU LOVED ME and install Tears 6.2.

Husband 1.0 should then automatically run the applications: Guilty 3.0 and Flowers 7.0. But remember, overuse can cause Husband 1.0 to default to Grumpy/Silence 2.5, Happy hour 7.0 or Beer 6.1. Beer 6.1 is a very bad program that will create "Snoring Loudly" wave files.

DO NOT install Mother In Law 1.0 or reinstall another Boyfriend program. These are not supported applications and will crash Husband 1.0.

In summary, Husband 1.0 is a great program, but it does have limited memory and cannot learn new applications quickly. Consider buying additional software to, improve performance. I personally recommend Hot Food 3.0 and Lingerie 5.3

From Tech Support

A woman walks into a supermarket and buys the following:

- 1 bar of soap
- 1 toothbrush
- 1 tube of toothpaste
- 1 loaf of bread
- 1 pint of milk
- 1 single serving cereal
- 1 single serving frozen dinner

The guy at the checkout looks at her and says, "So, you're single?" The woman replies very sarcastically, "How did you guess?"

He replies, "Because you're fucking ugly".

The Manliness Assessment: Choose a, b or c for each question

1. In the company of females, intercourse should be referred to as:
    a. Lovemaking
    b. Screwing
    c. the pigskin bus pulling into tuna town

2. You should make love to a woman for the first time only after you've both shared:
   a. your views about what you expect from a sexual relationship
   b. your blood-test results
   c. five tequila slammers

3. You time your orgasm so that:
   a. your partner climaxes first
   b. you both climax simultaneously
   c. you don't miss sports tonight

4. Passionate, spontaneous sex on the kitchen floor is:
   a. healthy, creative love-play
   b. not the sort of thing your wife/girlfriend would ever agree to
   c. not the sort of thing your wife/girlfriend need ever find out about

5. Spending the whole night cuddling a woman you've just had sex with is:
   a. the best part of the experience
   b. the second best part of the experience
   c. $100 extra

6. Your girlfriend says she's gained five pounds in the last month. You tell her that it is:
   a. No concern of yours
   b. not a problem, she can join your gym
   c. a very conservative estimate

7. You think today's sensitive, caring man is:
   a. a myth
   b. an oxymoron
   c. a moron

8. Foreplay is to sex as:
   a. appetizer is to entree
   b. primer is to paint
   c. a line is to an amusement park ride

9. Which of the following are you most likely to find yourself saying at the end of a relationship?
   a. "I hope we can still be friends."
   b. "I'm not in right now, please leave a message at the beep."
   c. "Welcome to Dumpsville population, YOU."

10. A woman who is uncomfortable watching you masturbate:
    a. probably needs a little more time before she can cope with that sort of intimacy
    b. is uptight and a waste of time
    c. shouldn't have sat next to you on the bus in the first place

Evaluating the results:

If you answered "a" more than 7 times, check your pants to make sure you really are a man.

If you answered "b" more than 7 times, check into therapy, you're a little confused.

If you answered "c" more than 7 times, "You the MAN!

Subject: Course for men

A new two year degree is being offered at Life University that many of you should be interested in: Becoming A Real Man. That's right, in just six trimesters, you, too, can be a real man. Please take a moment to look over the program outline.

FIRST YEAR

- Autumn Schedule:

MEN 101 Combating Stupidity

MEN 102 You, Too, Can Do Housework

MEN 103 PMS -Learn When to Keep Your Mouth Shut

MEN 104 We Do Not Want Sleazy Under things for Christmas

- Winter Schedule:

MEN 110 Wonderful Laundry Techniques

MEN 111 Understanding the Female Response to Getting In at 4 am

MEN 112 Parenting: It Doesn't End with Conception

EAT 100 Get a Life, Learn to Cook

EAT 101 Get a Life, Learn to Cook II

ECON 101A what's hers is hers

- Spring Schedule:

MEN 120 How NOT to Act like an Asshole When You're Wrong

MEN 121 Understanding Your Incompetence

MEN 122 YOU, the Weaker Sex

MEN 123 Reasons to Give Flowers I

MEN 124 Reasons to Give Flowers II

MEN 125 Reasons to Give Flowers III

SECOND YEAR

- Autumn Schedule:

SBX 101 You CAN Fall Asleep Without It

SBX 102 Morning Dilemma: If It's Awake, Take a Shower

MEN 201 How to Stay Awake After Sex

MEN 202 How to Put the Toilet Seat Down

MEN 203 Reasons to Give Flowers IV

Elective (See Electives Below)

- Winter Schedule:

MEN 210 The Remote Control: Overcoming Your Dependency

MEN 211 How to NOT Act Younger than Your Children

MEN 212 You, Too, Can Be a Designated Driver

MEN 213 Honest, You Don't Look Like Tom Cruise, Especially When Naked

MEN 230A Her Birthdays and Anniversaries Are Important I

MEN 214 Reasons to Give Flowers V

- Spring Schedule:

MEN 220 Omitting C\?@ from Your Vocabulary (Pass/Fail Only)

MEN 221 Fluffing the Blanket After Farting is NOT Necessary

MEN 222 Real Men Ask for Directions

MEN 223 Thirty Minutes of Begging is NOT Considered Foreplay

MEN 230B Her Birthdays and Anniversaries Are Important II

- Course Electives:

EAT 101 Cooking With Tofu

BAT 102 Utilisation of Baking Utensils

EAT 103 Burping and Belching Discreetly

MEN 231 Just Say "Yes, Sweetie"

ECON 001B Cheaper to Keep Her (Must Pass ECON 101A)

FIRST YEAR—A RESPONSE

- Autumn Schedule:

MEN 101 Combating Stupidity

DEALING WITH WOMEN AND THEIR HANGUPS

MEN 102 You, Too, Can Do Housework

WHILE YOU ARE SINGLE, WHEN YOU DECIDE TO DO A GIRL A FAVOUR AND MOVE IN

WITH HER, IT IS HER JOB, DON'T LET HER FORGET THAT

MEN 103 PMS-Learn When to Keep Your Mouth Shut

AFTER YOU TELL THE CRANKY BITCH TO GO AND LIVE WITH HER MOTHER UNTIL

SHE GETS OVER IT (AFTER SHE HAS COOKED ENOUGH MEALS FOR YOU TO EAT

UNTIL SHE GETS BACK)

MEN 104 We Do Not Want Sleazy Under things for Christmas

BUT IT IS NOT FOR YOU, IT IS FOR US

- Winter Schedule:

MEN 110 Wonderful Laundry Techniques

LEARN QUALITY CONTROL SO YOU CAN TELL HER WHAT SHE IS DOING WRONG

MEN 111 Understanding the Female Response to Getting In at 4 am

MAKE THEM COOK YOU BREAKFAST

MEN 112 Parenting: It Doesn't End with Conception

BUT IT CERTAINLY DOESN'T INCLUDE CHANGING NAPPIES OR WAKING UP IN THE

MIDDLE OF THE NIGHT—THAT IS HER JOB

EAT 100 Get a Life, Learn to Cook

WHILE YOU ARE SINGLE, AFTER THAT IT IS HER JOB

EAT 101 Get a Life, Learn to Cook II

YOU ARE ONLY ALLOWED TO COOK ON A BBQ WHILE WEARING AN APRON WITH FAKE TITS ON IT

ECON 001A what's hers is hers

UNLESS YOU WANT IT, THEN IT IS YOURS

M is for Male   341

- Spring Schedule:

MEN 120 How NOT to Act like an Asshole When You're Wrong

WE ARE NEVER WRONG, SUBJECT WITHDRAWN

MEN 121 Understanding Your Incompetence

WHY DID YOU GET MARRIED?

MEN 122 YOU, the Weaker Sex

HOW NERDS DESERVE TO BE TREATED BADLY BY WOMEN

MEN 123 Reasons to Give Flowers I YOU CHEATED ON HER

MEN 124 Reasons to Give Flowers II

SOMEBODY GAVE THEM TO YOU OR THEY WERE LEFT OVER AT WORK AT THE END OF THE WEEK

MEN 125 Reasons to Give Flowers III

ANAL SEX

SECOND YEAR

- Autumn Schedule:

SEX 101 You CAN Fall Asleep Without It

EVENTUALLY, AND IF SHE DENIES YOU MAKE SURE SHE DOESN'T FALL TO SLEEP BEFORE YOU.

SEX 102 Morning Dilemma: If It's Awake, Take a Shower AFTERWARDS

MEN 201 How to Stay Awake After Sex

I'M STARTING TO THINK I SHOULD GET BACK TO WORK, PLUS I CAN'T THINK OF A GOOD COMEBACK FOR THIS ONE

MEN 202 How to Put the Toilet Seat Down

AND HOW TO EFFECTIVELY PEE THROUGH THE GAP AT THE BACK

MEN 203 Reasons to Give Flowers IV THE ALWAYS FAVOURITE BLOW JOB

Elective (See Electives Below)

- Winter Schedule:

MEN 210 The Remote Control: Overcoming Your Dependency

MAKE THE BITCH DO IT

MEN 211 How to NOT Act Younger than Your Children

DONT HAVE ANY

MEN 212 You, Too, Can Be a Designated Driver

NEVER LET A WOMAN DRIVE YOUR CAR, ESPECIALLY AFTER SHE HAS BEEN DRINKING

MEN 213 Honest, You Don't Look Like Tom Cruise, Especially When Naked

TOM CRUISE IS A DWARFED RELIGIOUS FAGGOT WHO LIKES LITTLE BOYS

MEN 230A Her Birthdays and Anniversaries Are Important I

ITS A GREAT WAY TO GET A BLOWJOB IN RETURN

MEN 214 Reasons to Give Flowers V

FUCK THIS, WE HAVE BEEN THROUGH THIS ENOUGH TIMES

- Spring Schedule:

MEN 220 Omitting %?@ from Your Vocabulary (Pass/Fail Only)

GET FUCKED

MEN 221 Fluffing the Blanket After Farting is NOT Necessary

DUTCH OVEN THE BITCH INSTEAD

MEN 222 Real Men Ask for Directions of THE CLOSEST WHORE HOUSE

MEN 223 Thirty Minutes of Begging is NOT Considered Foreplay

YOU SHOULDN'T BE BEGGING, SHE IS YOUR WIFE, DEMAND IT

MEN 230B Her Birthdays and Anniversaries Are Important
II AS I SAID A BLOWJOB IS AT STAKE

- Course Electives:

EAT 101 Cooking With Tofu

WHAT THE FUCK IS TOFU AND WHO CARES GIVE ME SEX

EAT 102 Utilisation of Eating Utensils

AS GREAT SEX TOYS

EAT 103 Burping and Belching Discreetly

AND YOU ARE A POOF, THE LOUDER THE BETTER

MEN 231 Just Say "Yes, Sweetie"

AFTER THE 10 SUCCESSIVE WEEK OF DAILY BLOWJOBS

ECON 001B Cheaper to Keep Her (Must Pass ECON 001A) THAN TO HAVE TO BUY HOOKERS ALL THE TIME

REASONS ITS BEAUTY TO BE A BLOKE

1. You never get pissed as fast as the chick you're cracking on to.
2. If you wear a suit & tie no one will think you're a lesbian.
3. You have no trouble whatsoever putting stuff off until tomorrow.
4. You get to operate heavy machinery.
5. You don't collapse in floods of tears if your partner says you look fine.
6. You feel perfectly comfortable wearing clothes you wore yesterday & left on the floor all night.
7. You're allowed to (even expected to) sweat heavily.
8. You can eat a banana while walking past a building site.
9. Telephone conversations are over in 0 seconds, no worries.
10. Push-ups are a lot easier.
11. The remote is yours & yours alone.
12. The tab doesn't go quiet when you walk in.
13. You can buy condoms without the pharmacist imagining you naked.
14. You don't have to leave the room to make an emergency tackle rearrangement.
15. People never glance at your tits when you're talking to them.
16. Hot wax never comes near your genitals.
17. Ricky Martin doesn't live in your universe.

18. You can whip your shirt off on a hot day.
19. Cricket seems like a good idea.
20. You don't have to curl up next to a hairy arse every night.
21. Nobody secretly wonders if you swallow.
22. You can become a garbo.
23. Bucks parties shit all over hens nights.
24. Not liking a person does not preclude having an enjoyable root with them.
25. The world is your urinal.
26. Your bathroom lines are 0% shorter.
27. Guys in hockey masks don't attack you.
28. When flicking through the TV channels, you don't have to stop on every shot of someone crying.
29. You can open all your own jars.
30. Same work, more pay.
31. You can turn the bath into a beaut spa.
32. You can go years without having to see a doctor.
33. If you own a toaster you're never more than 2 minutes away from a tasty meal.
34. Your arse is never a factor in a job interview.
35. A -day holiday requires only 1 suitcase.
36. You know at least 20 ways to open a beer bottle.
37. Your undies are $1 for a three pack.
38. If another bloke shows up to a party in the same outfit, you might become lifelong mates.

39. As long as your mums still alive, you can get your washing done at her place.
40. Wedding dress $2000; suit rental $100.
41. You can be Prime Minister.
42. Porn movies are designed with your mind in mind.
43. Haircuts cost $1.
44. You can get a blow job.
45. You can become a catholic priest & have unlimited access to free wine.
46. You understand the offside rule.
47. None of your co-workers have the power to make you cry.
48. If you don't call a mate when you say you will, he won't tell all your other mates you've changed.
49. You know stuff about tanks.
50. You think the idea of drop kicking a small dog is funny.
51. Bachelor parties whimp ass over bridal showers.
52. You have a normal and healthy relationship with your mother.
53. You never have to sleep in the 'wet' spot.
54. You needn't pretend you're 'freshening up' to go to the bathroom.
55. If you don't call your buddy when you say you will, he won't tell your friends you've changed.
56. Someday you'll be a dirty old man.
57. You can rationalize any behaviour with the handy phrase 'Fuck it'

58. Princess Di's death was almost just another obituary.
59. The occasional well-rendered belch is practically excepted.
60. You never have to miss a sexual opportunity because you're not in the mood.
61. You think the idea of punting a small dog is funny.
62. If something mechanical didn't work, you can bash it was a hammer and throw it across the room.
63. New shoes don't cut, blister, or mangle your feet.
64. Porn movies are designed with you in mind.
65. You don't have to remember everyone's birthdays and anniversaries.
66. Not liking a person does not preclude having great sex with them.
67. Your pals can be trusted never to trap you with 'So.. notice anything different?'
68. Baywatch.
69. There is always a game on somewhere.
70. And, last but not least, you have a sense of humour for jokes against your gender and you never even consider taking whoever sent the sexiest joke to you to the anti-discrimination board for gender oppression.

If Men Really Ruled the World

1. Any fake phone number a girl gave you would automatically forward your call to her real number.
2. Nodding and looking at your watch would be deemed an acceptable response to 'I love you'

3. Hallmark would make "Sorry, what was your name again?" cards.
4. When your girlfriend really needed to talk to you during the game, she'd appear in a little box in the corner of the screen during an ad,
5. Breaking up would be a lot easier, smack to the ass and a "Nice hustle, you'll get ' next time" would pretty much do it.
6. Birth control would come in beer.
7. You'd be expected to fill your resume with gag names of people you'd worked for, like "Heywood J'blowme."
8. Each year, your raise would be pegged to the fortune of the football team of your choice.
9. The funniest guy in the office would get to be CFO
10. "Sorry I'm late, but I got really wasted last night' would be an acceptable excuse for tardiness.
11. At the end of the workday, a whistle would blow and you'd Jump out your window and slide down the tail of a brontosaurus and right into your car.
12. It'd be considered harmless fun to gather 30 friends, put on horned helmets, and go pillage a nearby town.
13. Lifeguards could remove citizens on beaches for violating the public ugliness ordinance.
14. Garbage would take itself out.
15. Instead of beer belly, you'd get "beer biceps."
16. Instead of an expensive engagement ring, you could present your wife-lo-be with a giant foam hand that said, "You're it!!!"
17. Valentine's day would be moved to February 29th so it would only occur in leap years.

18. On Christmas Eve, if you saw your shadow, you'd get the day off to go drinking. Mother's Day, too, St. Patrick's Day, however, would remain exactly the same, but it would be celebrated every month.
19. Cops would be broadcast live, and you could phone in advice to the pursuing Cops or to the crooks.
20. Two words: Ally McNaked
21. The victors in any athletic competition would get to kill and eat the losers.
22. The only show opposite Friday night Football would be from a different camera angle.
23. When a cop gave you a ticket, every smart ass answer you responded with would actually reduce your fine. As in; Cop: "You know how fast you were going?' You: "All I know is, I was spilling my beer all over the place. Cop: Nice one. That's $10 off."
24. Faucets would run "Hot" "Cold," and "100 proof."
25. The Statue of Liberty would get a bright red, 40-foot thong.
26. People would never talk about how fresh they felt.
27. Daisy Duke Shorts would never go out of style.
28. Telephones would automatically cut off after 30 seconds of conversation.

On a recent transatlantic flight, a plane passes through a severe storm. The turbulence is awful, and things go from bad to worse when one wing is struck by lightning. One woman in particular loses it. She stands up in the front of the plane. Screaming, "I'm too young to die," she wails. Then she yells, "Well, if I'm going to die, I want my last minutes to be memorable! Is there anyone on this plane who can make me feel like a woman?"

For a moment there is silence. Everyone has forgotten their own peril. They all stared, riveted, at the desperate woman in the front of the plane.

Then a man stands up in the rear of the plane. "I can make you feel like a woman," he says. He is gorgeous, tall, built with long, flowing black hair and jet black eyes. He starts to walk slowly up the aisle, unbuttoning his shirt....

.... One button at a time.

.... No one moves.

.... He removes his shirt.

.... Muscles ripple across his chest

.... As he reaches her, he extends the arm holding his shirt out to the trembling woman

.... And whispers:

.... "Iron this."

Why emails are like a penis

1. Those who have it would be devastated if it was ever cut off.
2. Those who have it think that those who don't are somewhat inferior.
3. Many of those who don't have it would like to try it—a phenomenon psychologists call "E-Male envy".
4. It's more fun when it's up, but this makes it hard to get any real work done.

5. In the distant past, its only real purpose was to transmit information vital to the survival of the species. Some people still think that is the only thing it should be used for, but most folks today use it only for fun.
6. If you don't take proper precautions, it can spread viruses.
7. If you use it too much, you'll find it becomes more and more difficult to think coherently.
8. We attach an importance to it that is far greater than its actual size and influence warrant.
9. If you are not careful what you do with it, it can get you into a lot of trouble.

And the number 10 reason why e-mail is like a male reproductive organ

10. If you play with it too much, you go blind.

THE MASTERCARD COMMERCIAL THAT NEVER MADE IT ON THE AIR

Cover charge: $15.00

Round of drinks: $23.00

Table dance: $30.00

Another round of drinks: $23.00

Couch dance and tips: $50.00

A round of shots: $34.00

Another round of drinks: $23.00

Lap Dance and Hand Job: $100.00

Private dance and hotel room: $500.00

Sending her on her way and never having to listen to her bitching

............Priceless

A man walks into a pharmacy and wanders up and down the aisles, the salesgirl notices him and asks him if she can help him. He answers that he is looking for a box of tampons for his wife. She directs him down the correct aisle.

A few minutes later, he deposits a huge bag of cotton balls and a ball of string on the counter.

She says, confused, "Sir, I thought you were looking for tampons for your wife?"

He answers, "You see, it's like this. Yesterday, I sent my wife to the store to get me a carton of cigarettes and she came home with a tin of tobacco and some rolling paper. So, I figure that if I have to roll my own, so does she!"

A guy walks into the psychiatrist wearing only cling wrap for shorts. The shrink says, "Well, I can clearly see you're nuts."

---

10 Simple Rules for dating my daughter

* Rule One: If you are delivering a package, you'd better pull into my driveway and honk because you're sure not picking anything up.

* Rule Two: You do not touch my daughter in front of me. You may glance at her, so long as you do not peer at anything below her neck. If you cannot keep your eyes or hands off of my daughter's body, I will remove them.

* Rule Three: I am aware that it is considered fashionable for boys of your age to wear their trousers so loosely that they appear to be falling off their hips. Please don't take this as an insult, but you and all of your friends are complete idiots. Still, I want to be fair and open-minded about this issue, so I propose this compromise: You may come to the door with your underwear showing and your pants ten sizes too big, and I will not object. However, In order to ensure that your clothes do not, in fact, come off during the course of your date with my daughter, I will take my electric nail gun and fasten your trousers securely in place to your waist.

* Rule Four: I'm sure you've been told that in today's world, sex without utilising a "barrier method" of some kind can kill you. Let me elaborate: when it comes to sex, I am the barrier, and I will kill you.

* Rule Five: In order for us to get to know each other, we should talk about sports, politics, and other issues of the day. Please do not do this. The only information I require from you is an indication of when you expect to have my daughter safely back at my house, and the only word I need from you on this subject is "early."

* Rule Six: I have no doubt you are a popular fellow, with many opportunities to date other girls. This is fine with me as long as it is okay with my daughter. Otherwise, once you have gone out with my little girl, you will continue to date no one but her until she is finished with you. If you make her cry, I will make you cry.

* Rule Seven: As you stand in my front hallway, waiting for my daughter to appear, and more than an hour goes by, do not sigh and fidget. If you want to be on time for the movie, you should not be dating. My daughter is putting on her makeup, a process that can take longer than painting the Golden Gate Bridge. Instead of just standing there, why don't you do something useful, like changing the oil in my car?

* Rule Eight: The following places are not appropriate for a date with my daughter: Places where there are beds, sofas, or anything softer than a wooden stool. Places where there are no parents, policemen, or nuns within eyesight. Places where there is darkness. Places where there is dancing, holding hands, or happiness. Places where the ambient temperature is warm enough to induce my daughter to wear shorts, tank tops, midriff, T-shirts, or anything other than overalls, a sweater, and a goose down parka zipped up to her throat. Movies with a strong romantic or sexual theme are to be avoided; movies which feature chainsaws are okay. Hockey games are okay. Old folk's homes are better.

* Rule Nine: Do not lie to me. I may appear to be a pot-bellied, balding, middle-aged, dim-witted has-been, but on issues relating to my daughter, I am the all-knowing, merciless god of your universe. If I ask you where you are going and with whom, you have one chance to tell me the truth, the whole truth and nothing but the truth. I have a shotgun, a shovel, and five acres behind the house. Do not trifle with me.

* Rule Ten: Be afraid. Be very afraid. It takes very little for me to mistake the sound of your car in the driveway for a chopper coming in over a rice paddy outside of Hanoi. When my Agent Orange starts acting up, the voices in my head frequently tell me to clean the guns as I wait for you to bring my daughter home. As soon as you pull into the driveway you should exit your car with both hands in plain sight, speak the perimeter password, announce in a clear voice that you have brought my daughter home safely and early, then return to your car, there is no need for you to come inside.

The camouflaged face at the window is mine.

- Why do men become smarter during sex? Because they are plugged into a genius.

- Why don't women blink during foreplay? They don't have time.
- Why does it take 1 million sperm to fertilise 1 egg? They won't stop for directions.
- Why did God put men on earth? Because a vibrator can't mow the lawn.
- Why don't women have men's brains? Because they don't have penises to put them in.
- What do electric trains and breasts have in common? They're intended for children, but it's the men who usually end up playing with them.
- Why do men snore when they lay on their backs? Because their balls fall over their assholes and they vapour lock.
- Why do men masturbate? It's sex with someone they love.
- Why were men given larger brains then dogs? So they won't hump women's legs at cocktail parties.
- Why did God make men before women? You need a rough draft before you have a final copy.
- Why is a man's sperm white and pee yellow? So he can tell if he is coming or going.
- How many men does it take to put a toilet seat down? Nobody knows. It hasn't happened yet.
- Why do doctors slap babies' butts right after they're born? To knock the penises off the smart ones.
- What is that insensitive bit at the base of the penis called? The man.

- Why is psychoanalysis quicker for men than for women? When it's time to go back to childhood, he's already there.
- What do you call a handcuffed man? Trustworthy.
- Why do so many women fake orgasm? Because so many men fake foreplay.
- What is the difference between a single 40 year old woman and a single 40 year old man?

The 40 year old woman thinks often of having children and the 40 year old man thinks often about dating them.

- What do most men think Mutual Orgasm is? An insurance company.
- Why do men have a hole in their penis? So oxygen can get to their brains.
- What do you call a man with 99% of his brain missing? Castrated.
- What's easier to make: a snowman or a snowwoman? A snowwoman is easier to make, 'cause with a snowman you have to hollow out the head and use all that extra snow to make its testicles.
- What is the one thing that all men at singles bars have in common? They're married.
- What women say: This place is a mess! C'mon, you and I need to clean up? Your stuff is lying on the floor and you'll have no clothes to wear if we don't do laundry right now!
- What a man hears: blah, blah, blah, blah, C'MON YOU AND I, blah, blah, blah blah, blah ON THE FLOOR blah, blah,blah, NO CLOTHES, blah blah, blah, blah, RIGHT NOW!

OK, here it is, the greatest formula ever, better then Plank's Photo-electric Theorem, more useful then Einstein's Theory of Relativity and less boring then Newton's, Boyle's and Rutherford's ramblings. It essentially determines to what extent your bird standards will fall while intoxicated in a social environments. [Note: Also applies to women pulling fella's]

$U = S—L$

Where: L (P x a) Ts / Tr x Wi

Values

U Ugly bird factor

S Sober attraction factor (see text below)

L Downward shift of Standards (to be subtracted from S)

P Pints consumed

A Strength of lager (see conversion table)

Ts Time since last shag (months)

Tr Time remaining at establishment (hours) Wi Number of witnesses present

Conversion table for (a) Hoffmeister/XXXX .5

Fosters/Heineken 1

Stella/Kronenbourg = 1.5

Exhibition Cider = 2.0

Before you do anything you have to be brutally honest and decide a figure (S) on a scale of 1 to 15 (budgieometer) as to what your average budgie pull is likely to look like while you are sober (1 being Jo Brand through to 15 being Claudia Schiffer).

The result of the formula (L) is the figure you MINUS from you sober score(S) in order to obtain (U). The value (U)

is then checked on the corresponding budgieometer. Hey presto, you have a value for your birds ugliness. Although this formula is purely for statistical purposes one usually finds their mates are highly calibrated indicators.

Men's English:

- I'm hungry—I'm hungry
- I'm sleepy—I'm sleepy
- I'm tired—I'm tired
- Do you want to go to a movie?—I'd eventually like to have sex with you
- Can I take you out to dinner?—I'd eventually like to have sex with you
- Can I call you sometime?—I'd eventually like to have sex with you
- May I have this dance?—I'd eventually like to have sex with you
- Nice dress!—Nice cleavage
- You look tense, let me give you a massage—I want to fondle you
- What's wrong?—I don't see why you are making such a big deal out of this
- What's wrong?—What meaningless self-inflicted psychological trauma are you going through now?
- What's wrong?—I guess sex tonight is out of the question
- I'm bored—Do you want to have sex?
- I love you—let's have sex now

- I love you, too. Okay, I said it... we'd better have sex now!
- I like the way you cut your hair—I liked it better before
- Yes, I like the way you cut your hair—$50 and it doesn't look that much different
- Let's talk. I am trying to impress you by showing that I am a deep person so then you'd like to have sex with me.
- Will you marry me?—I want to make it illegal for you to have sex with other guys.
- I like that one better (while shopping)—Pick any freaking dress and let's go home
- I don't think that blouse and that skirt go well together—I am gay.
- I want a divorce—I'm willing to lose all my stuff just so I don't have to put up with your crap anymore; and I'd like to have sex with women half my age.

Women's English:

- Yes—No
- Maybe—No
- I'm sorry—You'll be sorry
- We need—I want
- It's your decision—The correct decision should be obvious by now
- Do what you want—You'll pay for this later
- We need to talk—I need to complain
- Sure... go ahead—I don't want you to
- I'm not upset—Of course I'm upset, you moron!

- You're... so manly—You need a shave and you sweat a lot
- You're certainly attentive tonight—is sex all you ever think about?
- Be romantic, turn out the lights—I have flabby thighs
- This kitchen is so inconvenient—I want a new house
- Hang the picture there—NO, I mean hang it there!
- I heard a noise—I noticed you were almost asleep
- Do you love me?—I'm going to ask for something expensive
- How much do you love me?—I did something today you're really not going to like
- I'll be ready in a minute—kick off your shoes and find a good game on TV.
- I'm ready—kick off your shoes and find a good game on TV.
- Is my butt fat—Tell me I'm beautiful.
- You have to learn to communicate—Just agree with me.
- Are you listening to me—Too late, you're dead
- Was that the baby? –Why don't you walk with the baby until they go to sleep?
- I'm not yelling—Yea I am yelling because I think this is important.

- First guy (proudly): My wife's an angel! Second guy: you're lucky. Mine's still alive.

- How do most men define marriage? An expensive way to get laundry done for free.
- Just think, if it weren't for marriage, men would go through life thinking they had no fault at all.
- If you want your wife to listen and pay undivided attention to every word you say. Talk in your sleep.
- Then there was a man who said I never knew what real happiness was until l got married; and then it was too late.
- A little boy asked his father. "Daddy, how much does it cost to get married? And the father replied.—I don't know son. I'm still paying."

A married bloke was having an affair with his secretary. One day they went to her place and rooted all arvo.

Exhausted, they fell asleep and woke up at 8 PM. The bloke hurriedly dressed and told his lover to take his shoes outside and rub them in the grass and dirt. He put on his shoes and drove home.

"Where have you been?" his wife demanded.

"I can't lie to you," he replied, "I'm having an affair with my secretary. We had sex all afternoon."

She looked down at his shoes and said: "You lying bastard! You've been playing golf!"

---

5 Questions That Men Fear

The questions are:

1. What are you thinking about?
2. Do you love me?
3. Do I look fat?
4. Do you think she is prettier than me?
5. What would you do if I died?

What makes these questions so difficult is that everyone is guaranteed to explode into a major argument if the man answers incorrectly (i.e. tells the truth). Therefore, as a public service, each question is analysed below, along with possible responses.

Question # 1: What are you thinking about?

The proper answer to this, of course, is: "I'm sorry if I've been pensive, dear. I was just reflecting on what a warm, wonderful, thoughtful, caring, intelligent woman you are, and how lucky I am to have met you. "This response obviously bears no resemblance to the true answer, which most likely is one of the following:

a. Baseball.
b. Football.
c. How fat you are.
d. How much prettier she is than you.
e. How I would spend the insurance money if you died.

(Perhaps the best response to this question was offered by Al Bundy, who once told Peg, "If I wanted you to know what I was thinking, I would be talking to you!")

Question # 2: Do you love me?

The proper response is: "YES!" or, if you feel a more detailed answer is in order, "Yes, dear."

Inappropriate responses include:
- a. Oh Yeah, shit loads.
- b. Would it make you feel better if I said yes?
- c. That depends on what you mean by love.
- d. Does it matter?
- e. Who, me?

Question # 3: Do I look fat?

The correct answer is an emphatic: "Of course not!" Among the incorrect answers are:
- a. Compared to what?
- b. I wouldn't call you fat, but you're not exactly thin.
- c. A little extra weight looks good on you.
- d. I've seen fatter.
- e. Could you repeat the question? I was just thinking about how I would spend the insurance money if you died.

Question # 4: Do you think she's prettier than me?

Once again, the proper response is an emphatic: "Of course not!" Incorrect responses include:
- a. Yes, but you have a better personality
- b. Not prettier, but definitely thinner
- c. Not as pretty as you when you were her age
- d. Define pretty

e. Could you repeat the question? I was just thinking about how I would spend the insurance money if you died.

Question # 5: What would you do if I died?

A definite no-win question. (The real answer, of course, is "Buy a Corvette.")

No matter how you answer this, be prepared for at least an hour of follow-up questions, usually along these lines:

WOMAN: Would you get married again? MAN: Definitely not!

WOMAN: Why not—don't you like being married? MAN: Of course I do.

WOMAN: Then why wouldn't you remarry?

MAN: Okay, I'd get married again.

WOMAN: You would? (With a hurtful look on her face} , Would you sleep with her in our bed?

MAN: Where else would we sleep?

WOMAN: Would you put away my pictures, and replace them with pictures of her?

MAN: That would seem like the proper thing to do.

WOMAN: And would you let her use my golf clubs? MAN: She can't use them; she's left-handed

---

A man is driving up a steep, narrow mountain road. A woman is driving down the same road.

As they pass each other, the woman leans out of the window and yells -PIG!! The man immediately leans out of his window and replies, BITCH!! They each continue on their way, and as the man rounds the next corner, he crashes into a pig in the middle of the road.

If only men would listen.

Actual personal ad placed by a man........

WANTED

1 A tall women with good reputation, who can cook frog legs, who can stand a little future, Fun at parties and frolicking without getting serious froli

-

.

OK now go back up and read line one, three and five only

- How many men does it take to change a roll of toilet paper? We don't know; it has never happened.
- Why is it difficult to find men who are sensitive, caring & good looking? They all already have boyfriends.
- What do you call a woman who knows where her husband is every night? A widow.
- When do you care for a man's company? When he owns it.
- Why are married women heavier than single women? Single women come home, see what's in the fridge and go to bed. Married women come home, see what's in bed and go to the fridge.
- How did Pinocchio find out he was made of wood? His hand caught fire.

- How do you get a man to do sit-ups? Put the remote control between his toes

- What did God say after creating man? I must be able to do better than that.

- What did God say after creating Eve? Practice makes perfect.

- What is the one thing that all men at singles bars have in common? They're married.

- How many honest, intelligent, caring men in the world does it take to do the dishes? Both of them.

- Why does it take 1 million sperm to fertilise one egg? They won't stop to ask directions.

- What do men and sperm have in common? They both have a one-in-a-million chance of becoming a human being.

- How does a man show that he is planning for the future? He buys two cases of beer.

- What is the difference between men and government bonds? The bonds mature.

A few little pointers to show how they think!!! Ladies -

1. If you think you might be fat, you are. Don't ask us. Just get your arse in a gym.

2. Learn to work the toilet seat: if it's up, put the bloody thing down

3. Don't cut your hair. Ever. It causes arguments when we comment on it.
4. Birthdays, Valentines, and Anniversaries are not quests to see if we can find the perfect present again.
5. If you ask a question you don't want an answer to, expect an answer you don't want to hear.
6. Sometimes, we're not thinking about you. Live with it.
7. Anyone can buy condoms.
8. Get rid of your cat. And no, it's not different, it's just like every other cat.
9. Dogs are better than any cats.
10. Sunday = Football/Rugby/Any other sport. Let it be.
11. Shopping is not a sport.
12. Anything you wear is fine. Really.
13. You have enough clothes.
14. You have too many shoes.
15. Crying is blackmail. Use it if you must, but don't expect us to respond to it.
16. Your brother is an idiot, your ex-boyfriend is an idiot and your dad probably is too.
17. Ask for what you want. Subtle hints don't work.
18. Yes, peeing standing up is more difficult than peeing from point blank range. We're bound to miss sometimes.
19. Most blokes own two to three pairs of shoes, so what makes you think we'd be any good at choosing which pair, out of thirty, would look good with your dress?
20. 'Yes', 'No' and 'Mmm' are perfectly acceptable answers.

21. A headache that lasts for 17 months is a problem. See a doctor.
22. Your Mum doesn't have to be our best friend.
23. Foreign films are best left to foreigners.
24. Check your oil. It is an essential part of the car.
25. The relationship is never going to be like it was the first two months we were going out.
26. Don't fake orgasms. We'd rather be ineffective than deceived.
27. Anything we said 6 or 8 months ago is inadmissible in an argument. All comments become null and void after 7 days.
28. Telling us that the models in the men's magazines are airbrushed makes you look jealous and petty and it's certainly not going to deter us from reading them.
29. The male models with the great bodies you see in magazines are all gay.
30. If something we said could be interpreted two ways, and one of the ways makes you sad and angry, we meant the other one.
31. Let us ogle. If we don't look at other women, how can we rate how pretty you are?
32. Whenever possible, please say whatever you have to say during the commercials.
33. Women wearing Wonder bras, low-cut blouses, tight tops, no jackets, chest level logoed t- shirts etc. etc...., lose their right to complain about having their boobs stared at.

34. When we are in bed and look tired this means that we are tired and does not mean that we want to discuss the relationship.

35. If you want some dessert after a meal—have some. You don't have to finish it. You can just taste it if you like but don't say no. I couldn't/shouldn't/don't want any and then eat half of mine.

CHAPTER 14

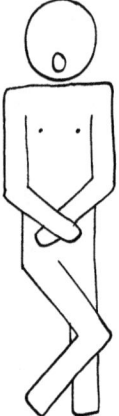

N is for Nude

Penny lost her husband almost four years ago and still has not gotten out of her depression, mourning as if it were only yesterday. Her daughter constantly calls her and urges her to get back into the world.

Finally, Penny agrees to go out, but didn't know anyone. Her daughter immediately replies, Mama! I have someone for you to meet.

Well, it was an immediate hit. They took to one another and after dating for six weeks he asks her to join him for a weekend at Niagara Falls. And we know what that means.

One room and the normal follow up to that. Their first night there she undresses. There she stood nude except for a pair of black lacy panties.

He in his birthday suit. Looking at her he asks -Why the panties?-

She replies, my breasts you can fondle, my body is yours to explore, but down there I am still in mourning. He knows he's not getting lucky that night.

The following night the same scenario. Her standing there with black panties on and he in his birthday suit; except that he has an erection on which he has a black condom. She looks at him and asks what's with this … a black condom?-

He replies, I'm going to offer my condolences.

Two parents take their son on a vacation and go to a nude beach. The father goes for a walk on the beach and the son goes and plays in the water.

The son comes running up to his mum and says, "Mummy, I saw ladies with boobies a lot bigger than yours!"

The mum says, "The bigger they are, the dumber they are."

So he goes back to play. Several minutes later he comes running back and says, "Mummy, I saw men with dingers a lot bigger than Daddy's!"

The mum says, "The bigger they are, the dumber they are."

So he goes back to play.

Several minutes later he comes running back and says, "Mummy, I just saw Daddy talking to the dumbest lady I ever saw and the more and more he talked, the dumber and dumber he got!"

Q: What did the elephant say to a naked man?

A: Hey that's cute but can you breath through it?

Q: Why should Playboy wait 5 years to shoot Lindsay Lohan nude?

A: In 5 years they can just go to the morgue!

Q: What do you call mobile porn?

A: Flash Drive

Q: How do you properly fuck a naked fat woman?

A: Role her around in flower and find the wet spot!

Q: What do you call a naked 18 year-old on a waterbed?

A: A cherry float.

Q: How do you know Adam was a Canadian?

A: Who else could stand beside a naked woman and be tempted by a fruit?

Q: What do naked fish play with?

A: Bare-a-cudas!

Man: If I could see you naked, I'd die happy.

Woman: If I saw you naked, I'd probably die laughing.

I'd like to give a shout out to all the women who don't need to dress half naked to get a man's attention. Stay classy! The rest of you, come with me.

A man and a woman were celebrating their 50th anniversary. They were talking before their dinner about how they should celebrate their big evening. The woman decided she would cook a big dinner for her husband. Then he said they should do what they did on their wedding night and eat at the dinner table naked. The woman agreed.

Later that night at the table, the woman says, "Honey, my nipples are as hot for you as they were fifty years ago."

The man replies, "That's because they are sitting in your soup."

An out-of-state couple are camping on the shores of a lake near a tiny hamlet. The young wife, stunningly built, decides to give the local town folk a thrill by sun bathing in the nude.

"That's OK with me, honey," says her husband. "I'll go get some wood for the fire."

About thirty minutes later, the husband returns to the campsite and finds his wife in tears. One of her breasts has been painted green, the other red and her ass is blue.

"What on earth happened to you dear?" he asks.

"Some of those rednecks from town came over and told me they don't allow any nakedness around these parts. Then they gave me this paint job!"

"Damn those trouble-makers! I'll fix them!" the husband shouts.

He rides into town and finds the rednecks in a bar. "Who is the SOB who painted my wife red, green and blue!" he shouts.

A huge redneck, about 6'-8," steps forward, a shotgun in his hand.

"I did it," he bellows. "What you got to say about it?"

The husband answers meekly, "I just wanted you to know the first coat of paint is dry."

A 60 year old woman is naked, jumping up and down on her bed laughing and singing. Her husband walks into the bedroom and sees her. He watches her awhile then says, "You look ridiculous, what on earth are you doing?"

She says, "I just got my check up and my doctor says I have the breasts of an eighteen-year-old."

She starts laughing and jumping again.

He says, "Yeah, right. And what did he say about your 60 year-old ass?" She says, "Well, your name never came up."

On their first night together, a newlywed couple go to change. The new bride comes out of the bathroom showered and wearing a beautiful robe.

The proud husband says, "My dear, we are married now, you can open your robe."

The beautiful young woman opens her robe, and he is astonished. "Oh, oh, aaaahhh," he exclaims, "My God you are so beautiful, let me take your picture. Puzzled she asks, "My picture?" He answers, "Yes my dear, so I can carry your beauty next to my heart forever".

She smiles and he takes her picture, and then he heads into the bathroom to shower.

He comes out wearing his robe and the new wife asks, "Why do you wear a robe? We are married now."

At that the man opens his robe and she exclaims, "oh, OH, OH MY, let me get a picture".

He beams and asks why and she answers, "So I can get it enlarged!"

- I always sleep naked. It's just more comfortable.
- This stewardess can fuck off. I don't care if there are young children on the plane.
- I get complaints from my neighbours because I always walk about my garden wearing only my boxers.

- I don't see what the problem is, I think they make a lovely hat.

A couple goes to an art gallery. They find a picture of a naked women with only her privates covered with leaves. The wife doesn't like it and moves on but the husband keeps looking.

The wife asks: "What are you waiting for?"

The husband replies: "Autumn."

A young couple were making passionate love in the guy's van (you know, shag carpets, big double mattress in the back ... all that) when suddenly the girl, being a bit on the kinky side, yells out "Oh big boy, whip me, whip me!"

The guy, not wanting to pass up this unique opportunity, obviously did not have any whips to hand, but in a flash of inspiration, he opens the window, snaps the antenna off his van and proceeds to whip the girl until they both collapse in sado-masochistic ecstasy.

About a week later, the girl notices that the marks left by the whipping session are starting to fester a bit so she goes to the doctor.

The doctor takes one look at the wounds and asks "Did you get these marks having sex?"

The girl is a little embarrassed but admits that, yes, she did. Nodding his head knowingly the doctor exclaims, "I thought so, because in all my years of doctoring you've got the worst case of van aerial disease that I've ever seen."

Little Johnny came home from school one day and went by his mom's room. The door was open, so he looked in and saw his mom lying on the bed naked moaning and touching herself saying, "Ooh, I need a man! I need a man!"

The next day, Little Johnny got home from school and saw his mom lying on the bed naked with a naked guy on top of her. So Little Johnny ran to his room, stripped down naked, and started to touch himself, while moaning, "Ooh, I need a bike! I need a bike!"

A little boy and girl are in a bathtub, and are naked because they are too little too understand anything like that. The girl and boy ask each other: "What's that?" and they both reply: "I'll ask my parents."

So the boy goes home and asks his dad what it is. The dad looks solemnly at him and says: "Son, that's your car. You park it in a girl's garage."

The girl goes home and says: "what's that?" The mother says: "That's your garage. Don't let any boy park his car in it."

The next day they are again in the tub. The boy says it's a car and remembers what his dad said. So he begins to put it in the girls "garage". But then the girl remembers what her mom said.

5 minutes later, the girl comes to the mom with blood all over her. The mother asks her what was wrong and she said: "Mommy, a boy tried to put his car in my garage, but I popped his two back tires."

CHAPTER 15

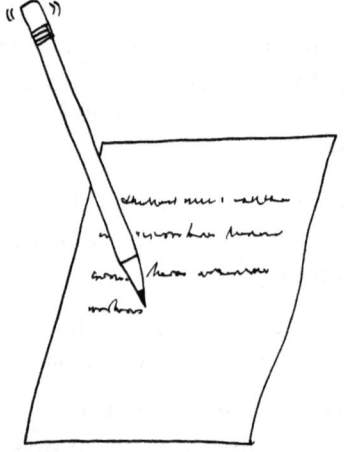

O is for One Liners

Monica Lewinsky (on CNN's Larry King Live discussing her miraculous Jenny Craig weight-loss): I've learned not to put things in my mouth that are bad for me.

- It's hard to understand how a cemetery raised its prices and blamed it on the cost of living.
- If the shoe fits, get another one just like it.
- The things that come to those that wait may be the things left by those who got there first.
- Give a man a fish and he will eat for a day. Teach a man to fish and he will sit in a boat drinking beer all day.
- Flashlight: A case for holding dead batteries.
- Shin: A device for finding furniture in the dark.
- As long as there are tests, there will be prayer in public schools.
- A fine is a tax for doing wrong. A tax is a fine for doing well.
- I wished the buck stopped here, as I could use a few.
- When you go into court, you are putting yourself in the hands of twelve people who weren't smart enough to get out of Jury duty.

- (On going to war over religion :) You're basically killing each other to see who's got the better imaginary friend. Rich Jeni
- I found my wife in bed naked one day next to a Vietnamese guy and a black guy. I took a picture and sent it to Benetton. You never know. Franck Dubosc

- I got kicked out of riverdance for using my arms.—Gary Valentine

- (On the difference between men and women): On the one hand, we'll never experience childbirth. On the other hand, we can open all our own jars. Jeff Green

- And God said: 'Let there be Satan, so people don't blame everything on me. And let there be lawyers, so people don't blame everything on Satan.—John Wing

- What are the three words guaranteed to humiliate men everywhere? 'Hold my purse.'—Francois Morency

- The web brings people together because no matter what kind of a twisted sexual mutant you happen to be, you've got millions of pals out there. Type in 'Find people that have sex with goats that are on fire' and the—computer will say, 'Specify type of goat.'—Rich Jeni

- Life strategy? Lie flat and try not to die.—Tim Steeves

- Women might be able to fake orgasms. But men can fake whole relationships.—Jimmy Shubert

- There are only two reasons to sit in the back row of an airplane Either you have diarrhoeas, or you're anxious to meet people who do.—Rich Jeni

- My girlfriend always laughs during sex-no matter what she's reading—Emo Philips

- What's with squeegee kids? I mean, they don't really wash the windshield, do they? They simply redistribute the dirt.—Ken Scott

- Clinton lied. A man might forget where he parks or where he lives, but he never forgets (oral sex) no matter how bad it is.—Lenny Clarke

- My cousin just died. He was only 19. He got stung by a bee—the natural enemy of a tightrope walker.—Emo Philips

- I saw a woman wearing a sweatshirt with 'Guess' on it. I said, 'Thyroid problem?'" Emo Philips

- "Honesty is the key to a relationship. If you can fake that, you're in—Rich Jeni

- "Hockey is a sport for white men. Basketball is a sport for black men. Golf is a sport for white men dressed like black pimps." Ren Hicks

- "Things you'll never hear a woman say 'My, what an attractive scrotum!' Jeff Green

- "I read somewhere that 77 per cent of all the mentally ill live in poverty. Actually, I'm more intrigued by the 23 per cent who are apparently doing quite well for themselves." Emo Philips

- "My parents saw the president they loved get shot in the head." I saw my president get head." Elon Gold

- "I discovered I scream the same way whether I'm about to be devoured by a Great White or if a piece of seaweed touches my foot." Kevin James

- Capital punishment turns the state into a murderer. But imprisonment turns the state into a gay dungeon-master." Emo Philips

- "My mother never saw the irony in calling me a son-of-a-bitch." Rich Jeni

---

- It is well documented that for every minute that you exercise, you add one minute to your life. This enables you at 85 years old to spend an additional 5 months in a nursing home at $5000 per month.

- My grandmother started walking five miles a day when she was 60. Now she's 97 years old and we don't know where the hell she is.
- The only reason I would take up exercising is so that I could hear heavy breathing again.
- I joined a health club last year, spent about 400 bucks. Haven't lost a pound. Apparently you have to show up.
- I have to exercise early in the morning before my brain figures out what I'm doing.
- I like long walks, especially when they are taken by people who annoy me.
- I have flabby thighs, but fortunately my stomach covers them.
- The advantage of exercising every day is that you die healthier.
- If you are going to try cross-country skiing, start with a small country.

---

1. Do not walk behind me, for I may not lead. Do not walk ahead of me, for I may not follow. Do not walk beside me, either. Just leave me the hell alone.
2. The journey of a thousand miles begins with a broken fan belt and a leaky tire.
3. It's always darkest before dawn, so if you're going to steal your neighbour's newspaper, that's the time to do it.

4. Don't be irreplaceable. If you can't be replaced, you can't be promoted.
5. No one is listening until you fart.
6. Always remember you're unique. Just like everyone else.
7. Never test the depth of the water with both feet.
8. It may be that your sole purpose in life is simply to serve as a bad example.
9. It is far more impressive when others discover your good qualities without your help.
10. If you think nobody cares if you're alive, try missing a couple of car payments.
11. Before you criticize someone, you should walk a mile in their shoes. That way, when you criticize them, you're a mile way and you have their shoes.
12. If at first you don't succeed, skydiving is not for you.
13. Give a man a fish and he will eat for a day. Teach him how to fish and he will sit in a boat & drink beer all day.
14. If you lend someone $20 and never see that person again, it was probably worth it.
15. Don't squat with your spurs on.
16. If you tell the truth, you don't have to remember anything.
17. Some days you are the bug, some days you are the windshield.
18. Don't worry, it only seems kinky the first time.
19. Good judgment comes from bad experience, and a lot of that comes from bad judgment.

20. The quickest way to double your money is to fold it in half and put it in your pocket.

21. Timing has an awful lot to do with the outcome of a rain dance.

22. A closed mouth gathers no foot.

23. Duct tape is like the Force. It has a light side & a dark side, and it holds the universe together.

24. There are two theories to arguing with women. Neither one works.

25. Generally speaking, you aren't learning much when your mouth is moving.

26. Experience is something you don't get until just after you need it.

27. Never miss a good chance to shut up.

28. We are born naked, wet, and hungry. Then things get worse.

BEST RECENT BRITISH NEWSPAPER HEADLINES

1. Something Went Wrong in Jet Crash, Experts Say
2. Police Begin Campaign to Run Down Jaywalkers
3. Drunks Get Nine Months in Violin Case
4. Iraqi Head Seeks Arms
5. Is There a Ring of Debris around Uranus?
6. Prostitutes Appeal to Pope
7. Panda Mating Fails; Veterinarian Takes Over
8. British Left Waffles on Falkland Islands

9. Clinton Wins Budget; More Lies Ahead
10. Plane Too Close to Ground, Crash Probe Told
11. Miners Refuse to Work After Death
12. Juvenile Court to Try Shooting Defendant
13. Stolen Painting Found by Tree
14. War Dims Hope for Peace
15. If Strike Isn't Settled Quickly, It May Last a While
16. Couple Slain; Police Suspect Homicide
17. Man Struck by Lightning Faces Battery Charge
18. New Study of Obesity Looks for Larger Test Group
19. Astronaut Takes Blame for Gas in Space
20. Kids Make Nutritious Snacks
21. Local High School Dropouts Cut in Half
22. Typhoon Rips through Cemetery; Hundreds Dead

---

1. Save the whales. Collect the whole set.
2. A day without sunshine is like, night.
3. On the other hand, you have different fingers.
4. I just got lost in thought. It was unfamiliar territory.
5. 42.7 percent of all statistics are made up on the spot.
6. I feel like I'm diagonally parked in a parallel universe.
7. You have the right to remain silent. Anything you say will be misquoted, then used against you.
8. I wonder how much deeper the ocean would be without sponges.

9. Honk if you love peace and quiet.
10. Remember half the people you know are below average.
11. Despite the cost of living, have you noticed how popular it remains?
12. Nothing is fool-proof to a talented fool.
13. Atheism is a non-prophet organisation.
14. He who laughs last thinks slowest.
15. Depression is merely anger without enthusiasm.
16. Eagles may soar, but weasels don't get sucked into jet engines.
17. The early bird may get the worm, but the second mouse gets the cheese.
18. I drive way too fast to worry about cholesterol.
19. I intend to live forever—so far so good.
20. Borrow money from a pessimist—they don't expect it back.
21. If Barbie is so popular, why do you have to buy her friends?
22. My mind is like a steel trap—rusty and illegal in 37 states.
23. Quantum mechanics: The dreams stuff is made of.
24. The only substitute for good manners is fast reflexes.
25. Support bacteria—they're the only culture some people have.
26. When everything's coming your way, you're in the wrong lane and going the wrong way.

27. If at first you don't succeed, destroy all evidence that you tried.
28. A conclusion is the place where you got tired of thinking.
29. Experience is something you don't get until just after you need it.
30. For every action there is an equal and opposite criticism.
31. Bills travel through the mail at twice the speed of check.
32. Never do card tricks for the group you play poker with.
33. No one is listening until you make a mistake.
34. Success always occurs in private and failure in full view.
35. The colder the x-ray table the more of your body is required on it.
36. The hardness of butter is directly proportional to the softness of the bread.
37. The severity of the itch is inversely proportional to the ability to reach it.
38. To steal ideas from one person is plagiarism; to steal from many is research.
39. To succeed in politics, it is often necessary to rise above your principles.
40. Monday is an awful way to spend 1/7th of your life.
41. You never really learn to swear until you learn to drive.
42. Two wrongs are only the beginning.

43. The problem with the gene pool is that there is no lifeguard.
44. The sooner you fall behind the more time you'll have to catch up.
45. A clear conscience is usually the sign of a bad memory.
46. Change is inevitable except from vending machines.
47. Get a new car for your spouse—it'll be a great trade!
48. Plan to be spontaneous—tomorrow.
49. Always try to be modest and be proud of it!
50. If you think nobody cares, try missing a couple of payments.
51. How many of you believe in telekinesis? Raise my hand ...
52. Love may be blind but marriage is a real eye opener.

Politically correct ways to say someone is STUPID

1. A few clowns short of a circus.
2. A few fries short of a happy meal.
3. The wheel's spinning, but the hamster's dead.
4. All foam, no beer.
5. The butter has slipped off his pancake.
6. The cheese slid off his cracker.
7. Body by Nautilus, brains by Mattel.
8. Warning: Objects in mirror are dumber than they appear.

9. Couldn't pour water out of a boot with instructions written on the heel.
10. He fell out of the stupid tree and hit every branch on the way down.
11. As smart as bait.
12. Doesn't have all his dogs on one leash.
13. His sewing machine's out of thread.
14. One fruit loop shy of a full bowl.
15. His antenna doesn't pick up all the channels.
16. His belt doesn't go through all the loops.
17. Gates are down, lights are flashing, but the train isn't coming.
18. Receiver is off the hook.
19. Not wired to code.
20. Skylight leaks a little.
21. His Slinky's kinked.
22. Too much yardage between the goal posts.
23. Got a full 6-pack, but lacks the plastic thingy to hold 'em together.
24. A photographic memory, but the lens cover is on.
25. During evolution, his ancestors were in the control group.
26. He's so dense, light bends around him.
27. If brains were taxed, he'd get a rebate.
28. Standing close to him, you can hear the ocean.
29. Some drink from the fountain of knowledge, but he just gargled.

30. He stayed on the Tilt-A-Whirl a bit too long.
31. His bubble is a little off centre

---

9 things I hate about everybody.

1. People who point at their wrist while asking for the time. I know where my watch is pal, where the f*ck is yours? Do I point at my crotch when I ask where the toilet is?

2. People who are willing to get off their arse to search the entire room for the TV remote because they refuse to walk to the TV and change the channel manually.

3. When people say "Oh you just want to have your cake and eat it too". F*cking right! What good is a cake if you can't eat it?

4. When people say "it's always the last place you look". Of course it is. Why the f*ck would you keep looking after you've found it? Do people do this? Who and where are they?

5. When people say while watching a film "did you see that?" No tosser, I paid $12 to come to the cinema and stare at the f*cking floor.

6. People who ask "Can I ask you a question?" Didn't really give me a choice there, did you sunshine?

7. When something is 'new and improved!' Which is it? If it's new, then there has never been anything before it. If it's an improvement, then there must have been something before it.

8. When people say "life is short". What the f*ck?? Life is the longest damn thing anyone ever f*cking does!! What can you do that's longer?

9. When you are waiting for the bus and someone asks "Has the bus come yet?" If the bus came would I be standing here, knob head?

Things you don't want to hear during surgery

- Better save that, we'll need it for the autopsy.
- Rats! Page 47 of this manual is missing!
- Rex! Come back with that! Bad Dog!
- Wait a minute, if this is his spleen, then what's that? Hand me that .... uh .... that uh .... thingie.
- Oh no! I just lost my Rolex.
- Oops! Hey, has anyone ever survived 500ml of this stuff before?
- Ya know, there's big money in kidneys, and heck, this guy's got two of 'em....'
- Could you stop that thing from beating? It's throwing my concentration off.
- That's cool! Now can you make his leg twitch?! I wish I hadn't forgotten my glasses.
- Well folks, this will be an experiment for us all. Sterile, shcmerile, the floor's clean, right? Anyone see where I left that scalpel?
- OK, now take a picture from this angle, this is truly a freak of nature.
- This patient has already had children, am I correct? Don't worry, I think it's sharp enough.
- Accept this sacrifice, oh lord of darkness.

Actual label instructions on consumer goods

On a blanket from Taiwan:

NOT TO BE USED AS PROTECTION FROM A TORNADO

On a helmet mounted mirror used by us cyclists:

REMEMBER. OBJECTS IN THE MIRROR ARE ACTUALLY BEHIND YOU

On a Korean kitchen knife:

KEEP OUT OF CHILDREN

On an Indonesian packet of nuts:

OPEN PACKET AND EAT CONTENTS

On a pack of Sainsbury's (UK) salted peanuts:

WARNING: CONTAINS NUTS

On a Taiwanese shampoo:

USE REPEATEDLY FOR SEVERE DAMAGE

On a Marks and Spencer's (UK) bread and butter pudding:

WARNING: PRODUCT WILL BE HOT AFTER HEATING

On the bottle-top of a flavoured milk drink:

AFTER OPENING. KEEP UPRIGHT

On an Aussie iron:

WARNING: NEVER IRON CLOTHES ON THE BODY.

On a New Zealand insect spray:

THIS PRODUCT NOT TESTED ON ANIMALS.

In an American guide to setting up a new computer:

TO AVOID CONDENSATION FORMING. ALLOW THE BOXES TO WARM UP TO ROOM TEMPERATURE

BEFORE OPENING. (Sensible. but the instruction was on the INSIDE of the box.)

On a Japanese product used to relieve painful haemorrhoids:

LIE DOWN ON BED AND INSERT POSCOOL SLOWLY UP TO THE PROJECTED PORTION LIKE A SWORD-GUARD INTO ANAL DUCT WHILE INSERTING POSCOOL FOR APPROXIMATELY 5 MINUTES. KEEP QUIET.

On Sears's hair dryer:

DO NOT USE WHILE SLEEPING.

On a bag of Fritos:

YOU COULD BB A WINNER! NO PURCHASE NECESSARY. DETAILS INSIDE.

On a bar of Dial soap:

DIRECTIONS: USE LIKE REGULAR SOAP.

On some Swann frozen dinners:

SERVING SUGGESTION: DEFROST.

On a hotel provided shower cap in a box:

FITS ONE HEAD.

On Tesco's tiramisu dessert:

DO NOT TURN UPSIDE DOWN. (Printed on bottom of the box)

On Boot's children's cough medicine:

DO NOT DRIVE CAR OR OPERATE MACHINERY.

On Nytol sleep aid:

WARNING: MAY CAUSE DROWSINESS.

On a string of Chinese-made Christmas lights:

FOR INDOOR OR OUTDOOR USE ONLY.

On a Japanese food processor:

NOT TO BE USED FOR THE OTHER USE.

On a child's Superman costume:

WEARING OF THIS GARMENT DOES NOT ENABLE YOU TO FLY.

On a Swedish chain saw:

DO NOT ATTEMPT TO STOP CHAIN WITH YOUR HANDS OR GENITALS.

- A bus station is where a bus stops. A train station is where a train stops. On my desk, I have a work station.
- Do Lipton tea employees take coffee breaks?
- What hair colour do they put on the driver's licenses of bald men?
- I was thinking that women should put pictures of missing husbands on beer cans.
- I was thinking about how people seem to read the Bible a whole lot more as they get older, then it dawned on me they were cramming for their finals.
- Why do they put pictures of criminals I up in the Post Office? What are we supposed to do, write to these men? Why don't they just put their pictures on the postage stamps so the mailmen could look for them while they deliver the mail?
- If it's true that we are here to help others, then what exactly are the OTHERS here for?

- If you can't be kind, at least have the decency to be vague.
- After eating, do amphibians need to wait an hour before getting OUT of the water?
- Why don't they just make mouse-flavoured cat food?
- If you're sending someone some Styrofoam, what do you pack it in?
- Is it true cannibals don't eat clowns because they taste funny?
- Since light travels faster than sound, isn't that why some people appear bright until you hear them speak?
- If it's zero degrees outside today and it's supposed to be twice as cold tomorrow, how cold is it going to be?
- Since Americans throw rice at weddings, shouldn't Asians throw hamburgers?

- Woody Allen: "Having sex is like bridge. If you don't have a good partner, you'd better have a good hand."
- Steven Wright: "I think it's wrong that only one company makes the game <u>Monopoly</u>."
- Demetri Martin: "The worst time to have a heart attack is during a <u>game</u> of <u>charades</u>."
- Groucho Marx: "I never forget a <u>face</u>, but in your case I'd be glad to make an exception."
- Zach Galifianakis: "I have a lot of growing up to do. <u>I realised</u> that the other day inside my fort."
- Jimmy Carr: "A big girl once came up to me after a show and said, 'I think you're <u>fatist</u>.' I said, 'No. I think you're fattest.'"

- Rodney Dangerfield: "I'm so ugly that my proctologist stuck his finger in my mouth."
- Bob Newhart: "I don't like country music, but I don't mean to denigrate those who do. And for the people who like country music, denigrate means 'put down'."
- Joan Rivers: "The people voting for the Oscars are so old. I haven't seen one Academy Award voter with a tampon in her purse."
- Jay Leno: "Remember the good old days when the only bomb you had to worry about on a plane was the Rob Schneider movie?"
- Jerry Seinfeld: "Looking at cleavage is like looking at the sun. You don't stare at it. It's too risky. You get a sense of it and then you look away."
- Louis C.K.: "There are two types of people in the world: People who say they pee in the shower and dirty fu**ing liars."
- Bill Bailey: "My first job was selling doors, door to door. That's a tough job isn't it? Bing Bong; 'Hello, can I interest you in a ... oh sh** you've got one already haven't you? Well never mind…'"
- Robin Williams: "We had gay burglars the other night. They broke in and rearranged the furniture."
- George Carlin: "Ever notice that anyone going slower than you is an idiot, but anyone going faster is a maniac?"
- Michael McIntyre: "Who's phoning radio stations to warn of traffic jams? Who in their right mind gets stuck and thinks: 'Get me the phone—I must warn the others. It's too late for me'?"
- Ricky Gervais: "Put a bet on the paralympics the other day; try telling the bookies that they're all winners."

- Lee Mack: "I remember the last thing my nanny said to me before she died. 'What are you doing here with that hammer?'"
- Phyllis Diller: "I do dinner in three phases; serve the food, clear the table, bury the dead."
- Russell Brand: "No wonder Bob Geldof is such an expert on famine. He's been dining off I Don't Like Mondaysfor 30 years."
- I hate Russian dolls, they're so full of themselves.
- I asked my North Korean friend how it was there, he said he couldn't complain.
- My girlfriend started smoking, so I slowed down and applied Lubricant.
- Don't let an extra chromosome get you down.
- I haven't talked to my wife in three weeks. I didn't want to interrupt her.
- People used to laugh at me when I would say 'I want to be a comedian', well nobody's laughing now.
- My wife told me to stop impersonating a flamingo. I had to put my foot down.
- Throwing acid is wrong, in some people's eyes.
- My wife and I were happy for twenty years; then we met.
- I haven't slept for three days, because that would be too long.
- The first time I got a universal remote control, I thought to myself 'This changes everything.'
- My girlfriend has the heart of a lion and a lifetime ban from the local zoo.

- Say what you want about deaf people.
- I've spent the past four years looking for my ex-girlfriend's killer, but no one will do it.
- I saw a sign that said 'watch for children' and I thought, 'that sounds like a fair trade'.
- I refused to believe my road worker father was stealing from his job, but when I got home, all the signs were there.
- I recently decided to sell my vacuum cleaner, all it was doing was gathering dust.
- People say I'm condescending. That means I talk down to people.
- You can never lose a homing pigeon—if your homing pigeon doesn't come back, what you've lost is a pigeon.
- Whiteboards are remarkable.
- I was at an ATM and this old lady asked me to help check her balance, so I pushed her over.

- I say no to alcohol, it just doesn't listen.
- I have an inferiority complex, but it's not a very good one.
- Shout out to all sidewalks; for keeping me off the streets.
- Love means nothing to a tennis player.
- Six out of seven dwarves are not happy.
- They took my mood ring, and I don't know how to feel about that.

- I loathe Russian nesting dolls. They are so full of themselves.
- My drug dealer cracks me up.
- Inspecting mirrors is a job I could really see myself doing.
- I'm so hip old ladies are trying to replace me.
- I'd give my left arm to be ambidextrous.
- Words cannot express how limited my vocabulary is.
- My girlfriend likes to do this really cute thing where she doesn't exist.
- Getting paid to sleep would be a dream job.
- My fear of moving stairs is escalating.
- I used to be a banker, but I lost interest.
- Asthma, it's breathtaking.
- I used to be indecisive, but now I'm not so sure.
- What do you get when you cross a rhetorical question with a joke?
- I'm a social smoker with lots of imaginary friends.
- Whiteboards are remarkable.

---

1. "I've decided to sell my Hoover, well, it was just collecting dust"—Tim Vine
2. "I've written a joke about a fat badger, but I couldn't fit it into my set"—Masai Graham
3. "Always leave them wanting more, my uncle used to say to me. Which is why he lost his job in disaster relief"—Mark Watson

4. "I was given some Sudoku toilet paper. It didn't work. You could only fill it in with number 1s and number 2s"—Bec Hill

5. "I wanted to do a show about feminism. But my husband wouldn't let me"—Ria Lina

6. "Money can't buy you happiness? Well, check this out, I bought myself a Happy Meal"—Paul F Taylor

7. "Scotland had oil, but it's running out thanks to all that deep frying"—Scott Capurro

8. "I forgot my inflatable Michael Gove, which is a shame 'cause halfway through he disappears up his own a***hole"—Kevin Day

9. "I've been married for 10 years, I haven't made a decision for seven"—Jason Cook

10. "This show is about perception and perspective. But it depends how you look at it"—Felicity Ward

11. "I go to the kebab shop so much that when they call me boss in there it's less a term of affection, more an economic reality"—Ed Gamble

12. "Leadership looks fun, but it's stressful. Just look at someone leading a conga"—James Acaster

13. "I bought myself some glasses. My observational comedy improved"—Sara Pascoe

---

TOP TEN Actual E-mail Addresses
================================

1. Helen Thomas Eatons (Duke University)—eatonsht@dku.edu

O is for One Liners 401

2. Mary Ellen Dickinson (Indiana University of Pennsylvania)—dickinme@iup.edu

3. Francis Kevin Kissinger (Las VerdesUniversity)—kissinfk@lvu.edu

4. Amanda Sue Pickering (Purdue University)—aspicker@pu.edu

5. Ida Beatrice Ballinger (Ball State University)—ibballin@bsu.edu

6. Bradley Thomas Kissering (Brady Electrical, Northern Division, Overton Canada)—btkisser@bendover.com

7. Isabelle Haydon Adcock (TOys "R" Us)—ihadcock@tru.com

8. Martha Elizibeth cummins (Fresno University)—cumminme@fu.edu

9. George David Blowmer (Drop Front Drawers & cabinets Inc.)—blowmegd@dropdrawers.com

...but at No 10, it had to be ...

10. Barbara Joan Beeranger (Myplace Home Decorating)—beeranbj@myplace.com

---

1. Two antennas met on a roof, fell in love and got married. The Ceremony wasn't much, but the reception was excellent.

2. A jumper cable walks into a bar. The bartender says, I'll serve you, but don't start anything."

3. A woman has twins and gives them up for adoption. One of them goes to a family in Egypt and is named "Ahmal." The other goes to a family In Spain; they

name him "Juan." Years later, Juan sends a picture of himself to his birth mother. Upon receiving the picture, she tells her husband that she wishes she also had a picture of Ahmal. Her husband responds, 'They're twins! If you've seen Juan, you've seen Ahmal."

4. A dyslexic man walks into a bra.

5. A man walks into a bar with a slab of asphalt under his arm and says: "A beer please, and one for the road."

6. Two cannibals are eating a clown. One says to the other: "Does this taste funny to you?"

7. "Doc, can't stop singing 'The Green, Green Grass of Home.' "That sounds like Tom Jones Syndrome." "Is it common?" Well, "It's Not Unusual."

8. Two cows are standing next to each other in a field. Daisy says to Dolly, "I was artificially inseminated this morning." "I don't believe you," says Dolly. "It's true, no bull!" exclaims Daisy.

9. An invisible man marries an invisible woman. The kids were nothing to look at either.

10. Deja Moo: The feeling that you've heard this bull before.

11. I went to buy some camouflage trousers the other day but I couldn't find any.

12. A man woke up in a hospital after a serious accident. He shouted, "Doctor, doctor, I can't feel my legs!" The doctor replied, "I know you can't I've cut off your arms!"

13. I went to a seafood disco last week and pulled a mussel.

14. What do you call a fish with no eyes? A fish.

15. Two fish swim into a concrete wall. The one turns to the other and says Dam!"

16. Two Eskimos sitting in a kayak were chilly, so they lit a fire in the craft. Unsurprisingly it sank, proving once again that you can't have your kayak and heat it too.

17. A group of chess enthusiasts checked into a hotel and were standing in the lobby discussing their recent tournament victories. After about an hour, the manager came out of the office and asked them to disperse. "But why," they asked, as they moved off. "Because," he said, "I can't stand chess-nuts boasting in an open foyer."

18. Two peanuts walk into a bar, and one was a salted.

19. Mahatma Gandhi, as you know, walked barefoot most of the time, which produced an impressive set of calluses on his feet. He also ate very little, which made him rather frail and with his odd diet, he suffered from bad breath. This made him. (Oh, man, this is so bad, it's good ...) A super calloused fragile mystic hexed by halitosis.

20. And finally, there was the person who sent twenty different puns to his friends, with the hope that at least ten of the puns would make them laugh. No pun in ten did!!!!!!!

Excerpted from the book "A Collection of Personal Ads From Alternative Newspapers," by Skippy Williams and Zohre Crumpton, Simon and Schuster:

1. Bitter, unsuccessful middle aged loser wallowing in an unending sea of inertia, draining loneliness looking for 24 year old needy leech-like hanger-on to abuse with dull stories, tired sex and Barry Manilow albums.

2. Me-trying to sleep on the bus station bench, pleading with you to give to me a cigarette; you-choking on my

odour, tripping over your purse trying to get away; at the last moment, our eyes meeting. Yours were blue. Can I have a dollar?

3. Imp and angel. Disembodied head in jar, 24, seeks pixie goddess to fiddle with while Rome burns. You bring marshmallows. No. I make joke. You like laugh? I like comebacks and confessions. Send photo of someone else.

4. I am spitting kitty. Ftt Ftttttt. I a mangy bear. Grrrrr. I am large watermelon seed stuck in your nose. Zermmmmm. I am small biting spider in your underwear. Yub, yub yub. No mimes.

5. Three toed mango peeler; searching for wicked lesbian infielder. Like screaming and marking territory with urine? Let's make banana enchiladas together in my bathtub. You bring the salsa.

6. Mongoloid spastic underwear model with extra limb (you guess where?) in search of bottle nosed dolphin and extra prickly cactus juice.

7. Soup is good food. I like eating mayonnaise and peanut butter sandwiches in the rain, watching Beverley Hills 90210 reruns, peeing on birds in the park and licking strangers on the subway; you eat beets raw, have climbed Kilimanjaro, and sweat freely and often. Must wear size five shoes.

8. Timber! Falling downward is the lumber of my love. You grind your axe of passion into my endangered headlands. Don't make me into a bureau. I want to be lots and lots of toothpicks.

9. Small lumpy squid monkey seeks healthy woman with no identifying scars, any age. Must have all limbs. Recommend appreciation of high-pitched, screeching

noises. Must like being bored and lonely. Must not touch the squids, ever.

10. There is a little place in the jumbled sock drawer of my heart where you match up all the pairs, throw out the ones with holes in them, and buy me some of those neat dressy ones with the weird black and red geometrical designs on them.

11. Mmmm Pez! Rabid Wonder Woman fan looking for someone in satin tights, fighting for our rights and the old red, white 'n blue. You look like Linda carter? Big plus. Know all words to theme song? Marry me.

12. Sanctimonious mordacious raconteur seeking same for hijinks and hiballs. SJM27 wants to look someone in the eye so don't be tall. Or, if you can't help it, enjoy lying down. Want to swim upstream?

13. Remember that summer you spent with your parents in Hawaii and how mad you were that they made you go? And how you were hopelessly bored until you saw the most gorgeous man you'd ever encountered strolling down the beach looking at you, skillfully removing your skimpy bikini with his piercing eyes? And how you spent the last month imagining him taking you in every possible way, masturbating feverishly day and night, wishing he would reappear, but he never did because you were 15 and he would have gone to jail? That was me, and you just turned 18.

14. Angry, simple-minded, balding, partially blind ex-circus flipper boy with a passion for covering lovers in sour cream and gravy seeks exotic, heavily tattooed piercing fanatic, preferably hairy, either sex, for whippings, bizarre sex and fashion consulting. No freaks.

15. Demented hunchback seeks humble wench to empty drool cup.

16. Parallel lines have so much in common. It's a shame they'll never meet.
17. My wife accused me of being immature. I told her to get out of my fort.
18. Women only call me ugly until they find out how much money I make. Then they call me ugly and poor.
19. How many Germans does it take to screw in a light bulb? One, they're efficient and not very funny.
20. What do you call a dog with no legs? It doesn't matter; it's not going to come.
21. Someone stole my Microsoft Office and they're going to pay. You have my Word.
22. What's green, fuzzy, and if it fell out of a tree, it would kill you? A pool table.
23. Apparently, someone in London gets stabbed every 52 seconds. Poor bastard.
24. How do you find Will Smith in the snow? You look for the fresh prints.
25. I went to a really emotional wedding the other day. Even the cake was in tiers.
26. We have a genetic predisposition for diarrhoea. Runs in our jeans.
27. A physicist sees a young man about to jump off the Empire State Building. He yells 'don't do it! You have so much potential!'
28. A hot blonde orders a double entendre at the bar. The bartender gave it to her.
29. Want to hear a word I just made up? Plagiarism.
30. Why do cows wear bells? Because their horns don't work.

31. What did the pirate say when he turned 80? Aye Matey.
32. To the handicapped guy who stole my bag—you can hide, but you can't run.
33. I took the shell off my racing snail, thinking it would make him run faster. If anything, it made him more sluggish.
34. And the Lord said unto James, 'Come forth and you will receive eternal life'. But James came fifth, and won a toaster.
35. Q: How do you think the unthinkable? A: With an iceberg.
36. Someone stole my mood ring, I don't know how I feel about that.
37. I tried to catch fog yesterday, Mist.
38. The first rule of Alzheimer's club, is don't talk about chess club.
39. Why does a chicken coop have two doors? If it had four doors, it would be a chicken sedan.
40. I told my wife she was drawing her eyebrows too high. She looked surprised.

Why did the chicken cross the road?

- Pat Buchanan: To steal a job from a decent, hardworking American.
- Louis Farrakhan: The road, you will see, represents the black man. The chicken crossed the "black man" in order to trample him and keep him down.
- Colonel Sanders: "I missed one?"

- LA Police Department: Give us five minutes with the chicken and we'll find out.
- Bill Clinton: The chicken did not cross the road. I repeat, the chicken did not cross the road. I don't know any chickens. I have never known any chickens.
- Dr. Seuss: Did the chicken cross the road? Did he cross it with a toad? Yes, the chicken crossed the road. But why it crossed, I've not been told!
- Ernest Hemingway: To die. In the rain.
- Martin Luther King Jr.: I envision a world where all chickens will be free to cross roads without having their motives called into question.
- Grandpa: In my day, we didn't ask why the chicken crossed the road. Someone told us that the chicken crossed the road, and that was good enough for us.
- Aristotle: It is the nature of chickens to cross the road.
- Karl Marx: It was an historical inevitability.
- Ronald Reagan: What chicken?
- Bill Clinton: I did not cross the road with that chicken. However, I did ask Vernon Jordan to find the chicken a job in New York.
- Captain James T. Kirk: To boldly go where no chicken has gone before.
- Fox Mulder: You saw it cross with your own eyes. How many more chickens have to cross before you believe it?
- Machiavelli: The point is that the chicken crossed the road. Who cares why? The end of crossing the road justifies whatever motive there was.

- Freud: The fact that you are at all concerned that the chicken crossed the road reveals your underlying sexual insecurity.
- Bill Gates: I have just released "Chicken Coop 98", which will not only cross roads, but will lay eggs, file your important documents, and balance your chequebook, and Explorer is an inextricable part of the operating system.
- Einstein: Did the chicken really cross the road or did the road move beneath the chicken?
- Bill Clinton: Define "cross"
- Kindergarten teacher—"to get to the other side"
- Plato—"for the greater good"
- Aristotle—"It is the nature of chickens to cross roads"
- Timothy Leary—"because that is the only trip the establishment would let it take"
- Sudam Hussein—"this was an unprovoked act of rebellion and we were quite justified in dropping 50 tonnes of nerve gas on it"
- Ronald Reagan—"I forget"
- Hippocrates—"because of an excess of phlegm in its pancreas"
- PriceWaterhouseCoopers—"Deregulation of the chicken's side of the road was threatening its dominant market position. The chicken was faced with significant challenges to create and develop the competencies required for the newly competitive market. PriceWaterhouseCoopers, in a partnering relationship with the client helped the chicken by rethinking its physical distribution strategy and implantation processes. Using the Poultry Integration

Model (PIM), Andersen helped the chicken use its skills, methodologies, knowledge, capital and experiences to align the chicken's people, processes and technology in support of its overall strategy within the Program Management framework.

PriceWaterhouseCoopers convened a diverse cross-spectrum of road analysts and best chickens along with Andersen consultants with deep skills in the transportation industry to engage in a two-hour itinerary of meetings in order to leverage their person knowledge capital, both tacit and explicit, and to enable them to synergize with each other in order to achieve the implicit goals of delivering and successfully architecting and implementing an enterprises-wide value framework across the continuum of poultry cross-median processes.

The meeting was held in a park-like setting, enabling and creating an impactful environment which was strategically based, industry-focused and built upon a consistent, clear and unified market message and aligned with the chicken's mission, vision and core values. This was conducive towards the creation of a total business integration solution.

PricewaterhouseCoopers helped the chicken's change to become more successful......

- Louis Farrakhan—"The road, you see, represents the black man ... The chicken 'crossed' the black man in order to trample him and keep him down"

- Moses—"And God came down from the Heavens and he said unto the chicken "Thou shalt cross the road." and the chicken crossed the road, and there was much rejoicing"

- Richard M Nixon—"The chicken did not cross the road. I repeat, the chicken did NOT cross the road"

- Jerry Seinfeld—"Why does anyone cross the road? I mean, why doesn't anyone ever think to ask, What the heck was this chicken doing walking around all over the place anyway?"
- Oliver Stone—"The question is not "Why did the chicken cross the road?" Rather, it is, "Who was crossing the road at the same time, whom we overlooked in our haste to observe the chicken crossing?"
- Darwin—"Chickens, over great periods of time, have been naturally selected in such a way that they are now genetically disposed to cross roads..."
- Buddha—"Asking this question denies your own chicken nature"
- Ralph Waldo Emerson—"The chicken did not cross the road. It transcended it...
- "Ernest Hemingway—"to die. In the rain ..."
- Colonel Sanders—"I missed one?"
- Bill Clinton—It depends on what the meaning of the word "chicken" means"

- Woman: Why did the man cross the road? He heard the chicken was a slut.
- Why did the penis toss on the road? Because it was a wanker.
- Why does the sun lighten our hair, but darken our skin?
- Why can't women put on mascara with their mouth closed?
- Why doesn't glue stick to the inside of the bottle?

- Why don't you ever see the headline "Psychic Wins Lottery"?
- Why is "abbreviated" such a long word?
- Why is a boxing ring square?
- Why is it called lipstick if you can still move your lips?
- Why is it considered necessary to nail down the lid of a coffin?
- Why is it that doctors and lawyers call what they do "practice"?
- Why is it that rain drops but snow falls?
- Why is it that to stop Windows 95 or 98, you have to click on "Start"?
- Why is it that when you're driving and looking for an address, you turn down the volume on the radio?
- Why is lemon juice made with artificial flavour, and dishwashing liquid made with real lemons?
- Why the man who invests all your money is called a broker?
- Why the third hand on the watch is called a second hand?
- Why is the time of day with the slowest traffic called rush hour?
- Why is the word dictionary in the dictionary?
- Why isn't there a special name for the tops of your feet?
- Why isn't there mouse-flavoured cat food?
- You know that little indestructible black box that is used on planes.

- Why can't they make the whole plane out of the same substance?
- Can fat people go skinny-dipping?
- Why do you need a driver's license to buy liquor when you can't drive?

---

1. I can only please one person per day. Today is not your day. Tomorrow is not looking good either.
2. I love deadlines. I especially like the whooshing sound they make as they go flying by.
3. Tell me what you need, and I'll tell you how to get along without it.
4. Accept that some days you are the pigeon and some days the statue.
5. Needing someone is like needing a parachute. If he isn't there the first time, chances are you won't need him again.
6. I don't have an attitude problem, you have a perception problem.
7. Last night I lay in bed looking up at the stars in the sky, and I thought to myself, where the heck is the ceiling?
8. My reality check bounced.
9. On the keyboard of life, always keep one finger on the escape key.
10. I don't suffer from stress. I am a carrier.
11. You are slower than a herd of turtles stampeding through peanut butter.

12. Do not meddle in the affairs of dragons, because you are crunchy and taste good with ketchup.
13. Everybody is somebody else's weirdo.
14. Never argue with an idiot. They drag you down to their level, then beat you with experience.
15. A pat on the back is only a few centimetres from a kick in the butt.
16. Don't be irreplaceable—if you can't be replaced, you can't be promoted.
17. After any salary raise, you will have less money at the end of the month than you did before.
18. The more crap you put up with, the more crap you are going to get.
19. You can go anywhere you want if you look serious and carry a clipboard.
20. Eat one live toad the first thing in the morning and nothing worse will happen to you the rest of the day.
21. If it wasn't for the last minute, nothing would get done.
22. When you don't know what to do, walk fast and look worried.
23. Following the rules will not get the job done.
24. When confronted by a difficult problem, you can solve it more easily by reducing it to the question, "How would the Lone Ranger handle this?"

Some bumper stickers seen around the place

1. Everyone has a photographic memory. Some just don't have film.

2. Save the whales. Collect the whole set.
3. A day without sunshine is like, night.
4. On the other hand, you have different fingers.
5. I just got lost in thought. It was unfamiliar territory.
6. When the chips are down, the buffalo is empty.
7. Those who live by the sword get shot by those who don't.
8. You have the right to remain silent. Anything you say will be misquoted, then used against you.
9. I wonder how much deeper the ocean would be without sponges.
10. Honk if you love peace and quiet.
11. Pardon my driving; I'm reloading.
12. Despite the cost of living, have you noticed how it remains so popular?
13. He who laughs last, thinks slowest.
14. It is well to remember that the entire universe, with one trifling exception, is composed of others.
15. Depression is merely anger without enthusiasm.
16. Eagles may soar, but weasels don't get sucked into jet engines.
17. Early bird gets the worm, but the second mouse gets the cheese.
18. I almost had a psychic girlfriend but she left me before we met.
19. I drive way too fast to worry about cholesterol.
20. I intend to live forever.... So far, so good.

21. I love defenceless animals, especially in a good gravy.
22. If Barbie is so popular, why do you have to buy her friends?
23. Mind like A Steel Trap ...Rusty and Illegal in 37 States.
24. Support bacteria ....They're the only culture some people have.
25. When everything's coming your way, you're in the wrong lane, going the wrong way.
26. If at first you don't succeed, destroy all evidence that you tried.
27. A conclusion is the place where you got tired of thinking.
28. Experience is something you don't get until just after you need it.
29. For every action, there is an equal and opposite criticism.
30. He who hesitates is probably right.
31. Never do card tricks for the group you play poker with.
32. No one is listening until you make a mistake.
33. Success always occurs in private, and failure in full view.
34. The colder the X-ray table, the more of your body is required on it.
35. The hardness of the butter is directly proportional to the softness of the bread.
36. The severity of the itch is inversely proportional to the ability to reach it.

37. To steal ideas from one person is plagiarism; to steal from many is research.
38. To succeed in politics, it is often necessary to rise above your principles.
39. You never really learn to swear until you learn to drive.
40. The problem with the gene pool is that there is no lifeguard.
41. Monday is an awful way to spend 1/7th of your life.
42. A clear conscience is usually the sign of a bad memory.
43. Change is inevitable ...except from vending machines.
44. Don't sweat petty things ...or pet sweaty things.
45. A fool and his money are soon partying.
46. Plan to be spontaneous tomorrow.
47. Always try to be modest. And be proud of it!
48. If you think nobody cares about you, try missing a couple of payments.
49. Get a new car for your spouse ....it'll be a great trade!
50. I'd kill for a Nobel Peace Prize.
51. Everybody repeat after me ...."We are all individuals." Death to all fanatics!
52. Love may be blind, but marriage is a real eye-opener.
53. Hell hath no fury like the lawyer of a woman scorned.
54. Bills travel through the mail at twice the speed of checks.
55. Hard work pays off in the future. Laziness pays off now.

56. Borrow money from pessimists ....They don't expect it back.//
57. Half the people you know are below average.
58. 99 percent of lawyers give the rest a bad name.
59. If at first you don't succeed, then skydiving definitely isn't for you.
60. Jesus loves you ... everyone else thinks you're an asshole.
61. If you women knew what men were thinking, you'd never stop slapping us.
62. Do you know the punishment for bigamy? Two mothers-in-law.

PICK UP LINES

1. Your name must be Daisy, because I have the incredible urge to plant you right here!
2. Roses are red, violets are blue, I like spaghetti, let's go screw.
3. Just call me milk; I'll do your body good.
4. Your body's name must be visa, because it's everywhere I want to be.
5. Can I buy you a drink, or do you just want the money?
6. I may not be Fred Flintstone, but I bet I can make your Bed Rock.
7. I may not be the best looking guy here, but I'm the only one talking to you.

8. My love for you is like the energizer bunny, it keeps going and going.

9. That shirt looks very becoming on you, but if I were on you, I'd be coming too.

10. Yo Baby, you be my Dairy Queen, I'll be your Burger King, you treat me right, and I'll do it your way right away.

11. I'd like to screw your brains out, but it appears that someone beat me to it.

12. I enjoy doing maintenance, you look like someone I would like to "tinker" around with.

13. You must be from Pearl Harbour, cause baby you're the Bomb-diggity.

14. If you were a new hamburger at McDonald's, you would be McGorgeous.

15. Is that Windex? Because I can see myself in your pants.

16. I'm a bird watcher and I'm looking for a Big Breasted Bed Thrasher, have you seen one?

17. I wish you were a Pony Carousel outside Walmart, so I could ride you all day long for a quarter.

18. Want a Play House? You be the screen door and I'll slam you all night long.

19. If you're going to regret this in the morning, we can sleep until the afternoon.

20. Oh, I'm sorry, I thought that was a Braille name tag.

21. If you were a car, I wax you and ride you all over town.

22. Guy: "Would you like to dance?"

23. Girl: "I don't care for this song and surely wouldn't dance with you."

24. Guy: "I'm sorry, you must have misunderstood me, I said you look fat in those pants"
25. Excuse me, do you have your phone number, I've seem to have lost mine.
26. I look good on you.
27. I'm new in town, could I have directions to your house.

- "You have to stay in shape. My grandmother, she started walking 5 miles a day when she was 60. She's 97 today and we don't know where the hell she is." — Ellen DeGeneres

- "If you ever see me getting beaten by the police, put down the video camera and come help me." —Bobcat Goldthwaite

- "Our bombs are smarter than the average high school student. At least they can find Kuwait." —A. Whitney Brown

- "I'm a psychic amnesiac. I know in advance what I'll forget." —Michael McShane

- "Maybe there is no actual place called hell. Maybe hell is just having to listen to our grandparents breathe through their noses when they're eating sandwiches." —Jim Carrey

- "Thou shall not kill. Thou shall not commit adultery. Don't eat pork. I'm sorry, what was that last one?? Don't eat pork. God has spoken. Is that the word of God or is that pigs trying to outsmart everybody?" — Jon Stewart

- "My mum said she learned how to swim. Someone took her out in the lake and threw her off the boat.

That's how she learned how to swim. I said, 'Mum, they weren't trying to teach you how to swim.'" -Paula Poundstone

- "In elementary school, in case of fire you have to line up quietly in a single file line from smallest to tallest. What is the logic? Do tall people bum slower?"—Warren Hutcherson

- "Ever wonder if illiterate people get the full effect of alphabet soup?" —John Mendoza

- "Relationships are hard. It's like a full-time job, and we should treat it like one. If your boyfriend or girlfriend wants to leave you, they should give you two weeks' notice. There should be severance pay, and before they leave you, they should have to find you a temp."—Bob Ettinger

- "A study in the Washington Post says that women have better verbal skills than men. I just want to say to the authors of that study: Duh!" —Conan O'Brien

- "I don't know what's wrong with my television set. I was getting C-Span and the Home Shopping

- Network on the same station. I actually bought a congressman." —Bruce Baum

- "Every time a baseball player grabs his crotch, it makes him spit. That's why you should never date a baseball player." —Marsha Warfield

- "I had a linguistics professor who said that it's man's ability to use language that makes him the dominant species on the planet. That may be. But I think there's one other thing that separates us from animals. We aren't afraid of vacuum cleaners."—Jeff Stimson

- "Did you ever walk in a room and forget why you walked in? I think that's how dogs spend their lives."—Sue Murphy

- "The statistics on sanity are that one out of every four Americans is suffering from some form of mental illness. Think of your three best friends. If they are okay, then it's you."—Rita Mae Brown

- "My grandfather's a little forgetful, but he likes to give me advice. One day, he took me aside and left me there." —Ron Richards

- "I worry that the person who thought up Muzak may be thinking up something else."—Lily Tomlin

- "Some women hold up dresses that are so ugly and they always say the same thing: 'This looks much better on.' On what? On fire?"—Rita Rudner

- "The ad in the paper said 'Big Sale. Last Week.' Why advertise? I already missed it. They're just rubbing it in."—Yakov Smirnoff

- "Everything that used to be a sin is now a disease."—Bill Maher

- "You know how to tell if the teacher is hung over?? Movie Day."—Jay Mohr

- "A women broke up with me and sent me pictures of her and her new boyfriend in bed together. Solution? I sent them to her dad."—Christopher Case

- "Now they show you how detergents take out bloodstains, a pretty violent image there. I think if you've got a T-shirt with a bloodstain all over it, maybe laundry isn't your biggest problem. Maybe you should get rid of the body before you do the wash."—Jerry Seinfeld

- "I ask people why they have deer heads on their walls. They always say because it's such a beautiful animal. There you go. I think my mother is attractive, but I have photographs of her.—Ellen DeGeneres
- "USA Today has come out with a new survey: Apparently three out of four people make up 75 percent of the population."—David Letterman
- "I was in a supermarket and I saw Paul Newman's face on salad dressing and spaghetti sauce. I thought he was missing."—Bob Saget
- "If God doesn't destroy Hollywood Boulevard, he owes Sodom and Gomorrah an apology."—Jay Leno
- "Chihuahua. There's a waste of dog food. Looks like a dog that is still far away."—Billiam Coronell
- "I just broke up with someone and the last thing she said to me was, 'You'll never find anyone like me again!' I'm thinking, 'I should hope not! If I don't want you, why would I want someone like you?'-Larry Miller
- "A lady came up to me on the street and pointed at my suede jacket.' You know a cow was murdered for that jacket?' she sneered. I replied in a psychotic tone, 'I didn't know there were any witnesses. Now I'll have to kill you too."-Jake Johansen
- "If your parents never had children, chances are you won't either."-Dick Cavett
- I have such poor vision I can date anybody."-Garry Shandling
- "I was a vegetarian until I started leaning towards sunlight."—Rita Rudner
- "I always wanted to be somebody, but I should have been more specific."—Lily Tomlin

- "The Swiss have an interesting army. Five hundred years without a war. Pretty impressive. Also pretty lucky for them. Ever see that little Swiss Army knife they have to fight with? Not much of a weapon there corkscrews. Bottle openers. 'Come on, buddy, let's go. You get past me, the guy in back of me, he's got a spoon. Back off. I've got the toe clippers right here.' —Jerry Seinfeld

- "Why does Sea World have a seafood restaurant? I'm halfway through my fish burger and I realize, Oh my God.... I could be eating a slow learner."—Lynda Montgomery

- "What do people mean when they say the computer went down on me?"-Marilyn Pittman

- "I met a new girl at a barbecue, very pretty, a blond I think. I don't know, her hair was on fire, and all she talked about was herself. You know these kind of girls: 'I'm hot. I'm on fire. Me, me, me: You know. 'Help me, put me out: Come on, could we talk about me just a little bit?—Garry Shandling

- Sometimes I think war is God's way of teaching us geography."—Paul Rodriguez

- "I don't do drugs anymore 'cause I find I get the same effect just by standing up really fast." —Johnathan Katz

- "Why is it that when we talk to God we're said to be praying, but when God talks to us we're schizophrenic?" —Lily Tomlin

- "When you look at Prince Charles, don't you think that someone in the Royal family knew someone in the Royal family?" —Robin Williams

- "Where lipstick is concerned, the important thing is not colour, but to accept God's final word on where your lips end." —Jerry Seinfeld

- "I think that's how Chicago got started. A bunch of people in New York said, 'Gee, I'm enjoying the crime and the poverty, but it just isn't cold enough. Let's go west.'" -Richard Jeni

---

1. Well, this day was a total waste of makeup.
2. A hard-on doesn't count as personal growth.
3. Do I look like a fucking people person?
4. This isn't an office. It's Hell with fluorescent lighting.
5. I've found Jesus. He was behind the sofa the whole time.
6. If I throw a stick, will you leave?
7. You! Off my planet!
8. Therapy is expensive, popping bubble wrap is cheap. You choose.
9. I like cats, too. Let's exchange recipes.
10. Does your train of thought have a caboose?
11. The Bible was written by the same people who said the earth was flat.
12. Did the aliens forget to remove your anal probe?
13. And just how may I fuck you over today?
14. And your cry baby whiny-assed opinion would be?
15. I'm not an asshole, I've just been in a very bad mood for 0 years.
16. See no evil, hear no evil, date no evil.
17. Sarcasm is just one more service we offer.

18. Whisper my favourite words: I'll buy it for you.
19. Whatever kind of look you were going for, you missed.
20. Sure it's user—friendly...if you know what you're doing.
21. I majored in liberal arts. Will that be to eat here or take away?
22. Living proof that nature does not abhor a vacuum.
23. I can't remember if I'm the good twin or the evil one.
24. Can you out-think a doorknob?
25. How many times do I have to flush before you go away?
26. I have a computer, a vibrator, and pizza delivery. Why should I leave the house?
27. I just want revenge. Is that so wrong?
28. It's sick the way you people keep having sex without me.
29. Vertically-fornicated mind.
30. You say I'm a bitch like it's a bad thing.
31. Can I trade this job for what's behind door?
32. Okay, okay, I take it back! UnFuck you!
33. Macho Law prohibits me from admitting I'm wrong.
34. Nice perfume. Must you marinate in it?
35. Not all men are annoying. Some are dead.
36. Too many freaks, not enough circuses.
37. Chaos, panic, & disorder-my work here is done.
38. A woman's favourite position is CEO.

39. Ambivalent? Well, yes and no.
40. Is it time for your medication or mine?
41. Does this condom make me look fat?
42. Did I mention the kick in the groin you'll be receiving if you touch me?
43. And which dwarf are you?
44. I thought I wanted a career, turns out I just wanted pay checks.
45. I'm not tense, just terribly, terribly alert.
46. It isn't the size, It's no, it's the size.

- I've just been on a once-in-a-lifetime holiday. I'll tell you what, never again—Tim Vine
- I worked out that on average I sleep with a little over three people every week. You could say I'm Pi-sexual—James Bennison
- You can't lose a homing pigeon. If your homing pigeon doesn't come back, then what you've lost is a pigeon—Sara Pascoe
- I was walking along the other day, and on the road I saw a small, dead, baby ghost. Although thinking about it, it might have been a handkerchief—Milton Jones
- I sold my guitar to a bloke with no arms recently. I asked him how it was going to work, he replied, 'I'm going to play it by ear'—Lloyd Griffith
- Whenever I'm in England someone invariably says to me: "Oh you are Australian. We really don't think it's

right what you people did to the Aborigines." And I always reply, "Hang on, wasn't that you?"—Greg Fleet

- Love is like a fart. If you have to force it it's probably s**t—Stephen K Amos

- I used to think an ocean of soda existed, but it was just a Fanta sea—Bec Hill

- My wife told me: "Sex is better on holiday." That wasn't a very nice postcard to receive—Joe Bor

- I wonder how long it will be until airlines aren't only charging for physical baggage, but for emotional baggage too? Not that it'd bother me. I'm fine. Really. Just ask my dad. Who's never there!—Tegan Higginbotham

- My name is Fin, which means it's very hard for me to end emails without sounding pretentious.—Fin Taylor

- My dad said, always leave them wanting more. Ironically, that's how he lost his job in disaster relief—Mark Watson

- Have you heard about the evil group of men who control all the world's cheese? The hallouminati—Nick Helm

- When my wife and I argue, we're like a band in concert: we start with some new stuff, and then we roll out our greatest hits—Frank Skinner

- I did a gig recently where I got booed off stage for saying that I live at home with my parents. As soon as I said it the whole audience went: "Booooo!" That's the last time I do a charity gig for an orphanage—Nathan Caton

CHAPTER 16

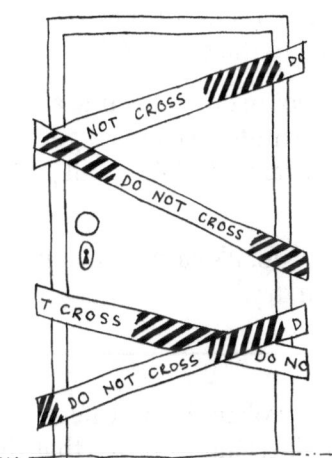

P is for Police

A girl was a prostitute, but she didn't want her grandma to know. One day, the police raided a whole group of prostitutes at a sex party in a hotel and the girl was among them. The police took them outside and had all the prostitutes line up along the driveway when suddenly, the girl's grandma came by and saw her granddaughter.

Grandma asked, "Why are you standing in line here, dear?" Not willing to let her grandmother know the truth, the girl told her grandmother that the policemen were there passing out free oranges and she was just lining up for some. "Why, that's awfully nice of them. I think I'll get some for myself," and she proceeded to the back of the line.

A policeman was going down the line asking for information from all of the prostitutes. When he got to Grandma, he was bewildered and exclaimed, "Wow, still going at it at your age? How do you do it?"

Grandma replied, "no, it's easy, dear. I just take my dentures out and suck them dry."

The Los Angeles Police Department (LAPD), The FBI, and the CIA are all trying to prove that they are the best at apprehending criminals. The President decides to give them a test.

He releases a rabbit into a forest and each of them has to catch it. The CIA goes in. They place animal informants throughout the forest. They question all plant and mineral witnesses.

After three months of extensive investigations they conclude that rabbits do not exist. The FBI goes in. After two weeks with no leads they burn the forest, killing everything in it, including the rabbit, and they make no apologies. "The rabbit had it coming". The LAPD goes in. They come out two hours later with a badly beaten bear. The bear is yelling: "Okay! Okay! I'm a rabbit! I'm a rabbit!"

There's this little guy sitting at a bar just looking at his drink. He stays like that for half-an-hour. Then this big trouble-making truck driver sits next to him takes the drink from the guy, and just drinks it all down.

The poor man starts crying. The truck driver says: "Come on man, I was just joking. Here, I'll buy you another drink. I just can't stand seeing a man cry."

"No, it's not that. Today is the worst day of my life. First, I overslept and was late for an important meeting. My boss, outraged, fired me.

When I left the building to get into my car, I found out it was stolen. The police, they said they could do nothing. I got a cab to return home, and after I paid the cab driver and the cab had gone, I found that I left my wallet in the cab. Again the police said there was nothing to do.

I got home only to find my wife was in bed with a policeman. I left home and came to this bar. And when I was thinking about putting an end to my life, you show up and drink my poison."

A man who is driving a car is stopped by a police officer. The following exchange takes place:

The man says, "What's the problem officer?"

Officer: "You were going at least 75 in a 55 zone." Man: "No sir, I was going 65"

Wifc: "No!, Harry. You were going 80" (The man gives his wife a dirty look.)

Officer: "I'm also going to give you a ticket for your broken tail light."

Man: "Broken tail light? I didn't know about a broken tail light!"

Wife: "Oh Harry, you've known about that tail light for weeks." (The man gives his wife another dirty look.)

Officer: "I'm also going to give you a citation for not wearing your seatbelt."

Man: "Oh I just took it off when you were walking up to the car."

Wife: "Oh Harry, you never wear your seatbelt."

The man turns to his wife and yells, "Shut your mouth!"

The Officer turns to the woman and asks "Ma'am, does your husband talk this way all the time?"

Wife says, "No, only when he's drunk."

A woman and a man are involved in a car accident and it is a bad one. Both of their cars are totally destroyed but amazingly, neither the man nor the woman is hurt. After they crawl out of their Cars, The woman says to the man, "So, you're a man. That's interesting. I'm a woman. Just look at our cars! There's nothing left, but fortunately, we are unhurt. This must be a sign from God that we should meet and be friends and live together in peace for the rest of our days." The man replied, "I agree with you completely. This must be a sign from God!"

The woman continued, "And look at this, here's another miracle! My car is completely demolished but this bottle of wine didn't break.

Surely God wants us to drink this wine and celebrate our good fortune! "

Then she hands the bottle to the man. The man nods his head in agreement, opens the bottle, drinks half of it and hands it back to the woman.

The woman takes the bottle, immediately puts the cap back on and hands it back to the man.

The man asks, "Aren't you going to have any?"

The woman replies, "No. I think I'll just wait for the police ..."

A man went to the Police Station wishing to speak with the burglar who had broken into his house the night before. "You'll get your chance in court." said the Desk Sergeant. "No, no no!" said the man. "I want to know how he got into the house without waking my wife. I've been trying to do that for years!"

A police officer attempts to stop a car for speeding and the guy gradually increases his speed until he's topping 100 mph. He eventually realizes he can't escape and finally pulls over. The cop approaches the car and says, "It's been a long day and my tour is almost over, so if you can give me a good excuse for your behaviour, I'll let you go." The guy thinks for a few seconds and then says, "My wife ran away with a cop about a week ago. I thought you might be that officer trying to give her back!"

A woman was reporting her car as stolen, and mentioned that there was a car phone in it. The policeman taking the report called the phone and told the guy that answered that he had read the ad in the newspaper and wanted to buy the car. They arranged to meet, and the thief was arrested.

A true story out of San Francisco: A man, wanting to rob a downtown Bank of America, walked into the branch and wrote "this iz a stikkup. Put all your muny in this bag."

While standing in line, waiting to give his note to the teller, he began to worry that someone had seen him write the note and might call the police before he reached the teller window. So he left the Bank of America and crossed the street to Wells Fargo.

After waiting a few minutes in line, he handed his note to the Wells Fargo teller. She read it and, surmising from his spelling errors that he was not the brightest light in the harbour, told him that she could not accept his stickup note because it was written on a Bank of America deposit slip and that he would either have to fill out a Wells Fargo deposit slip or go back to Bank of America. Looking somewhat defeated, the man said, "OK" and left.

The Wells Fargo teller then called the police who arrested the man a few minutes later, as he was waiting in line back at Bank of America.

Drug Possession Defendant Christopher Jansen, on trial in March in Pontiac, Michigan, said he had been searched without a warrant.

The prosecutor said the officer didn't need a warrant because a "bulge" in Christopher's jacket could have been a gun. Nonsense said Christopher, who happened to be wearing the same jacket that day in court. He handed it over so the judge could see it.

The judge discovered a packet of cocaine in the pocket and laughed so hard he required a five-minute recess to compose himself.

Detroit: R.C. Gaitlan, 21, walked up to two patrol officers who were showing their squad car computer equipment to children in a Detroit neighbourhood. When he asked how the system worked, the officer asked him for identification.

Gaitlan gave them his driver's license, they entered it into the computer, and moments later they arrested Gaitlan because information on the screen showed Gaitlan was wanted for a two year old armed robbery in St. Louis, Missouri.

Colorado Springs: A Guy walked into a little corner store with a shotgun and demanded all the cash from the cash drawer. After the cashier put the cash in a bag, the robber saw a bottle of scotch that he wanted behind the counter on the shelf. He told the cashier to put it in the bag as well, but he refused and said "Because I don't believe you are over 21."

The robber said he was, but the clerk still refused to give it to him because he didn't believe him. At this point the robber took his Drivers' license out of his wallet and gave it to the clerk. The clerk looked it over, and agreed that the man was in fact over 21 and he put the scotch in the bag

The robber then ran from the store with his loot. The cashier promptly called the police and gave the name and address of the robber that he got off the license. They arrested the robber two hours later.

Another from Detroit: A pair of Michigan robbers entered a record shop nervously waving revolvers. The first one shouted, "Nobody move!" When his partner moved, the startled first bandit shot him.

Florida, A thief burst into the bank one day wearing a ski mask and carrying a gun. Aiming his gun at the guard, the thief yelled, "FREEZE, MOTHER-STICKERS, THIS IS AN F—UP!" For a moment, everyone was silent. Then the snickers started.

The guard completely lost it and doubled over laughing. It probably saved his life, because he'd been about to draw his gun. He couldn't have drawn and fired before the thief got him. The thief ran away and is still at large. In memory of the event, the bank later put a plaque on the wall engraved "Freeze, mother-stickers, this is an f— up!"

An elderly couple was just settled down for bed when the old man realized he left the lights on in the greenhouse in the back yard. Then they heard voices.

Three men had broken into the greenhouse. Scared, they called the police. The dispatcher replied, he would send an officer as soon as one became available as they were all out on calls. The old man waited for a few minutes and called Dispatch again. He told Dispatch, "Don't worry about sending an officer, I shot the robbers and now the dogs are eating their bodies!" In no time at all, police were all over the place and captured the robbers red-handed!

One of the cops asked the old man, "I thought you said you shot the robber and your dogs were eating them." The old man replied, "I thought you said, there weren't any officers available."

Cop on horse says to a little girl on bike, "Did Santa get you that?" "Yes," replies the little girl. "Well tell him to put a reflector light on it next year!" and fines her $5.

The little girl looks up at the cop and says, "Nice horse you've got there, did Santa bring you that?" The cop chuckles and replies, "He sure did!" "Well," says the little girl, "Next year tell Santa that the d*ck goes under the horse, not on top of it!"

A mature (over 40) lady gets pulled over for speeding

Older Woman: Is there a problem, Officer?

Officer: Ma'am, you were speeding.

Older Woman: Oh, I see.

Officer: Can I see your license please?

Older Woman: I'd give it to you but I don't have one.

Officer: Don't have one?

Older Woman: Lost it, 4 years ago for drunk driving.

Officer: I see...Can I see your vehicle registration papers please.

Older Woman: I can't do that.

Officer: Why not?

Older Woman: I stole this car.

Officer: Stole it?

Older Woman: Yes, and I killed and hacked up the owner.

Officer: You what?

Older Woman: His body parts are in plastic bags in the trunk if you want to see.

The Officer looks at the woman and slowly backs away to his car and calls for back up. Within minutes 5 police cars circle the car. A senior officer slowly approaches the car, clasping his half drawn gun.

Officer 2: Ma'am, could you step out of your vehicle please! The woman steps out of her vehicle.

Older woman: Is there a problem sir?

Officer2: One of my officers told me that you have stolen this car and murdered the owner.

Older Woman: Murdered the owner?

Officer2: Yes, could you please open the trunk of your car, please. The woman opens the trunk, revealing nothing but an empty trunk.

Officer2: Is this your car, ma'am?

Older Woman: Yes, here are the registration papers. The officer is quite stunned.

Officer2: One of my officers claims that you do not have a driving license. The woman digs into her handbag and pulls out a clutch purse and hands it to the officer. The officer examines the license. He looks quite puzzled.

Officer2: Thank you ma'am, one of my officers told me you didn't have a license, that you stole this car, and that you murdered and hacked up the owner.

Older Woman: Bet the liar told you I was speeding, too.

Three highly decorated police officers die in a wild shoot out with narcotics dealers and go to heaven. God greets them and asks, "When you are laid out in your casket, and your fellow officers and family are mourning you, what would you like to hear them say about you?

The first cop says, "I would like to hear them say, that I was the bravest cop on the force."

The second police officer says, "I would like to hear that I was a terrific cop who died in the line of duty."

The last cop replies, "I would like to hear them say ... Look, He's Moving!"

A police officer pulls over this guy who had been weaving in and out of the lanes. He goes up to the guy's window and says, "Sir, I need you to blow into this breathalyzer tube."

The man says, "Sorry officer I can't do that. I am an asthmatic. If I do that I'll have a really bad asthma attack." "Okay, fine. I need you to come down to the station to give a blood sample." "I can't do that either. I am a hemophiliac. If I do that, I'll bleed to death." "Well, then we need a urine sample." "I'm sorry officer I can't do that either. I am also a diabetic. If I do that I'll get really low blood sugar." "Alright then I need you to come out here and walk this white line." "I can't do that, officer." "Why not?" "Because I'm too drunk to do that."

A motorist gets caught in an automated speed trap that photographs his car. He later receives a ticket in the mail for $40 with a photo of his car. Instead of payment, he sends the police department a photograph of $40. A few days later, he gets a letter from the police department with a picture of handcuffs.

A police officer pulls over an elderly female for speeding while driving her husband to a doctor's appointment. The officer approaches the vehicle and attempts to explain that he stopped her for speeding. She looks at her husband and asks,

"What did he say?" The husband replies, "He said he stopped you for speeding."

The officer asked the elderly female for her driver's license and she turned and asked her husband, "What did he say? The husband replies, "He wants to see your driver's license."

The women hands the officer her license and he sees that she is from his old home town. The officer tells the couple that he remembered the town because he had the worst sexual experience of his life there. The women looks at her husband and asked, "What did he say?" The husband replies, "He says he knows you."

The top 20 things not to say to a cop when he pulls you over.

1. I can't reach my license unless you hold my beer.
2. Sorry officer, I didn't realize my radar detector wasn't plugged in.
3. Aren't you the guy from the village people?
4. Hey, you must have been doing 125 to keep up with me, good job.
5. I thought you had to be in relatively good physical shape to be a police officer.
6. I was going to be a cop, but I decided to finish high school instead.
7. Bad cop, No donut.
8. You're not going to check the trunk, are you?
9. Gee, that gut sure doesn't inspire confidence.
10. Didn't I see you get your butt kicked on Cops?

11. Is it true that people become cops because they are too dumb to work at McDonalds?
12. I pay your salary.
13. So uh, you on the take or what?
14. Gee officer, that's terrific. The last officer only gave me a warning.
15. Do you know why you pulled me over? Okay, just so one of us does.
16. I was trying to keep up with traffic. Yes, I know there are no other cars around, that's how far they are ahead of me.
17. What do you mean have I been drinking? You are the trained specialist.
18. Well, when I reached down to pick up my bag of crack, my gun fell off of my lap and got lodged between the brake and the gas pedal, forcing me to speed out of control.
19. Hey, is that a 9mm? That's nothing compared to this 44 magnum.
20. Hey, can you give me another one of those full cavity searches?

EXTREME Game of Hide and Seek

The boss of a big company needed to call one of his employees about an urgent problem with one of the main computers. He dialled the employee's home phone number and was greeted with a child's whispered, "Hello?"

Feeling put out at the inconvenience of having to talk to a youngster the boss asked, "Is your Daddy home?"

"Yes", whispered the small voice." May I talk with him?" the man asked.

To the surprise of the boss, the small voice whispered, "No." Wanting to talk with an adult, the boss asked, "Is your Mummy there?"

"Yes," came the answer." May I talk with her?"

Again the small voice whispered, "No."

Knowing that it was not likely that a young child would be left home alone, the boss decided he would just leave a message with the person who should be there watching over the child." Is there anyone there besides you?" the boss asked the child.

"Yes," whispered the child, "A policeman."

Wondering what a cop would be doing at his employee's home, the boss asked "May I speak with the policeman?"

"No, he's busy," whispered the child. "Busy doing what?" asked the boss.

"Talking to Daddy and Mummy and the Fireman," came the whispered answer. Growing concerned and even worried as he heard what sounded like a helicopter through the ear piece on the phone the boss asked, "What is that noise?"

"A hello-copper," answered the whispering voice.

"What is going on there?" asked the boss, now alarmed. In an awed whispering voice the child answered, "The search team just landed the hello-copper."

Alarmed, concerned, and more than just a little frustrated, the boss then had to ask, "Why are they there?"

Still whispering, the young voice replied along with a muffled giggle ... "They're looking for me!"

63 WAYS TO PISS OFF A COP

1. When you get pulled over, say "What's wrong, officer, there's no blood in my alcohol?"
2. When he asks why you were speeding, tell him you wanted to race.
3. When he talks to you, pretend you are deaf.
4. If he asks if you knew how fast you were going, say no, my speedometer only goes to .
5. Ask if you can see his gun.
6. When he says you aren't allowed, tell him I just wanted to see if mine was bigger.
7. Touch him.
8. When he asks why you were speeding, tell him you had to buy a hat.
9. Ask him where he bought his cool hat.
10. Refer to him by his first name.
11. Pretend you are gay and ask him out.
12. When he says no, cry.
13. If he says yes, accuse him of sexual harassment.
14. If the cop is a woman, tell her how ugly she is, but in a nice way.
15. If he asks you to step out of the car, automatically throw yourself on the hood.
16. When he asks you to spread them, tell him you don't go that way.

17. When he puts the handcuffs on, say "Usually my dates buy me dinner first"
18. Ask to be fingerprinted with candy, because you don't like ink on your fingers.
19. After you get the ticket and give it to him, say "Oops' that's the wrong name."
20. Bribe him with donuts, and when he agrees, tell him sorry, I just ate the last one.
21. When he comes up to the car say "License and registration, please" right when he says it.
22. When he goes to read you your rights, sing "La La La, I can't hear you!"
23. Trip and fall into him.
24. Accuse him of police brutality when he pushes you away.
25. Before you sign the ticket, pick your nose, then ask to use his pen to sign the ticket.
26. Chew on the pen, nervously.
27. Clean your ear with the pen.
28. If it's a click pen, take it apart and play with the spring.
29. Ask if he has a daughter. If he says yes, say I thought the name sounded familiar.
30. Ask him if he ever worked in a prison. If he says yes, ask him how the plumbing was.
31. Act like you are retarded.
32. When he's telling you what you did wrong, start repeating him, quietly.
33. Mumble to yourself.

34. When he tells you to stop, say what are you talking about, DUDE?
35. Drive to Dunkin Donuts and say hrnmm...only of you here tonight.
36. Ask if they know how to make the donuts.
37. When he comes to the car, say I have a badge just like yours!
38. Ask if he watches Cops.
39. Ask if ever watched Cop Rock.
40. Giggle if he did.
41. Talk to your hand
42. When he frisks you, say you missed a spot, and grin.
43. When he asks to inspect your car, say there is no alcohol in my car, sir, the last cop got it.
44. Try to sell him your car.
45. Ask if you can buy his car.
46. If he takes you to the station, ask to sit in front.
47. Play with the siren.
48. If you know him, say you had his wife for dinner.
49. If you don't know him, ask if you can have his wife for dinner; Oops, I meant over for dinner.
50. Ask if he ever had pu-tang.
51. If he asks what it is, point at him and giggle.
52. If there is someone else in the car, talk to each other in tongues.
53. When he acts confused, keep talking, look at him and laugh.

54. When you are in the back, touch his neck through the fencing.
55. Turn your head and whistle.
56. When he pulls out his night stick, say what you going to do with that.
57. If you are female, say I don't do that on the first date.
58. If he sticks you in the back of the car, cower in the corner, suck your thumb, and whine.
59. Stare at his lights and say "Look at the pretty colours!"
60. Tell him you like men in uniform.
61. Ask if you can borrow his uniform for a Halloween party

CHAPTER 17

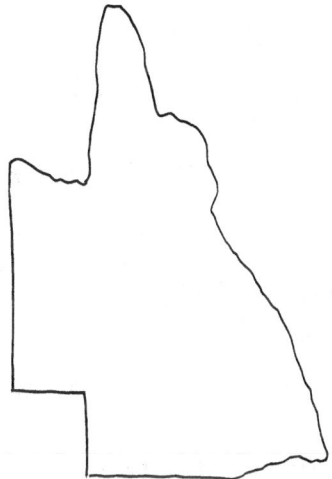

Q is for Queensland

Complaints received by the Queensland Housing commission from their tenants: (actual comments taken from forms)....

1. I want some repairs done to my cooker as it has back-fired and burnt my knob off.
2. I wish to complain that my father hurt his ankle very badly when he put his foot in the hole in his back passage.
3. The 18 year old next door is continuously banging his balls against my fence. Not only is this making a hell of a noise, but the fence is now sagging in the centre.
4. This is to let you know there is a smell coming from the man next door.
5. I am writing on behalf of my sink, which is running away from the wall.
6. Wish to report that tiles are missing from the roof of the outside toilet and I think it was bad wind the other night that blew them off.
7. I request your permission to remove my drawers in the kitchen.
8. This toilet is blocked and we cannot bath the children until it is cleared.
9. Will you please send a man to look at my water, it is a funny colour and not fit to drink.
10. Would you please send a man to repair my spout I am an old aged pensioner and need it straight away?
11. I want to complain about the farmer across the road. Every morning at 5, his cock wakes me up and it's getting too much.
12. It is all right when my husband is on day-shift. But when he is on back shifts or nights I get it several

times a week from Mr Docherty next door and at my age it's too much.

13. The man next door has a large erection in the back garden, which is unsightly and dangerous.

14. Our kitchen floor is very deep, we have two children and would like a third so will you please send someone to do something about it.

15. The toilet seat is cracked - where do I stand?

16. I am a single woman living in a downstairs flat and would be pleased if you could do something about the noise made by the man I have on top of me every night.

17. Please send a man with clean tools to finish the job and satisfy the wife.

18. Can you send a carpenter to the house? When the woman next door closed the door the other night, she pulled at my knob too hard and now it's ready to falloff.

19. I have had the Works Superintendent down on the floor six times, but still have no satisfaction.

20. We are getting married in September and would like it in the garden before we move into the house.

The story behind the letter below is that there is nut ball in Queensland, named Jim Scott who digs things out of his backyard and sends the stuff to the Queensland Museum, labelling them with scientific names, insisting that they are actual archaeological finds. This guy really exists and does this in his spare time.

Anyway here's the actual response from the Queensland Museum.

Bear this in mind next time you think you are challenged in your duty to respond to a difficult situation in writing.

Dear Mr Scott

Thank you for your latest submission to the Museum, labelled 9J211-0, layer seven, next to the clothesline pole - Hominid skull.

We have given this specimen actual and detailed examination, and regret to inform you that we disagree with your theory that it represents conclusive proof of the presence of early man in Queensland over two million years ago.

Rather, it appears that what you have found is the head of a Barbie doll of the variety that one of our staff, who has small children, believes to be "Malibu Barbie." It is evident that you have given a great deal of thought to the analysis of this specimen, and you may be quite certain that those of us who are familiar with your prior work in the field were loath to come to contradiction with your findings.

However, we do feel that there are a number of physical attributes of the specimen which might have tipped you off to its modern origin:

1. The material is moulded plastic. Ancient hominid remains are typically fossilized bone.

2. The cranial capacity of the specimen is approximately 9 cubic centimetres, well below the threshold of even the earliest identified proto-hominids.

3. The dentition pattern evident on the skull is more consistent with the common domesticated dog than it is with the ravenous man-eating Pliocene clams you speculate roamed the wetlands during that time. This latter finding is certainly one of the most intriguing hypotheses you have submitted in your history with this institution, but the evidence seems to weigh

rather heavily against it. Without going into too much detail, let us say that:

a. The specimen looks like the head of a Barbie doll that a dog has chewed on.

b. Clams don't have teeth.

It is with feelings tinged with melancholy that we must deny your request to have the specimen carbon-dated. This is partially due to the heavy load our lab must bear in its normal operation, and partly due to carbon-dating's notorious inaccuracy in fossils of recent geologic record. To the best of our knowledge, no Barbie dolls were produced prior to 1956AD, and carbon-dating is likely to produce wildly inaccurate results.

Sadly, we must also deny your request that we approach the National Science Foundation Phylogeny Department with the concept of assigning your specimen the scientific name Australopithecus Back-yardicus. Speaking personally, I, for one, fought tenaciously for the acceptance of your proposed taxonomy, but was ultimately voted down because the species name you selected was hyphenated, and didn't really sound like it might be Latin.

However, we gladly accept your generous donation of this fascinating specimen to the museum. While it is undoubtedly not a Hominid fossil, it is, nonetheless, yet another riveting example of the great body of work you seem to accumulate here so effortlessly. You should know that our

Director has reserved a special shelf in his own office for the display of the specimens you have previously submitted to the Institution, and the entire staff speculates daily on what you will happen upon next in your digs at the site you have discovered in your back yard.

We eagerly anticipate your trip to our nation's capital that you proposed in your last letter, and several of us are pressing the

Director to pay for it. We are particularly interested in hearing you expand on your theories surrounding the transpositating fillifitation of ferrous metal in a structural matrix that makes the excellent juvenile tyrannosaurus rex femur you recently discovered take on the deceptive appearance of a rusty 9-mm Sears Craftsman automotive crescent wrench.

Yours in research.

The following are all replies that have been included on the Queensland Child Support Agency forms in the section for listing father's details.

- Regarding the identity of the father of my twins child A was fathered by [name removed]. I am unsure as to the identity of the father of child B, but I believe that he was conceived on the same night.

- I am unsure as to the identity of the father of my child as I was being sick out of a window when taken unexpectedly from behind. I can provide you with a list of names of men that I think were at the party if this helps.

- I do not know the name of the father of my little girl. She was conceived at a party [address and date given] where I had unprotected sex with a man I met that night. I do remember that the sex was so good that I fainted. If you do manage to track down the father can you send me his phone number? Thanks

- I don't know the identity of the father of my daughter. He drives a BMW that now has a hole made by my stiletto in one of the door panels. Perhaps you can contact BMW service stations in this area and see if he's had it replaced.

- I have never had sex. I am awaiting a letter from Pope confirming that my son's conception was immaculate and that he is Christ risen again.

- I cannot tell you the name of child A's dad as he informs me that to do so would blow his cover and that would have cataclysmic implications for the Queensland economy. I am torn between doing right by you and right by my country please advise.

- I do not know who the father of my child was as all squadies look the same to me. I can confirm that he was a Royal Green Jacket.

- [name given] is the father of child A. If you do catch up with him can you ask him what he did with my AC/DC CDs?

- From the dates it seems that my daughter was conceived at Euro Disney maybe it really is the Magic Kingdom.

- So much about that night is a blur. The only thing that I remember for sure is Master Chef did a programme about eggs earlier in the evening. If I'd have stayed in and watched more TV rather than going to the party at [address given] mine might have remained unfertilised.

From the State where drink driving is considered a sport comes a true story from the Sunshine Coast, Queensland.

Recently a routine police patrol parked outside a local neighbourhood tavern. Late in the evening the officer noticed a man leaving the bar so intoxicated that he could barely walk. The man stumbled around the car park for a few minutes, with the officer quietly observing.

After what seemed an eternity and trying his keys on five vehicles, the man managed to find his car which he fell into.

He was there for a few minutes as a number of other patrons left the bar and drove off. Finally he started the car, switched the wipers on and off (it was a fine dry night), flicked the indicators on and off, tooted the horn and then switched on the lights. He moved the vehicle forward a few inches, reversed a little and then remained stationary for a few more minutes as more patrons left in their vehicles.

At last he pulled out of the car park and started to drive slowly down the road.

The police officer, having patiently waited all this time, now started up the patrol car, put on the flashing lights, promptly pulled the man over and carried out a Breathalyser test.

To his amazement the Breathalyser indicated no evidence of the man having consumed alcohol at all!!

Dumbfounded, the officer said" I'll have to ask you to accompany me to the Police Station, this Breathalyser equipment must be broken."

"I doubt it," said the man, "Tonight I'm the designated decoy."

A young woman, down on her luck, decided to end it all one night by casting herself into the cold, dark waters of Sydney Harbour. As she stood on the edge of the dock, pondering the infinite, a young sailor noticed her as he strolled by.

"You're not thinking of jumping, are you?" he asked.

"Yes, yes I am." replied the sobbing girl.

Putting his arm around her, the kind sailor coaxed her back from the edge, "Look, nothing's worth that. I tell you what, I'm sailing off for Europe tomorrow. Why don't you stowaway on board and start a new life over there? I'll set you up in one of the lifeboats on the deck, bring you food and water every night, and I'll look after you if you 'look after' me." The girl, having no better prospects, agreed and the sailor snuck her on board that night.

For the next 3 weeks the sailor would come to her lifeboat every night, bringing food and water, and making love to her until dawn. Then, during the fourth week, the captain was performing a routine inspection of the ship & its lifeboats. He peeled back the cover to find the startled young woman and demanded an explanation. The young woman came clean.

"I've stowed away to get to Europe. One of the sailors is helping me out, he set me up in here and brings me food and water every night, and he's screwing me."

The puzzled captain stared at her for a moment before a small grin cracked his face and he replied; "He sure is, this is the Brisbane City Council!".

Be careful what you wear (or don't wear), when working under your vehicle ... especially in public.

This story of a central west couple who drove their car to Springfield, Brisbane K-Mart only to have their car break down in the parking lot.

The man told his wife to carry on with the shopping while he fixed the car. On closer inspection she saw a pair of male legs protruding from under the chassis. Although the man was in shorts, his lack of underpants turned private parts into glaringly public ones.

Unable to stand the embarrassment she dutifully stepped forward, quickly put her hand up his shorts and tucked everything back into place.

On regaining her feet she looked across the hood and found herself staring at her husband who was standing idly by.

The mechanic, however, had to have three stitches in his head.

An older Queensland gentleman marries a younger lady and they are very much in love. However, no matter what the husband does sexually, the woman never achieves orgasm. Since a Queensland wife is entitled to sexual pleasure, they decide to ask the State Government sex counsellor.

The counsellor listens to their story and makes the following suggestion. "Hire a strapping young man. While the two of you are making love, have the young man wave a towel over you. That will help the wife fantasize and should bring on an orgasm."

They go home and follow the advice. They hire a handsome young man and he waves a towel over them as they make love. But it doesn't help and she is still unsatisfied.

Perplexed, they go back to the counsellor. "Okay", says the rabbi, "let's try it reversed. Have the young man make love to your wife and you wave the towel over them."

Once again, they follow the advice. The young man gets into bed with the wife and the husband waves the towel. The young man gets to work with great enthusiasm and the wife soon has an enormous, room-shaking, screaming orgasm.

The husband smiles, looks at the young man and says to him triumphantly, "You see, that's how you wave a towel!"

Bruce took his wife Sheila to the Ekka in Brissie and one of the first exhibits they stopped at was the breeding bulls. They went up to the first pen and there was a sign attached that said, "This bull mated 50 times last year." Sheila playfully nudged Bruce in the ribs and said, "He mated 50 times last year."

They walked to the second pen which had a sign attached that said, "This bull mated 120 times last year." Sheila gave Bruce a healthy jab and said, "That's more than twice a week! You could learn a lot from him."

They walked to the third pen and it had a sign attached that said, in capital letters, "This bull mated 365 times last year." Sheila, so excited that her elbow nearly broke Bruce's ribs, said, that's once a day, you could really learn something from this one."

Bruce looked at her and said, "Go over and ask him if all those times it was with the same old cow."

Ad in Queensland' Courier Mail newspaper –

Important Notice - see if you can do this

Read each line aloud

This is this cat

This is is cat

This is how cat

This is to cat

This is keep cat

This is a cat

This is dumbass cat

This is busy cat

This is for cat

This is forty cat

This is seconds cat

Now go back and read the third word in each line from the top.

The Queensland Government is concerned that some individuals working for the government have been using foul language to other employees during the execution of their duties. Due to the complaints from some other employees who are more easily offended, this type of language will no longer be tolerated.

However we do realise the importance of staff being able to clearly express their feelings when communicating with other employees.

With this in mind the Queensland Department of Human Resource has compiled a list of code phrases requirements so that the proper exchange of ideas and information can continue in an effective manner without risking offence to our sensitive co-workers.

Old Phrase	New Phrase
No fucking way	I'm fairly sure that's not feasible
You're fucking kidding	Really
Tell someone who gives a fuck	Have you run this by the boss
No cunt told me	I wasn't involved on that project
I won't have no fucking time	Perhaps I can work late
Who fucking cares	Are you sure that's a problem
Eat shit and die	You don't say
Eat shit you mother fucker	You don't say sir

Q is for Queensland

Kiss my fucking ass	Well there you go
She's a ball busting bitch	She's an aggressive go-getter
You haven't got a fucking clue	You're the supervisor and I respect you
This place is fucked	We're a little disorganised today
What sort of fuck wit are you	You could use more training
Fuck off shit head	I no longer require your assistance
You're a fucking wanker*	You're new here aren't you?
Fuck off	I'm fairly sure that's not feasible
Fuck off dick head	My apologies, however I can't seem to get motivated to assist you today
How'd you get this piece of shit work	Have you run this by the boss
You lying prick	Could you clarify that for me
What are you fucking doing	Are you within your delegation
You fucking loser	Are you sure that's a problem
Those fuckers fucked up my pay	Gee, that was unfortunate**

*Bucket mouth may be used to replace wankers

**If you work for the Department of Health, you may continue using the old phrase

An elderly couple is vacationing in Western Queensland. Sam always wanted a pair of authentic RW Williams cowboy boots. Seeing some on sale one day, he buys them, wears them home, walking proudly. Upon arriving home, he walks into their room and says to his wife, "Notice anything different, Bessie?"

Bessie looks him over, "Nope."

Sam says excitedly, "Come on, Bessie, take a good look. Notice anything different about me?"

Bessie looks again, "Nope."

Frustrated, Sam storms off into the bathroom, undresses, and walks back into the room completely naked except for his boots. Again, he asks, a little louder this time, "Notice anything different?"

Bessie looks up and says, "Sam, what's different? It's hanging down today, it was hanging down yesterday, and it'll be hanging down again tomorrow."

Furious, Sam yells, "AND DO YOU KNOW WHY IT IS HANGING DOWN, BESSIE? IT'S HANGING DOWN BECAUSE IT'S LOOKING AT MY NEW BOOTS!!!"

To which Bessie replies, "Should have bought a hat, Sam. Should have bought a hat".

The Ferrari F1 Team recently fired the whole Pit-Crew to employ some young unemployed youths from the Inala – Forest Lake Area. The decision to hire them was brought on by a documentary on how unemployed youth in the area can remove a set of car wheels in less than 6 seconds without proper equipment.

This was thought to be a good move as most races are won & lost in the pits these days & Ferrari would have an advantage.

However Ferrari soon encountered a major problem not only were "the boyz" changing the tyres in under 6 seconds, but within 12 seconds they had resprayed, rebadged and sold the vehicle to the McLaren Team.

Three guys - a Tasmanian, a New South Welshman & a Queenslander are out walking along the beach together one day. They come across a lantern and after a gentle rub a genie pops out of it.

"I will give you each one wish, that's three wishes total", says the genie.

'The Tasmanian says, "I am a fisherman, my dad's a fisherman, his dad was a fisherman and my son will be one too. I want all the oceans full of fish for all eternity.

"With a blink of the genie's eye, 'FOOM' the oceans were teeming with fish.

The New South Welshman was amazed, so he said, "I want a wall around New South Wales so that we can run our own State how we feel, and no boofhead, south or north of the border can tell us what to do in our State. I want it so nothing and no-one will get in for all eternity."

Again, with a blink of the genie's eye, 'POOF' there was a huge wall around New South Wales.

"The Queenslander asks, "I'm very curious. Please tell me more about this wall."

The genie explains, "Well, it's about 150 feet high, 50 feet thick and nothing can get in or out."

"The Queenslander says, "Fill it up with water."

CHAPTER 18

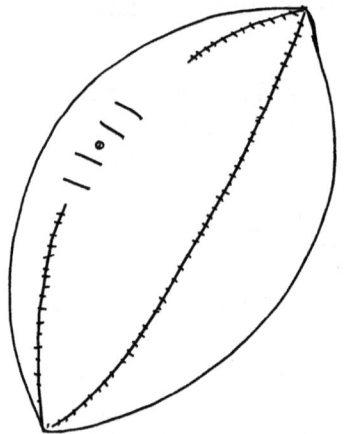

R is for Rugby

Q: What is the function of the All Black coach?

A: To transport the team from the hotel to the ground.

Q: What's the All Black version of a hat-trick?

A: Conceding three tries in three minutes.

Q: Why don't the All Black backline need pre-tour travel injections?

A: Because they never catch anything.

Q: What's the most proficient form of footwork displayed by the All Black backline?

A: The walk back to the dressing room.

Q: What do the All Blacks and drug addicts have in common?

A: Both spend most of their time wondering where their next score will come from.

The seven dwarves are down in the mines when there is a cave-in.

Snow White runs to the entrance and yells down to them. In the distance a voice shouts out says- New Zealand are good enough to win the World Cup. Snow White says, well at least Dopey's alive!

Q: How does John Hart change a light bulb?

A: He holds it in the air, and the world revolves around him.

A man desperate at the All Blacks current situation decides to top himself. In his living room, alone, he prepares to hang himself. At the very last moment, he decides upon wearing his full All Black kit as his last statement.

A neighbour, catching sight of the impending incident, informs the police. On arrival, the police quickly remove the Jersey and dress the man in stockings and suspenders. The man, totally confused asks why. The policeman simply replies, it's to avoid embarrassing your family.

Rumour has it that the All Blacks have got a new sponsor: Tampax.

The NZRB thought it was an appropriate change as the team is going through a very bad period.

When I was studying in New Zealand, I took up rugby. As my first season wore on, the lads and I were eventually scheduled to play a team which had a reputation for violent play considering that we weren't the most talented outfit to have ever taken the field, we decided to accept the challenge with a "do or die" attitude hoping things would eventually swing our way.

They didn't and to make matters worse our star player Alan dislocated his hip after a particularly ferocious tackle. He was clearly in a lot of pain, so we all stood back to watch the medic who, in one swift movement, managed to slot the hip back into place.

There was a long blood-curdling scream. To our horror, we realised that one of his testicles had also been jammed into the socket and was now firmly held in the place by the hip. Incidentally, Alan managed to rip a vocal chord with his screaming.

The All Blacks were playing England and after the half time whistle blew they found themselves up by 90 points to nil with Jonah Lomu scoring 8 tries on his own. The rest of the team decided to go down to the pub instead of playing the second half and told Jonah that he was on his own.

No problems- Jonah told the captain, -I'll come down after the game and report back. Well, after the game Jonah found the rest of the team at the pub." What was the final score Jonah? - asked one of the players. -It ended up 95 points to 3. What!!!!! Exclaimed the captain...." How did you let them get 3 points????- To which Jonah replied...." I got sent off with 20 minutes to go."

An All Black fan dies on match day and goes to heaven in his All Black jumper.

He knocks on the old pearly gates and out walks St Peter in a Wallabies scarf.

"Hello, mate," says St Peter, "I'm sorry, no All Black fans in heaven."

"What?" exclaims the man, astonished. "You heard. No All Black fans."

"But, but, but, I've been a good man," replies the All Black supporter.

Oh, really?" says St Peter. "What have you done then?"

"Well," says the guy, "three weeks before I died, I gave 20 bucks to the starving children in Africa."

"Oh," says St Peter. "Anything else?"

"Well, two weeks before I died, I also gave 20 bucks to the homeless."

"Hmm. Anything else?"

"Yeah. A week before I died, I gave 20 bucks to the Albanian orphans."

"Okay," says St Peter, "you wait here a minute while I have a word with the boss."

Ten minutes pass before St Peter returns. He looks the bloke in the eye and says, "I've had a word with God and he agrees with me.

Here's your sixty bucks back, now fuck off."

A little boy from Australia had gone to Rome on holiday with his family hoping to see the Pope. A couple of days after they'd arrived, the Pope was doing a tour of the city in his Pope mobile.

The little lad was a bit worried that the Pope wouldn't be able to pick him out in the crowd, so his Mum said "Don't worry, the Pope is a rugby fan, so wear your Wallaby top and he's bound to pick you out and talk to you."

So, they're in the crowd, but the Pope mobile drives past them, and stops a bit further down the street where John Paul gets out and speaks to a little kiwi boy in an All Blacks Rugby top. The lad is distraught and starts crying. His Mum says "Don't worry, the Pope's driving around tomorrow as well, so we'll get you an All Blacks top and then he's bound to stop to see you."

The next day arrives, and the Aussie boy's got on his new All Blacks top. The Pope mobile stops right by him, John Paul gets out, bends down and says to the lad "I thought I told you yesterday to fuck off".

Rugby culture

Seeing how the All Blacks were motivated by performing "The Haka" before their rugby world cup games, the other nations were asked to suggest pre-match rituals of their own.

The England team will chat about the weather, wave hankies in the air and attach bells to their ankles for a while before moaning about how they invented the game, and gave it to the world, and how it's not fair that everyone can beat them now.

The Scotland team will chant "You lookin' at me Jimmy?" before smashing a beer bottle over their opponents heads.

The Ireland team will spilt into two, with the Southern half performing a Riverdance, while the Northerners march the Traditional route from their dressing room to the pitch, via their opponents' dressing room.

Unfortunately the Welsh suggestion has been vetoed by the RSPCA.

Argentina will unexpectedly invade a small part of opposition territory claim it as their own "Las In-Goals-Areas" and then be forcibly removed by the Stewards.

Two members of the South African team will claim to be more important than the other thirteen whom they will coral between the posts whilst they claim the rest of the pitch for themselves.

The Americans will not be there until half time. In future years they will alter the records to show that they were in fact the most important team in the tournament and Hollywood will make a film called "Saving No 8 Lyle".

Five of the Canadian team will sing La Marsaillaise and hold the rest of the side to ransom.

The Italian team will arrive in red penis substituting cars, sexually harass the female stewards and then run away.

The Spanish will sneak into the other half of the pitch mow it and then claim that it was all in line with the European "grass quotas."

They will then curl up under the posts and have a kip until half time.

The Japanese will attempt to strengthen their team by offering good salaries to the key opposition players (over 35) and then run around the pitch at high speed in a highly efficient manner before buying the ground (with a subsidy from the UK Government).

The French will declare they have new scientific evidence that the opposition are in fact all mad. They will then park Lorries across the halfway line, let sheep loose In the opposition half and burn the officials.

The Australians will have a barbie before negotiating lucrative singing and TV contracts in the UK. They will invite their mates to come and live with them in Shepherds Bush before beating up all the women on the touchline.

A man had tickets for the Rugby World Cup Final. As he sits down, a man comes down and asks if anyone is sitting in the seat next to him.

"No", he says, "The seat is empty."

"This is incredible," said the man.

"Who in their right mind would have a seat like this for the World Cup Final, the biggest sporting event in the world, and not use it?"

He says "Well, actually, the seat belongs to me. I was supposed to come with my wife, but she passed away. This is the first Rugby Final we haven't been together since we got married in 1987".

"Oh ... I'm sorry to hear that. That's terrible. But couldn't you find someone else - a friend or relative, or even a neighbour to take the seat?"

The man shakes his head." No. They're all at the funeral."

Official proof that the world is a crazy place - this is just bonkers....

On Sunday 14th March this year, Spain played Romania at home in the first of the IRB Rugby World Cup European Zone preliminaries. The other team in the group is Portugal. The idea is that the 3 teams play each other to see who goes into the seed pool (decided after this year's World Cup) for the next world cup. They play home and away so 6 games in all.

Halfway through the first half the Spanish prop forward Iganez was sent off for stamping on the Romanian fly half Corin Abrazu. The Romanian was taken off the field for treatment to two wounds, a head wound and a leg wound. After the physio had tried to staunch the flow of blood to the head wound, (and failed) he called for an ambulance to get Abrazu into hospital. At the hospital, a broken knife blade was removed from Abrazu's leg. He was allowed home from hospital and flew home a few days later.

Iganez was arrested for attempted murder by the Spanish Police in Pamplona. Iganez has continually denied any wrong doing (and video evidence supports this).

Last week Abrazu withdrew from the Rumanian team to play Portugal, complaining of headaches. It was thought he had banged his head in a club match the previous weekend. He collapsed at his home, and was rushed to hospital. X-Rays showed a .22 calibre bullet lodged in his brain. The entrance wound had been stitched by a Spanish doctor in belief that it had been caused by a boot stud.

Iganez was then questioned by Spanish police about the bullet.... The truth is always so much more surreal. Apparently, Abrazu had received death threats before the Spanish game via post (the letter was sent from Cadiz). He laughed them off until fifteen minutes into the game he felt what he thought was a bee sting on the back of his head. He felt the wound and found that he was bleeding. Not knowing what had happened, he continued until four minutes later when the incident with Iganez occurred.

Iganez plays for Bilbao in the Basque country. He had received a letter before the match saying that unless he helped with the murder of Abrazu, his family would be murdered. He was told that someone on the pitch would kill the Romanian. All he had to do was to "rough up" the Romanian to allow a doctor on to the pitch. This is what he was attempting to do when he was called aside by the ref. Only, he had done nothing up to that point.

Spanish authorities, investigating the incidents found that:

1. Abrazu was targeted because he had been "seeing" (euphemism) Inja Felipe de Compostilla ... (the ETA bosses daughter (ETA being the Basque extremists), the year before while he played for Spain. She was up the duff.

2. The knife wound was administered by a stretcher assistant, the knife used is an ETA speciality called a "Juanez", where the blade is intended to break inside the wound.
3. The bullet was fired from the crowd by a hired assassin hired by Inja Felipe de Campostilla because she was up the duff ....

Complicated or what ....

also

All of the suspects have now been rounded up. Spanish Authorities want to extradite Abrazu, since the young Lady in question is just 14 the years old...

CHAPTER 19

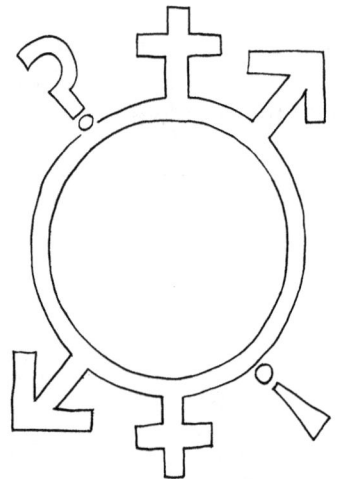

S is for Sex

There were three young priests about to take their final vows. The last test that they had to pass was the CELIBACY test. For this, all three had to strip naked and tie a little bell around their penises. A belly dancer entered the room, and started slinking around the first priest. "Ting-a-ling."

The chief priest said "Oh, Patrick, I'm so disappointed, you've failed. Go and have a shower."

The belly dancer had stripped as far as her last veil for the second guy when the chief priest heard. "Ting-a-ling." "Joseph, I'm very disappointed. You can't resist the temptation of a woman. Go for a shower," said the chief priest.

The belly dancer started dancing totally naked now around the last priest. She did everything erotic she could think of ... but no bell rang!

James, I'm delighted. You've passed! You can resist the temptation of women. Now, go relax and take a shower with Patrick and Joseph.

"Ting-a-ling"...

A bloke picks this girl up in a bar, one thing leads to another and he ends up going back to her house.

°Once inside her bedroom he was surprised to see a whole wall-unit FULL of soft toys, from the floor to the ceiling. Everything from the Pink Panther to Winnie the Pooh.

After a night of passion he asks her "so, how was it?"

She says "Well, put it this way, You can have anything on the bottom shelf!"

A very confident James Bond walks into a bar and takes a seat next to a very attractive woman. He gives her a quick glance, then casually looks at his watch for a moment. The woman notices this and asks, is your date running late? No, he replies, Q's just given me this state-of-the-art watch and I was just testing it.

The intrigued woman says, a state-of-the-art watch? What's so special about it?

Bond explains, it uses alpha waves to talk to me telepathically.

The lady says, what's it telling you now?

Well, it says you're not wearing any knickers.

The woman giggles and replies, well it must be broken because I am wearing knickers!

Bond tuts, taps his watch, and says, Damn thing's an hour fast.

On July 20, 1969, as commander of the Apollo 11 Lunar Module, Neil Armstrong was the first person to set foot on the moon. His first words after stepping on the moon, that's one small step for a man, one giant leap for mankind, were televised to Earth and heard by millions.

But just before he re-entered the lander, he made the enigmatic remark: Good luck, Mr Gorsky. Many people at NASA thought it was a casual remark concerning some rival Soviet Cosmonaut. However, upon checking, there was no Gorsky in either the Russian or American space programs.

Over the years many people questioned Armstrong as to what the Good luck Mr Gorsky statement meant, but Armstrong always just smiled. On July 5, 1995, in Tampa Bay, Florida, while answering questions following a speech, a reporter brought up the 26 year old question to Armstrong. This time he finally responded. Mr Gorsky had died and so Neil Armstrong felt he could answer the question.

In 1938 when he was a kid in a small Midwest town, he was playing baseball with a friend in the backyard. His friend hit a fly ball, which landed in his neighbour's yard by the bedroom windows. His neighbours were Mr and Mrs Gorsky.

As he leaned down to pick up the ball, young Armstrong heard Mrs Gorsky shouting at Mr Gorsky. Sex! You want sex?! You'll get sex when the kid next door walks on the moon…!!!

The pope had become very ill and was taken to many doctors, whom could not figure out how to cure him. Finally he was brought to an old physician, who stated that he could figure it out.

After about an hour's examination he came out and told the cardinals that he knew what was wrong. He said that the bad news was that it was °a rare disorder of the testicles. He said that the good news was that all the pope had to do to be cured was to have sex.

Well, this was not good news to the cardinals, who argued about it at length. Finally they went to the pope with the doctor and explained the situation.

After some thought, the pope stated, "I agree, but under four conditions."

The cardinals were amazed and there arose quite an uproar. Over all of the noise there arose a single voice that asked, "And what are the four conditions?"

The room stilled. There was a long pause … The pope replied, "First the girl must be blind, so that she cannot see with whom she is having sex."

"Second, she must be deaf, so that she cannot hear with whom she is having sex."

"And third she must be dumb so that if somehow she figures out with who she is having sex, she can tell no one."

After another long pause a voice arose and asked, "And the fourth condition?"

"Fucking huge tits," he replied.

A cabbie picks up a nun. She gets into the cab, and the cab driver won't stop staring at her.

She asks him why he is starting and he replies "I have a question to ask you but I don't want to offend you."

She answers, "My dear son, you cannot offend me, when you're as old as I have been a nun a long as I have, you get a chance to see and hear just about everything. I'm sure that there's nothing you could say or ask that I would find offensive."

"Well, I've always had a fantasy to have a nun kiss me."

She responds, "Well, let's see what we can do about that: #1. you have to be single and #2. you have to be Catholic."

The cab driver is very excited and says, "Yes, I am single and I'm Catholic."

The nun says "OK, pull into the next alley."

He does and the nun fulfils his fantasy. But when they get back on the road, the cab driver starts crying.

"My dear child, said the nun, why are you crying?"

"Forgive me sister, but I have sinned. I lied, I must confess, I'm married and I'm Jewish."

The nun says, "That's OK, my name is Bruce and I'm on my way to a Halloween party."

Steve is shopping for a new motorcycle.

He finally finds one for a great price, but it's missing a seat. So whenever it rains, he has to smear Vaseline over the spot where the seat should be.

Anyway, his girlfriend is having him over for dinner to meet her parents. He drives his new bike to her house, where she is outside waiting for him.

No matter what happens at dinner tonight, don't say a word, she tells him. Our family had a fight a while ago about doing dishes. We have not done any since, but the first person to speak at dinner has to do them. Steve sits down for dinner and it is just how she described it.

Dishes are piled up to the ceiling in the kitchen and nobody is saying a word. So Steve decides to have a little fun. He grabs his girlfriend, throws her on the table and has sex with her in front of her parents. His girlfriend is a little flustered, her dad is obviously livid, and her mum horrified when he sits back down, but no one says a word.

A few minutes later, he grabs her mum, throws her on the table and does a repeat performance. Now his girlfriend is furious, her dad is boiling, and her mother is a little happier. But still there is complete silence at the table. All of a sudden, there is a loud clap of thunder, and it starts to rain. Steve remembers his motorcycle. He jumps up and grabs his jar of Vaseline.

Upon witnessing this, his girlfriend's father backs away from the table and screams OKAY ENOUGH ALREADY, I'll DO THE DAMN DISHES…!!

When Bill and Hillary first got married, Bill said, "I am putting a box under our bed. You must promise never to look in it." In all their 30 years of marriage, Hillary never looked. However, on the afternoon of their 30th anniversary, curiosity got the better of her and she lifted the lid and peeked inside. In the box there were 3 empty beer cans and $1,874.25 in cash.

After dinner, Hillary could no longer contain her guilt and she confessed, saying, "I am so sorry. For all these years I kept my promise and never looked in the box under our bed. However, today the temptation was too much and I gave in. But now I need to know why do you keep the empty cans in the box?"

Bill thought for a while and said, "I guess that after all these years you deserve to know the truth. Whenever I was unfaithful to you, I put an empty beer can in the box under the bed to remind myself not to do it again."

Hillary was shocked, but said, "I am very disappointed and saddened, but I guess after all those years away from home on the road, temptation does happen and I guess that 3 times is not that bad considering the number of years we've been together."

They hugged and made their peace. A little while later, Hillary asked Bill, "why do you have all that money in the box?"

Bill answered, "Well, whenever the box filled up with empty cans, I took them to the recycling centre and redeemed them for cash."

A girl goes to the doctor's office for a check-up. As she takes off her blouse, he notices a red "H" on her chest.

"How did you get that mark on your chest?", asks the doctor.

"Oh my boyfriend went to Harvard and he's so proud of it that he never takes off his sweatshirt, even when we make love", she replies.

A couple of days later, another girl comes in for a check-up. As she takes off her blouse, he notices a blue "Y" on her chest.

"How did you get that mark on your chest?" asks the doctor.

"Oh my boyfriend went to Yale and he's so proud of it that he never takes off his sweatshirt, even when we make love", she replies.

A couple of days later, another girl comes in for a check-up. As she takes off her blouse, he notices a green "M" on her chest.

"Do you have a boyfriend at Michigan?" asks the doctor.

She replies, "No, but I have a girlfriend at Wisconsin. Why do you ask?"

An old lady is rocking away the last of her days on her front porch, reflecting on her long life, when—all of a sudden—a fairy godmother appears in front of her and informs her that she will be granted three wishes.

"Well, now," says the old lady, "I guess I would like to be really rich." Her rocking chair turns to solid gold.

"And, gee, I guess I wouldn't mind being a young, beautiful princess." She turns into a beautiful young woman.

"Your third wish?" asked the fairy godmother. Just then the old woman's cat wanders across the porch in front of them.

"Ooh—can you change him into a handsome prince?" she asks.

There before her stands a young man more handsome than anyone could possibly imagine.

She stares at him, smitten. With a smile that makes her knees weak, he saunters across the porch and whispers in her ear:

"I bet you're sorry you had me neutered."

A priest and a rabbi found themselves sharing a compartment on a train. After a while, the priest put down his book and opened a conversation by saying, I know that, in your religion, you're not supposed to eat pork ... but have you really never even tasted it?

The rabbi closed his newspaper and responded, I must tell you the truth.

Yes I have, on the odd occasion." The rabbi had his turn of interrogation. He asked, I know that in your religion, you're supposed to be celibate ... but ...

The priest interjected, "Yes, I know what you are going to ask, and yes, I have succumbed to temptation once or twice.

The two resumed their reading. There was silence for a while.

Then the rabbi peeked around his newspaper with a smile and said, "Better than pork, isn't it!"

A social misfit walks into his local pub with a big grin on his face. 'What are you so happy about?' asks the Barman.

"Well, I'll tell You, replies the ugly bloke, you know I live by the railway, on my way home last night I noticed a young woman tied to the tracks, like in the movies. I, of course, went and cut her free and took her back to my place. Anyway, to cut a long story short, I scored big time! We made love all night, all over the house. We did everything, me on top sometimes, her on top!"

"Fantastic, exclaimed the barman, you lucky sod. Was she pretty?"

"I dunno replied the bloke, I never found her head."

A blind man walks into a restaurant and sits down. The waiter who is also the owner, walks up to the blind man and hands him a menu. I'm sorry sir, I am blind and can't read the menu. Just bring me a dirty fork from previous customer, I'll smell it and order from there.

A little confused, the owner walks over to the dish pile and picks up a greasy fork. He returns to the blind man's table and hands it to him. The man puts the fork up to his nose and takes in a deep breath. "oh yes that's what I'll have, meat loaf and mashed potatoes." Unbelievable the owner says to himself as he walks towards the kitchen. The cook happens to be the owner's wife and he tells her what just happened.

The blind man eats his meal and leaves. Several days later the blind man returns and the owner mistakenly brings him a menu again. "Sir, remember me? I'm the blind man."

"I'm sorry, I didn't recognize you, I'll go get a dirty fork."

The owner again retrieves a dirty fork and brings it to the blind man. After another deep breath, the blind man says, "That smells great, I'll take the macaroni and cheese with broccoli."

Once again walking in disbelief, the owner thinks the blind man is screwing around with him and tells his wife that the next time the blind man comes in he's going to test him. The blind man eats and leaves. He returns the following week, but this time the owner sees him coming and runs to the kitchen. He tells his wife, "Mary rub this fork on your panties before I take it to the blind man."

Mary complies and hands her husband the fork back. As the blind man walks in and sits down, the owner is ready and waiting.

"Good afternoon sir, this time I remembered you and I already have the fork ready for you" The blind man puts the fork to his nose, takes a deep whiff and says, "Hey I didn't know Mary worked here?"

This big, nasty, sweaty woman, wearing a sleeveless sundress, walks into a bar. She raises her right arm, revealing a big, hairy armpit as she points to all the people sitting at the bar and asks, "What man out there will buy a lady a drink?" The whole bar goes dead silent, as the patrons try to ignore her.

At the end of the bar, a skinny little drunk slams his hand on the bar and says, "Bartender! I want to buy that ballerina a drink!" The bartender pours the drink and the woman chugs it down.

After she's completed the drink, she turns again to the patrons and points around at all of them, again revealing her hairy armpit, saying, "What man out there will buy a lady a drink?" Once again, the little drunk slaps his hand down on the bar and says, "Bartender! I'd like to buy the ballerina another drink!"

After serving the lady her second drink, the bartender approaches the little drunk and says, "It's your business if you want to buy the lady a drink, but why do you call her a ballerina?" The drunk replies, "Sir! In my eyes, any woman who can lift her leg up that high has got to be a ballerina."

An obese fellow was reading the paper one day lamenting the fact that his doctor has ordered him to lose 75 pounds.

Next thing he sees is an advertisement for a "guaranteed" weight loss program. "Guaranteed like heck" he thinks to himself. "But let's see what they think they can do."

He calls them on the phone and subscribes to the 3-day, 10 lbs. weight loss program.

The next day there comes a knock at his door, and when he answers, there stands before him a voluptuous, athletic 19 year old babe dressed in nothing but a pair of Nike's and a sign hanging around her neck. She introduces herself as a representative of the weight loss company.

The sign reads, "If you can catch me, you can have me."

Well, without a second thought he takes off after her. A few miles later, huffing and puffing, he finally catches her and has his way with her. After they are through the kisses the girl one last time and thinks to himself with a nod.

"I like the way this company does business."

For the next two days, the same girl shows up and the same thing happens each time. On the fourth day, he weighs himself and, sure enough, he has lost 10 pounds.

Deciding that he likes his somewhat more slender physique, not to mention the method of "treatment", he calls the company back and subscribes to their 5-day, 20 lbs. weight loss program. He thinks that losing 20 pounds in only 5 days seems like a lot, but he is intrigued by what their "workout" schedule might be like this time.

As expected, the next day there comes a knock at his door. When he answers it there stands a 22 year old knockout dressed in nothing but a pair of Reebok's and a sign hanging around her neck. She is simply stunning, the most beautiful woman he has ever seen. She introduces herself as a representative of the weight loss company.

The sign reads, "If you can catch me, you can have me." He's out the door like a shot!

This gal is in excellent shape and it takes a while to catch her. But when he does, it is worth every cramp and wheeze. She is wonderful, the best he has ever had. He is really looking forward to the next four days.

For the next four days, the same girl shows up and the same thing happens each time, much to his delight. On the sixth day, he weighs himself and unbelievably, he has lost another 20 pounds.

"I love this company," he thinks to himself, "I never knew losing weight could be so easy and so much fun."

Feeling much better about himself, he decides to go for broke and subscribe to the company's 7-day, 50 pound weight loss program.

"Are you sure, sir?" asks the representative on the phone. "This is our most rigorous program."

"Absolutely," says he, "I love your program. Haven't felt this good in years!"

The next day there comes a knock at his door and he enthusiastically answers it. There stands before him a 200 pound perfect specimen of a man dressed in nothing but racing spikes and a sign around his neck.

He introduces himself as a representative of the weight loss company. The sign reads, "If I can catch you, I can have you."

After a long night of making love the young guy rolled over, pulled out cigarette from his jeans and searched for his lighter. Unable to find it, he asked the girl if she had one at hand.

"There might be some matches in the top drawer," she replied. He opened the drawer of the bedside table and found a box of matches setting neatly on top of a framed picture of another man. Naturally, the guy began to worry.

"Is this your husband?" he inquired nervously. "No, silly," she replied, snuggling up to him. "Your boyfriend then?" he asked.

"No, not at all," she said, nibbling away at his ear.

"Well, who is he then?" demanded the bewildered guy.

Calmly the girl replied, "That's just a photo of me before the operation."

A rich couple was going out for the evening. The lady of the house decided to give the butler, Throckmorton, the night off. She said they would be home very late and he should just enjoy his evening. As it turned out, the wife didn't have a good time at the party, so she came home early. She walked into the house and eyed Throckmorton sitting alone in the dining room. She called for him to follow her and led him to the master bedroom where she closed and locked the door.

There, the woman looked at him and smiled. "Throckmorton. Take off my dress." He did so, carefully. "Throckmorton. Take off my stockings and garter." He silently obeyed. "Throckmorton. Remove my bra and panties." The tension mounted as he complied.

Finally she looked at him and said, "Throckmorton, if I ever catch you wearing my clothes again, you're fired."

I take it that bus passes have photographs on them.

This appeared in Sky Magazine a few months ago—who says the 90's man isn't caring and sensitive.

From Laura. 24:

Last year at a Christmas party. I got off with this gorgeous bloke called Mark Digby. He was a real arrogant git. But I've always been attracted to bastards. Little did I know this bloke was the biggest shit imaginable?

We went back to my place and he pounced on me straight away. Within minutes, he was shagging me frantically from behind on the sofa. I began to think that doing it that way was really impersonal in this drunken state. But Mark just carried on regardless. I tried to move round myself, but he held me in place grunting something about his jeans around his ankles making it difficult to move.

I was getting well cheesed off and I could feel he was about to finish.

I suddenly found myself groaning, "I want to see your face as you come".

I felt him reach down into his pocket and just as he reached orgasm, he thrust his bus pass in front of my face. I stared miserably at a bus pass of the git as he shot his load behind me.

Subject: Top 10 Reasons To Go To Work Naked—(actually 11)

1. Your boss is always yelling, "I wanna see your ass in here by 8.00."
2. Can take advantage of computer monitor radiation to work on your tan.
3. Inventive way to finally meet that hottie in Human Resources.
4. "I'd love to chip in, but I left my wallet in my pants."
5. To stop those creepy guys in Marketing from looking down yourblouse.
6. You want to see if it's like the dream.

7. So that, with a little help from Muzak, you can add "Exotic Dancer" to your exaggerated resume.

8. People stop stealing your pens after they've seen where you keep them.

9. Diverts attention from the fact that you also came to work stoned.

10. Gives "bad hair day" a whole new meaning.

11. No one steals your chair.

A young single guy finds himself stranded on a deserted island. As he washes ashore, he sees a women passed out in the sand. Able to perform CPR on her, he saves her life. Suddenly, he realizes that the woman is Cindy Crawford. Immediately, Cindy falls in love with the man. Days and weeks go by, and they're making passionate love morning, noon and night. True Heaven on earth in the man's eyes. Alas, one day she notices he's looking kind of glum.

"What's the matter, sweetheart?" she asks. "We have a wonderful life together and I'm in love with you. Is there something wrong? Is there anything I can do?"

He says, "Actually, Cindy, there is. Would you mind, putting on my shirt and pants?" "Sure," she says, "if it'll help." He takes off his shirt and pants and she puts it on. "Okay, would you put on my hat now, and draw a little moustache on your face?" he asks. "Whatever you want, sweetie," she says, and does so.

Then he says, "Now, would you start walking around the edge of the island?" She starts walking around the perimeter of the island. He sets off in the other direction. They meet up half way around the island a few minutes later.

He rushes up to her, grabs her by the shoulders, and says, "Dude! You'll never believe who I'm sleeping with!"

The Smiths had no children and decided to use a proxy father to start their family. On the day the proxy father was to arrive, Mr Smith kissed his wife and said, "I'm off. The man should be here soon".

Half an hour later, just by chance, a door-to-door baby photographer rang the doorbell, hoping to make a sale.

"Good morning madam. You don't know me, but I've come to...."

"No, no need to explain. I've been expecting you," Mrs. Smith cut in." Really?" the photographer asked. "Well, good! I've made a specialty of babies."

"That's what my Husband and I had hoped. Please come in and have a seat. Just where do we start?" asked Mrs Smith, blushing.

"Leave everything to me. I usually try two in the bathtub, one on the couch and perhaps a couple on the bed. Sometimes the living room floor is fun too, you can really spread out."

"Bathtub, living room floor? No wonder it didn't work for Harry and me." "Well, madam, none of us can guarantee a good one every time. But if we try several different positions and I shoot from six or seven angles, I'm sure you'll be pleased with the results."

"I hope we can get this over with quickly," gasped Mrs Smith.

Madam, in my line of work, a man must take his time. I'd love to be in and out in five minutes, but you'd be disappointed with that, I'm sure."

"Don't I know!!?" Mrs Smith exclaimed.

The photographer opened his briefcase and pulled out a portfolio of his baby pictures. "This was done on the top of a bus in downtown London."

"Oh my God!!" Mrs Smith exclaimed, tugging at her handkerchief.

"And these twins turned out exceptionally well when you consider their mother was so difficult to work with." The photographer handed Mrs Smith the picture.

"She was difficult?" asked Mrs Smith.

"Yes, I'm afraid so I finally had to take her to Hyde Park to get the job done right. People were crowding around four and five deep, pushing to get a good look."

"Four and five deep?" asked Mrs Smith, eyes widened in amazement.

"Yes," the photographer said. "And for more than three hours too. The mother was constantly squealing and yelling. I could hardly concentrate. Then darkness approached and I began to rush my shots. Finally, when the squirrels began nibbling on my equipment I just packed it all in."

Mrs Smith leaned forward. "You mean they actually chewed on your, er .., um.., ah .... equipment?"

"That's right. Well madam, if you're ready, I'll set up my tripod so that we can get to work."

"Tripod??" Mrs Smith looked extremely worried now.

"Oh yes, I have to use a tripod to rest my Canon on. It's much too big for me to hold while I'm getting ready for action. Madam? Madam? Good Lord, she's fainted!!"

A guy in a balaclava bursts into a sperm bank with a shotgun.

'Open the fucking safe' he yells at the girl behind the counter.' But we're not a real bank' she replies, 'we don't have any money, this is a sperm bank'

'Don't argue, open the fucking safe or I'll blow your head off' says the guy with the gun.

She obliges and once she's opened the safe door the guy says 'Take out one of the bottles and drink it.'

'But it's full of sperm!' she replies nervously. 'Don't argue, just drink it' he says.

She prises the cap off and gulps it down.

'Take out another one and drink it too' he demands. She takes out another and drinks it as well.

Suddenly the guy pulls off the balaclava and to the girl's amazement it's her husband.

'There,' he says 'it's not that fucking difficult is it!?!"

There's a pensioner couple on holiday, back in the place where they first met.

They're sitting in the pub and he says to her:

"Remember our first time together, almost fifty years ago? We went round the corner to the gasworks. You leaned against the fence and I gave you one from behind." "Yes", she says, "I remember it well". "OK", he says, "how about taking a stroll round there and I'll give you one again—for old times' sake".

"Sounds good to me", she answers.

There's a bloke sitting at the next table listening to all this, having a chuckle to himself and thinking, I've got to see this, two pensioners having sex against the gasworks fence. So he follows them out.

They get to the gas works, she lifts her skirt, takes her knickers down and leans against the fence. He takes her from behind and goes hell for leather like an eighteen year-old.

The other chap is peeping round the corner at this, thinking "F**k's sake, he can half go for a pensioner!" After about forty minutes, the old couple finish and get their clothes back on. The guy watching thinks "That was amazing, he was going like a train. I've got to ask him what his secret is".

As the couple pass by, he says, "That was something else, you must have been shagging for about forty minutes. How do you manage it, what's your secret?"

"No secret", the man says breathlessly, "but fifty years ago that f**king fence wasn't electrified."

A guy walks into a bar with an octopus. He sits the octopus down on a stool and tells everyone in the bar that this is a very talented octopus. "He can play any musical instrument in the world."

Everyone in the bar laughs at the man, calling him an idiot.

So he says that he will wager $50 to everyone who has an instrument that the octopus can't play.

A guy walks up with a guitar and sets it beside the octopus. Immediately the octopus picks up the guitar and starts playing better than Jimi Hendrix. The guitar man pays up his $50.

Another guy walks up with a trumpet. This time the octopus plays the trumpet better than Miles Davis. This guy pays up his $50.

Then a Scotsman walks up with some bagpipes. He sits them down and the octopus fumbles with it for a minute and then sits down with a confused look. "Ha" the Scot says. "Can ye nae plae it?"

The octopus looks up at him and says, "Play it? I'm going to fuck it as soon as I figure out how to get its pyjamas off!"

There was this old man who everyday would go to the central park in his town and sit on the park bench by the lake.

He would just sit there and do nothing, watch people go by, until one day an old lady came and sat next to him.

And every day for the next week, the old lady would turn up at the same time and sit next to the old man. One day the old man decided that he would flop out his "love machine", and surprisingly the old lady responded by gently holding it.

For the next two weeks the same thing would happen, the old lady would turn up and hold the old man's hunk of meat. Then one day the old man didn't turn up. The old lady was a bit worried, but she kept going back day after day, but the old man still didn't turn up.

A few days later the old lady was out doing the weekly food shopping when she bumped into the old man.

Old lady: "Why have you stopped coming to the park bench" Old Man: "Well you know I haven't really felt like it" Old lady: "What ..., why. ... Is it another women??"

Old Man:"Well actually now that you mentioned there is someone else" Old lady:"But why? What does she have that I haven't got?

Old Man: "well Parkinson's disease for one thing!!!!"

Bill Clinton and Al Gore go into a local diner for lunch. As they read the menu the waitress comes over and asks Clinton, "Are you ready to order?"

Clinton replies, "Yes, I'd like a quickie."

"A quickie?!?" the waitress replies. "Sir, given the current situation of your personal life I don't think that is a good idea. I'll come back when you are ready to order from the menu."

She walks away.

Gore leans over to Clinton and says, "It's pronounced Quiche."

The following test was developed by a combination of top U.S. and European psychologists. The results are extremely accurate in describing your personality with one simple question.

Which is your favourite Teletubbie?

A. Yellow—La La

B. Purple—Tinky Winky

c. Green—Dipsy

D. Red—Po

Scroll down to get your profile

A. You chose the Yellow Teletubbie. You are gay.

B. You chose the Purple Teletubbie. You are gay.

C. You chose the Green Teletubbie. You are gay.

D. You chose the Red Teletubbie. You are gay.

A young woman was preparing for her wedding. She asked her mother to go out and buy a nice, long black, negligee and carefully place it in her suitcase so it would not wrinkle. Well, Mum forgot until the last minute. She dashed out and could only find a short pink nighty. She bought it and threw it into the suitcase.

After the wedding, the bride and groom entered their hotel room. The groom was a little self-conscious, so he asked his new bride to change in the bathroom and promise not to peek while he got ready for bed. While she was in the bathroom, the bride opened her suitcase and saw the negligee her mother had thrown in there.

"Oh no! It's short, pink, and wrinkled!" She exclaimed.

Then her groom cried out, "I told you not to peek."

A company takes out a newspaper advertisement claiming to be able to supply imported hard core pornographic videos. As their prices seem reasonable, people place orders and make payments via check.

After several weeks, the company writes back explaining that under the present law they are unable to supply the materials and do not wish to be prosecuted. So they return their customers' money in the form of a company check.

However, due to the name of the company, few people ever bother to present these to their banks. The name of the company:

"The Anal Sex and Fetish Perversion Company".

A couple had been married 15 Years. One afternoon they were working in the garden together. As the wife was bending over pulling weeds, the husband exclaimed, "honey you sure are getting fat. Your butt is really getting huge. I bet it is as big as the gas grill by now."

The husband, feeling be needed to prove his point, got a yardstick and measured the grill, then measured his wife's butt. "Yep, just what I thought, about the same size."

The wife got very incensed and decided to let him do the gardening alone. She went inside didn't speak to her husband the rest of the day. That evening when they went to bed, the husband cuddled up to his wife and said "How about a little lovemaking?!!!" The wife rolled over and turned her back to him, giving him the cold shoulder. What's the matter he asked? To which she replied, "you don't think I am going to fire up this big ass grill just for one little weenie, do you?"

After having been commissioned by God to take a survey of how man was doing on Earth, St. Peter now stood before his boss ready to present his findings.

"Tell me, St. Peter, what have you found out?" God asked. "I'm very sorry to have to tell you this, but the people are behaving in a sinful manner. There's drugs, alcohol, murders, you name it—a regular Sodom and Gomorrah. But the worst is this new obsession with oral sex. According to my survey, 88% of the population is doing it. Even four out of five dentists recommend it. I'm afraid it has reached epidemic proportions.

"Hmmm," God said thoughtfully, "Do you have any recommendations as to what should be done to put an end to this sexual perversion? I think we should send a message to everyone on Earth who engages in oral sex. The contents of that message should tell them exactly what will happen to them on Judgment Day if they do not stop this type of activity." replied St. Peter.

"That is an effective solution," God stated, "but I think that instead of punishing those who practice oral sex, we should reward those who refrain from it. Let's send a letter that's personally signed by me to each one of these good people." And so they did. "Do you know what the letter said?"

(scroll down)

"No?" (Scroll down a little more)

"Hmmm ...You didn't get the letter either, huh??"

Your Favourite Colour is the Key to Your Sexual Life.

The clothes you wear, your home furnishings and the car you drive all give clues to your sexual personality. Think of this colour and, (scroll down). Don't change your colour either! The key is the colours you select for your possessions. Most people claim they haven't a favourite colour. But look around you, and you ll notice a pattern, especially in your clothing and home decor. The predominant colour for you is the one that appears most frequently—it's the one that mirrors the sexual you. A panel of psychologists, speaking at the Home Interior Design Forum, explained the association between colour and sexual patterns.

RED: People who like red tend to be tigers in the sack. They are easily aroused and enjoy sex in every way imaginable. Once the sexual spark is ignited, it may take hours to extinguish. When two reds get together, the ensuing erotica could make Lady Chatterley blush. Lovers of red tend to be aggressors and weaker colours should be aware.

YELLOW: If you tend to favour yellow, your sexual drives are complex and turn toward the adaptable. In most cases the person will consent to the stronger partner's desires in a passive manner. You will never enjoy sex to the fullest, but you will never turn down an invitation from somebody you enjoy or admire.

PINK: Persons who like pink show a reluctance to mature in sexual matters: women tend to tease, to promise more than they intend to deliver. In some cases they flaunt their femininity—but because they secretly hate men. A great percentage of prostitutes boast entire wardrobes in pink. Men who like pink are the philanderers and flirts. They are the type who will make three dates for the same evening and not keep one, preferring to pick up a dish in some bar instead. Women whose husbands like pink should keep a secret nest egg.

PURPLE: Lovers of purple frequently consider themselves to be too sophisticated for a fun romp in the sack. Women sometimes are the type who hates to mess their hair. Men are business-like in their approach to lovemaking. In both sexes purple partners are more concerned with their fulfilment than anyone else's gratification.

BLACK: Black colour preferences point to black sex. These people are the misfits of the sex world and seek out each other in kinship. They tend to prefer perverted sex and are usually masochistic or sadistic in nature. They are moody people and often perform at their peak when under stress or during unhappy times. Police psychiatrists claim that sex offenders prefer the colour black. And it is no coincidence that the uniform of mobsters and teenage gangs is black attire.

GREEN: Those who prefer green are fresh and innocent in their approach to sex. Women who love green will always make love like virgins all their life. And a man may always be a clumsy and awkward but in a charming and endearing sort of way. Green lovers are gentle, but not passionate. If chosen as a mate, one will never need worry about infidelity.

ORANGE: Lovers of the colour orange lean toward sexual fantasies. The sex act is regarded as a dramatic one-act play in which they are the star. Foreplay is as important as the act of love. They whisper sweet nothings, meaningless dialogue; they feel it is their image. Orange people often do not experience orgasm—but they put on a dam good act. Men tend to pull their partner's hair, and women leave red welts on the sex partner's back.

BROWN: If you love brown, you're a real treasure for the right mate. Brown lovers tend to be warm and deep, sensitive to the needs and desires of their partners. Sex is a 24 hour a day thing. Where you can't say "I love you" often enough. Snuggling by the fire, walking in the rain or catching snowflakes on their tongue is a turn-on to a lover of brown. They need lots of time and privacy to make love. But their emotions are such that one harsh word could end the affair.

GREY: The colour grey a preferred by people who are indecisive. They can't get excited about anything—including colour—so they choose a noncommittal shade. Men who prefer grey look at sex as a way of relieving tension—but nothing more, nothing less. It's "wham, bam, thank you ma'am. Women don't make love, they have intercourse. And for one of two reasons only: to accommodate their mate, or to become pregnant. They count the cracks in the bedroom plaster until the sex act is over with and done. But when teamed with another colour, the grey spouse considers the other's infidelity a blessing. When a grey marries another grey, the marriage is made in heaven.

BLUE: Lovers of blue are wonderful sex partners. They are sinners, affectionate and sensitive to their partner's needs. They consider love making a fine art and their approach is elegant. Men who love blue are like concert pianists, delicately ravaging their partner like they would play a baby grand. Women in the blue category enjoy sex to the fullest. They are exciting partners but their passion may be compared to a tidal wave rather than fiery aggression. Both women and men enjoy foreplay and the aftermath of lovemaking, as much as the sex act itself. In marriage a blue person is a wonderful mate—never seeking outside interests.

WHITE: If a person is infatuated with white, sex often seems filthy. These people are puritanical in nature. French kissing is obscene and to make love in the daylight in unheard of. Women who love white will undress beneath the covers. Men will shower before and after the sex act. These people still use pet names for their genitals.

Jim invited his mother over for dinner with him and his flatmate. His mother had long been suspicious of a relationship between Jim and his flatmate and this only made her more curious. Reading his mum's thoughts, Jim volunteered,—I know what you must be thinking, but I assure you, Jim and I are just mates.

About a week later, Jim said to Jim—Ever since your mother came to dinner, I've been unable to find the beautiful silver gravy ladle. You don't suppose she took it, do you?—Jim said, well, I doubt it, but I'll write her a letter just to be sure.—SO, he sat down and wrote: "Dear Mother, I'm not saying you 'did' take a gravy ladle from my house, and I'm not saying you 'did not' take a gravy ladle. But the fact remains that one has been missing ever since you were here for dinner." Several days later, Jim received a letter from his mother which read: "Dear Son, I'm not saying that you 'do' sleep with Jim, and I'm not saying that you don't sleep with Jim. But the fact remains that if he was sleeping in his own bed, he would have found the gravy ladle by now."

Love, Mum

Lesson of the Day—Don't lie to your Mother.

Bob goes to the doctors and says, "Doctor, I've got this problem you see, only you've got to promise not to laugh".

The doctor replies, "Of course I won't laugh! That would be thoroughly unprofessional. In over twenty years of being a doctor I've never laughed at a patient."

"OK then," says Bob, and he drops his trousers. The doctor is greeted by the sight of the tiniest penis he has ever seen in his life.

Despite his best efforts, he begins laughing, softly at first, then uncontrollably. Several minutes later he manages to compose himself and wipes the tears from his eyes. "I'm so sorry," he says to Bob, "I don't know what came over me, I won't let it happen again. Now what seems to be the problem?

Bob looks up at the doctor with sad eyes and says, "It's swollen."

Two Aliens in Brisbane, next to a petrol station. The Aliens waddle out of their ship and look around. The first thing they see that resembles a being is the petrol pump. The two Aliens approach. The first one says "Earthling take me to your leader!"

He gets no response. The first Alien looks at his buddy then addresses the pump again. "Earthling, I said Take me to your leader!" Still no response.

The first Alien then turns to the second and says "If this Earthling doesn't show me some respect I'm going to blast him!" The second Alien replies "OK but I think that I'll just go & stand down on the next block."

The first Alien looks a little puzzled, but waits for the other to waddle to the next block. He then addresses the pump a third time. "Earthling take me to your leader!"

No response. The Alien then pulls out his ray-gun and shoots the pump. After the explosion the Alien gets up dusts himself off then goes down the block to his buddy, He then says to the second Alien "If you knew that was going to happen why didn't you warn me?"

The second Alien replies "Well, I didn't really know what was going to happen, but I'm f*cked if I'm going to mess with anyone who's penis can hang to the ground, wrap around his body twice, and still stick it in his ear!"

A bloke escapes from prison where he has been for 15 years.

He breaks into a house to look for money, beer and guns and finds a young couple in bed. He orders the guy out of bed and ties him to a chair. While tying the girl to the bed he gets on top of her, kisses her neck, then goes into the bathroom.

While the man is in the bathroom, the husband tells the wife: Listen, this guy's an escaped convict, look at his clothes! He probably spent lots of time in jail and hasn't seen a woman in years... I saw how he kissed your neck. If he wants sex, don't resist, don't complain. Do whatever he tells you. Satisfy him no matter how much he nauseates you. This guy is probably dangerous. If he gets angry, he'll kill us. Be strong, honey. I love you."

To which the wife responds: "He wasn't kissing my neck. He was whispering in my ear. He told me he was gay, thought you were cute, and asked if we had any Vaseline. I told him it was in the bathroom. Be strong honey, I love you too!!"

CHAPTER 20

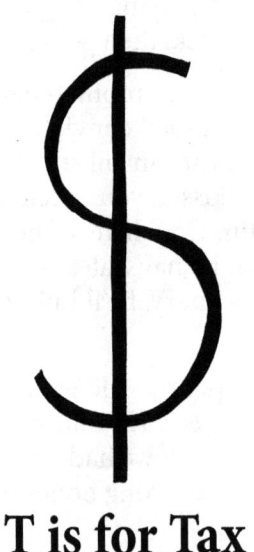

T is for Tax

A man called to testify at the ATO, asked his accountant for advice on what to wear.

"Wear your shabbiest clothing. Let him think you are a pauper", the accountant replied.

Then he asked the lawyer the same question, but got the opposite advice—"Do not let them intimidate you. Wear your most elegant suit and tie."

Confused, the man went to his Rabbi, told him of the conflicting advice and requested some resolution of the dilemma "Let me tell you a story" replied the rabbi.

A woman, about to be married, asked her mother what to wear on her wedding night. 'Wear a heavy, long, flannel nightgown that goes right up to your neck.' But when she asked her best friend, she got conflicting advice. 'Wear your most sexy negligee, with a V neck right down to your navel.'

The man protested: "Rabbi, what does all this have to do with my problem with the IRS?"

"No matter what you wear, you are going to get screwed."

NEW TAX RATES

The only thing that we have not yet taxed is the penis.

To date this has been due to the fact that 40% of the time it is hanging around unemployed. 30% of the time it is hard up, 20% of the time it is pissed off and 10% of the time it is in the hole. On top of that, it has two dependents and they are both nuts.

Effective July 1, your penis will be taxed according to length.

The brackets are as follows:

€10-12" Luxury Tax

€8-10" Pole Tax

€5-8" Privilege Tax

€4-5" Nuisance Tax

Note: If you exceed 12 inches you will be required to declare capital gains.

If you measure below 4 inches you will be eligible for a refund but may not ask for an extension.

All measurements will be effected by me from an under desk kneeling position. I am still considering rulings on the following questions:

- Are there penalties for early withdrawals?
- What if one's penis is self-employed?
- Are multiple partners dealt with as a corporation?
- Are condoms a deductible as work attire?
- Is there an additional tax if you are not circumcised?
- Is dry-cleaning demanded of an employee deductible as a work related expense?
- Are Cuban cigars a legitimate substitution and thereby deductible?

Consideration is being given to a girth size tax (GST). Under this proposal, if girth exceeds 6 inches you may be deemed to be more than a handful and subject to a 10% loading.

If subjected to this tax, lost opportunities are likely to be deductible although I have yet to settle on a solution that satisfies me in this respect.

Sincerely,

Monica Lewinsky

Head pecker Checker

IRS

- I'm tired because I'm overworked.
- The population of this country is 18 million. 4 million are retired. That leaves 14 million to do the work.
- There are 4 million that are below the age of five, which leaves 10 million to do the work.
- There are 3 million in school, which leaves 7 million to do the work.
- Of this there are 3 million employed by the Federal government. This leaves 4 million to do the work.
- One million are in the Armed Forces, which leaves 3 million to do the work.
- One million are unemployed, which leaves 2 million to do the work.
- Take from the total the 1,800,000 people who work for State and Local Government and that leaves 200,000 to do the work.
- There are 188,000 in hospitals, so that leaves 12,000 to do the work.
- Now, there are 11,998 people in Prisons.

- That leaves just two people to do the work. You and me.
- And you're sitting there stuffing around on email.

"I'm not going to pay taxes. When they say I'm going to prison, I'll say no, prisons cost taxpayers a lot of money. You keep what it would have cost to incarcerate me, and we'll call it even."—Jimmy Kimmel

Amazing, but true, if you think about it, and it shows the importance of accuracy in your tax return.

"The government is really asking a lot of us this month—first we're supposed to count how many people live in our home—then we're supposed to count how much money we owe them. I actually got confused and accidentally sent a check to the census and a member of my household to the IRS. Sorry grandma."—Jimmy Kimmel

---

The CRA has returned the Tax Return to a man in Canada after he apparently answered one of the questions incorrectly.

In response to the question, ... "Do you have anyone dependent on you?" The man wrote: ... "2.1 million illegal immigrants, 1.1 million crackheads, 4.4 million unemployable scroungers, 80,000 criminals in over 85 prisons plus 650 idiots in Parliament and the entire group that call themselves Politicians".

The CRA stated that the response he gave was unacceptable.

The man's response back to the CRA was, ... "Sorry but who did I leave out?"

A man goes to the doctor. "Doctor, that medicine you gave me isn't working. Is there anything else I could try?".

"Fill out this tax form," suggests the doctor.

"How's that going to help me?", asks the man.

"I'm not sure," replies the doctor, "but some of my patients say it gives them relief."

What's the difference between a dead rat and a dead tax inspector found on the road? There are skid marks by the rat.

If a tax man and a lawyer were both drowning and you could only save one, would you go to lunch or read the paper?

How do you know you've got a good tax accountant? He's had a loophole named after him.

What did the Tax Accountant do to liven up the office party? Not show up.

"The U.S. Senate is considering a bill that would tax Botox. When Botox users heard this, they were horrified. Well, I think they were horrified. It's difficult to tell." —Craig Ferguson

---

A businessman on his deathbed called his friend and said, "Bill, I want you to promise me that when I die, you will have my remains cremated." "And what," his friend asked, "What do you want me to do with your ashes?" The businessman said, "Just put them in an envelope and mail them to the Internal Revenue Service. Write on the envelope, "Now, you have everything."

The taxman was surprised to receive a letter which read, "Dear Sir, Last year I cheated on my tax and I can't sleep for thinking about it. I am therefore enclosing a cheque for 2,000 pounds. If I find that I still can't sleep, I'll send you the balance."—Anonymous

---

Taken from the Guardian, an actual letter sent by the Inland Revenue (Tax Office):

Dear Mr Addison,

I am writing to you to express our thanks for your more than prompt reply to our latest communication, and also to answer some of the points you raise. I will address them, as ever, in order. Firstly, I must take issue with your description of our last as a 'begging letter'. It might perhaps more properly be referred to as a 'tax demand'. This is how we, at the Inland Revenue have always, for reasons of accuracy; traditionally referred to such documents.

Secondly, your frustration at our adding to the 'endless stream of crapulent whining and panhandling vomited daily through the letterbox on to the doormat' has been noted. However, whilst I have naturally not seen the other letters to which you refer I would cautiously suggest that their being from 'pauper councils, Lombardy pirate banking houses and pissant gas-mongerers' might indicate that your decision to 'file them next to the toilet in case of emergencies' is at best a little ill-advised. In common with my own organisation, it is unlikely that the senders of these letters do see you as a 'lackwit bumpkin' or, come to that, a 'sodding charity'. More likely they see you as a citizen of Great Britain, with a responsibility to contribute to the upkeep of the nation as a whole.

Which brings me to my next point. Whilst there may be some spirit of truth in your assertion that the taxes you pay 'go to shore up the canker-blighted, toppling folly that is the Public Services', a moment's rudimentary calculation ought to disabuse you of the notion that the government in any way expects you to 'stump up for the whole damned party' yourself. The estimates you provide for the Chancellor's disbursement of the funds levied by taxation, whilst colourful, are, in fairness, a little off the mark. Less than you seem to imagine is spent on 'junkets for Bunterish lickspittles' and 'dancing whores' whilst far more than you have accounted for is allocated to, for example, 'that box-ticking façade of a university system.'

A couple of technical points arising from direct queries:

1. The reason we don't simply write 'Muggins' on the envelope has to do with the vagaries of the postal system; and

2. You can rest assured that 'sucking the very marrows of those with nothing else to give' has never been considered as a practice because even if the Personal Allowance didn't render it irrelevant, the sheer medical logistics involved would make it financially unviable.

I trust this has helped. In the meantime, whilst I would not in any way wish to influence your decision one way or the other, I ought to point out that even if you did choose to 'give the whole foul jamboree up and go and live in India' you would still owe us the money.

Please forward it by Friday.

Yours Sincerely,

H J Lee

Customer Relations

Inland Revenue (Tax Office)

"The House passed a bill where there's a tax now of 90% on the bonuses that these people get. So, half the Republicans voted against this. They said this is exactly the kind of punitive taxation that's going to drive good people out of the fraud business." —Bill Maher

---

Two junior doctors were involved in a fight in the hospital. A senior consultant had to pull them apart.

"What's all this about?" asked the consultant angrily.

"It's the Tax Inspector in C ward," said one.

"He's only got 2 days to live."

"He had to be told." said the second doctor.

"I know," said the first, "but I wanted to be the one to tell him…!"

At the end of the tax year the Tax Office sent an inspector to audit the books of a synagogue. While he was checking the books he turned to the Rabbi and said, "I notice you buy a lot of candles. What do you do with the candle drippings?"

"Good question," noted the Rabbi. "We save them up and send them back to the candle makers, and every now and then they send us a free box of candles." "Oh," replied the auditor, somewhat disappointed that his unusual question had a practical answer. But on he went, in his obnoxious way: "What about all these matzo purchases? What do you do with the crumbs?"

"Ah, yes," replied the Rabbi, realising that the inspector was trying to trap him with an unanswerable question. "We collect them and send them back to the manufacturers, and every now and then they send a free box of matzo balls."

"I see," replied the auditor, thinking hard about how he could fluster the know-it-all Rabbi. "Well, Rabbi," he went on, "what do you do with all the leftover foreskins from the circumcisions you perform?"

"Here, too, we do not waste," answered the Rabbi. "What we do is save up all the foreskins and send them to the Tax Office, and about once a year they send us a complete dick."

"Nobody likes taxes, but they've been around forever. Taxes date back all the way back to the year one, when baby Jesus was visited by two wise men and an IRS agent, who demanded half the family's frankincense."—Jimmy Kimmel

"Tax day is the day that ordinary Americans send their money to Washington, D.C., and wealthy Americans send their money to the Cayman Islands."—Jimmy Kimmel

"Every year, I include a piece of chicken in the envelope with my taxes. Not as a bribe, just a little treat for the guy at the IRS who opens it."—Jimmy Kimmel

---

AUSTRALIAN TAXATION OFFICE

INCOME TAX FORM —1040 EZ 2 00

New Simplified Tax Form for all future Income Taxes

1. How much money did you make this year? $—
2. Send it to us.

CHAPTER 21

U is for Urban Myths

58 THINGS PEOPLE HAVE DONE IN AN ELEVATOR

1. When there's only one other person in the elevator, tap them on the shoulder- and then pretend it wasn't you.
2. Push the buttons and pretend they give you a shock. Smile, and go back for more.
3. Ask if you can push the button for other people, but push the wrong ones.
4. Call the Psychic Hotline from your cell phone and ask if they know what floor you're on.
5. Hold the doors open and say you're waiting for your friend. After a while, let the doors close, look at an empty space and say, "Hi Greg. How's your day been?"
6. Bring a cat basket and take a nap in the corner.
7. Bounce a superball around the elevator.
8. Light a cigarette and tell people, "Smokey Bear doesn't know what the hell he's talking about!"
9. Drop a pen and wait until someone reaches to help pick it up, then Scream. "That's mine!"
10. Stand in the corner reading a telephone book, laughing uproariously.
11. Bring a camera and take pictures of everyone in the elevator.
12. Move your desk in to the elevator and whenever someone gets on, ask if they have an appointment.
13. When the doors close, use duct tape and work furiously to tape the doors together. Ask for help.
14. Lay down a Twister mat and ask people if they'd like to play.

15. Bring a hammer and nails and hang pictures of yourself on the walls. Ask people, "Isn't that a good picture of me?"
16. Leave your—foot long python alone in the elevator.
17. Turn off the lights in the elevator to "conserve energy."
18. Leave a box in the corner, and when someone gets on ask them if they hear something ticking.
19. Pretend you are a flight attendant and review emergency procedures and exits with the passengers.
20. Clean your gun.
21. Ask, "Did you feel that?"
22. Dressed in coveralls, get in a full elevator and when the door closes, push the stop button, post an "out of order" sign inside and go to work on the access panel, saying "This may take a minute."
23. Push the call button, and when the voice answers ask, "God?"
24. Stand really close to someone, sniffing them occasionally.
25. When the doors close, announce to the others, "It's okay. Don't panic, hey open up again."
26. Push your floor button with your tongue.
27. Stand alone, and when the doors open tell people trying to get on that the car is full and that they should wait for the next one.
28. Swat at flies that don't exist.
29. Shoot rubber bands at everyone.
30. When the doors open, pretend that you bounce off a force field when you try to leave.

31. Ask people not to look, and then change your clothes.
32. When people get on, ask for their tickets and check that they meet the "height" requirements.
33. Push the top floor button and announce that you tried to kill yourself yesterday but the other building wasn't high enough.
34. Talk to people about the "golden age" of elevators in the 0's. Explain why modern elevators can't compete with the gas- powered lifts.
35. Borrow small items from other people in the elevator, then shout "Whee! as you drop them through the crack in the floor when the elevator doors open.
36. Jump rope.
37. Bring a shovel and try to dig a hole.
38. When the doors close, menacingly announce that "it's going to be a bumpy ride."
39. Tell people that you can see their aura.
40. Callout, "group hug!", then enforce it.
41. Walk-on with a cooler that has "HUMAN HEAD" on the side.
42. Grimace painfully while smacking your forehead and muttering "Shut up, all of you, just shut up"
43. Crack open your briefcase or purse, and while peering inside, ask, "Got enough air in there?"
44. Stand silently and motionless in the corner, facing the wall, without getting off.
45. When arriving at your floor, grunt and strain to yank the doors open, then act embarrassed when they open by themselves.

46. Greet everyone getting on the elevator with a warm handshake and ask them to call you Admiral.
47. Meow occasionally.
48. Bet the other passengers you can fit a quarter in your nose.
49. Stare at another passenger for a while, then announce in horror, "You're one of THEM" and back away slowly.
50. Wear a puppet on your hand and use it to talk to the other passengers.
51. Listen to the elevator walls with your stethoscope.
52. Announce in a demonic voice, "I must find a more suitable host body."
53. Say "Ding" at each floor.
54. Say "I wonder what all these do?" and push all the red buttons.
55. Make explosion noises when anyone presses a button.
56. Stare, grinning at another passenger for a while, and then announce "I have new socks on."
57. When the elevator is silent, look around and ask, "Is that your beeper?"
58. Draw a little square on the floor with chalk and announce to the other passengers, "This is my personal space."

Super Grannie: Defender of Justice (True Story).

An elderly lady did her shopping and, upon returning to her car, found four males in the act of leaving with her car. She dropped her shopping bags and drew her handgun, proceeding to scream at them at the top of her voice, "I have a gun and I know how to use it! Get out of the car you scum bags! "

The four men didn't wait for a second invitation but got out and ran like mad, whereupon the lady, somewhat shaken, proceeded to load her shopping bags into the back of the car and got into the driver's seat. She was so shaken that she could not get her key into the ignition. She tried and tried and then it dawned on her why.

A few minutes later she found her own car parked four or five spaces farther down. She loaded her bags into her car and drove to the police station. The sergeant to whom she told the story nearly tore himself in two with laughter and pointed to the other end of the counter where four white males together with their lawyers were reporting a carjacking by a mad elderly woman described as white, less than 5' tall, glasses, and curly white hair carrying a large handgun.

No charges were filed.

An Amish boy and his father almost were visiting a mall. They were amazed by everything they saw, but especially by two shiny, silver walls that could move apart and back together again.

The boy asked his father, "What is this father?"

The father (never having seen an elevator) responded, "Son, never seen anything like this in my life, I don't know what it is."

While the boy and his father were watching wide-eyed, an old lady in a wheelchair rolled up to the moving walls and pressed a button. The walls opened and the lady rolled between them and into a small room. The walls closed and the boy and his father watched small circles of light with numbers above the wall light up. They continued to watch the circles light up in the reverse direction.

The walls opened up again and a beautiful 24 year old woman stepped out.

The father said to his son, "Go get your Mother."

A woman was helping her computer illiterate husband set up his computer, and at the appropriate point in the process, told him that he would now need to choose and enter a password. Something he will use to log on.

The husband was in a rather amorous mood and figured he would try for the shock effect to bring this to his wife's attention.

So when the computer asked him to enter his password, he made it plainly obvious to his wife that he was keying in penis.

His wife nearly fell off her chair laughing when the computer replied: **PASSWORD REJECTED NOT LONG ENOUGH**...

Today's Touching Story…

A small boy named Hameed lived in a village in Morocco. None of his classmates liked him because of his stupidity, especially his teacher, who was always yelling at him 'you are driving me crazy Hameed!!!!'

One day Hameed's mother came into school to check on how he was doing. The teacher told his mother honestly, that her son is simply a disaster, getting very low marks and even she had never seen such a dumb boy in her entire teaching career!!!!

The mother was shocked at the feedback and withdrew her son from the school and even moved to another town!!!!

25 years later, the teacher was diagnosed with an incurable cardio disease! All the doctors strongly advised her to have an open heart operation, which only one surgeon could perform . . . Left with no other options, the teacher decided to have the operation, which was successful . . . . .

When she opened her eyes after the surgery, she saw a handsome doctor smiling down at her! She wanted to thank him, but could not talk. Her face started to turn blue, she raised her hand, trying to tell him something, but eventually died!

The doctor was shocked and was trying to work out what went wrong, when he turned around he saw our friend Hameed, working as a cleaner in the clinic, who had unplugged the oxygen equipment to connect his Hoover!!!!

"Don't tell me, you thought that Hameed became a fucking doctor."

WHENEVER I FEEL PARTICULARLY STUPID, I READ THIS...

1. Question: If you could live forever, would you and why?

Answers: 1 "I would not live forever, because we should not live forever, forever, then we would live because if we were supposed to live forever, which is why I would not live but we cannot live forever, forever." Miss Alabama Miss USA contest

2. "Whenever I watch TV and see those poor starving kids all over the world, I can't help but cry. I mean I'd love to be skinny like that but not with all those flies and death and stuff." Mariah Carey

3. "Researchers have discovered that chocolate produces some of the same reactions in the brain as marijuana. The researchers also discovered similarities between

the two, but can't remember what they are." Matt Lauer on NBC's Today show, August 22

4. "I haven't committed a crime. What I did was fail to comply with the law" * David Dinkins, New York City Mayor, answering accusations that he failed to pay his taxes.

5. "Smoking kills. If you're killed, you've lost a very important part of your life." * Brooke Shields, during an interview to become spokesperson for a federal anti-smoking campaign

6. "I've never had major knee surgery on any other part of my body." Winston Bennett, University of Kentucky basketball forward

7. "Outside of the killings, Washington has one of the lowest crime rates in the country." * Mayor Marion Barry, Washington, D.C .

8. "They're multipurpose. Not only do they put the clips on, but they take them off." * Pratt & Whitney spokesperson explaining why the company charged the Air Force nearly $1000 for an ordinary pair of pliers.

9. "We're going to turn this team around 360 degrees." * Jason Kidd, upon his drafting to the Dallas Mavericks

10. "I'm not going to have some reporters pawing through our papers. We are the president." * Hillary Clinton commenting on the release of subpoenaed documents

11. "China is a big country, inhabited by many Chinese." * Former French President Charles De Gaulle

12. "That lowdown scoundrel deserves to be kicked to death by a jackass, and I'm just the one to do it." * A congressional candidate in Texas

13. "The government is not doing enough about cleaning up the environment. This is a good planet." *Mr. New

Jersey contestant when asked what he would do with a million dollars.

14. "When I have been asked during these last weeks who caused the riots and the killing in L.A., my answer has been direct and simple: Who is to blame for the riots? The rioters are to blame. Who is to blame for the killings? The killers are to blame." * Former U.S. Vice-President Dan Quayle on the complex social issues behind the Los Angeles Riots.

15. "I don't feel we did wrong in taking this great country away from them. There were great numbers of people who needed new land, and the Indians were selfishly trying to keep it for themselves." John Wayne

16. "Half this game is ninety percent mental." Philadelphia Phillies manager Danny Ozark

17. "It isn't pollution that's harming the environment. It's the impurities in our air and water that are doing it." Former U.S. Vice-President Dan Quayle

18. "Without censorship, things can get terribly confused in the public mind." General William Westmoreland

19. "What a waste it is to lose one's mind. Or not to have a mind is being very wasteful. How true that is." Former U.S. Vice-President Dan Quayle at a fundraising event for United Negro College Fund. (He was attempting to quote the line "a mind is a terrible thing to waste".)

20. "If you let that sort of thing go on, your bread and butter will be cut right out from under your feet." Former British foreign minister Ernest Bevin

21. "I love California. I practically grew up in Phoenix." Former U.S. Vice-President Dan Quayle

Long ago, when sailing ships ruled the sea, a captain and his crew were in danger of being boarded by a pirate ship.

As the crew became frantic, the captain bellowed to his First Mate, Bring me my red shirt!"

The First Mate quickly retrieved the captain's red shirt, the captain put it on and led the crew to battle the pirate ship.

Although some casualties occurred among the crew, the pirates were repelled.

Later that day, the lookout screamed that there were two pirate vessels about to attack.

The crew cowered in fear, but the captain, calm as ever, bellowed, "Bring me my red shirt!" And once again the battle was on.

This time, the Captain and his crew repelled both pirate ships, although this time more casualties occurred.

Weary from the battles, the men sat around on deck that night recounting the day's occurrences when an ensign looked to the Captain and asked, "Sir, why did you call for your red shirt before the battles?"

The Captain, giving the ensign a look that only a captain can give, exhorted, "If I am wounded in battle, the red shirt does not show the wound, and thus, you men will continue to fight unafraid."

The men sat in silence marvelling at the courage of such a man.

As dawn came the next morning, the lookout screamed more pirate ships were approaching, 10 of them, all ready to attack.

The men became silent and looked to the Captain, their leader, for his usual command. The Captain, calm as ever, bellowed, "Bring me my brown pants!"

U is for Urban Myths 523

Important Warning for those who have been drawn unsuspectingly into the use of bread:

1. More than 98 percent of convicted felons are bread users.

2. Fully HALF of all children who grow up in bread-consuming households score below average on standardized tests.

3. In the 18th century, when virtually all bread was baked in the home, the average life expectancy was less than 50 years; infant mortality rates were unacceptably high; many women died in childbirth; and diseases such as typhoid, yellow fever, and influenza ravaged whole nations.

4. More than 90 percent of violent crimes are committed within 24 hours of eating bread.

5. Bread is made from a substance called "dough". It has been proven that as little as one pound of dough can be used to suffocate a mouse. The average Australian eats more bread than that in one month!

6. Primitive tribal societies that have no bread exhibit a low incidence of cancer, Alzheimer's, Parkinson's disease, and osteoporosis.

7. Bread has been proven to be addictive. Subjects deprived of bread and given only water to eat begged for bread after as little as two days.

8. Bread is often a "gateway" food item, leading the user to "harder" items such as butter, jam and even peanut butter.

9. Bread has been proven to absorb water. Since the human body is more than 90 percent water, it follows that eating bread could lead to your body being taken

over by this absorptive food product, turning you into a soggy, gooey bread-pudding person.

10. Newborn babies can choke on bread.
11. Bread is baked at temperatures as high as 200 degrees Cl. That kind of heat can kill an adult in less than one minute.
12. Most Australian bread eaters are utterly unable to distinguish between significant scientific fact and meaningless statistical babbling.

In light of these frightening statistics, we propose the following bread restrictions:

13. No sale of bread to minors.
14. A nationwide "Just Say No to Toast" campaign, complete celebrity TV spots and bumper stickers.
15. A 300 percent tax on all bread to pay for all the societal ills we might associate with bread.
16. No animal or human images nor any primary colours (which may appeal to children) may be used to promote bread usage.
17. The establishment of "Bread-free zones around schools."

A game warden was driving down the road when he came upon a boy carrying a wild turkey under his arm. He stopped and asked the boy, "Where did you get that turkey?"

The boy replied, "What turkey?" The game warden said, "That turkey you're carrying under your arm." The boy looks down and said, "Well, look here, a turkey done roosted under my arm!"

The game warden said, "Now look, you know turkey season is closed, so whatever you do to that turkey, I'm going to do to you. If you break his leg, I'm gonna break your leg. If you break his wing, I'll break your arm. Whatever you do to him, I'll do to you. So, what are you gonna do with him?"

The little boy said, "I guess I'll just kiss his ass and let him go!"

A cop got out of his car and walked towards the kid driving a car, who was stopped for speeding following a speed gun trap. The kid rolled down his window.

"I've been waiting for you all day," the cop said.

The kid replied, "Yeah, well I got here as fast as I could." When the cop finally stopped laughing, he sent the kid on his way without a ticket.

A farmhand is driving around the farm, checking the fences.

After a few minutes he radios his boss and says, "Boss, I've got a problem. I hit a pig on the road and he's stuck in the bull-bars of my truck. He's still wriggling. What should I do?" "In the back of your truck there's a shotgun. Shoot the pig in the head and when it stops wriggling you can pull it out and throw it in a bush."

The farm worker says okay and signs off.

About 10 minutes later he radios back. "Boss I did what you said, I shot the pig and dragged it out and threw it in a bush." "So what's the problem now?" his Boss snapped. "The blue light on his motorcycle is still flashing!"

From the United States comes the following story which reinforces the need to get email addresses correct:

After being nearly snowbound for two weeks during the winter, a Seattle man departed for Miami Beach, where he was to meet his wife the next day, at the conclusion of her business trip to Minneapolis.

They were looking forward to some warm, pleasant weather and enjoying a break from the children.

Unfortunately, there was a mix-up at the Departure Gate and the man was informed he would have to travel on a later flight.

He tried to have the decision reversed but was told he had no alternative but to travel on the later flight.

On arrival, he found Miami Beach was having a heat wave and the weather was as uncomfortably hot, as Seattle's was cold.

The receptionist gave him a message that the wife would arrive later in the day.

He could hardly wait to get to the pool.

So he hurriedly sent his wife an email message, but because of his haste made an error in the address.

As a result, his message arrived at the home of an elderly widow, whose preacher husband had been buried the day before.

The grieving widow opened her email, took one look at the monitor, let out an anguished scream and promptly had a heart attack.

When her family found her, the following message was still on the screen:

Dearest Wife,

U is for Urban Myths

Departed yesterday, as you know.

Just now checked in.

Some confusion at the gate.

Appeal was denied.

Received confirmation of your arrival

Your loving husband

P.S. Things are not as we thought

You will be surprised how hot it is down here.

"We'd go and sit on the balcony at Terminal 3 at Heathrow, directly under one of the speakers as the roof is low. We put the tape machine in our bag with the microphone poking out of the top. We'd look for a flight that'd arrived in the last 40 minutes from somewhere where you'd expect mental names, then write a letter saying "Could you go and pick up etc. etc. from flight, etc. U"—

That way, it looked like it'd been arranged in advance as the flight arrival details were written on the note. We also wore an ID-style badge and carried a mobile so that we looked like taxi drivers. One of us would get the first one read out and then the other did the second. We'd pretend to be unable to pronounce it and then hand them the bit of paper with the name written on it. Long winded, but well worth it!

Looks like . . .	Reads like . . .
Arheddis Varkenjaab and Aywellbe Fayed	I hate this fucking job, and I will be fired
Arhevbin Fayed and Bybeiev Rhibodie	I've just been fired, and bye-bye everybody

Aynayda Pizaqvick and Malexa Kriest	I need a piss quick, and my legs are crossed
Awul Dasfilshabeda and Nowaynayda Zheet	Oo-ah, that's better and now I need a shit
Makollig Jezvahted and Levdaroum DeBahzted	My colleague just farted, and left the room, the bastard
Steelaygot Maowenbach and Tuka Piziniztee	Still, I got my own back and took a piss in his tea

---

Two couples were playing cards. John accidentally dropped some cards on the floor. When he bent down under the table to pick them up, he noticed that Bill's wife was not wearing any underwear! Shocked by this, John hit his head on the table and emerged red-faced.

Later, John went to the kitchen to get some refreshments. Bill's wife followed him and asked, "Did you see anything that you liked under there?" John admitted that, well, yes he did.

She said "You can have it, but it will cost you $100." After a minute since two, John indicates that he is interested. She tells him that Bill works Friday afternoons and John doesn't, John should come to her house around 2:00 pm on Friday. Friday came and John went to her house at 2:00 pm.

After paying her $100 they went to the bedroom, had sex, and then John left. Bill came home about 6:00 pm. He asked his wife, "Did John come by this afternoon?" Reluctantly, she replied, "Yes, he did stop by for a few minutes." Next Bill asked, "Did John give you $100?" She thinks 'Oh hell, he knows!' Finally she says, "Yes, he did give me $100."

"Good," Bill says.

"John came by the office this morning and borrowed $100 from me. He said that he would stop by our house on his way home and pay me back.

Have a think about this one first...

You are driving along on a wild stormy night. You pass by a bus stop, and you see three people waiting for the bus:

1. An old lady who is about to die.
2. An old friend who once saved your life.
3. The perfect man (or) woman you have been dreaming about.

Which one would you choose, knowing that there could only be one passenger in your car? This is a moral/ethical dilemma that was once actually used as part of a job application.

You could pick up the old lady, because she is going to die, and thus you should save her first; or you could take the old friend because he once saved your life, and this would be the perfect chance to pay him back. However, you may never be able to find your perfect dream lover again.

The candidate who was hired (out of 200 applicants) had no trouble coming up with his answer. Think before you continue reading. Think about it then (scroll down),,,,,,,,,

"WHAT DID HE SAY?" He simply answered: "I would give the car keys to my old friend, and let him take the lady to the hospital. I would stay behind and wait for the bus with the woman of my dreams."

A valid warning.

I got this today and the warning is genuine—especially after Sept 11.

Yesterday, a friend was travelling on a Brisbane train line. A man of Arabic-appearance got off the train and my friend noticed that he had left his bag behind. She grabbed the bag and ran after him, caught up with him at the top of the escalator and handed him back his bag.

He was extremely grateful and reached into his bag which appeared to contain large bundles of money and white powder.

He looked around to make sure nobody was looking and whispered "I can never repay your kindness, but I will try to ....with a word of advice for you: Stay away from Ipswich".

My friend was genuinely terrified.

"Is there going to be an attack?" she asked him.

"No", he whispered back." It's a sh*ithole."

There was a guy in a bar one night that got really drunk, I mean REALLY, REALLY, REALLY drunk.

When the bar closed the guy got up to go home and as he stumbled out the door he saw a nun walking on the sidewalk.

So the REALLY DRUNK guy stumbled over to the nun and punched her right in the face. Well, the nun was really surprised but before she could say or do anything the REALLY DRUNK guy punched her again. This time she fell down and the REALLY DRUNK guy stumbled over to her and kicked her in the butt. He then picked her up and threw her into a wall.

BY this time the nun was pretty weak and could hardly move. So the REALLY DRUNK guy stumbled over to her, looked down at her and said, "NOT VERY F'**KIN' STRONG TONIGHT, ARE YOU BATMAN?"

The CIA has three candidates, two men and a woman, for one assassin position.

On the final day of testing, the CIA proctor leads the first male candidate to a large steel door and hands him a gun. "We must know that you will follow our instructions, regardless of the circumstances," he explains. "Inside this room, you will find your wife sitting in a chair. Take this gun and kill her." The man is horrified, "You can't be serious! I could never shoot my wife!" "Well," says the proctor, "you're definitely not the right man for this job then."

The CIA proctor leads the second male candidate to another large steel door and hands him a gun. "We must know that you will follow instructions, no matter what the circumstances," the proctor explains. "Inside this room, you will find your wife sitting in a chair. Take this gun and kill her." The second man steadies himself, takes the gun and enters the room.

After three quiet minutes, the man exits the room with tears in his eyes. "I wanted to do it I just couldn't pull the trigger and shoot my wife. I guess I'm not the right man for the job." Finally, the CIA proctor leads the female candidate to yet another large steel door and hands her a gun. "We must be sure that you will follow instructions, no matter what the circumstances. Inside this room, you will find your husband sitting in a chair. Take this gun and kill him."

The woman takes the gun, enters the room, and before the door even closes completely behind her, she's fired off six shots. Then all hell breaks loose behind the door cursing, screaming, crashing. Suddenly, all goes quiet. The door opens slowly, the woman exits, and wiping the sweat from her brow, she says, "Did you guys know the gun was loaded with blanks? I had to beat the son of a bitch to death with the chair!"

Jon and Amanpreet were in a mental institution. This place had an annual contest, picking two of the best patients and giving them two questions. If they got them correct, they're deemed cured and free to go.

Jon was called into the doctor's office first and asked if he understood that he'd be free if he answered the questions correctly. The doctor said, "Jon, what would happen if I poked out one of your eyes?"

Jon said, "I'd be half blind."

"That's correct. What if I poked out both of your eyes?"

"I'd be completely blind." The doctor got up, shook his hand and told him he was free.

On Jon's way out, as the doctor filled out the paperwork, Jon mentioned the exam to Amanpreet. He told him what questions were going to be asked, and told him the answers. Amanpreet was called in. The doctor went through the formalities and asked, "What would happen if I cut off one of your ears?"

Amanpreet, remembering what Jon said was the correct answer, he said, "I'd be half blind."

The doctor looked a little puzzled, but went on. "What if I cut off both of your ears?"

"I'd be completely blind." Amanpreet answered. "Amanpreet, can you explain how you'd be blind?" "My hat would fall over my eyes."

Police arrested Malcolm Davidson, a 27 year old white male, resident of Wilmington, NC, in a pumpkin patch at 11:38 pm Friday. Davidson will be charged with lewd and lascivious behaviour, public indecency, and public intoxication the County Courthouse on Monday. The suspect allegedly stated that as he was passing a pumpkin patch, he decided to stop.

"You know, a pumpkin is soft and squishy inside, and there was no one around here for miles. At least I thought there wasn't." He stated in a phone interview from the County Courthouse Jail.

Davidson went on to state that he pulled over to the side of the road, picked out a pumpkin that he thought was appropriate for his purposes, cut a hole in it and proceeded to satisfy his alleged "need" "I guess I was just really into it, you know?" he commented with evident embarrassment. In the process, Davidson apparently failed to notice the Wilmington Municipal Police car approaching him and was unaware of his audience until Officer Brenda Taylor approached him.

"It was an unusual situation, that's for sure" said Officer Taylor." I walked up to Davidson and he's just working away at this pumpkin." Taylor went on to describe what happened when she approached Davidson. "I just went up and said Excuse me sir, but do you realize that you're doing it with a pumpkin? 'He got real surprised as you would expect and then looked me straight and said, 'A pumpkin? Damn... Is it midnight already?'"

After hearing that one of the patients in a mental hospital had saved another from a suicide attempt by pulling him out of a bathtub, the director reviewed the rescuer's file and called him into his office.

Mr James, your records and your heroic behaviour indicate that you're ready to go home. "I'm only sorry that the man you saved later killed himself with a rope around his neck."

"Oh, he didn't kill himself," Mr James replied. "I hung him up to dry."

This is spooky—especially the last one.

You've probably seen this before, but it's still spooooooooooooky! These little "Jedi mind tricks" are kind of freaky, till you think about them for a little while—then they become more weird. Just follow so the instructions below:

DON'T scroll down too fast—do it slowly and follow the instructions below exactly. Do the math in your head as fast as you can.

It may help to say the answers aloud quietly.

Follow the instructions one at a time, and as QUICKLY as you can!

QUIZ 1..

What is:

2+2?

4+4?

16+16?

Quick! Pick a number between 12 and 5.

Got it?

The number you picked was 7.

Right!!!

Isn't that weird???

Quiz 2.

Again, as quickly as you can, but don't advance until you've done each of them, really.

Now, ARROW down (but not too fast, you might miss something). What is:

1+5?

2+4?

3+3?

4+2?

5+1?

Now repeat saying the number 6 to yourself as you can for 15 seconds.

Then scroll down.

QUICK!! ! Think of a vegetable.

Then scroll down.

Keep going.

You're thinking of a carrot, right?

If not, you're among the 2% of the population whose minds are warped enough to think of something else. 98% of people will answer with carrot when given this exercise.

#3. Here is another one. You'll need a pencil and paper for this one.

DON'T CHEAT BY SCROLLING DOWN FIRST !!!!

It only takes 30 seconds. Work this out as you read. Don't read the bottom until you've worked it out.

    a. First, pick the number of days a week you would like to eat out.

    b. Multiply this number by 2.

    c. Add 5.

    d. Multiply this by 50.

    e. If you have already had your birthday this year, add 1749. If not, add 1748.

    f. Now subtract the" digit year that you were born in.

See below:

You should now have a three digit number.

The first digit of this was your original number (i.e. how many times you want to go out to eat each week.)

The second 2 digits are your age.

This is the only year (1999) it will ever work.

Do you know the, probably apocryphal story of the wealthy client of a bank who told the loan officer he was going abroad for a fortnight and wanted a $5,000 loan? The bank official said security would be required and the applicant offered his Rolls Royce which was parked outside the bank. All was in order so the bank official had the vehicle driven to the bank's underground carpark. When the customer returned from his holiday he returned the $5,000 he had borrowed and the $25 interest. As he handed over the keys of the car the loan officer asked why such a wealthy man would trouble himself with such a transaction. He replied "I became wealthy by not wasting money—where else can you find safe covered parking for a month in this city for $25?"

WHY I FIRED MY SECRETARY?

Two weeks ago, was my forty-fifth birthday, and I wasn't feeling too hot that morning anyway. I went into breakfast. Knowing my wife would be pleasant and Say "Happy Birthday" and probably have a present for me.

She didn't even say Good Morning, let alone any "Happy Birthday." I thought, "Well, that's wives for you. The children will remember." The children came in to breakfast and didn't say a word.

When I started to the office I was feeling pretty low and despondent. As I walked into my office, my secretary, Janet said, "Good Morning, Boss, Happy Birthday."

And I felt a little better; someone had remembered.

I worked until noon.

About noon, Janet knocked on my door and said, "You know, it's such a beautiful day outside and it's your birthday, let's go to lunch, just you and me."

I said, "By George, that's the greatest thing I've heard all day. Let's go."

We went to lunch. We didn't go where we normally go; we went out into the country to a little private place. We had two martinis and enjoyed lunch tremendously.

On the way back to the office, she said, "You know, it's such a beautiful day. We don't need to go back to the office, do we?"

I said "No, I guess not."

She said, "Let's go to my apartment." After arriving at her apartment, we had another martini and smoked cigarette and she said, "Boss, if you don't mind, I think I'll go into the bedroom and slip into something more comfortable."

"Sure," I excitedly replied.

She went into the bedroom and, in about six minutes, she came out ... carrying a big birthday cake, followed by my wife, children, and dozens of our friends.

All were singing Happy Birthday and there on the couch I sat... with nothing on but my socks...!!!!

A young couple was invited to a swanky masked party. The wife came down with a terrible headache and told her husband to go to the party and have a good time. Being the devoted husband, he protested, but she argued and said she was going to take some aspirin and go to bed. She told him there was no need for him to miss the fun. So he took his costume and away he went.

The wife, after sleeping soundly for one hour, awakened without pain, and as it was still early, she decided to go to the party.

Because hubby did not know what her costume was, she thought she would have some kicks watching her husband to see how he acted when she was not around.

She joined the party and soon spotted her husband cavorting around on the dance floor. He was dancing with every nice woman he could, and taking a little kiss here and there. His wife sidled up to him and being a rather seductive woman herself, he left his partner high and dry and devoted his time to the new "action".

She let him go as far as he wished; naturally, since he was her husband. Finally he whispered a little proposition in her ear and she agreed, so off they went to one of the cars and they took care of business. Just before unmasking at midnight, she slipped out, went home and put the costume away and got into bed, wondering what kind of explanation he would have for his notorious behaviour.

She was sitting up reading when he came in, and she asked him what he had done. He said, "Oh, the same old thing. You know I never have a good time when you're not there." Then she asked, "Did you dance much?" He replied, "I'll tell you, I never even danced one dance. When I got to the party, I met Pete, Bill and some other guys, so we went into the den and played poker all evening. But I'll tell you ... the guy that I loaned my costume to sure had one unforgettable time!"

At a Presidential, White House Dinner Party Hillary and Bill Clinton hosted a large bipartisan dinner party in their personal residence quarters at the White House including a number of current and former members of Congress: former Presidents Carter, Ford and Bush, along with former Vice presidents Mondale and Quayle. After the introductory speeches, during dinner, Vice President Dan Quayle excused himself to use the bathroom, one adjacent to the First Family's private living room.

After a couple of minutes, he returns to his seat, looking rather smug but says nothing to his wife at the time. After the dinner, as the Quayles returned home, Dan turned to Marilyn and said, "Did you know Bill has a solid gold urinal in his bathroom? How can he pretend to be serious about cutting the budget after buying that?"

Marilyn's initial look of shock turns to a sly grin as she turns to her husband and says, "We've really caught him with his pants down this time! As soon as we get home, why don't you call up the paper give them a little 'insider' information, dear?"

"Excellent idea Marilyn!" says Dan to his lovely wife. "You know, sometimes you're just so smart, dear, as he leans over to gives his wife a quick kiss on the cheek."

The following morning, after the early editions of the papers have been delivered to the White House residence, Hillary Clinton opens the newspaper over breakfast only to see a bold headline stating "Clintons SPLURGE ON GOLD URINAL, SAYS QUAYLE." Shaking her head, Hillary smirks and shouts up to the bedroom, "Bill! I think I know who peed in your Saxophone!"

Some days it just doesn't pay to get out of bed.

STILL THINK YOU'RE HAVING A BAD DAY? THINK AGAIN.

The following is taken from a Florida newspaper:

A man was working on his motorcycle on his patio and his wife was in the house in the kitchen. The man was racing the engine on the motorcycle and somehow, the motorcycle slipped into gear. Then, still holding the handlebars, the man was dragged through a glass patio door and along with the motorcycle dumped onto the floor inside the house.

The wife, hearing the crash, ran into the dining room, and found her husband laying on the floor, cut and bleeding, the motorcycle laying next to him and the patio door shattered. The wife ran to the phone and summoned an ambulance.

Because they lived on a fairly large hill, the wife went down several flights of long steps to the street to direct the paramedics to her husband. After the ambulance arrived and transported the husband to the hospital, the wife uprighted the motorcycle and pushed it outside.

Seeing that gas had spilled on the floor, the wife obtained some paper towels, blotted the gasoline, and threw the towels in the toilet.

The husband was treated at the hospital and was released to come home.

After arriving home, he looked at the shattered patio door and the damage done to his motorcycle.

He became despondent, went into the bathroom, sat on the toilet and smoked a cigarette. After finishing the cigarette, he flipped it between his legs into the toilet bowl while still seated.

The wife, who was in the kitchen, heard a loud explosion and the husband screaming. She ran into the bathroom and found her husband lying on the floor. His trousers had been blown away and he was suffering burns on the buttocks, the back of his legs and groin. The wife again ran to the phone and called for an ambulance. The same ambulance crew was dispatched and the wife met them at stairs to the street.

The paramedics loaded the husband on the stretcher and began carrying him to the street. While they were going down the street accompanied by the wife, one of the paramedics asked the wife how the husband had burned himself. She told them and the paramedics started laughing so hard, one of them tipped the stretcher and dumped the husband out. He fell down the remaining steps and broke his arm.

Now, That is a bad day...

Ivan Milat and a young lass were walking deeper and deeper into the forest when the lass said, "I don't like this it's getting darker and darker and I'm scared."

"You're scared!" replied Ivan. "I have to walk back out on my own."

This is a bricklayer's accident report that was printed in the newsletter of the English equivalent of the Workers Compensation Board a true story.

Dear Sir,

I am writing in response to your request for additional information in Block #3 of the accident reporting form. I put "Poor Planning" as the cause of my accident. You asked for a fuller explanation and I trust the following details will be sufficient. I am a bricklayer by trade. On the day of the accident, I was working alone on the roof of a new six-story building. When I completed my work, I found I had some bricks left over which when weighed later were found to weigh 240 lbs.

Rather than carry the bricks down by hand, I decided to lower them in a barrel by using a pulley which was attached to the side of the building at the sixth floor. Securing the rope at ground level, I went up to the roof, swung the barrel out and loaded the bricks into it. Then I went down and untied the rope, holding it tightly to ensure a slow descent of the 240 Lbs of bricks. You will note on the accident reporting form that my weight is 135 lbs.

Due to my surprise at being jerked off the ground so suddenly, I lost my presence of mind and forgot to let go of the rope. Needless to say, I proceeded at a rapid rate up the side of the building. In the vicinity of the third floor, I met the barrel which was now proceeding downward at an equally impressive speed. This explains the fractured skull, minor abrasions and the broken collarbone, as listed in Section 3, accident reporting form.

Slowed only slightly, I continued my rapid ascent, not stopping until the fingers of my right hand were two knuckles deep into the pulley which I mentioned in Paragraph 2 of this correspondence. Fortunately by this time I had regained my presence of mind and was able to hold tightly to the rope, in spite of the excruciating pain I was now beginning to experience. At approximately the same time, however, the barrel of bricks hit the ground and the bottom fell out of the barrel.

Now devoid of the weight of the bricks, the barrel weighed approximately 50 lbs. I refer you again to my weight. As you might imagine, I began a rapid descent down the side of the building. In the vicinity of the third floor, I met the barrel coming up. This accounts for the two fractured ankles, broken tooth and several lacerations of my legs and lower body. Here my luck began to change slightly.

The encounter with the barrel seemed to slow me enough to lessen my injuries when I fell into the pile of bricks and fortunately only three vertebrae were cracked.

I am sorry to report, however, as I lay there on the pile of bricks, in pain, unable to move and watching the empty barrel six stories above me, I again lost my composure and presence of mind and let go of the rope and I lay there watching the empty barrel begin its journey back onto me.

A small white guy goes into an elevator, when he gets in he notices a huge black dude standing next to him.

The big black dude looks down upon the small white guy and says "7 foot tall, 350 pounds, 20 inch dick, 3 pound left ball, 3 pound right ball, Turner Brown." The small white guy faints!! The big black dude picks up the small white guy and brings him to, slapping his face and shaking him and asks the small white guy "What's wrong?"

The small white guy says, "Excuse me but what did you say?" The big black dude looks down and says "7 foot tall, 350 pounds, 20 inch dick, 3 pound left ball, 3 pound right ball, my name is Turner Brown."

The small white guy says "Thank god, I thought you said turn around".

The following are ACTUAL answers given by contestants on the "Family Fortunes" Quiz show in the UK.

- Name something a blind person might use—A sword.
- Name a song with moon in the title—Blue Suede Moon.
- Name a bird with a long neck—Naomi Campbell.
- Name an occupation where you need a torch—A burglar.
- Name a famous brother and sister—Bonnie & Clyde.
- Name a dangerous race—The Arabs.
- Name an item of clothing worn by the Three Musketeers—A horse.
- Name something that floats in the bath—Water.
- Name something you wear on the beach—A deckchair.
- Name something Red—My cardigan.
- Name a famous cowboy—Buck Rogers.
- Name a famous royal—Mail.
- Name a number you have to memorize—7.
- Name something you do before going to bed—Sleep.
- Name something you put on walls—Roofs.
- Name something in the garden that's green—Shed.
- Name something that flies that doesn't have an engine—A bicycle with wings.
- Name something you might be allergic to—Skiing.
- Name a famous bridge—The Bridge over troubled waters.

U is for Urban Myths

- Name something a cat does—Goes to the toilet Name something you do in the bathroom—Decorate.
- Name an animal you might see at the zoo—A dog Name something associated with the police—Pigs.
- Name a sign of the zodiac—April.
- Name something slippery—A conman.
- Name a kind of ache—Fillet '0' Fish.
- Name a food that can be brown or white—Potato.
- Name a jacket potato topping—Jam.
- Name a famous Scotsman—Jock.
- Name another famous Scotsman—Vinnie Jones Name something with a hole in it—Window.
- Name a non-living object with legs—Plant.
- Name a domestic animal—Leopard.
- Name a part of the body beginning with 'N'—Knee.
- Name a way of cooking fish—Cod.
- Name something you open other than a door—Your.

CLASSFIED ADS:

FREE PUPPIES.

1/2 COCKER SPANIEL.

1/2 SNEAKY NEIGHBOR'S DOG.

FREE Yorkshire TERRIER.

8 YEARS OLD UNPLEASANT LITTLE DOG.

1 MAN, 7 WOMAN HOT TUB——$850 OFFER.

WASHER $100. OWNED BY CLEAN BACHELOR WHO SELDOM WASHED.

SNOW BLOWER FOR SALE... ONLY USED ON SNOWY DAYS.

FREE PUPPIES... PART GERMAN SHEPHERD—PART DOG.

2 WIRE MESH BUTCHERING GLOVES.

15-FINGER, 13-FINGER, PAIR: $15.

TICKLE ME ELMO, STILL IN BOX, COMES WITH IT'S OWN MUSTANG, 5L, AUTO, EXCELLENT CONDITION.

COWS, CALVES NEVER BRED... ALSO 1 GAY BULL FOR SALE.

SOFT GENITAL BATH TISSUES OR FACIAL TISSUE 89 cents.

GERMAN SHEPHERD 85 Lbs. NEUTERED. SPEAKS GERMAN. FREE.

FULL SIZED MATTRESS. 20 YR. WARRANTY. LIKE NEW. SLIGHT URINE SMELL.

FOR SALE, LEE MAJORS (6 MILLION DOLLAR MAN) $50.

BILL'S SEPTIC CLEANING-"WE HAUL AMERICAN MADE PRODUCTS."

GET A LITTLE JOHN, THE TRAVELING URINAL—HOLDS 2 1/2 BOTTLES OF BEER.

NICE PARACHUTE, NEVER OPENED—USED ONCE—SLIGHTLY STAINED.

FREE, FARM KITTENS. READY TO EAT.

AMERICAN FLAG—60 STARS—POLE INCLUDED—$100.

TIRED OF WORKING FOR ONLY $9.75 PER HOUR? WE OFFER PROFIT SHARING AND FLEXIBLE HOURS. STARTING PAY, $7—$9 PER HOUR.

NOTICE:

TO THE PERSON OR PERSONS WHO TOOK THE LARGE PUMPKIN ON HIGHWAY 87 NEAR SOUTHRIDGE STORAGE, PLEASE RETURN PUMPKIN AND BE CHECKED. PUMPKIN MAY BE RADIOACTIVE. ALL OTHER PLANTS IN VICINITY ARE DEAD.

QUEEN SIZE MATTRESS AND BOX SPRINGS—$175.

OUR SOFA SEATS THE WHOLE MOB. AND IT'S MADE OF 100% Italian LEATHER.

JOINING NUDIST COLONY! MUST SELL WASHER & DRYER $300.

LAWYER SAYS CLIENT IS NOT THAT GUILTY.

ALZHEIMER'S CENTRE PREPARES FOR AN AFFAIR TO REMEMBER.

GAS CLOUD CLEARS OUT TACO BELL.

OPEN HOUSE BODY SHAPES TONING SALON, FREE COFFEE & DONUTS.

FULLY COOKED BONELESS SMOKED MAN.

FOR SALE BY OWNER Complete Set of Encyclopaedia Britannica. 45 volumes. Excellent condition. $1.000.00 or best offer. No longer needed. Got married last weekend. Wife knows everything.

This is an email that a friend of mine received the other day from a guy she knows nothing at all about. She met him while out dancing and gave him her email address. When he emailed her, she emailed him back with a few get-to-know-you questions... like "what's your last name?"

This is how he responded:

I am at a stage in my life where I'm looking seriously and systematically for someone I can share my life with. You seem like a nice person, and I don't mean this as badly as it might sound, but I don't have time for twenty questions by email. I met five girls Saturday night, have already booked a first coffee with three of them, and meet more every time I go dancing... and I go dancing at least three times a week. I immediately rule out women who put up too many barriers. I don't do this because I think there's anything wrong with them, nor do I do it because I'm arrogant. I do this simply to economize on time.

I know that dating in this city is difficult and scary for women. But keep in mind it's that way for the guys, too. Most of all, remember that you're competing with thousands of other women who don't insist that that the man do all of the work of establishing a connection. And they live closer.

Now, maybe you'll find someone who's so taken by a single dance with you that he's willing to negotiate by email for a chance to trek to your suburban hideout to plead his case. But you might not.

And if such a person does exist, and you do happen to cross paths with him-what do you imagine a guy that desperate would have to offer?

—Bryan Winter

In the hopes that this email might get back to him after being seen by countless thousands of young women along the way... please send on to a friend!!!

Would you believe?

I left Brisbane heading towards Maryborough, when I decided to stop at a comfort station for a 'number 2'. The first stall was occupied, so I went into the second one. I was no sooner seated than I heard a voice from the next stall:

"HI, how are you doing?"

Well, I am not the type to chat with strangers in highway comfort stations, and I really don't know quite what possessed me... But anyway, I answered—a little embarrassed: "Not bad."

Then stranger asked, "And, what are you up to?"

Talk about your dumb question. I was really beginning to think this was too weird! But I said, "well, just like you, I'm driving east." Then, I heard the stranger, sounding very upset, says, "look, I'll call you back. There's some idiot in the next stall answering all the questions I'm asking you."

A man and his wife are awakened at 3 o'clock in the morning by a loud banging on the door. The man gets up and goes to the door where an unknown stranger, standing in the pouring rain, is asking for a push.

"Not a chance", says the husband, "it is three o'clock in the morning!" He slams the door and returns to bed. "Who was that?" Asked his wife "Just some drunk guy asking for a push," he answers. "Did you help him?" She asks.

"No, I did not, it is three in the morning and it is pouring out!"

"Well, you have a short memory," says his wife. "Can't you remember about 'three months ago when we broke down and those two guys helped us?—I think you should help him, and should be ashamed of yourself."

The man does as he is told, gets dressed, and goes out into the pounding rain. He calls out into the dark, "Hello, are you still there? "Yes" comes back the answer.

"Do you still need a push?" calls out the husband. "Yes, please!" Comes the reply from the dark.

"Where are you?" asks the husband.

"Over here on the swing!" replies the drunk?

---

1. Phone hackers, managed to break into the telephone system of 'Weight Watchers' in Glasgow, and changed the outgoing message to 'Hello, you fat bastard'.

2. From the Churchdown Parish Magazine: "Would the Congregation please note that the bowl at the back of the Church, labelled 'For the Sick', is for monetary donations only."

3. From The Guardian concerning a sign seen in a Police canteen in Christchurch, New Zealand: "Will the person who took a slice of cake from the Commissioner's Office return it immediately. It is needed as evidence in a poisoning case."

4. From The Daily Telegraph in a piece headed "Brussels Pays 200,000 Pounds to Save Prostitutes": "... the money will not be going directly into the prostitutes' pocket, but will be used to encourage them to lead a

better life. We will be training them for new positions in hotels."

5. From The Derby Abbey Community News: "We apologise for the error in the last edition, in which we stated that 'Mr Fred Nicolme is a Defective in the Police Force'. This was a typographical error. We meant of course that 'Mr Nicolme is a Detective in the Police Farce. "'

6. From The Guardian: "After being charged 20 pounds for a 10 pounds overdraft, 30 year old Michael Howard of Leeds changed his name by deed poll to "Yorkshire Bank Plc is Fascist Bastards". The Bank bas now asked him to close his account, and Mr Bastards has asked them to repay the 69p balance by cheque, made out in his new name."

7. From The Manchester Evening News: An Austrian circus dwarf died recently when he bounced sideways from a trampoline and was swallowed by a hippopotamus. Seven thousand people watched as little Franz Dasch popped into the mouth of Hilda the Hippo and the animal's gag reflex forced it to swallow. The crowd applauded wildly before other circus people realized what had happened.

8. An elderly woman at a unit for sufferers of senile dementia passed round a box of mothballs thinking that they were mints. Eleven people were taken to hospital for treatment.

9. After a heavy drinking session in Weymouth, 51 year old Philip Pyne fancied a nap on a bench. To stop himself rolling off, he put 12 nails through his trousers and in the process, drove several of them through his leg. Fortunately he was discovered by police.

10. An operation at Nottingham hospital ended prematurely when the patient exploded. The casualty, an

82-year old woman, was undergoing electro surgery for cancer. The blast was attributed to an unusual build-up of stomach gases ignited by the sparks.

The following is a direct quote from the Centre for Strategic and International Studies report on Global organized Crime.

FBI agents conducted a raid of a psychiatric hospital in San Diego that was under investigation for medical insurance fraud. After hours of reviewing thousands of medical records, the dozens of agents had worked up quite an appetite. The agent in charge of the investigation called a nearby pizza parlour with delivery service to order a quick dinner for his colleagues.

The following telephone conversation was recorded by the FBI because they were taping all conversations at the hospital:

Agent: "Hello. I would like to order 19 large pizzas and 67 cans of soda."

Pizza Man: "And where would you like them delivered?"

Agent: "We're over at the psychiatric hospital."

Pizza Man: "The psychiatric hospital?"

Agent: "That's right. I'm an FBI agent."

Pizza Man: "You're an FBI agent?"

Agent: "That's correct. Just about everybody here is."

Pizza Man: "And you're at the psychiatric hospital?"

Agent: "That's correct. And make sure you don't go through the front doors. We have them locked. You will have to go around to the back to the service entrance to deliver the pizzas."

Pizza Man: "And you say you're all FBI agents?"

Agent: "That's right. How soon can you have them here?"

Pizza Man: "And everyone at the psychiatric hospital is an FBI agent?"

Agent: "That's right. We've been here all day and we're starving."

Pizza Man: "How are you going to pay for all of this?"

Agent: "I have my cheque book right here."

Pizza Man: "And you're all FBI Agents?"

Agent: "That's right. Everyone here is an FBI agent. Can you remember to bring the pizzas and sodas to the service entrance in the rear? We have the front doors locked."

Pizza Man: "I don't think so." (Click)

---

1. The average cost of rehabilitating a seal after the Exxon Valdez oil spill in Alaska was $80,000. At a special ceremony, two of the most expensive saved animals were released back into the wild amid cheers and applause from onlookers. A minute later they were eaten by a killer whale.

2. A psychology student in New York rented out her spare room to a carpenter in order to nag him constantly and study his reactions. After weeks of needling, he snapped and beat her repeatedly with an axe leaving her mentally retarded.

3. Fran Perkins of Los Angeles made an attempt on the world flag-pole sitting record. Suffering from flu he came down eight hours short of the 400 day record, his sponsor had gone bust, his girlfriend had left him and his phone and electricity had been cut off.

4. A woman came home to find her husband in the kitchen, shaking frantically with what looked like a wire running from his waist towards the electric kettle. Intending to jolt him away from the deadly current she whacked him with a handy plank of wood, breaking his arm in two places until then he had been happily listening to his iPod.

5. Two animal rights protesters were protesting at the cruelty of sending pigs to the slaughterhouse in Bonn. Suddenly the pigs, all two thousands of them, escaped through a broken fence and stampeded, trampling the two hapless protesters to death.

6. Terrorist, Khay Rahnajet, didn't pay enough postage on a letter bomb. It came back with 'return to sender' stamped on it. Forgetting it was the bomb, he opened it and was blown to bits.

Bizarre accidents suffered by men...

Flower Power (I defy any of you not to wince at this one.)

A man turned up at a hospital wearing an overcoat, and with blood dripping down his leg. When he removed the coat, the doctor saw he had a geranium inserted into his penis. The man got the flower in without any difficulty, but when he tried to remove it, the hairs on the stem of the flower had dug into the urethra and ripped it to shreds.

Dog's Dinner

A policeman in Staffordshire returned home from a night shift to find his wife preparing breakfast. For some unknown reason, he wrapped a slice of bread around his penis, at which point the dog leapt up and took a bite out of it. The man needed cosmetic surgery to restore the damage.

Make Mine a Stiff One

A 34-year old New Yorker injected a cocaine solution into his penis to heighten his sexual pleasure. After enjoying intercourse with his girlfriend, however, and after three days he went to the doctor in search of help. Shortly afterwards, he developed blood clots in various parts of his body, gangrene set in, and he lost both legs, nine fingers and his penis.

The following are all bizarre-but-true news stories, courtesy of Private Eye magazine:

1. Bristol Evening Post:

    "I have promised to keep his identity confidential," said Jane Setherton, a spokeswoman for the Marriott Hotel, Bristol, "but I can confirm that he is no longer in our employment. We asked him to clean one lift, and he spent four days on the job."

    When I asked him why, he replied; "well, there are twelve of them, one on each floor, and sometimes some of them aren't there.' Eventually, we realized that he thought each floor had a different lift, and he'd cleaned the same one twelve times. We had to let him go. It seemed best all round. I understand he is now working for Woolworths."

2. The Star (Johannesburg):

    "The situation is absolutely under control," Transport Minister Ephraem Magagula told the Swaziland parliament in Mbabane. "Our nation's merchant navy is perfectly safe. We just don't know where it is, that's all."

Replying to an MP's question, Minister Magagula admitted that the landlocked country had completely lost track of its only ship, the Swazimar: "We believe it is in a sea somewhere. At one time, we sent a team of men to look for it, but there was a problem with drink and they failed to find it, and so, technically, yes, we've lost it a bit. But I categorically reject all suggestions of incompetence on the part of this government. The swazimar is a big ship painted in the sort of nice bright colours you can see at night.

Mark my words, it will turn up. The right honourable gentleman opposite is a very naughty man, and he will laugh on the other side of his face when my ship comes in."

3. The Standard (Kenya):

"What is all the fuss about?" Weseka Sambu asked a hastily convened news conference at Jomo Kenyatta International Airport. "A technical hitch like this could have happened anywhere in the world. You people are not patriots. You just want to cause trouble."

Sambu, a spokesman for Kenya Airways, was speaking after the cancellation of a through flight from Kisumu, via Jomo Kenyatta, to Berlin: "The forty-two passengers had boarded the plane ready for take-off, when the pilot noticed one of the tyres was flat. Kenya Airways did not possess a spare tyre, and unfortunately the airport nitrogen canister was empty."

"A passenger suggested taking the tyre to a petrol station for inflation, but unluckily the jack had gone missing so we couldn't get the wheel off. Our engineers tried heroically to reinflate the tyre with a bicycle pump, but had no luck, and the pilot even blew into the valve with his mouth, but he passed out. When I announced that the flight had to be abandoned, one of the passengers, Mr Mutu, suddenly struck me about the face with a life-jacket whistle and said we were a national disgrace. I told him he was being ridiculous, and that there was to be another flight in a fortnight."

"And, in the meantime, he would be able to enjoy the scenery around. Kisurnu, albeit at his own expense."

You gotta love people who can turn a tragedy into at least a little humour. After the May 3rd tornado, many Oklahoma City residents have tried to deal with their loss through humour. Many home owners have spray-painted their homes or put up signs claiming:

"FOR SALE: FIXER UPPER or OPEN HOUSE".

However, the best one comes from a man in Moore, who, before President Clinton's visit, put a sign in his yard saying: "HEY BILL, HOW'S THIS FOR A BLOW JOB?"

Unfortunately, the Secret Service asked him to remove it since there was so much media coverage.

If you receive an e-mail entitled "Crazy Times" delete it immediately. Do not open it! Apparently this one is pretty nasty.

It will not only erase everything on your hard drive, but it will also delete anything on disks within 20 feet of your computer.

It demagnetizes the stripes on ALL of your credit cards.

It reprograms your ATM access code, messes up the tracking on your VCR and uses subspace field harmonics to scratch any CD's you attempt to play.

It will re-calibrate your refrigerator's coolness settings so all your ice cream melts and your milk curdles.

It will program your phone autodial to call only your mother-in- law's number.

This virus will mix antifreeze into your fish tank. It will drink all your beer.

It will leave dirty socks on the coffee table when you are expecting company.

Its radioactive emissions will cause your toe jam and bellybutton fuzz (be honest, you have some) to migrate behind your ears.

It will replace your shampoo with Nair and your Nair with Rogaine, all while dating your current boy/girlfriend behind your back and billing their hotel rendezvous to your Visa card.

It will cause you to run with scissors and throw things in a way that is only fun until someone loses an eye.

It will give you Dutch elm disease and Lupus.

It will rewrite your backup files, changing all your active verbs to passive tense and incorporating undetectable misspellings which grossly change the interpretations of key sentences.

If the "Crazy Times" message is opened in a Windows 95 environment, it will leave the toilet seat up and leave your hair dryer plugged in dangerously close to a full bathtub.

It will not only remove the tags from your mattresses and pillows, but it will also refill your skimmed milk with whole milk.

It will replace all your luncheon meat with Spam.

It will molecularly rearrange your cologne or perfume, causing it to smell like dill pickles. (Remember Brut 33?)

It is insidious and subtle.

It is dangerous and terrifying to behold.

It is also a rather interesting shade of mauve. These are just a few signs of infection.

PLEASE FORWARD THIS MESSAGE TO EVERYONE YOU KNOW!! !

(For the benefit of non-Americans—Nair is a brand name hair remover)

I think you should all give this a go!

Even if you've seen this one before it's important that you do complete it again (promise)....and it only takes 30 secs anyway.

It's very important you don't cheat with this, as it really does spoil it...

Best personality test I've seen in a long time...

First, get a pen and paper.

Second, write the numbers one to six. Next to number one, write any number...

Next to number two, write the name of anyone to whom you are really attracted... to

Next to three, write down the first colour you can think

Next to number four, write the name of your first pet....

Next to number five and six write down the names of two members of your family.

Remember...no cheating. Keep scrolling down.

Here's the answers....

The number next to number one show how many times you should smashed over the head with a baseball hat for thinking that stupid e-mails like this actually mean anything....

The person named next to number two is someone who will never sleep with you because you're stupid enough to waste your time on something like this....

The colour you picked means nothing. It's a friggin' colour for Christ sake....

Number four gives you the name of a dead animal....

Numbers five and six represent family members who are embarrassed to be related to you..

Pass this on to everyone you know, so they can feel like a twat too.

DON'T CHEAT BY SCROLLING DOWN FIRST

It only takes 30 seconds.

Work this out as you read.

Make sure you don't read the bottom until you've worked it out.

This is not one of those waste of time things, it's GOOD.

1. First of all, pick the number of times a week that you would like to have sex. (try for more than once)
2. Multiply this number by 2. (Just to be bold)
3. Add 5. (for Sunday)
4. Multiply it by 50. (being a bit stupid). I'll wait while you get the calculator.
5. If you have already had your birthday this year add 1750. If you haven't, add 1749.

6. Now subtract the four digit year that you were born.

You should now have a three digit number.

The first digit of this was your original number. (i.e. how many times you want to have sex each week.)

The second two digits are your age and it shows.

THIS IS THE ONLY YEAR (2000) IT WILL EVER WORK, SO SPREAD IT AROUND WHILE IT LASTS. IMPRESSIVE ISN'T IT?

The following are actual stories told by travel agents.

1. I had someone ask for an aisle seat so that their hair wouldn't get messed up by being near the window.
2. A client called in inquiring about a package to Hawaii. After going over all the cost info, she asked, "would it be cheaper to fly to California and then take the train to Hawaii?"
3. I got a call from a woman who wanted to go to Capetown. I started to explain the length of the flight and the passport information when she interrupted me with "'I'm not trying to make you look stupid, but Capetown is in Massachusetts". Without trying to make her look like the stupid one, I calmly explained, "Capecod is in Massachusetts, Capetown is in Africa". Her response....click
4. A secretary called in looking for a hotel in Los Angeles. She gave me various names off a list, none of which I could find. I finally had her fax me the list. To my surprise, it was a list of hotels in New Orleans, Louisiana. She thought the LA stood for Los Angeles, and that New Orleans was a suburb of L.A. Worst of all, when I called her back, she was not even embarrassed.

5. "A man called, furious about a Florida package we did. I asked what was wrong with the vacation in Orlando. He said he was expecting an ocean-view room. I tried to explain that is not possible, since Orlando in the middle of the state. He replied, 'Don't lie to me. I looked on the map and Florida is a very thin state."

6. "I got a call from a man who asked, "Is it possible to see England from Canada?" I said, 'No'. He said 'but they look so close on the map.' Another man called and asked if he could rent a car in Dallas. When I pulled up the reservation, I noticed he had a 1-hour lay-over in Dallas. When I asked him why he wanted to rent a car, he said, 'I heard Dallas was a big airport, and I need a car to drive between the gates to save time.'"

7. "A nice lady just called. She needed to know how it was possible that her flight from Detroit left at 8:20am and got into Chicago at 8:33am. I tried to explain that Michigan was an hour ahead of Illinois, but she could not understand the concept of time zones. Finally I told her the plane went very fast, and she bought that!"

8. "A woman called and asked, 'Do airlines put your physical description on your bag so they know whose luggage belongs to who?' I said, 'No, why do you ask?' She replied, 'Well, when I checked in with the airline, they put a tag on my luggage that said FAT, and I'm overweight, is there any connection?' I explained the city code for Fresno is FAT, and that the airline was just putting a destination tag on her luggage".

9. "I just got off the phone with a man who asked, 'How do I know which plane to get on?' I asked him what exactly he meant, which he replied, 'I was told my flight number is 823, but none of these darn planes have numbers on them.'"

10. "A woman called and said, 'I need to fly to Pepsi-cola on one of those computer planes.' I asked if she meant to fly to Pensacola on a commuter plane. She said, 'Yea, whatever'"

11. "A business man called and had a question about the documents he needed in order to fly to China. After a lengthy discussion about passports, I reminded him he needed a visa. 'Oh no I don't, I've been to China many times and never had to have one of those'. I double checked, and sure enough, his stay required a visa. When I told him this he said, 'Look, I've been to China 4 times and every time they have accepted my American Express.'"

12. "A woman called to make reservations, 'I want to go from Chicago to Hippopotamus, New York'. The agent was at a loss for words. Finally, the agent: 'Are you sure that's the name of the town?' 'Yes, what flights do you have?' replied the customer. After some searching, the agent came back with, 'I'm sorry, ma'am, I've looked up every airport code in the country and can't find a Hippopotamus anywhere.' The customer retorted, 'Oh don't be silly. Everyone knows where it is. Check your map.' The agent scoured a map of the state of New York and finally offered, 'You don't mean Buffalo, do you?' 'That's it! I knew it was a big animal!'"

As a joke, my brother used to hang a pair of panty hose over his fireplace before Christmas. He said all he wanted was for Santa to fill them. What they say about Santa checking the list twice must be true because every Christmas morning, although Jay's kids' stockings were overflowed, his poor pantyhose hung sadly empty and grew increasingly threadbare.

One year I decided to make his dream come true. I put on sunglasses and fake beard and went in search of an inflatable love doll. Of course, they don't sell those things at Wal-Mart. I had to go to an adult bookstore downtown. If you've never been in an X-rated store, don't go.

You'll only confuse yourself. I was there almost three hours saying things like, "What does this do?" "You're kidding me!" "Who owns that?" "Do you have their phone number?"

Finally, I made it to the inflatable doll section. I wanted to buy a standard, uncomplicated doll suitable for a night of romance that could also substitute as a passenger in my truck so I could use the car pool lane during rush hour. I'm not sure what a complicated doll is. Perhaps one that is subject to wild mood shifts and using a French accent.

That also describes a few ex-girlfriends. Finding what I wanted was difficult. Love dolls come in many different models. The top of line, according to the side of the box, could do things I'd only seen in a book on animal husbandry. I figured the "vibro-motion" was a feature I could live without, so I settled for Lovable Louise. She was at the bottom of the price scale. To call Louise a "doll" took a huge leap of imagination.

On Christmas Eve, with the help of an old bicycle pump, Louise came to life.

My sister-in-law was in on the plan and cleverly left the front door key hidden under the mat. In the wee morning hours, long after Santa had gone, I snuck into the house and filled the dangling panty hose with Louise's pliant legs and bottom. I also ate some cookies and drank what remained of a glass of milk on a nearby tray. Then I let myself out and went home, and giggled for a couple of hours.

The next morning my brother called to say that Santa had been to his house and left a present that had made him VERY happy but had left the dog confused. He would bark, start to walk away, then come back and bark some more. I suggested he purchase an inflatable Lassie to set Rover straight.

We also agreed that Louise should remain in her panty hose so the rest of the family could admire her when they came over for the traditional Christmas dinner. It seemed like a great idea, except that we forgot that Grandma and Grandpa would be there.

My grandmother noticed Louise the moment she walked in the door. "What the hell is that?" she asked. My brother quickly explained. 'It's a doll."

"Who would play with something like that?" Granny snapped. I had several candidates in mind, but kept my mouth shut.

"Where are her clothes?" Granny continued.

"I hadn't seen any in the box, but I kept this information to myself."

"Boy, that turkey sure smells nice, Gran," Jay said, trying to steer her into the dining room. But Granny was relentless.

"Why doesn't she have any teeth?"

Again, I could have answered, but why would I? It was Christmas and no one wanted to ride in the back of the ambulance saying, "Hang on Granny, Hang on!"

My grandfather, a delightful old man with poor eyesight, sidled up to me and said, "Hey, who's the naked gal by the fireplace?" I told him she was Jay's friend. A few minutes later I noticed Grandpa by the mantel, talking to Louise. Not just talking, but actually flirting. It was then that we realized this might be Grandpa's last Christmas at home.

The dinner went well. We made the usual small talk about who had died, who was dying, and who should be killed, when suddenly Louise made a noise that sounded a lot like my father in the bathroom in the morning. Then she lurched from the panty hose, flew around the room twice, and fell in a leap in front of the sofa.

The cat screamed, I passed cranberry sauce through my nose, and Grandpa ran across the room, fell to his knees, and began administering mouth-to-mouth resuscitation. My brother wet his pants and Granny threw down her napkin, stomped out of the room, and sat in the car.

It was indeed a Christmas to treasure and remember.

Later in my brother's garage, we conducted a thorough examination to decide the cause of Louise's collapse. We discovered that Louise had suffered from a hot ember to the back of her right thigh. Fortunately, thanks to a drug called duct tape, we restored her to perfect health. Louise went on to star in several bachelor party movies. I think Grandpa still calls her whenever he can get out of the house.

CHAPTER 22

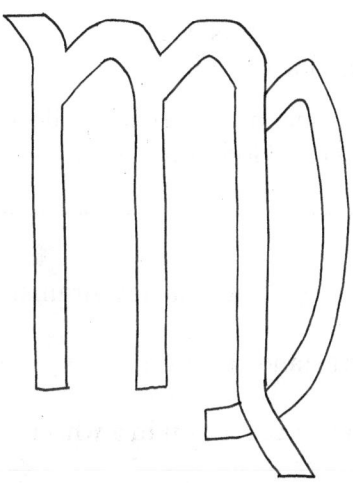

V is for Virgin

A middle aged man and woman meet, fall in love, and decide to get married. On their wedding night they settle into the bridal suite at their hotel and the bride says to her new groom, "Please promise to be gentle,... I am still a virgin."

The startled groom says "How can that be? You've been married 3 times before."

The bride responds...

"Well you see it was this way: My first husband was a psychiatrist and all he ever wanted to do was talk about it."

"My second husband was a gynaecologist and all he ever wanted to do was look at it."

"And my third husband was a stamp collector and all he ever wanted to do was...... God I miss him!"

Q: Why do men want to marry virgins?

A: They can't stand criticism.

Q: What do you call a Nun in a wheel chair?

A: Virgin Mobile.

They told me that god and chocolate are great ways to substitute sex. Now, i'm a Nun, a virgin and now have diabetes.

Q: Tiger Woods once visited the Virgin Islands?

A: They are now just called the Islands.

Q: What do you call a 13 year old girl from Kentucky who can run faster than her six brothers?

A: A virgin.

Q: Did you hear about the spread that lost its virginity?

A: It got marmalaid.

Q: Where does Extra Extra Virgin Olive Oil come from?

A: Really ugly olives

Q: What do virgins and screen doors have in common?

A: The more they get slammed the looser they get.

Dear young girls losing their virginity... if your age is on the clock, you're too young for the cock.

Dear virgins... if you're old enough to flirt, you're old enough to squirt.

Q: "Father, how am I going to tell my husband that I am still a virgin?"

A: "My child, you have been a married woman for many years. You have had three husbands! Surely that cannot be." "Well, father, my first husband was a psychologist, and all he wanted to do was talk, and the next one was in construction and he always said he'd get to it tomorrow. The last one was a gynecologist and all he did was look. But this time, father, I'm marrying a lawyer and I'm sure I'm going to get screwed."

Prisoner Woman: "Honey you no I'm a virgin and I no nothing about sex. Explain.."

Man: "Honey lets put it this way your privates a prison and mines a prisoner so you put the prisoner in the prison."

So they have sex for the first time then the man gets tired to take a break the woman says honey the prisoner escaped so they have sex again then he took his dick out for a while because he was so exhausted and the woman says "Honey the prisoner escaped again."

Man: "ITS NOT A LIFE LONG SENTENCE, OK!"

Church One Sunday in church the priest told the ladies. If you know you are virgin you stand up. A lady carrying a baby stood up and everyone laughed in tears but the lady said it's not me. It's my baby.

Your stereotypes of virgins are pathetic.

"I am a twenty three year old virgin and

1. I don't play world of Warcraft;
2. I don't have ginger hair; and
3. I am not on COD twenty hours a day.

   It's strange really.

   I'm just a normal size 18 girl."

My girlfriend's dad was pissed off that I took her virginity. I said "Sorry, it won't happen again."

A new priest at his first mass was so nervous he could hardly speak. After mass, he asked the monsignor how he had done. The Monsignor replied, "When I am worried about getting nervous on the pulpit, I put a glass of vodka next to the water glass. If I start to get nervous, I take a sip".

So next Sunday, the priest took the monsignor's advice. At the beginning of the sermon, he got nervous and took a drink. He proceeded to talk up a storm.

Upon his return to his office after mass, he found the following note on the door:

Sip the Vodka, don't gulp.

There are 10 commandments, not 12.

There are 12 disciples, not 10.

Jesus was consecrated, not constipated.

Jacob wagered his donkey, he did not bet his ass.

We do not refer to Jesus Christ as the late J.C..

The Father, Son and Holy Ghost are not referred to as Daddy, Junior and the Spook.

David slew Goliath, he did not kick the shit out of him.

When David was hit by a rock and knocked off his donkey, don't say he was stoned off his ass.

We do not refer to the cross as the "Big T".

When Jesus broke the bread at the Last Supper, he said, "Take this and eat it, for it is my body." He did not say, "Bite me".

The Virgin Mary is not called "Mary with the Cherry".

The recommended grace before a meal is not: Rub-A-Dub-Dub thanks for the grub, yeah God.

Next Sunday, there will be a taffy-pulling contest at St Peter's, not a Peter pulling contest at St Taffy's.

Virgin flight staff occasionally makes an effort to ensure the "In-flight safety lecture" is a lot more than just "entertaining." Here are some real examples that have been heard or reported.

1. "There may be 50 ways to leave your lover, but there are only 4 ways out of this aircraft ..."
2. "Your seat cushions can be used for floatation and—In the event of an emergency water landing—Please take them with our compliments."
3. "We do feature a smoking section on this flight; if you must smoke, contact a member of the flight crew who will escort you to the wing of the aircraft."
4. "Smoking in the lavatories is prohibited. Any person caught smoking in the lavatories will be asked to leave the plane immediately."
5. Pilot—"Folks, we have reached our cruising altitude now, so am going to switch the seat belt sign off. Feel free to move about as you wish, but please stay inside the plane till we land... It's a bit cold outside, and if you walk on the wings it affects the flight pattern."
6. Pilot, after landing: "Thank you for flying with us. We hope you enjoyed giving us the money as much as we enjoyed taking you for a ride."
7. As we waited just off the runway for another airliner to cross in front of us, some of the passengers began to retrieve luggage from the overhead bins. The "Head Purser" announced on the intercom, "This aircraft is

equipped with a video surveillance system that monitors the cabin during taxiing. Any passenger leaving their seat before the aircraft comes to a full and complete stop at the gate will be strip-searched as they leave the aircraft."

8. Pilot: "We've reached our cruising altitude now, so I'm turning off the seat belt sign. I'm also switching to auto pilot. This means I can come back there and, for the remainder of the flight, go for a nap."

9. The plane landed and was coming to a stop, when a shout came over the loudspeakers: "Whoa, BIG fella ... WHOA ..!"

10. "Should the cabin lose pressure, oxygen masks will drop from the overhead area. Please place the bag over your own mouth and nose before assisting children. Or adults acting like children."

11. "As you exit the plane, please make sure to sure to gather all of your belongings. Anything left behind will be distributed evenly among the flight attendants. Please do NOT leave children or spouses!" The purser then continued, "Last one off the plane must clean it."

12. And from a Captain during his welcome message: "You'll be pleased to know we have some of the best flight attendants in the industry ... Unfortunately none of them are on this aircraft!"

13. A Captain reported that, on a particular flight, he had hammered his ship into the runway really hard. The airline had a policy which required the first officer to stand at the door while the passengers exited, give a smile, and a "Thanks for flying with us." He said that, in light of the terrible landing, he had a difficult time looking passengers in the eye, thinking that someone would have a smart comment. Finally everyone had

departed, except for a little old lady walking with a cane. She said, "Sonny, mind if I ask you a question?" "Why no Ma'am," replied the first officer, "What is it?" The little old lady commented, "Did we land. Or were we shot down?"

14. Overheard on a flight, on a particularly windy and bumpy day. During the final approach the Captain was really having to fight it. After an extremely hard landing, a female Flight Attendant came on the PA and announced, "Ladies and Gentlemen, welcome. Please remain in your seats with your seatbelts fastened while the Captain taxis what's left of our aircraft to the gate!"

15. Flight attendant's comment on a less than perfect landing: "We ask you to please remain seated whilst 'Captain Kangaroo' bounces us towards a terminal."

16. After a particularly rough landing during thunderstorms, a flight attendant announced: "Please take care when opening the overhead compartments because, after a landing like that, sure as HELL everything has shifted."

17. From a flight attendant ... "Welcome aboard this flight. To operate your seatbelt, insert the metal tab into the buckle, and pull tight. It works just like every other seatbelt, and if you don't know how to operate one, you probably shouldn't be out in public unsupervised. In the event of a sudden loss of cabin pressure, oxygen masks will descend from the ceiling. Stop screaming, grab the mask, and pull it over your face. If you have a small child travelling with you, secure your mask before assisting with theirs. If you are travelling with two small children, we now suggest you think VERY seriously, and rapidly decide which one you love most."

18. "Weather at our destination is 27 degrees with some broken clouds, but we'll try to have them fixed before we arrive."

19. "Thank you for flying with us and remember. Nobody loves you, or your money, more than us."

20. After a real crusher of a landing, the Flight Attendant came on with, "Ladies and Gentlemen, please remain in your seats until Captain Crash and the Crew have brought the aircraft to a screeching halt up against the gate. And, once the tire smoke has cleared and the warning bells are silenced, we'll open the door and you can pick your way through the wreckage to the terminal."

21. Part of a Flight Attendant's arrival announcement: "We'd like to thank you folks for flying with us today. And, the next time you get the insane urge to go blasting through the skies in a pressurized metal tube, we hope you'll think of us."

22. "Your seat cushions can be used for flotation, and in the event of an emergency water landing, please take them with our compliments."

CHAPTER 23

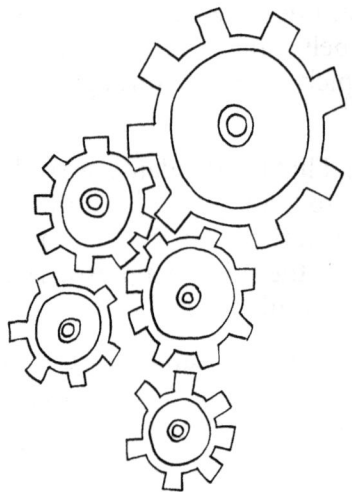

W is for Work

PERFORMANCE EVALUATIONS

1. "Since my last report, this employee has reached rock bottom and has started to dig."
2. "His men would follow him anywhere, but only out of morbid curiosity."
3. "I would not allow this employee to breed".
4. "This employee is really not so much of a has-been, but more of a definite won't be."
5. "Works well when under constant supervision and cornered like a rat in a trap."
6. "When she opens her mouth, it seems that it is only to change feet."
7. "He would be out of his depth in a parking lot puddle"
8. "This young lady has delusions of adequacy."
9. "He sets low personal standards and then consistently fails to achieve them"
10. "This employee is depriving a village somewhere of an idiot"
11. "This employee should go far, and the sooner he starts, the better."
12. "Got a full -pack, but lacks the plastic thing to hold it all together."
13. "A gross ignoramus—times worse than an ordinary ignoramus."
14. "He certainly takes a long time to make his pointless observations."
15. "He doesn't have ulcers, but he's a carrier."

16. "I would like to go hunting with him sometime."
17. "He's been working with glue too much."
18. "He would argue with a signpost."
19. "He has a knack for making strangers immediately uncomfortable."
20. "He brings a lot of joy whenever he leaves the room."
21. "When his IQ reaches, he should sell."
22. "If you see two people talking and one looks bored, he's the other one."
23. "A photographic memory but with the lens cover glued on."
24. "A prime candidate for natural de-selection."
25. "Donated his brain to science before he was done using it."
26. "Gates are down, the lights are flashing, but the train isn't coming."
27. "Has two brains: one is lost and the other is out looking for it."
28. "If he were any more stupid, he'd have to be watered twice a week."
29. "If you give him a penny for his thoughts, you'd get change."
30. "If you stand close enough to him, you can hear the ocean."
31. "It's hard to believe that he beat out, other sperm."
32. "One neuron short of a synapse."

33. "Some drink from the fountain of knowledge; he only gargled."
34. "Takes him 2 hours to watch minutes."
35. "The wheel is turning, but the hamster is dead."

TEN BEST THINGS TO SAY IF YOU GET CAUGHT SLEEPING AT YOUR DESK

10. They told me at the blood bank this might happen.
9. This is just a 15-minute power nap like they raved about in that time-management course you sent me to.
8. WWhew! Guess I left the top off the Whiteout. You probably got here just in time!
7. I wasn't sleeping! I was meditating on the mission statement and envisioning a new paradigm.
6. I was testing my keyboard for drool resistance.
5. I was doing a highly specific Yoga exercise to relieve work-related stress. Are you discriminating toward people who practice Yoga?
4. Why did you interrupt me? I had almost figured out a solution to our biggest problem.
3. The coffee machine is broken...
2. Someone must've put decaf in the wrong pot...
1. ...And in Jesus' name. Amen.

"What I've learned at work..."

1. I've learned that you cannot make someone love you. All you can do is stalk them and hope they panic and give in.
2. I've learned that it takes years to build up trust, and only suspicion, not proof, to destroy it.
3. I've learned- that you can get by on charm for about fifteen minutes.
4. After that, you'd better have a big dick or huge tits.
5. I've learned that you shouldn't compare yourself to others—they are more fucked up than you think.
6. I've learned that you can keep puking long after you think you're finished.
7. I've learned that money is a great substitute for character.
8. I've learned that sometimes the people you expect to kick you when you're down will be the ones who do.
9. I've learned that your family won't always be there for you. Of course, you win the lottery, the nag, the philanderer, the fuck-up, the missing one will be there for "You."
10. I've learned that we don't have to ditch bad friends because their dysfunction makes us feel better about ourselves.
11. I've learned that no matter how you try to protect your children, they will eventually get arrested and end up in the local paper.
12. I've learned that overzealous customs agents can change your life in a matter of hours.

13. I've learned that the people you care most about in life are taken from you too soon. And all the less important ones just never go away.

TIPS FROM EMPLOYEES TO THEIR MANAGERS:

1. Never give me work in the morning. Always wait until 4pm and then bring it to me. The challenge of a deadline is refreshing.
2. If it's really a rush job, run in and interrupt me every 10 minutes to inquire how it's going. That helps. Or even better, hover behind me, advising me at every keystroke.
3. Always leave without telling anyone where you're going. It gives me a chance to be creative when someone asks where you are.
4. If my arms are full of papers, boxes, books, or supplies, don't open the door for me. I need to learn how to function as a paraplegic and opening doors with no arms is good training in case I should ever be injured and lose all use of my limbs.
5. If you give me more than one job to do, don't tell me which is the priority. I am psychic.
6. Do your best to keep me late. I adore this office and really have nowhere to go or anything to do. I have no life beyond work.
7. If a job I do pleases you, keep it a secret. If that gets out, it could mean a promotion.
8. If you don't like my work, tell everyone. I like my name to be popular in conversations. I was born to be whipped.

9. If you have special instructions for a job, don't write them down. In fact, save them until the job is almost done. No use confusing me with useful information.
10. Never introduce me to the people you're with. I have no right to know anything. In the corporate food chain, I am plankton. When you refer to them later, my shrewd deductions will identify them.
11. Be nice to me only when the job I'm doing for you could really change your life and send you straight to manager's hell.
12. Tell me all your little problems. No one else has any and it's nice to know someone is less fortunate. I especially like the story about having to pay so much taxes on the bonus check you received for being such a good manager.
13. Wait until my yearly review and then tell me what my goals should have been.
14. Give me a mediocre performance rating with a cost of living increase. I'm not here for the money anyway.

All the organs of the body were having a meeting, trying to decide who was in charge.

'I should be in charge', said the brain, because I run all the body's systems, so without me nothing would happen'.

'I should be in charge', said the blood, 'because I circulate oxygen all over, so without me you'd all waste away'.

'I should be in charge', said the stomach, 'because I process food and give all of you energy'.

'I should be in charge', said the rectum, 'because I'm responsible for waste removal'.

All the other body parts laughed at the rectum and insulted him, so in a huff, he shut down tight.

Within a few days, the brain had a terrible headache, the stomach was bloated, and the blood was toxic. Eventually the other organs gave in. They all agreed that the rectum should be the boss.

The moral of the story? You don't have to be smart or important to be in charge...just an asshole.

YOU KNOW YOU WORKED IN AN OFFICE DURING THE 1990s IF—

1. You've sat at the same desk for 4 years and worked for three different organisations.
2. Your resume is on a diskette in your pocket. You get really excited about a 2% pay raise.
3. You learn about your layoff on the ABC.
4. Your biggest loss from a system crash is that you lose your best jokes.
5. Your supervisor doesn't have the ability to do your job.
6. Salaries of the members on the Executive Board are higher than all the Third World countries' annual budgets combined.
7. It's dark when you drive to and from work.
8. Communication is something your section is having problems with.
9. You see a good looking person and know it is a visitor.
10. Free food left over from meetings is your main staple.

11. Being sick is defined as can't walk or you're in the hospital.
12. You're already late on the work task you just got.
13. You work 200 hours for the $100 bonus check and jubilantly say "Oh wow, thanks!"
14. Your supervisors' favourite lines are "when you get a few minutes", "in your spare time", "when you're freed up", and "I have an opportunity for you."
15. Vacation is something you rollover to next year or a cheque you get every January.
16. Your relatives and family describe your job as "works with computers".
17. You read this entire list and understood it.

Answering machine answers recorded and verified -

1. My wife and I can't come to the phone right now, but if you'll leave Your name and number, we'll get back to you as soon as we're finished.
2. A is for academics, B is for beer. One of those reasons is why we're not here. So leave a message.
3. Hi this is John. If you are the phone company, I already sent the money, If you are my parents, please send money. If you are my financial institution, you didn't lend me enough money. If you are my friends, you owe me money. If you are a female, don't worry, I have plenty of money.
4. Hi. Now you say something.
5. Hi, I'm not home right now but my answering machine is, so you can talk to it instead. Wait for the beep.

6. Hello. I am David's answering machine. What are you?

7. (From a Japanese man in Toronto:) He-ro! This is Sato. If you leave message, I call you soon. If you leave sexy message, I call sooner!

8. Hi! Bob's answering machine is broken. This is his refrigerator. Please speak very slowly, and I'll stick your message to myself with one of these magnets.

9. Hello, this is Sally's microwave. Her answering machine just eloped with her tape deck, so I'm stuck with taking her calls. Say, if you want anything cooked while you leave your message, just hold it up to phone.

10. Hello, you are talking to a machine. I am capable of receiving messages. My owners do not need siding, windows, or a hot tub, and their carpets are clean. They give to charity through their office and do not need their picture taken. If you're still with me, leave your name and number and they will get back to you.

11. This is not an answering machine-this is a telepathic thought-recording device. After the tone, think about your name, your reason for calling and I'll think about returning your call.

12. Hi, this is George. I'm sorry I can't answer the phone right now. Leave a message, and then wait by your phone until I call you back.

13. Hi I am probably home. I'm just avoiding someone I don't like. Leave me a message, and if I don't call back, it's you.

14. If you are a burglar, then we're probably at home cleaning our weapons right now and can't come to the home phone. Otherwise, we probably aren't and it's safe to leave us a message.

15. You're growing tired. Your eyelids are getting heavy. You feel very sleepy now. You are gradually losing your willpower and your ability to resist suggestions. When you hear the tone you will feel helplessly compelled to leave your name, number, and a message.

16. Please leave a message. However, you have the right to remain silent. Everything you say will be recorded and will be used by us.

One particular Christmas season a long time ago, Santa was getting ready for his annual trip ... but there were problems everywhere.

Four of his elves got sick, and the trainee elves did not produce the toys as fast as the regular ones. So Santa was beginning to feel the pressure of being behind schedule.

Then Mrs Claus told Santa that her mom was coming to visit. This stressed Santa even more. When he went to harness the reindeer, he found that three of them were about to give birth and two had jumped the fence and went out, heaven knows where. More stress.

Then when he began to load the sleigh one of the boards cracked and the toy bag fell to the ground and scattered the toys.

So, frustrated, Santa went into the house for a cup of coffee and a shot of whiskey. When he went to the cupboard, he discovered that the elves had hidden the liquor and there was nothing to drink.

In his frustration, he accidentally dropped the coffee pot and it broke into hundreds of little pieces all over the kitchen floor.

He went to get the broom and found that mice had eaten the straw it was made from.

Just then the doorbell rang and Santa cussed on his way to the door.

He opened the door and there was a little angel with a great big Christmas tree.

The angel said, very cheerfully, "Merry Christmas Santa. Isn't it just a lovely day? I have a beautiful tree for you. Isn't it just a lovely tree? Where would you like me to stick it?"

Thus began the tradition of the little angel on top of the Christmas tree.

STAFF CHRISTMAS PARTY

FROM: Pauline, Human Resources Director

TO: All Employees

DATE: 1st November

RE: Staff Christmas Party

I'm happy to inform you that the company Christmas Party will take place on December 23rd, starting at noon in the private function room at the Grill House. There will be a free bar and plenty of drinks! We'll have a small band playing traditional carols ... please feel free to sing along. And don't be surprised if the MD shows up dressed as Santa Claus! A Christmas tree will be lit at 1.00p.m. Exchange of gifts among employees can be done at that time; however, no gift should be over $10.00 to make the giving of gifts easy on everyone's pocket. This gathering is only for employees! The MD will make a special announcement at the Party.

Merry Christmas to you and your Family.

Pauline.

FROM: Pauline, Human Resources Director

TO: All Employees

DATE: 2nd November

RE: Holiday Party

In no way was yesterday's memo intended to exclude our Jewish employees. We recognise that Chanukah is an important holiday, which often coincides with Christmas, though unfortunately not this year. However, from now on we're calling it our 'Holiday Party'. The same policy applies to any other employees who are not Christians. There will be no Christmas tree, nor will Christmas carols be sung. We will have other types of music for your enjoyment.

Happy now?

Happy Holidays to you and your family.

Pauline.

FROM; Pauline, Human Resources Director

TO: All Employees

DATE: 6th November

RE: Holiday Party

Regarding the note I received from a member of Alcoholics Anonymous requesting a non-drinking table ... you didn't sign your name. I'm happy to accommodate this request, but if I put a sign on a table that reads, "AA Only", you wouldn't be anonymous anymore!!!! How am I supposed to handle this? Suggestion somebody? Forget about the gift exchange, no gift exchange allowed now since the Union Officials feel that $10.00 is too much money and Management believe

$10.00 is a little cheap. NO GIFT EXCHANGE WILL BE ALLOWED.

Pauline.

FROM: Pauline, Human Resources Director

TO: All Employees

DATE: 7th November

RE: Holiday Party

What a diverse group we are! I had no idea that December 20th begins the Muslim holy month of Ramadan, which forbids eating and drinking during daylight hours. There goes the party! Seriously, we can appreciate how a luncheon at this time of year does not accommodate our Muslim employees' beliefs, perhaps the Grill House can hold off on serving your meal until the end of the party—or else package everything up for you to take home in a little foil doggy bag. Will that work? Meanwhile, I've arranged for members of Weight Watchers to sit farthest from the dessert buffet and pregnant women will get the table closest to the toilets. Gays are allowed to sit with each other, Lesbians do not have to sit with gay men, each will have their own table. Yes, there will be flower arrangements for the gay men's table too. To the person asking permission to cross dress—no cross dressing allowed. We will have booster seats for short people. Low fat food will be available for those on a diet. As we cannot control the amount of salt used in the food we suggest those people with high blood pressure taste the food first. There will be fresh fruit as dessert for Diabetics; the restaurant cannot supply "No Sugar" desserts. Sorry! Did I miss anything?!?!?!?!?!

Pauline.

FROM: Pauline, Human Resources Director

TO: All F****** Employees

DATE: 8 November

RE: The F******* Holiday Party.

Vegetarian bastards, I've had it with you people !!! We're going to keep this party at the Grill House whether you like it or not, so you can sit quietly at the table furthest from the "grill of death", as you so quaintly put it, you'll get your f****** salad bar, including organic tomatoes. But you know tomatoes have feelings too, they scream when you slice them. I've heard them scream. I'm hearing the scream right NOW!!

I hope you all have a rotten holiday—drink, drive and die.

The Bitch from HELL!!!!!!!!!!!!!!!!!!!!!!!!!!!!!!!!!!

FROM: James, Acting Human Resources Director

TO: All Employees

DATE: 9th November

RE: Pauline Lewis and Holiday Party

I'm sure I speak for all of us in wishing Pauline a speedy recovery, and I'll continue to forward your cards to her. In the meantime, Management has decided to cancel our Holiday Party and instead, give everyone the afternoon of the 23rd December off with full pay.

James.

IMMEDIATE DOWNSIZING MEASURES EMPLOYED

The recent announcement that Donner and Blitzen have elected to take the early reindeer retirement package has triggered a good deal of concern about whether they will be replaced, and about other restructuring decisions at the North Pole.

Streamlining is due to the North Pole's loss of dominance of the season's gift distribution business. Home shopping channels, the Internet, and mail order catalogs have diminished Santa's market share. He could not sit idly by and permit further erosion of the profit picture.

The reindeer downsizing was made possible through the purchase of a late model Japanese sled for the CEO's annual trip. Improved productivity from Dasher and Dancer—who summered at the Harvard Business School—is anticipated. Reduction in reindeer will also lessen airborne environmental emissions for which the North Pole has received unfavourable press.

I am pleased to inform you that Rudolph's role will not be disturbed. Tradition still counts for something at the North Pole. Management denies, in the strongest possible language, the earlier leak that Rudolph's nose got that way, not from the cold, but from substance abuse.

Calling Rudolph sluggish, who was into the sauce and never did pull his share of the load was an unfortunate comment, made by one of Santa's helpers and taken out of context at a time of year when he is known to be under executive stress.

Today's global challenges require the North Pole to continue to look for better, more competitive steps. Effective immediately, the following economic measures are to take place in the Twelve Days of Christmas subsidiary.

The partridge will be retained, but the pear tree never turned out to be the cash crop forecasted. It will be replaced by a plastic hanging plant, providing considerable savings in maintenance.

The two turtle doves represent a redundancy that is simply not cost-effective. In addition, their romance during working hours could not be condoned. The positions are therefore eliminated.

The three French hens will remain intact. After all, everyone loves the French.

The four calling birds were replaced by an automated voice mail system, with a call-waiting option. An analysis is underway to determine who the birds have been calling, how often and how long they talked.

The five golden rings have been put on hold by the Board of Directors. Maintaining a portfolio based on one commodity could have negative implications for institutional investors. Diversification into other precious metals as well as a mix of T-Bills and high technology stocks appear to be in order.

The six geese-a-laying constitutes a luxury which can no longer be afforded. It has long been felt that the production rate of one egg per goose per day is an example of the decline in productivity. Three geese will be let go, and an upgrading in the selection procedure by personnel will assure management that from now on every goose it obtains will be more productive.

The seven swans-a-swimming is obviously a number chosen in better times. Their function is primarily decorative. Mechanical swans are on order. The current swans will be retrained to learn some new strokes and therefore enhance their outplacement.

As you know, the eight maids-a-milking concept has been under heavy scrutiny by the Equal Opportunity Commission. A male/female balance in the workforce is being sought. The more militant maids consider this a dead-end job with no upward mobility. Automation of the process may permit the maids to try a-mending, a-mentoring, or a-mulching.

Nine ladies dancing has always been an odd number. This function will be phased out as these individuals grow older and can no longer do the steps.

Ten Lords-a-leaping is overkill. The high cost of Lords plus the expense of international air travel prompted the compensation Committee to suggest replacing this group with ten out-of-work Councillors. While leaping ability may be somewhat sacrificed, the savings are significant because we expect an oversupply of unemployed congresspersons this year.

Eleven pipers piping and twelve drummers drumming is a simple case of the band getting too big. A substitution with a string quartet, a cutback on new music, and no uniforms will produce savings which will drop right down to the bottom line.

We can expect a substantial reduction in assorted people, fowl, animals and other expenses. Though incomplete, studies indicate that stretching deliveries over twelve days is inefficient. If we can drop ship in one day, service levels will be improved.

Regarding the lawsuit filed by the lawyer's association seeking expansion to include the legal profession ("thirteen lawyers-a-suing"), action is pending.

Lastly, it is not beyond consideration that deeper cuts may be necessary in the most efficient number.

A LITTLE OFFICE PRAYER

Grant me the serenity to accept the things I cannot change, The courage to change things I cannot accept, And the wisdom to hide the bodies of those people I had to kill today because they pissed me off And also, help me to be careful of the toes I step on today As they may be connected to the arse that I might have to kiss tomorrow Help me to always give 100% at work.

12% on Monday

23% on Tuesday

40% on Wednesday

20% on Thursday

5% on Fridays

And help me to remember when I'm having a really bad day, and it seems that people are trying to piss me off, That it takes 42 muscles to frown And only 4 to extend my finger and tell them to FUCK OFF.

TOP 25 SAYINGS WE'D LIKE TO SEE ON THOSE OFFICE INSPIRATIONAL POSTERS:

1. Rome did not create a great empire by having meetings, they did it by killing all those who opposed them.
2. If you can stay calm, while all around you is chaos ...then you probably haven't completely understood the seriousness of the situation.
3. Doing a job RIGHT the first time gets the job done. Doing the job WRONG fourteen times gives you job security.
4. Eagles may soar, but weasels don't get sucked into jet engines.
5. We put the "k" in "kwality."
6. Artificial Intelligence is no match for Natural Stupidity.
7. A person who smiles in the face of adversity ...probably has a scapegoat.

8. Plagiarism saves time.
9. If at first you don't succeed, try management.
10. Never put off until tomorrow what you can avoid altogether.
11. TEAMWORK ...means never having to take all the blame yourself.
12. The beatings will continue until morale improves.
13. Never under-estimate the power of very stupid people in large groups.
14. We waste time, so you don't have to.
15. Hang in there, retirement is only thirty years away!
16. Go the extra mile. It makes your boss look like an incompetent slacker.
17. A snooze button is a poor substitute for no alarm clock at all.
18. When the going gets tough, the tough take a coffee break.
19. INDECISION is the key to FLEXIBILITY.
20. Succeed in spite of management.
21. Aim Low, Reach Your Goals, Avoid Disappointment.
22. We waste more time by 8:00 in the morning than other companies do all day.
23. You pretend to work, and we'll pretend to pay you.
24. Work: It isn't just for sleeping anymore.
25. If you do a good job and work hard, you may get a job with a better company someday.

26. The light at the end of the tunnel has been turned off due to budget cuts. Sure, you may not like working here, but we pay your rent.

27. If you think we're a bad firm, you should see our rivals!

28. ABANDON ALL HOPE, HE WHO ENTER HERE.....

29. We make great money! We have great benefits! We do no work! We are union members!

30. 2 days without a Human Rights Violation!

31. It's only unethical if you get caught.

32. Never put off until tomorrow what you can avoid altogether.

33. Never quit until you have another job.

34. Work harder slaves!

35. The beatings will continue until morale improves.

36. If you can read this, you're not working!

HOW TO KEEP A HEALTHY LEVEL OF INSANITY AT WORK

1. At lunch time, sit in your parked car and point a hair dryer at passing cars to see if they slow down.

2. Page yourself over the intercom. (Don't disguise your voice.)

3. Insist that your email address is Xena-goddess-of-fire@companyname.com, Elvis-the-king@companyname.com.

4. Every time someone asks you to do something, ask if they want fries with that.

5. Encourage your colleagues to join you in a little synchronized chair dancing.
6. Put your garbage can on your desk and label it "IN TRAY."
7. Develop an unnatural fear of staplers.
8. Put decaf in the coffee maker for 3 weeks. Once everyone has gotten over their caffeine addictions, switch to espresso.
9. In the memo field of all your checks, write 'for sexual favours.'
10. Reply to everything someone says with, -That's what you think.-
11. Finish all your sentences with -In accordance with the prophecy.-
12. Adjust the tint on your monitor so that the brightness level lights up the entire work area. Insist to others that you like it that way.
13. Don't use any punctuation.
14. As often as possible, skip rather than walk.
15. Ask people what sex they are.
16. Specify that your drive-through order is "to go."
17. Sing Along at the opera.
18. Go to a poetry recital and ask why the poems don't rhyme.
19. Find out where your boss shops and buy exactly the same outfits. Wear them one day after your boss does. (This is especially effective if your boss is the opposite gender.)

20. Send e-mail to the rest of the company to tell them what you're doing. For example: If anyone needs me, I'll be in the bathroom.

21. Put mosquito netting around your cubicle.

22. Five days in advance, tell your friends you can't attend their party because you're not in the mood.

23. Call and ask if is for emergencies.

24. Call the psychic hotline and just say, "Guess."

25. Have your co-workers address you by your wrestling name, Rock-hard.

26. When the money comes out of the ATM, scream "I Won!", "I Won!""3rd time this week!!!"

27. When leaving the Zoo, start running towards the parking lot, yelling Run for your lives, they're loose!"

28. Tell your boss, "It's not the voices in my head that bother me, it's the voices in your head that do."

29. Tell your children over dinner. "Due to the economy, we are going to have to let one of you go."

Subject: The Work Poop.

We've all been there but don't like to admit it. We've all kicked back in our cubicles and suddenly felt something of a brew down below. As much as we try to convince ourselves, the WORK poop is inevitable. For those of you who hate pooping at work as much as I do. I give you the.... Survival Guide for Taking a Dump at Work.

Memorize these definitions and pooping at work will become a pure pleasure.

ESCAPE: A fart that slips out while taking a leak at the urinal or forcing poop in a stall. This is usually accompanied by a sudden wave of panic/embarrassment. This is similar to the hot flash you receive when passing an unseen police car while speeding. If you release an escapee, do not acknowledge it. Pretend it did not happen. If you are standing next to the farter at the urinal, pretend that you did hear it -no one likes an escapee, it is uncomfortable for all involved.

Making a joke or laughing makes both parties feel uneasy.

JAILBREAK (Used in conjunction with escapee): When forcing several farts slip out at a machine gun's pace _ this is usually side effect of diarrhoea or a hangover. If this should happen do not panic, remain in the stall until everyone has left the bathroom. So to spare everyone the awkwardness of what just occurred

COURTESY FLUSH: The act of flushing the toilet the instant the nose cone of the poop log hits the water and the poop is whisked away to an undisclosed location. This reduces the amount of air time the poop has to stink up the bathroom. This can help you avoid being caught doing the WALK OF SHAME.

WALK OF SHAME: Walking from the stall, to the sink, to the door after you have just stunk-up the shitter. This can be a very unforgettable moment if someone walks in and busts you. As with all farts, it is best to pretend that the smell does not exist. Can be avoided with the use of a COURTESY FLUSH.

OUT OF THE CLOSET POOPER: A colleague who poops at work and is proud of it. You will often see an Out of the Closet Pooper enter the bathroom with a newspaper or magazine under their arm. Always look around the office for the Out Of THE CLOSET POOPER before entering the bathroom.

THE POOPING FRIENDS NETWORK (KPPM): This is a group of co-workers who band together to ensure emergency pooping goes off without incident. This group can help you to monitor the whereabouts of OUT OF THE CLOSET POOPERS and identify SAVE HAVENS.

SAFE HAVENS: a seldom used bathroom somewhere in the building where you can least expect visitors. Try floors that are predominantly of the opposite sex. This will reduce the odds of a pooper of your sex entering the bathroom.

TURD BURGLAR: A pooper who does not realize that you're in the stall and tries to force the door open. This is one of the most shocking and vulnerable moments that occur when taking a dump at work...

If this occurs, remain in the stall until the TURDBURGLAR leaves. This way you will avoid all uncomfortable eye contact. TURD BURGLARS you have been known to cause premature pinchage, which inevitably causes you to pinch one off in the middle.

CAMO-COUGH: A phony cough which alerts all new entrants into bathroom that you are in a stall. This can be used to cover-up a WATERMELON or to alert potential TURD BURGLARS. Very effective when used in conjunction with an ASTAIRE.

ASTAIRE: This is a subtle toe-tap that is used to alert all potential TURD BURGLARS that you are occupying a stall. This will remove doubt that the stall is occupied. If you hear an ASTAIRE, leave the bathroom immediately so the pooper can poop in peace.

WATERMELON: A turd that creates a loud splash when hitting the toilet water. This is also an embarrassing incident. If you feel a WATERMELON coming on, create a diversion. See CAMO-COUGH.

HAVANA OMELET: A load of diarrhoea that creates a series of loud splashes in the toilet water. Often accompanied by an Escapee. Try using CAMO-COUGH with an ASTAIRE.

UNCLE TED: A bathroom user who seems to linger around forever spend extended lengths of time in front of the mirror or pot. An UNCLE TED makes it difficult to relax while on the crapper, you should always wait to drop your load when the bathroom is empty. This benefits you as well as the other bathroom attendee.

FLY BY: The act of scouting out a bathroom before pooping. Walk in, check for other poopers. If there are others in the bathroom, come back again. Be careful not to become a FREQUENT FLYER. People become suspicious if they catch you constantly going into the bathroom.

Tips for success in the business world.

Brag. Remember, your work is of unparalleled significance and inestimable value. Constantly referring to your achievements will help others to understand your key role in running the universe. Good leadership is all about giving the troops confidence.

Use that personal pronoun. Every sentence should begin with "I". "We", on the other hand, is the beginning of the word weakling. "It's so easy to remember the masculine plurals," observes a female fellow student in my Italian class. "They all end in I, and that's a man's favourite word."

Talk rubbish. If you advance rational arguments, people will talk back. Learn to jabber disconnected subclauses full of malapropisms, then no one will Question you. Learn to say the name of some huge international intellect and toss it around at every opportunity. Don't worry if you can't actually remember what Dostoevsky, Kierkegaard or Iacocca were on about.

Assume, don't ask. Do not acquire information—it's a waste of time and may threaten your status. Never diminish your self-esteem by taking a training course or doing research.

Information is confusing and pointless, so there is no need to use it. Your opinion is what counts.

Delegate. Your intelligence is too precious to waste on actual work, which is why others are employed to support you. Your role is to make sure that they perform the work for which you are responsible. That way, if things go pear-shaped. You can simply fire somebody and demonstrate your effectiveness as a manager. And if things go well, the credit is where it belongs—with you.

Interrupt. Since nobody is as smart as you. It's a waste of time listening to what they may want to say. Especially if they try to come in with some negative commentary such as "I told you so". Your views are crucial and should be stated often enough for employees of lesser intelligence to understand them.

Never sweat the small stuff. It is extremely diminishing to a manager's credibility to know anything of minor significance. Technological tips and tricks are someone else's job. Your organisation must employ enough assistants and anoraks to know everything necessary to facilitate your performance. An advance in technology should mean employing more appropriately skilled staff. If your system crashes, fire somebody. Nothing trivial should ever be allowed to impinge on your mental processes. The really great executives can't even use a keyboard.

Network. Since awareness of your superior intelligence is the key factor in corporate success, spreading that awareness is your most important function. Never cut back on time spent at lunch or in the pub, making contacts with people who need to understand how clever you are. Make sure that these activities are adequately resourced your company platinum card should spend a minimum of five nights a week behind the best bars in town.

Don't look busy. Appearing busy implies that you actually need to work to achieve. You should give the impression that achievement will be attracted to your superior intelligence by some kind of intellectual magnetism. Keep an empty desk and learn to sit behind it in a conspicuously idle manner.

Lie. All the great leaders of history have understood the power of lying. The really effective lies are those that you believe yourself, so relating to reality will only obstruct this process. Just visualise the outcome you desire and apply the concepts necessary to achieve your goal.

Finally, don't forget that being a team player means only recognising the achievements of your own team.

Any modest, reality-based thinking should firmly be rejected to avoid the development of a hostile business culture in which you may be exposed as a great big fraud.

THINGS YOU'D LOVE TO SAY AT WORK, BUT CAN'T!

1. Ahhh… I see the fuck-up fairy has visited us again.
2. I don't know what your problem is, but I'll bet it's hard to pronounce.
3. How about never? Is never good for you?
4. I see you've set aside this special time to humiliate yourself in public.
5. I'm really easy to get along with once you people learn to worship me.
6. I'll try being nicer if you'll try being smarter.
7. I'm out of my mind, but feel free to leave a message.
8. I don't work here. I'm a consultant.

9. It sounds like English, but I can't understand a word you're saying.
10. I can see your point, but I still think you're full of shit.
11. I like you. You remind me of when I was young and stupid.
12. You are validating my inherent mistrust of strangers.
13. I have plenty of talent and vision. I just don't give a damn.
14. I'm already visualizing the duct tape over your mouth.
15. I will always cherish the initial misconceptions I had about you.
16. Thank you. We're all refreshed and challenged by your unique point of view.
17. The fact that no one understands you doesn't mean you're an artist.
18. Any connection between your reality and mine is purely coincidental.
19. What am I? Flypaper for freaks!?
20. I'm not being rude. You're just insignificant.
21. It's a thankless job, but I've got a lot of Karma to burn off.
22. Yes, I am an agent of Satan, but my duties are largely ceremonial.
23. And your cry-baby whiny-butt opinion would be...?
24. Do I look like a people person?
25. This isn't an office. It's Hell with fluorescent lighting.
26. I started out with nothing & still have most of it left.
27. Sarcasm is just one more service we offer.

28. If I throw a stick, will you leave?
29. Errors have been made. Others will be blamed.
30. Whatever kind of look you were going for, you missed.
31. I'm trying to imagine you with a personality.
32. A cubicle is just a padded cell without a door.
33. Can I trade this job for what's behind door #1?
34. Too many freaks, not enough circuses.
35. Nice perfume. Must you marinate in it?
36. Chaos, panic, & disorder—my work here is done.

CHAPTER 24

X is for Xenophobia

A woman was very distraught at the fact she had not had a date nor any sex in quite some time. Afraid she might have something wrong with her, she decided to employ the medical expertise of a sex therapist.

Her personal physician recommended Dr Wang, a well-known Chinese sex therapist. So she went and saw him.

Upon entering the examination room, Dr Wang took one look at her and said, "OK, take off aw your crows."

She quickly disrobed and stood naked before him.

"Now," said Wang, "get down on knees and craw reery, reery, fass away from me to the other side of room."

Having done that, then Dr Wang said, "Okay, now turn around and craw reery, reery fass to me."

Once again she obliged. Dr Wang slowly shook his head, "OK, your problem vaywe, vaywe bad, you have Ed Zachary Disease .... worse case I ever see ... that why you not have dates, that why you not have sex."

Confused, the woman asked, "What is Ed Zachary Disease?"

Wang replied, "It when your face rook Ed Zachary rike your ass."

President Boris Yeltsin called Clinton with an emergency:

"Our largest condom factory has exploded!" the Russian President cried "my people's favourite form of birth control! This is a true disaster!"

"Boris, the American people would be happy to do anything within their power to help you," replied the President.

"I do need your help," said Yeltsin. "Could you possibly send 1,000,000 condoms ASAP to tide us over?"

"Why certainly! I'll get right on it!" said Clinton.

"Oh, and one more small favour, please?" said Yeltsin.

"Could the condoms be red in colour and at least 10" long and 4" in diameter?" said Yeltsin.

"No problem," replied the President and, with that, Clinton hung up and called the President of Trojan.

"I need a favour, you've got to make 1,000,000 condoms right away and send them to Russia."

"Consider it done," said the President of Trojan.

"Great! Now listen, they have to be red in colour, 10" long and 4" wide."

"Easily done. Anything else?"

"Yeah," said the President, print 'MADE IN AMERICA, SIZE MEDIUM' on each one.

The lineage is finally revealed. Many people are at a loss for a response when someone says "You don't know Jack Schitt." Now you can intellectually handle the situation. Jack is the only son of Awe Schitt and O. Awe Schitt, the fertilizer magnate, married O. Schitt, the owner of Needeep N. Schitt Inc. They had one son, Jack. In turn Jack Schitt married Noe Schitt, and the deeply religious couple produced 6 children: Holie Schitt, Fulla Schitt, Giva Schitt, Bull Schitt and the twins: Deap Schitt and Dip Schitt.

Against her parent's objections Deap Schitt married Dumb Schitt, a High school dropout. However, after being married 15 years, Jack and Noe Schitt divorced. Noe Schitt later remarried Ted Sherlock and, because her kids were living with them, she wanted to keep her previous name.

She was then known as Noe Schitt-Sherlock. Meanwhile, Dip Schitt married Loda Schitt and they produced a son of nervous disposition, Chicken Schitt. Two others of the six children, Fulla Schitt and Giva Schitt, were inseparable throughout childhood and subsequently married the Happens brothers in a dual ceremony.

The wedding announcement in the newspaper announced the Schitt-Happens wedding. The Schitt-Happens children were Dawg, Byrd, and Hoarse. Bull Schitt, the prodigal son, left home to tour the world. He recently returned from Italy with his new Italian bride, Pisa Schitt. So now when someone says, "You don't know Jack Schitt" you can correct them. (Family History Recorded By crock O. Schitt)

STRESS REDUCTION COURSE

- Picture yourself near a stream.
- Birds are softly chirping in the crisp cool mountain air. Nothing can bother you here.
- No one knows this secret place.
- You are in total seclusion from that place called "the world."
- The soothing sound of a gentle waterfall fills the air with a cascade of serenity.
- The water is clear.
- You can easily make out the face of the person whose head you're holding under the water.
- Look. It's that annoying South African manager who caused you all this stress in the first place.

- What a pleasant surprise. You let them up ... just for a quick breath then poof! ... back under they go.
- You allow yourself as many deep breaths as you want. There now ... feeling better?

A man was getting a haircut prior to a trip to Rome. He mentioned the trip to the barber who responded, "Rome? Why would anyone want to go there? It's crowded & dirty and full of Italians. You're crazy to go to Rome. So, how are you getting there?" "We're taking TWA," was the reply. "We got a great rate!" "TWA!" exclaimed the barber. "That's a terrible airline. Their planes are old, their flight attendants are ugly, and they're always late. So, where are you staying in Rome?" "We'll be at the downtown International Marriott." "That dump! That's the worst hotel in the city. The rooms are small, the service is surly and they're overpriced. So, what are doing when you get there?"

"We're going to go to see the Vatican and we hope to see the Pope."

"That's rich," laughed the barber. "You and a million other people trying to see him. He'll look the size of an ant. Boy, good luck on this lousy trip of yours. You're going to need it."

A month later, the man again came in for his regular haircut.

The barber asked him about his trip to Rome.

"It was wonderful," explained the man, "Not only were we on time in one of TWA's brand new planes, but it was overbooked and they bumped us up to first class.

The food and wine were wonderful and I had a beautiful 28-year-old stewardess who waited on me hand and foot. And the hotel was great! They'd just finished a $25 million remodeling job and now it's the finest hotel in the city.

They, too, were overbooked, so they apologized and gave us the presidential suite at no extra charge!" "Well," muttered the barber, "I know you didn't get to see the pope."

"Actually, we were quite lucky. As we toured the Vatican, a Swiss Guard tapped me on the shoulder and explained that the pope likes to personally meet some of the visitors, and if I'd be so kind as to step into his private room and wait the pope would personally greet me. Sure enough, five minutes later the pope walked through the door and shook my hand! I knelt down as he spoke a few words to me."

"Really?" asked the barber. "What'd he say?"

He said, "Where'd you get that shitty haircut?"

People in other countries sometimes go out of their way to communicate with their English-speaking tourists.

Cocktail lounge, Norway:

LADIES ARE REQUESTED NOT TO HAVE CHILDREN IN THE BAR.

At a Budapest zoo:

PLEASE DO NOT FEED THE ANIMALS. IF YOU HAVE ANY SUITABLE FOOD, GIVE IT TO THE GUARD ON DUTY

Doctor's office, Rome:

SPECIALIST IN WOMEN AND OTHER DISEASES.

Hotel, Acapulco:

THE MANAGER HAS PERSONALLY PASSED ALL THE WATER SERVED HERE.

Information booklet about using a hotel air conditioner, Japan:

COOLES AND HEATES: IF YOU WANT JUST CONDITION OF WARM AIR IN YOUR ROOM, PLEASE CONTROL YOURSELF.

Car rental brochure, Tokyo:

WHEN PASSENGER OF FOOT HEAVE IN SIGHT, TOOTLE THE HORN. TRUMPET HIM MELODIOUSLY AT FIRST, BUT IF HE STILL OBSTACLES YOUR PASSAGE THEN TOOTLE HIM WITH VIGOR.

Dry cleaner's, Bangkok:

DROP YOUR TROUSERS HERE FOR THE BEST RESULTS.

Sign in men's rest room in Japan:

TO STOP LEAK TURN COCK TO THE RIGHT.

In a Nairobi restaurant:

CUSTOMERS WHO FIND OUR WAITRESSES RUDE OUGHT TO SEE THE MANAGER.

On the grounds of a private school:

NO TRESPASSING WITHOUT PERMISSION.

On an Athi River highway:

TAKE NOTICE: WHEN THIS SIGN IS UNDER WATER, THIS ROAD IS IMPASSABLE.

On a poster at Kencom:

ARE YOU AN ADULT THAT CANNOT READ? IF SO, WE CAN HELP.

In a City restaurant:

OPEN SEVEN DAYS A WEEK AND WEEKENDS.

One of the Mathare buildings:

MENTAL HEALTH PREVENTION CENTRE.

A sign seen on an automatic restroom hand dryer:

DO NOT ACTIVATE WITH WET HANDS.

In a Pumwani maternity ward:

NO CHILDREN ALLOWED.

In a cemetery:

PERSONS ARE PROHIBITED FROM PICKING FLOWERS FROM ANY BUT THEIR OWN GRAVES.

Sign in Japanese public bath:

FOREIGN GUESTS ARE REQUESTED NOT TO PULL COCK IN TUB.

Tokyo hotel's rules and regulations:

GUESTS ARE REQUESTED NOT TO SMOKE OR DO OTHER DISGUSTING BEHAVIOURS IN BED.

On the menu of a Swiss restaurant:

OUR WINES LEAVE YOU NOTHING TO HOPE FOR.

In a Tokyo bar:

SPECIAL COCKTAILS FOR THE LADIES WITH NUTS.

In a Bangkok temple:

IT IS FORBIDDEN TO ENTER A WOMAN EVEN A FOREIGNER IF DRESSED AS A MAN.

Hotel room notice, Chiang-Mai, Thailand:

PLEASE DO NOT BRING SOLICITORS INTO YOUR ROOM.

Hotel brochure, Italy:

THIS HOTEL IS RENOWNED FOR ITS PEACE AND SOLITUDE. IN FACT, CROWDS FROM ALL OVER THE WORLD FLOCK HERE TO ENJOY ITS SOLITUDE.

Hotel lobby, Bucharest:

THE LIFT IS BEING FIXED FOR THE NEXT DAY. DURING THAT TIME WE REGRET THAT YOU WILL BE UNBEARABLE

Hotel elevator, Paris:

PLEASE LEAVE YOUR VALUES AT THE FRONT DESK.

Hotel, Yugoslavia:

THE FLATTENING OF UNDERWEAR WITH PLEASURE IS THE JOB OF THE CHAMBERMAID.

Hotel, Japan:

YOU ARE INVITED TO TAKE ADVANTAGE OF THE CHAMBERMAID.

In the lobby of a Moscow hotel across from a Russian Orthodox monastery:

YOU ARE WELCOME TO VISIT THE CEMETERY WHERE FAMOUS RUSSIAN AND SOVIET COMPOSERS, ARTISTS, AND WRITERS ARE BURIED DAILY EXCEPT THURSDAY.

Hotel catering to skiers, Austria:

NOT TO PERAMBULATE THE CORRIDORS IN THE HOURS OF REPOSE IN THE BOOTS OF ASCENSION.

Taken from a menu, Poland:

SALAD A FIRM'S OWN MAKE; LIMPID RED BEET SOUP WITH CHEESY DUMPLINGS IN THE.

FORM OF A FINGER; ROASTED DUCK LET LOOSE; BEEF RASHERS BEATEN IN THE COUNTRY PEOPLE'S FASHION.

Supermarket, Hong Kong:

FOR YOUR CONVENIENCE, WE RECOMMEND COURTEOUS, EFFICIENT SELF-SERVICE.

From the "Soviet Weekly":

THERE WILL BE A MOSCOW EXHIBITION OF ARTS BY 15,000 SOVIET REPUBLIC PAINTERS AND SCULPTORS. THESE WERE EXECUTED OVER THE PAST TWO YEARS.

In an East African newspaper:

A NEW SWIMMING POOL IS RAPIDLY TAKING SHAPE SINCE THE CONTRACTORS HAVE THROWN IN THE BULK OF THEIR WORKERS.

Hotel, Vienna:

IN CASE OF FIRE, DO YOUR UTMOST TO ALARM THE HOTEL PORTER.

A sign posted in Germany's Black Forest:

IT IS STRICTLY FORBIDDEN ON OUR BLACK FOREST CAMPING SITE THAT PEOPLE OF DIFFERENT SEX, FOR INSTANCE, MEN AND WOMEN, LIVE TOGETHER IN ONE TENT UNLESS THEY ARE MARRIED WITH EACH OTHER FOR THIS PURPOSE.

Hotel, Zurich:

BECAUSE OF THE IMPROPRIETY OF ENTERTAINING GUESTS OF THE OPPOSITE SEX IN THE BEDROOM, IT IS SUGGESTED THAT THE LOBBY BE USED FOR THIS PURPOSE.

An advertisement by a Hong Kong dentist:

TEETH EXTRACTED BY THE LATEST METHODISTS.

A laundry in Rome:

LADIES, LEAVE YOUR CLOTHES HERE AND SPEND THE AFTERNOON HAVING A GOOD TIME.

Tourist agency, Czechoslovakia:

TAKE ONE OF OUR HORSE-DRIVEN CITY TOURS. WE GUARANTEE NO MISCARRIAGES.

Advertisement for donkey rides, Thailand:

WOULD YOU LIKE TO RIDE ON YOUR OWN ASS?

In the window on a Swedish furrier:

FUR COATS MADE FOR LADIES FROM THEIR OWN SKIN.

The box of a clockwork toy made in Hong Kong:

GUARANTEED TO WORK THROUGHOUT ITS USEFUL LIFE.

In a Swiss mountain inn:

SPECIAL TODAY—NO ICE-CREAM.

Airline ticket office, Copenhagen:

WE TAKE YOUR BAGS AND SEND THEM IN ALL DIRECTIONS.

On the door of a Moscow hotel room:

IF THIS IS YOUR FIRST VISIT TO THE USSR, YOU ARE WELCOME TO IT.

Fancy telling people that you live In these places?

Nobber (Donegal, Ireland).

Arsoli (Lazio, Italy).

Muff (Northern Ireland).

Bastard (Norway).

Twatt (Shetland, UK).

Twatt (Orkney, UK).

Dildo (Newfoundland, Canada).

WanJde (Zimbabwe).

Climax (Colorado, USA).

Lickey End (West Midlands, UK).

Shafter (California, USA).

Dongo (Congo—Democratic Republic).

Dong Rack (Thailand-Cambodia border).

Donk (Belgium).

Intercourse (Pennsylvania, USA).

Brown Willy (every schoolboy's favourite, Cornwall, UK).

Stains (Near Paris, France).

Seymen (Turkey).

Turdo (Ranania).

Fukum (Yemen).

Fukue (Honshu, Japan).

Fukui (Honshu, Japan).

Fuku (Shensi, China).

Wankie Colliery (Zimbabwe).

Wanks River (Nicaragua).

Wankendorf (Schleswig-Holstein, Germany).

Wankener (India).

Shag Island (Indian Ocean).

Sexmoan (Luzon, Philippines).

Hold With Hope (Greenland).

Beaver (Oklahana, USA).

Beaver Head (Idaho, USA).

Wet Beaver Creek (Australia).

Pis River (Nicaragua).

Tittybong (Australia).

Dikshit (India).

Middle Intercourse Island (Australia).

Chinaman's Knob (Australia).

Subject: Iraqi Prime Time Television Schedule.

MONDAYS:

8:00—"Husseinfeld"

8:30—"Mad About Everything."

9:00—"Suddenly Sanctions."

9:30—"The Brian Benben Bin Laden Show."

10:00—"Allah McBeal."

TUESDAYS:

8:00—"Wheel of Fortune and Terror."

8:30—"The Price is Right If Saddam Says It's Right."

9:00—"Children Are Forbidden from saying The Darndest Things."

9:30—"Iraq's Wackiest Public Execution Bloopers."

10:00—"Buffy the Yankee Imperialist Dog Slayer."

WEDNESDAYS:

8:00—"U.S. Military Secrets Revealed."

8:30—"When Kurds Attack."

9:00—"Two Guys, a Girl, and a Fatwah."

9:30—"Just Shoot Me."

10:00—"Veilwatch."

THURSDAYS:

8:00—"Matima Loves Chachi."

8:30—"M*U*S*T*A*S*H."

9:00—"Veronica's Closet Full of Long, Black, Shapeless Dresses."

9:30—"My Two Baghdads."

10:00—"Diagnosis: Heresy."

FRIDAYS:

8:00—"Judge Saddam."

8:30—"Funniest Super 8 Home Movies."

9:00—"Captured Iranian Soldiers Say the Darndest Things."

9:30—"Achmed's Creek."

10:00—"No-witness News."

A Chinese man had three daughters, he asked his eldest daughter what kind of man she would like to marry.

"I would like to marry a man with three dragons on his chest," said the eldest daughter.

He then asked his second daughter who she would like to marry.

"I would like to marry a man with two dragons on his chest," said the second daughter.

He finally asked his youngest daughter who she would like to marry.

"I would like to marry a man with one draggin' on the ground," said the youngest daughter.

International Love:

There are these beautiful deserted islands in the middle of nowhere. On these islands the following people are stranded:

2 Italian men and 1 Italian woman.

2 French men and 1 French woman.

2 German men and 1 German woman.

2 Greek men and 1 Greek woman.

2 English men and 1 English woman.

2 Bulgarian men and 1 Bulgarian woman.

2 Japanese men and 1 Japanese woman.

2 American men and 1 American woman.

2 Irish men and 1 Irish woman.

This is the situation one month later:

One Italian man had killed the other Italian man for the Italian woman. The two French men and the French woman are living happily together in a ménage a trois.

The 2 German men have a strict weekly schedule of when they alternate with the German woman.

The 2 Greek men are sleeping with each other and the Greek woman is cleaning and cooking for them.

The 2 English men are waiting for someone to introduce them to the English woman.

The Bulgarian men have looked at the endless ocean, taken one look at the Bulgarian woman and started swimming.

The American woman keeps on bitching about her body being her own, the true nature of feminism, how she can do everything that they can do, about the necessity for fulfilment, the equal division of household chores, how her last boyfriend respected her opinion and treated her much nicer and how her relationship with her mother is improving. The two American men are contemplating the virtues of suicide.

The two Japanese men have faxed Tokyo and are waiting for instructions.

and finally ...

The Irish began by dividing the island into North and South then setting up a distillery. They do not remember if sex is in the picture because it gets sort of foggy after the first few litres of coconut whisky, but they are satisfied that at least the English are not getting any.

An Indian chief decided it was time to give his 3 sons their adult names once they had reached manhood. So he gathered them in to his tent, together the elders of the tribe.

He turns to the 1st son, "Son, you will be called Bagle,"

The 3rd son interrupts, "Father, father, what will I be called?"

"All in good time, my son", he continues, "you will be called Bagle, because you are strong and wise."

The Elders agreed.

He then turns to the second son, but the 3rd son says "Father, father, what will I be called?"

"All in good time, my son" he replies. He then continues to the 2nd son "Son you will be called Swallow". '

The 3rd son says again "Father, father, what will I be called?"

"All in good time my son" comes the reply. He then continues, "you will be named Swallow because you are quick and cunning."

The elders agree.

He then turns to the 3rd son who is asking, "Father Father, what will I be called?"

"Son, you will be called Thrush" he said to his 3rd Son. "Why that father?" he asked excitedly, "Because you are an irritating cunt" the father replied. The elders agreed.

Funny signs in Kenya:

In a Nairobi restaurant:

- "Customers who find our waitresses rude ought to see the manager."
- In a Westland's Jewellery store.

- "Ears pierced while you wait."
- In the window of an Indian store along River Road.
- "Why go elsewhere to be cheated, when you can come here?"
- On the grounds of a private school.
- "No trespassing without permission."

A bunch of Indians capture a cowboy named "Clint", and bring him back to their camp to meet the chief. The chief says to Clint, "You going to die. But we sorry for you, so give you one wish a day for three days. On sundown of third day, you die. What is your first wish?" Clint says, "I want to see my horse." The Indians get his horse. Clint grabs the horse's ear and whispers something, then slaps the horse on the ass. The horse takes off. Two hours later, the horse comes back with a naked blonde. She jumps off the horse and goes into the teepee with Clint. The Indians look at each other, figuring, "Typical white man—can only think of one thing." The second day, the chief says, "What's your wish today?" Clint says, "I want to see my horse again." The Indians bring him his horse. Clint leans over to the horse and whispers something in the horse's ear, then slaps it on the ass. Two hours later, the horse comes back with a naked redhead. She gets off and goes in the teepee with Clint. The Indians shake their heads, figuring, "Typical white man—going to die tomorrow and can only think of one thing." The last day comes, and the chief says, "This is your last wish, white man. What you want?" Clint says, "I want to see my horse again." The Indians bring him his horse. Clint grabs the horse by both ears, twists them hard and yells, "Read my lips! POSSE, damn it! P-O-S-S-E!"

Actual quote from Abdul Aziz, Chief Minister of the Malaysian State of Kelantan, during a recent lecture to Govt. employees:

"There are far too many pretty women in the government offices at the moment, distracting male workers and lowering business efficiency with their pert and yielding tightness. We must be ever watchful for possible, immoral activities and it is well-known that pretty women cause unhealthy activities that lead to insanity, blindness, sickness and bends. That is why from now on thorough ugliness must be considered a deciding factor at all job interviews. Since the prettier candidate has already been blessed by God it is only right that we should hire the uglier one. After all if we do not choose the ugly candidates, who will?"

An Aussie and a little man were sitting at a bar in Sydney when this huge, burly American guy walks in. As he passes the Aussie, he hits him on the neck knocking him to the floor. The big, burly Yank says,"That's a karate chop from Korea." Well, the Aussie gets back on his barstool and resumes drinking his beer.

The burly Yank then gets up to go to the bathroom and, as he walks by the Aussie, he hits him on the other side of the neck and knocks him to the floor. "That's a judo chop from Japan", he says.

The Aussie decides he's had enough and leaves. A half hour later he comes back and sees the burly Yank bastard sitting at the bar. He walks up behind him and smacks him on the head, knocking

him out. The Aussie says to the bartender, "When he wakes up mate, tell him that was a f*ckin' crowbar from Bunnings."

X is for Xenophobia

(Read with and Italian accent)—One day ima going to Malta to bigga hotel. Ina morning, I go down to eat breakfast. I tella waitress I wanan two pissis toast. She brings me only one piss. I tella her I want two piss on my plate. She say you better not piss onna plate. You sonna ma bitch. I don't even know the lady and she call me a sonna ma bitch. Later I go to eat at the bigga restaurant. The waitress brings me a spoon and knife, but no fock. I tella her I wanna fock. She tell me everyone wanna fock. I tell her she no understand, I wanna fock on the table. She say you better not fock on the table, you bitch. So I go back to my room inna hotel and there is no shits onna my bed. Call the manager and tella him I want to shit. He tella me to go to the toilet. I say you no understand. I wanna shit on my bed. He say you better not shit onna bed You sonna ma bitch. I don't even know the man and he call me a sonna ma bitch. I go to the checkout and the man at the desk say: peace on you. I say piss onna you too, you sonna ma bitch. I gonna back to Italy.

CHAPTER 25

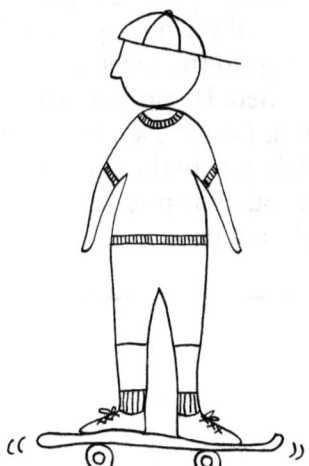

Y is for Youth

A girl asks her boyfriend to come over Friday night and have dinner with her parents. Since this is such a big event, the girl announces to her boyfriend that after dinner, she would like to go out and have sex for the first time.

Well, the boy is ecstatic, but he has never had sex before, so he takes a trip to the pharmacist to get some condoms. The pharmacist helps the boy for about an hour. He tells the boy everything that there is to know about condoms and sex. At the register the pharmacist asks the boy how many condoms he'd like to buy, a 3 pack, 10 pack or a family pack.

The boy insists on the family pack, he explains to the pharmacist that he is expecting to have a big night with his girlfriend tonight.

That night the boy shows up at the girl's parent's house, and meets his girlfriend at the door. "Oh I'm so excited that you're meeting my parents, come on in!" she says. The boy goes inside and is taken to the dinner table where the girl's parents are seated.

The boy quickly offers to say grace and bows his head. A minute passes, and the boy is still deep in prayer, with his head down. 10 minutes passes, and still no movement from the boy. Finally, after 20 minutes with his head down the girlfriend leans over and whispers to the boyfriend, "I had no idea that you were this religious."

The boy turns and whispers back, "I had no idea that your father was a pharmacist."

A little girl is in line to see Santa. When it's her turn, she climbs up on Santa's lap.

"What would you like Santa to bring you for Christmas?" Santa asks.

"I want a Barbie and GI Joe," the little girl replies.

Santa looks at the little girl for a moment and says, "I thought Barbie comes with Ken."

"No," the little girl says. "She comes with GI Joe. She fakes it with Ken."

Barbie's Letter To Santa:

Dear Santa,

Listen you fat troll, I've been saving your ass every year, being the perfect Christmas Present, wearing skimpy bathing suits in December and dressing in fake Chanel at sappy tea parties.

I hate to break it to ya', Santa, but it's payback time. There had better be some changes around here, or I'm gonna call for a nationwide meltdown, and trust me, you don't wanna be around to smell it.

These are my demands for Christmas:

1. Sweat pants and an oversized sweatshirt. I'm sick of looking like a hooker in hot pink bikinis. Do you have any idea what it feels like to have nylon and Velcro up your butt? I don't suppose you do.

2. Real underwear that can be pulled on and off. The cheap-o moulded underwear some genius at Mattel came up with looks like cellulite!!!!

3. A Real man... I don't care if you have to go to HasBro to get him, bring me GI Joe. Hell, I'd take Tickle-Me-Elmo over that pathetic bump of a boytoy, Ken. And what was up with that earring anyways? Hullo!?!

4. It's about time you made us all anatomically correct. Give me arms that actually bend so I can push the aforementioned Ken-wimp away once he is anatomically correct.

5. Breast reduction surgery. Nuff said.

6. A jog-bra. To wear until I get the surgery.

7. A new career. Pet doctor and school teachers make real money.

8. A new, more 90s persona. Maybe "PMS Barbie," complete with a pint of cookie dough ice cream and a bag of chips.

9. No more McDonald's endorsements. The grease is wrecking my vinyl complexion.

10. Mattel stock options. It's been 40 years—I think I deserve a piece of the action.

Considering my valuable contribution to society and Mattel, I think these demands are reasonable. If you don't like it, you can find yourself a new bitch for next Christmas. It's that simple.

As ever, ...

Barbie

Ken's Letter To Santa:

Dear Santa,

It has come to my attention that one of my colleagues has petitioned for changes in her contract, specifically asking for anatomical and career changes. In addition, it is my understanding that disparaging remarks were made about me, my sexuality, and some of my fashion choices.

I would like to take this opportunity to inform you of issues concerning Ms Barbie, as well as some of my own needs and desires: First, I, along with several of my colleagues feel Ms Barbie does not deserve the preferential treatment she has received over the years. That bitch has everything. Neither I, nor Joe, Jem nor The Raggedys, Ann & Andy, have dream houses, Corvettes, dune buggies, evening gowns, and some of us do not even have the ability to change out hairstyle. I have a limited wardrobe, obviously designed to complement but never upstage Ms Barbie.

My decision to accessorize with an earring was immediately quashed, which I protest, for it was my decision and reflects my lifestyle choice. I would like a change in my career to further explore my creative nature. Some options which could be considered are "Decorator Ken," "Beauty Salon Ken," or "Broadway Ken."

Other avenues which could be considered are: "Go-Go Ken," Impersonator Ken" (with wigs and gowns), or "West Hollywood Ken." These would more accurately reflect my interests and, I believe open up markets that have been underserved.

As for Ms Barbie needing bendable arms so she can "pushme away", I need bendable knees so I can kick the bitch to the curb. Bendable knees would also be helpful in other situations of which you are aware.

In closing, further concessions to the Blonde Bimbo from Hell, while the needs of others within my coalition are ignored, will result in legal action to be taken by myself and others. And kindly tell Ms Barbie she can forget about G.I. Joe ... he's mine, at least that's what he said last night.

Sincerely,

Ken

A middle-aged woman has a heart attack and is taken to the hospital. While on the operating table she has a near death experience. During that experience she sees God and asks if this is it. God says no and explains that she has another 30-40 years to live. Upon her recovery she decides to just stay in the hospital and have a face-lift, liposuction, breast augmentation, tummy tuck, etc.

She even has someone come in and change her hair colour. She figures since she's got another 30 or 40 years she might as well make the most of it. She walks out the hospital after the last operation and is killed by an ambulance speeding up to the hospital.

She arrives in front of God and asks, "I thought you said I had another 30-40 years?"

God replies, "I didn't recognize you."

Mark decided to propose to Juanita, but prior to her acceptance, Juanita had to confess to her man about her childhood illness. She informed Mark that she suffered a disease that left her breasts the maturity of a 12 year old.

He stated that it was ok because he loved her soooo much. However, Mark felt this was also the time for him to open up and admit that he also had a deformity too. Mark looked Juanita in the eyes and said I too have a problem. My penis is the same size as an infant and I hope you could deal with that once we are married.

She said "Yes I would marry you and learn to live with your infant size penis."

Juanita and Mark got married and they could not wait for the honeymoon so Mark whisked Juanita off to their hotel suite and they started getting funky, touching and teasing one another ...

As Juanita put her hands in Mark's pants she screamed and ran out of the room. Mark ran after her to find out what was wrong. Juanita you told me your penis was the size of an infant!

Mark said "Yes, it is 8 lbs., 7 oz., and 19 inches long!!

A mother is in the kitchen making supper for her family when her youngest daughter walks in. The Child asks "Mother, where do babies come from?"

After thinking about it for a moment the mother says "Well dear ....a mummy and daddy fall in love and get married. One night they go into their room ...they kiss and hug and have sex."

The child looks puzzled so the Mother continues "That means the daddy puts his penis in the mummy's vagina. That's how you get a baby, honey."

The child replies "Oh I see, but the other night when I came into yours and daddy's room, you had daddy's penis in your mouth. What do you get when you do that?

The Mother says "Jewellery, dear."

A group of kindergarteners were trying to become accustomed to first grade. The biggest hurdle they faced was that the teacher insisted on no baby talk.." You need to use 'big people' words," she'd always remind them. She asked Wendy what she had done over the weekend.

"I went to visit my Nana.—

"No, you went to visit your GRAND-MOTHER. Use big people words!"

She then asked Joey what he had done.

"I took a ride on a choo-choo."

She said, "No, you took a ride on a TRAIN." Use big people words.

She then asked Eddie what he had done.

"I read a book" he replied.

"That's wonderful," the teacher said.

"What book did you read?" Eddie thought about it, then puffed out his chest with great pride and said, "Winnie the SHIT."

What's the difference between greyhound racing and Gary Glitter? The greyhounds wait for the hare.

What is the worst thing about being Gary Glitter? You have to go to bed before 7.00.

How do you know when it is bedtime at the Glitter residence? When the big hand touches the small hand.

"Have you heard about Gary Glitter's New Book?" It's called, "The In's and Out's of Child Rearing."

A young boy and Gary Glitter are out at night, walking towards the forest. The boy says, It's dark! I don't like it! I'm scared!" Gary Glitter says, you're scared! I've got to walk back out of here on my own!"

Gary Glitter is sitting in his living room surfing the internet on his laptop. All of a sudden, the door of the apartment whips open and his girlfriend storms through.

She screams, You f**king asshole" and she heads into the bedroom.

Stunned, Gary flips off the computer and walks toward the bedroom wondering, Now what have I done?"

Inside the bedroom he finds the girl furiously packing a suitcase.

He asks her what's up. She responds with a hiss, my therapist says that I should leave you and that you're a paedophile.

Gary responds, "Wow, that's a big word for an 8 year old."

Have you beard? Gary Glitter has pulled out of Children In Need…

An elderly couple, a middle-aged couple and a young newly-wed couple wanted to join a church.

The priest said, "We have special requirements for new parishioners. You must abstain from having sex for two weeks."

The couples agreed and came back at the end of two weeks.

The pastor went to the elderly couple and asked, "Were you able to abstain from sex for the two weeks?"

The old man replied, "No problem at all, Priest." "Congratulations! Welcome to the church!" said the priest.

The priest went to the middle-aged couple and asked, "Well, were you able to abstain from sex for the two weeks?"

The middle-aged man replied, "The first week was not too bad. The second week I had to sleep on the couch for a couple of nights but, yep we made it." "Congratulations! Welcome to the church," said the priest.

The priest then went to the newly-wed couple and asked, "Well, were you able to abstain from sex for two weeks?"

"NO Pastor, we were not able to go without sex for the two weeks," the young man replied sadly.

"What happened?" inquired the priest.

"My wife was reaching for a can of corn on the top shelf and dropped it" said the young man. 'When she bent over to pick it up, I was overcome with Lust; and took advantage of her right there."

"You understand, of course, this means you will not be welcome in our church" stated the priest .

"We know," said the young man. "We're not welcome at the supermarket anymore either."

A young married couple returned to their house after being on honeymoon. "Care to go upstairs and have a bop?" the husband asked.

"Shhhh!" said the bride "All the neighbours will know what we're about to do. These walls are paper thin. In the future, we'll have to ask each other in code. For example, how about asking 'Have you left the washing machine door open instead?"

So the following night, the husband asks, "I don't suppose you left the washing machine door open, did you?"

"No, I definitely shut it", replied the wife who rolled over and fell asleep.

When she woke up however, she was feeling a little amorous herself and she nudged her husband and said, "I think I did leave the washing machine door open after all. Would you like to do some washing?"

"No thanks" said the husband, "It was only a small load and I've done it by hand."

An old man gets on a crowded bus and no one gives him a seat. As the bus shakes and rattles, the old man's cane slips on the floor and he falls.

As the old man gets up and composes himself, a young kid, sitting nearby, turns to him and says, "you know, if you put a little rubber thingy on the end of your stick, it won't slip."

The old geezer man snaps back, "well, if your daddy did the same thing seven years ago, I'd have a seat on this here bus."

This boy just takes his girlfriend back to her home after being out together, and when they reach the front door he leans with one hand on the wall and says to her, "Sweetie, why don't you give me a blowjob?"

"What? You're crazy???!!!"

"Don't worry, it will be quick, no problem."

"No!! Someone may see; a relative, a neighbour ..."

"At this time of the night no one will show Up .."

"I've already said NO, and NO!"

"Honey, it's just a small blowie ... I know you like it too.."

"NO!!! I've said NO!!!"

"My love .. don't be like that .."

At this moment the younger sister shows up at the door in nightgown with hair totally in disorder, rubbing her eyes and says. Dad says either you have to blow him, I have to blow him, or he will come down and give the guy a blowjob himself, but for God's sake to tell your boyfriend to take his hand off the intercom!

This is an actual job application a 17 year old boy submitted at a fast-food establishment and they hired him because he was so honest and funny!

NAME: "Greg Bulmash."

SEX: "Not yet." "Still waiting for the right person."

DESIRED POSITION: "Company's President or Vice President. But seriously, whatever's available. If I was in a position to be picky, I wouldn't be applying here in the first place."

DESIRED SALARY: "$185,000 a year plus stock options and a huge CEO style severance package. If that's not possible, make an offer and we can haggle."

EDUCATION: "Yes."

LAST POSITION HELD: "Target for middle management hostility."

SALARY: "Less than I'm worth."

MOST NOTABLE ACHIEVEMENT: "My incredible collection of stolen pens and post-it notes."

REASON FOR LEAVING: "It sucked."

HOURS AVAILABLE TO WORK: "Any."

PREFERRED HOURS: "1:30-3:30 p.m., Monday, Tuesday, And Thursday."

DO YOU HAVE ANY SPECIAL SKILLS?: "Yes, but they're better suited to a more intimate environment."

MAY WE CONTACT YOUR CURRENT EMPLOYER?: "If I had one, would I be here?"

DO YOU HAVE ANY PHYSICAL CONDITIONS THAT WOULD PROHIBIT YOU FROM LIFTING UP TO 50 LBS?: "Of what?"

DO YOU HAVE A CAR?: I think the more appropriate question here would be "DO you have a car that runs?"

HAVE YOU RECEIVED ANY SPECIAL AWARDS OR RECOGNITION?: "I may already be a winner of the Publishers Clearing house Sweepstakes."

DO YOU SMOKE?: "On the job no, on my breaks yes."

WHAT WOULD YOU LIKE TO BE DOING IN FIVE YEARS?: "Living in the Bahamas with a fabulously wealthy dumb sexy blonde super model who thinks I'm the greatest thing since sliced bread."

"Actually, I'd like to be doing that now."

DO YOU CERTIFY THAT THE ABOVE IS TRUE AND COMPLETE TO THE BEST OF YOUR KNOWLEDGE?: "Yes. Absolutely."

SIGN HERE: "Aries."

A traveling salesman knocks on the door of a house. A kid, about 12 years old, answers the door—He's wearing a pink tutu, has a cigar in one hand, and a martini with one olive in the other. The salesman is a little taken aback, so he asks "Excuse me son, are your parents' home?" The kid takes a big puff on the cigar and answers, "What the fuck do you think?"

One fine, sunny morning, a priest took a walk in the local forest. He was walking by a small stream when, sitting on a nearby toadstool, he noticed a sad, sad-looking frog.

What's wrong with you? said the priest. Well, said the frog, the reason I am so sad on this fine day is because I wasn't always a frog. Really! said the priest.

Can you explain? Once upon a time I was an 11-year-old Choirboy at your very church. I too was walking by this stream when I was confronted by the wicked witch of the forest. 'Let me pass!' I cried, but to no avail. She called me a cheeky little boy and with a flash of her wand, turned me into the frog you now see before you.

"That's an incredible story!" said the priest. "Is there no way of reversing the witch's spell? Yes," said the frog. "It is said that if a nice kind person would pick me up, take me home, give me food and warmth and a good night's sleep, I will wake up as a boy again."

"Today's your lucky day!" Said the priest, and forthwith picked up the frog and took him home. He gave him lots of food, placed him by the fire, and at bedtime put the frog on the pillow beside him. And, lo miracle of miracles, when he awoke the next morn, there was the 11 year old Choirboy beside him in bed. "And that, your honour is the case for the Defence."

A father asks his son, "now aged 10, if he knows about the birds and the bees." I don't want to know! the child said, "bursting into tears."

Confused, the father asked his son "what was wrong."

"Oh dad" he sobbed, "at age six I got the 'there's no Santa' speech. At age seven I got the ' there's no Easter bunny speech. Then at age 8 you hit me with the 'there's no tooth fairy' speech! If you're going to tell me now that grown-ups don't really f*ck, I've got nothing left to live for!"

A professor is giving the first year medical students their first lecture on autopsies, and decides to give them a few basics before starting. "You must be capable of two things to do an autopsy. The first thing is that you must have no sense of fear." At this point, the lecturer sticks his finger into the dead man's anus, and then licks it.

He asks all the students to do the same thing with the corpses in front of them. After a couple of minute's silence, they follow suit.

"The second thing is that you must have an acute sense of observation: I stuck my middle finger into the corpse's anus, but I licked my index finger."

You too can have a cool Star Wars name—How to determine your Star Wars name:

For your new first name:

1. Take the first three letters of your first name;
2. Add the first two letters of your last name; and
3. Add a dash somewhere, if you want.

For your new last name:

4. Take the first two letters of your mother's maiden name; and
5. Add the first three letters of the city in which you were born.

How to determine your Star Wars honorific and title:

6. Take the last three letters of your last name and reverse them;
7. Add the name of the first car/vehicle you drove/owned;
8. Insert the word "of"; and
9. Tack on the name of the last medication you took.

YOU MAY BE NO LONGER YOUNG IF . . . . .

1. You find yourself listening to talk radio.
2. You daughter says she got pierced and you look at her ears.
3. All the cars behind you turn on their headlights.
4. Your wife buys a flannel nighty and you find that sexy.
5. You call the police on a noisy party next door instead of grabbing beer and joining it.
6. You actually ask for your father's advice.
7. You turn down free tickets to a rock concert because you have to work the next day.
8. Sex becomes "All that foolishness".
9. Getting a little action means your prune juice is working.
10. You bought your first car for the same price you paid for your son's new running shoes.
11. What's all this stuff about E-mail?" comes out from your voice
12. When someone mentions SURFING you picture waves and a surf board.

A boy was walking down the road when a car pulled over if you get in, the driver said, "I'll give you $10." The boy refused and kept on walking.

A bit further along, the man pulled over again "Ok, how about $20 and a bag of lollies?" The driver asks.

The boy told the man "to piss off," and kept on walking. Further up the road, the driver tried once more.

"Right this is my final offer, I'll give you $50 and all the lollies you can eat."

The boy finally snaps and says "dad – you bought the Volvo, live with it!".

Little Johnny and Susie are only 10 years old, but they just know that they are in love.

One day they decide that they want to get married, so Johnny goes to Susie's father to ask him for her hand. Johnny bravely walks up to him and says "Mr Smith, me and Susie are in love and I want to ask you for her hand in marriage."

Thinking that this was the cutest thing, Mr Smith replies, "Well Johnny, you are only 10 where will you two live?"

Without even taking a moment to think about it, Johnny, replies "In Susie's room. It's bigger than mine and we can both fit there nicely." Still thinking this is just adorable Mr Smith says with a huge grin, "Okay then how will you live. You're not old enough to get a job. You'll need to support Susie."

Again, Johnny instantly replies, "Our allowance ... Susie makes 5 bucks a week and I make 10 bucks a week. That's about 60 bucks a month, and that should do us just fine."

By this time Mr Smith is a little shocked that Johnny has put so much thought into this. So, he thinks for a moment trying to come up with something Johnny won't have an answer to. After a second, Mr Smith says you have got everything all figured out. I just have one more question for you. What will you do if the two of you should have little ones of your own?

Johnny just shrugs his shoulders and says "Well, we've been lucky so far . . ."

Dear Mum and Dad:

Our Scout Master told us to write to our parents in case you saw the flood on TV and worried. We are OK. Only 1 of our tents and 2 sleeping bags got washed away. Luckily, none of us got drowned because we were all up on the mountain looking for Davey when it happened.

Oh yes, please call Davey's mother and tell her he is OK. He can't write because of the cast. I got to ride in one of the search & rescue jeeps. It was neat. We never would have found him in the dark if it hadn't been for the lightening. Scout master Chris got mad at Davey for going on a hike alone without telling anyone. Davey said he did tell him, but it was during the fire so he probably didn't hear him.

Did you know that if you put gas on a fire, the gas can will blow up? The wet wood still didn't burn, but one of our tents did. Also some of our clothes. Dylan is going to look weird until his hair grows back.

We will be home on Saturday if Scout master Chris gets the car fixed. It wasn't his fault about the wreck. The brakes worked OK when we left.

Scout master Chris said that a car that old you have to expect something to break down; that's probably why he can't get insurance on it. We think it's a neat car. He doesn't care if we get it dirty, and if it's hot, sometimes he lets us ride on the fenders. It gets pretty hot with 10 people in the car. He let us take turns riding in the trailer until the highway patrolman stopped and talked to us.

Scout master Chris is a neat guy. Don't worry, he is a good driver. In fact, he is teaching Robbie how to drive. But he only lets him drive on the mountain roads where they isn't any traffic. All we ever see up there are logging trucks.

This morning all of the guys were diving off the rocks and swimming out in the lake. Scout master Chris wouldn't let me because I can't swim and Davey was afraid he would sink because of his cast, so he let us take the canoe across the lake. It was great. You can still see some of the trees under the water from the flood.

Scout master Chris isn't crabby like some Scout masters. He didn't even get mad about the life jackets. He has to spend a lot of time working on the car so we are trying not to cause him any trouble. Guess what? We have all passed our first aid merit badges. When Brad dove into the lake and cut his arm, we got to see how a tourniquet works.

Also Tyler G. and I threw up, but scout master Chris said it probably was just food poisoning from the leftover chicken, he said they got sick that way with the food they ate in prison. I'm so glad he got out and became our Scout master. He said he sure figured out how to get things done better while he was doing his time.

With love, James.

CHAPTER 26

Z is for Zoo

One day little Timmy was in his back yard filling in a hole, carefully shovelling earth in and packing it down with his foot.

When he's almost finished, his neighbour decided to investigate.

"Whatcha doin?" he asks.

Timmy replies, "My goldfish died and I've just buried him."

"That was an awful big hole for a goldfish, wasn't it?" asked the neighbour.

Timmy shot back, "That's because he's inside your f**king cat."

About Sheep and such matters:

Once upon a time there was a shepherd tending his sheep at the edge of a country road. A brand new Jeep Grand Cherokee screeches to a halt next to him.

The driver, a young man dressed in a Brioni suit, Cerrutti shoes, Ray-Ban glasses, Jovial Swiss wrist watch and a BHS tie gets out and asks the shepherd: "If I guess how many sheep you have, will you give me one of them?"

The shepherd looks at the young man, then looks at the sprawling field of sheep and says: "Okay."

The young man parks the SUV, connects his notebook and wireless modem, and enters a NASA site, scans the ground using his GPS, opens a database and 60 Excel tables filled with algorithms, then prints a 150 page report on his high tech mini printer. He then turns to the shepherd and says: "You have exactly 1,586 sheep here."

The shepherd answers: "That's correct, you can have your sheep."

The young man takes one of the animals and puts it in the back of his vehicle.

The shepherd looks at him and asks: "Now, if I guess your profession, will you pay me back in kind?"

The young man answers: "Sure."

The shepherd says: "You are a consultant." "Exactly! How did you know," asks the young man?

Very simple, answers the shepherd.

"First, you came here without being called."

"Second, you charged me a fee to tell me something I already knew."

"Third, you do not understand anything about my business and I'd really like to have my dog back."

A chicken and an egg are lying in bed.

The chicken looks quite content and he is puffing away on a cigarette....

The egg looks very dissatisfied and she looks very aggravated as well....

The egg looks over to the chicken and tells him, "I guess that answers that question !"

A man goes into a cafe and sits down. A waitress comes to take his order, and he asks her, "What's the special of the day?"

"Chili," she says, "but the gentleman next to you got the last bowl."

The man says he'll just have coffee, and the waitress goes to fetch it. As he waited, he noticed the man next to him was eating a full lunch and the bowl of chili remained uneaten. "Are you going to eat your chili?" he asked.

"No, help yourself," replied his neighbour.

The man picked up a spoon and eagerly began devouring the chili. When he got halfway through the bowl, he noticed the body of a dead mouse in the bottom of the bowl. Sickened, he puked the chili he had just eaten back into the bowl.

The man sitting next to him says, "Yeah, that's as far as I got, too."

A man was leaving a 7-11 with his morning coffee and newspaper when he noticed a most unusual funeral procession approaching the nearby cemetery.

A long black hearse was followed by a second long black hearse about 50 feet behind. Behind the second hearse was a solitary man walking a pit-bull on a leash. Behind him were 200 men walking single file.

The guy couldn't stand the curiosity. He respectfully approached the man walking the dog and said "Sir, I know now is a bad time to disturb you, but I've never seen a funeral like this. Whose funeral is it? "

The man replied "Well, that first hearse is for my wife."

"What happened to her?"

The man replied "My dog attacked and killed her."

He inquired further, "Well, who is in the second hearse?"

The man answered, "My mother-in-law. She was trying to help my wife when the dog turned on her."

A poignant and thoughtful moment of silence passes between the two men.

"Sir, could I borrow that dog?"

"Get in line."

While proudly showing off his new apartment to friends late one night, the drunk led the way to his bedroom where there was a big brass gong.

"What's that big brass gong for?" one of the guests asked. "Why, that's the talking clock" the man replied.

"How does it work?"

"Watch", the man said, giving it an ear-shattering pound with a hammer. Suddenly, a parrot on the other side of the wall screamed, "For fuck's sake, you wanker, it's 2 o'clock in the morning!!"

A Polar bear was taking his young baby polar bear to teach him how to fish.

They went out onto an iceberg, and after a few hours of catching many wonderful salmon, the father polar bear took the polar bear home, feeling very proud of his son on this wonderful day.

On the way home, the baby polar bear tuned to his father and said "Dad, am I a polar bear?" His father replied—"Of course you are a polar bear—you have white fur, you catch fish—yes, you're a polar bear."

"OK" says the baby polar bear.

The next day once again Dad and baby polar bear go out fishing, continuing on the proud tradition of fish catching which had been in that family of polar bears for centuries. Once again, Baby polar bear did Dad proud, catching a wonderful yellow fin tuna.

They were walking home, Dad's arm round baby polar bear's shoulder when once again baby polar bear turned to his father and said "Dad, am I a polar bear?"

"Of course you are a polar bear—your fur's white, you catch fish, your mother's a polar bear, I'm a polar bear—yes, you are a polar bear!"

"OK" replies baby polar bear.

The Third day, they once again go fishing, and once again baby polar bear exhibits all the signs that he will one day be a great fisherman amongst the Polar bear Clan. Dad stands proudly by as baby polar bear catches fish after fish.

They go home, skipping together and whistling, Dad rubbing baby polar bears head in admiration.

Suddenly, baby polar bear turns around to his Dad and says (you guessed it) "Dad, are you sure I am a polar bear?"

Dad is starting to get quite angry with this persistent line of questioning.

"Look you are a polar bear. Your fur is white, you catch fish, your mother is a polar bear, I am a polar bear your sister is a polar bear, your grandmother and grandfather is a polar bear.

There's no' doubt you're a polar bear. Now stop this nonsense."

Baby polar bear is quiet for a while, then turns to his Dad and says "Then why am I so fucking cold???"

Two vampire bats are hanging up in their cave.

One says to the other "I'm really hungry—I'm going to get something to eat." (Yes they can talk) "Are you coming?"

"No" says the other bat, "I had a big feed last night, and I'm still full. You go ahead" The first bat drops off the roof and flies out of the mouth of the cave.

He's back about 30 seconds later, with fresh blood all over his nose and mouth.

"Wow" says the other bat "That was quick! I've never found a meal as fast as that. What happened?"

"You see that big rock just outside the cave?" says the first bat. "Yep" says the second bat.

"Well I didn't."

Guy Just Bought A Dead Horse Without Knowing. What He Does Next Is Genius.

A young man, named Chuck bought a horse from a farmer for $250. The farmer agreed to deliver the horse the next day. The next day, the farmer drove up to Chucks house and said, 'Sorry son, but I have some bad news, the horse died.'

Chuck replied, "Well, then just give me my money back.'

The farmer said, 'Can't do that. I went and spent it already.'

Chuck said, 'Ok, then" just bring me the dead horse.'

The farmer asked 'What ya gonna do with him?'

Chuck said, 'I'm going to raffle him off.'

The farmer said, 'You can't raffle off a dead horse! '

Chuck said" 'Sure I can" Watch me. I just won't tell anybody he's dead.'

A month later, the farmer met up with Chuck and asked, "What happened with that dead horse?"

Chuck said, 'I raffled him off. I sold 500 tickets at five dollars a piece and made a profit of $2495.'

The farmer said, 'Didn't anyone complain?' Chuck said, 'Just the guy who won. So I gave him his five dollars back.'

Chuck grew up and works now for the government.

A couple drove several miles down a country road, not saying a word. An earlier discussion had led to an argument, and neither wanted to concede their position.

As they passed a paddock of goats and pigs, the wife sarcastically asked, "Relatives of yours?"

"Yep," the husband replied, "In-laws."

The Seven Dwarfs go to the Vatican and, because they have requested an audience, and as they are THE Seven Dwarfs, they are ushered in to see the Pope. Dopey leads the pack.

"Dopey, my son," says the Pope, "what can I do for you?" Dopey asks, "Excuse me, Your Excellency, but are there any dwarf nuns in Rome?"

The pope wrinkles his brow at the odd question, thinks for a moment, and answers, "No, Dopey, there are no dwarf nuns in Rome."

In the background a few of the dwarfs start giggling. Dopey turns around and gives them a glare, silencing them.

Dopey turns back, "your Worship," are there any dwarf nuns in all of Europe?

The Pope, puzzled now, again thinks for a moment and then answers, "No, Dopey, there are no dwarf nuns in Europe."

This time, all of the other dwarfs burst into laughter. Once again, Dopey turns around and silences them with an angry glare.

Dopey turns back and says, "Mr Pope! Are there ANY dwarf nuns anywhere in the world?"

"I'm sorry, my son, there are no dwarf nuns anywhere in the world." The other dwarfs collapse into a heap, rolling and laughing, pounding the floor, tears rolling down their cheeks as they begin chanting.

Dopey shagged a penguin! Dopey shagged a penguin!

A woman goes to her boyfriend's parents' house for dinner.

This is to be her first time meeting the family, and she is very nervous.

They all sit down and begin eating a fine meal.

The woman is beginning to feel a little discomfort, thanks to her nervousness and the broccoli casserole.

The gas pains are almost making her eyes water.

Left with no other choice, she decides to relieve herself a bit and lets out a dainty little fart.

It wasn't loud, but everyone at the table heard the poot.

Before she even had a chance to be embarrassed, her boyfriend's father looked over at the dog that had been snoozing at the women's feet, and said in a rather stern voice, Ginger! The woman thought, this is great! and a big smile came across her face.

A couple minutes later, she was beginning to feel the pain again.

This time, she didn't even hesitate. She let a much louder and longer fart rip.

The father again looked at the dog and yelled, darn it Ginger!

Once again the woman smiled and thought, yes!

A few minutes later the woman had to let another one rip. This time she didn't even think about it.

She let rip with a fart that rivalled a train whistle blowing.

Again, the father looked at the dog with disgust and yelled, Darn it Ginger, get away from her before she shits on you!

THE FISHING TRIP:

A woman is in bed with her lover who also happens to be her husband's best friend. They make love for hours, and afterwards, while they're just laying there, the phone rings.

Since it is the woman's house, she picks up the receiver. Her lover looks over at her and listens, only hearing her side of the conversation ...

(She is speaking in a cheery voice)

"Hello? Oh, hi. I'm so glad that you called. Really? That's wonderful. I am so happy for you. That sounds terrific. Great! Thanks. Okay. Bye bye." She hangs up the telephone and her lover asks, "Who was that?"

"Oh," she replies, "that was my husband telling me all about the wonderful time he's having on his fishing trip with you."

THE PARROT:

A lady was walking down the street to work and she saw a parrot on a perch in front of a pet store. The parrot said to her, "Hey lady, you are really ugly." Well, the lady is furious! She stormed past the store to her work.

On the way home she saw the same parrot and it said to her, "Hey lady, you are really ugly." She was incredibly ticked now. The next day the same parrot again said to her, "Hey lady, you are really ugly."

The lady was so ticked that she went into the store and said that she would sue the store and kill the bird. The store manager replied profusely and promised he would make sure the parrot didn't say it again.

When the lady walked past the store that day after work the parrot called to her, "Hey lady."

She paused and said, "Yes?" The bird said, "You know."

Here are some management strategies that we can all recognize.

The tribal wisdom of the Dakota Indians, passed on from one generation to the next, says that when you discover you are riding a dead horse, the best strategy is to dismount.

However, in modern business, because of the heavy investment factors to be taken into consideration, often other strategies have to be tried with dead horses, including the following:

1. Buying a stronger whip.
2. Changing riders.

3. Threatening the horse with termination.
4. Appointing a committee to study the horse.
5. Arranging to visit other sites to see how they ride dead horses.
6. Lowering the standards so that dead horses can be included.
7. Appointing an intervention team to reanimate the dead horse.
8. Creating a training session to increase the riders load share.
9. Reclassifying the dead horse as living-impaired.
10. Change the form so that it reads: "This horse is not dead."
11. Hire outside contractors to ride the dead horse.
12. Harness several dead horses together for increased speed.
13. Donate the dead horse to a recognized charity, thereby deducting its full original cost.
14. Providing additional funding to increase the horse's performance.
15. Do a time management study to see if the lighter riders would improve productivity.
16. Purchase an after-market product to make dead horses run faster.
17. Declare that a dead horse has lower overhead and therefore performs better.
18. Form a quality focus group to find profitable uses for dead horses.

19. Rewrite the expected performance requirements for horses.

20. Promote the dead horse to a supervisory position.

Subject: "IF NOAH LIVED ON THE GOLD COAST TODAY"

And the Lord spoke to Noah and said, "In one year, I am going to make it rain and cover the whole earth with water until all flesh is destroyed. But I want you to save the righteous people and two of every kind of living thing on the earth. Therefore, I am commanding you to build an Ark."

In a flash of lightning, God delivered the specifications for an Ark. In fear and trembling, Noah took the plans and agreed to build the Ark.

"Remember" said the Lord, "You must complete the Ark and bring everything onboard in one year. Exactly one year later, fierce storm clouds covered the earth and all the seas of the earth went into a tumult. The Lord saw that Noah was sitting in his front yard weeping. "Noah," He shouted. "Where is the Ark?"

"Lord, please forgive me!," cried Noah. "I did my best, but there were big problems. First, I had to get a permit for construction and your plans did not meet the specifications. I had to hire an engineering firm and redraw the plans. Then I got into a fight with occupational Safety people over whether or not the Ark needed a fire sprinkler system and flotation devices.

Then my neighbour objected, claiming I was violating City Council zoning ordinances by building the Ark in my front yard, so I had to get a variance from the city planning department. Then I had problems getting enough wood for the Ark, because there was a ban on cutting trees to protect the Spotted owl.

I finally convinced the Department of Forestry that I needed the wood to save the owls. However, the Department of Environmental won't let me catch any owls. So, no owls.

The carpenters union went out on strike I had to negotiate a settlement with the National Labour Relations Board before anyone would pick up a saw or a hammer. Now I have 16 carpenters on the Ark, but still no owls.

When I started rounding up the other animals, I got sued by an animal rights group. They objected to me only taking two of each kind aboard.

Just when I got the suit dismissed, the Federal Department of the Environment notified me that I could not complete the Ark without filing an environmental impact assessment on your proposed flood. They didn't take very kindly to the idea that they had no jurisdiction over the conduct of the Creator of the universe.

Then the City Engineer demanded a map of the proposed new flood plan. I sent them a globe. Right now, I am trying to resolve a complaint filed with the Equal Employment Opportunity Commission that I am practising discrimination by not taking godless, unbelieving people aboard.

The ATO has seized my assets, claiming that I'm building the Ark in preparation to flee the country to avoid paying taxes. I just got a notice from the Licensing Department that I owe them some kind of tax and failed to register the Ark as a recreational watercraft.

Finally, the Constitutional Court issued an injunction against further construction of the Ark, saying that "since God is flooding the earth, a religious event and therefore unconstitutional. I really don't think I can finish the Ark for another five or six years" Noah wailed.

The sky began to clear, the sun began to shine and the seas began to calm.

A rainbow arched across the sky. Noah looked up hopefully. You mean "You are not going to destroy the earth, Lord?"

"No", said the Lord. "I don't have to. The government already has."

Two sea monsters were swimming around in the ocean, looking for something to do. They came up underneath a ship that was hauling potatoes. Seymour, the first sea monster, swam underneath the ship, tipped it over and ate everything on the ship.

A little while later, they came up to another ship, again hauling potatoes. Seymour again capsizes the ship and eats everything on board.

The third ship they found was also hauling potatoes and Seymour once again capsized it and ate everything.

Finally his buddy Heathcliffe asked him, "Why do you keep tipping over those ships full of potatoes and eating everything on board?"

Seymour replied, "I wish I hadn't, but I just can't help myself once I start. Everyone knows you can't eat just one potato ship."

STORY: DO NOT DRIVE AND EAT.

This woman went through the drive-thru of Burger King for lunch a couple of years ago. She ordered a chicken sandwich (the breaded kind... before spicy chicken or grilled chicken became big sellers) and specifically requested NO MAYO because she couldn't stand the stuff.

She drove away without confirming that she got what she ordered. As she drove, she began to eat the sandwich and realised that there was Mayo on it. She was none too pleased but was so hungry that she ate it anyway. When she got about halfway through the sandwich, she began to feel very ill. She stopped eating the sandwich but felt increasingly worse as she continued to drive.

She felt so bad that she drove herself to the hospital emergency room. She took her sandwich with her since she started feeling bad after eating the sandwich. The hospital performed tests on both her and the sandwich and found out the following... the sandwich actually didn't have any Mayo on it. In reality, the chicken had a tumour on its breast. When the chicken was breaded and fried, the tumour burst inside the breaded chicken breast. The mayo-like substance was actually puss from the tumour.

Kind of makes you want to swear off fast food and mayo, doesn't it!

STORY: MUMMY DOWN THE HATCH.

This girl was really in a hurry one day so she just stopped off at a Taco Bell and got a Chicken taco and ate it on the way home. That night she noticed her jaw was kind of tight and swollen. The next day it was a little worse so she went to her doctor.

He said she was just having an allergic reaction to something and gave her some cream to rub on her jaw to help. After a couple of days the swelling had just gotten worse and she could hardly move her jaw.

She went back to her doctor to see what was wrong. Her doctor had no idea so he started to run some tests.

They scrubbed out the inside of her mouth to get tissue samples and they also took some saliva samples.

Well, they found out what was wrong.

Apparently her chicken taco had a pregnant cockroach in the one she ate!!!

The eggs then somehow got into her saliva glands and she was incubating them. They had to remove couple layers of her inner mouth to get all the eggs out. If they hadn't figured out what was going on, the eggs would have hatched inside the lining of her mouth!!!!!!!!!

Scientists at NASA have developed a gun, whose purpose it is to launch dead chickens. It is used to shoot a dead chicken at the windshields of airline jets, military jets, and the space shuttle, at that vehicle's maximum travelling velocity. The idea being, that it will simulate the frequent incidents of collisions with airborne fowl (bird strike), and therefore determine if the windshields are strong enough.

British engineers, upon hearing of the gun, were eager to test the gun out on the windshield of their new high speed trains. However, upon the firing of the 'gun, the engineers watched in shock as the chicken shattered the windshield, smashed through the control console, snapped the engineer's backrest in two, and embedded itself in the back wall of the cabin.

Horrified, the engineers sent NASA the results of the experiment, along with the designs of the windshield, and asked the NASA scientists for any suggestions. The NASA scientists sent back a one sentence response:

"THAW THE F*&##%@* CHICKEN."

One person who used to work for British Aerospace tells a similar story (which he swears is true) that these machines are actually used to fire chickens into jet engines to simulate bird strikes on the compressor blades. To cut a long story short, to thaw the chicken, someone left it in the gun overnight and performed the test in the morning. The results were somewhat different to be expected and close examination of the high speed video footage showed a very startled looking stray cat clinging to a half-eaten chicken as it exited the gun at MACH O.7.

This guy walks into a quiet bar. He is carrying three ducks, one in each hand and one under his left arm. He places them on the bar, then has a few drinks and chats with the Bartender.

The Bartender is experienced and has learned not to ask people about the animals that they bring into the bar, so he doesn't mention the ducks.

They chat for about half an hour before the guy with the ducks has to go to the toilet, leaving them on the bar. So the bartender is alone with the ducks.

There is an awkward silence.

The Bartender decides to try to make some conversation. "What's your name?" he says to the first duck.

"Huey" said the first duck. "How's your day been, Huey?"

"Great. Lovely day. Had a ball. Been in and out of puddles all day".

"That's good" He turns to the second duck and asks him, "What's your name?"

"Dewey" says the second duck.

"So how's your day been, Dewey?"

"Brilliant day. Had a fantastic time. Been in and out of puddles all day. If I had the chance another day I would do the same again".

So the Bartender turns to the third duck and says "So, you must be Louie". "No", growls the third duck, "My name is Puddles. And don't ask about my fucking day".

Three mice are sitting in a bar in a pretty rough neighbourhood late at night trying to impress each other about how tough they are.

The first mouse pounds a shot of scotch, slams the shot glass to the bar, turns to the second mouse and says: When I see a mousetrap, I get on it, lie on my back, and set it off with my foot. When the bar comes down, I catch it in my teeth, and then bench press it 100 times.

The second mouse orders up two shots of tequila. He grabs one in each paw, slams the shots, and pounds the glasses to the bar. He turns to the other mice and replies: Yeah, well when I see rat poison, I collect as much as I can and take it home. In the morning, I grind it up into a powder and put it in my coffee so I get a good buzz going for the rest of the day. The first mouse and the second mouse then turn to the third mouse.

The third mouse lets out a long sigh and says to the first two, I don't have time for this bullshit. I gotta go home and fuck the cat.

Three women had a very late night drinking. They left in the early morning hours and went home their separate ways. The next day, they all met and compared notes about who was drunker the night before. The first girl claims that she was the drunkest, saying, "I drove straight home and walked into the house. As soon as I got through the door, I blew chunks."

The second said, you think that was drunk? Hell, I got into my car and wrapped my car around the first tree I saw. I don't even have insurance!"

The third proclaimed, "Damn, I was the drunkest by far. When I got home, I got into a big fight with my husband, knocked a candle over, and burned the whole house down!"

The room was silent for a moment.

Then, the first girl spoke out again, "Listen, girls, I don't think you understand . . . Chunks is my dog".

A Captain in the foreign legion was transferred to a desert outpost. On his orientation tour he noticed a very old, seedy looking camel tied out back of the enlisted men's barracks.

He asked the Sergeant leading the tour, "What's the camel for?" The Sergeant replied "Well sir it's a long way from anywhere, and the men have natural sexual urges, so when they do, uh, we have the camel."

The captain said "Well if it's good for moral, then I guess it's all right with me."

After he had been at the fort for about 6 months the captain could not stand it anymore so he told his Sergeant, "BRING IN THE CAMEL!!!" The Sergeant shrugged his shoulders and led the camel into the captain's quarters. The captain got a foot stool & proceeded to have vigorous sex with the camel.

As he stepped, satisfied, down from the stool, and was buttoning his pants he asked the Sergeant, "Is that how the enlisted men do it?"

The Sergeant replied, "Well sir, they usually just use it to ride into town."

A duck walks into a bar and says "Got any duck food?" And the barman says "No."

And the duck says "Got any duck food?" The barman says "No, Got any duck food?"

I said"NO, N-O, NO! Got any duck food?" For cryin' out loud – "NO spells NO and I mean NO!! Got any duck food?"

"NO NO NO NO NO NO NO NO NO NO NO NO NO NO NO!! Got any duck food?"

"Look, if you ask me one more f--ing time if I've got any duck food, I'm going to nail your f--ing webbed feet to the f--ing bar! !"

"WE HAVE NO F--KING DUCK FOOD!!"

"Got any nails?"

"No!"

"Got any duck food?"

A farmer goes out one day and buys a brand new stud rooster for his chicken coop. The young rooster walks over to the old rooster and says,

"Ok, old fellow, time to retire."

The old rooster says, "You can't handle all these chickens ... look at what it did to me!"

The young rooster replies, "Now, don't give me a hassle about this."

"Time for the old to step aside and the young to take over, so take a hike."

The old rooster says, "Aw, c'mon. Just let me have the two old hens over in the corner. I won't bother you."

The young rooster says, "Scram! Beat it! You're washed up! I'm taking over!"

The old rooster thinks for a minute and then says to the young rooster, "I'll tell you what, young fellow, I'll have a race around the farmhouse with you. Whoever wins the race gets domain of the chicken coop."

The young rooster says, "You know I'm going to beat you, old man, so just to be fair, I'm even going to give you a head start."

They line up in back of the farm house, get a chicken to cluck "Go!" and the old rooster takes off running. About 15 seconds later the young rooster takes off after him. They round the front of the farm house and the young rooster is only about 5 inches behind the old rooster and gaining fast.

The farmer, sitting on the porch, looks up, sees what's going on, grabs his shotgun and BOOM!, he blows the young rooster to bits.

He sadly shakes his head and says, "Dangit, third gay rooster I bought this week!"

WHY DOGS ARE BETTER THAN WOMEN:

1. Dogs don't cry.
2. Dogs love it when your friends come over.
3. Dogs don't care if you use their shampoo.
4. Dogs think you sing great.
5. A dog's time in the bathroom is confined to a quick drink.

6. Dogs don't expect you to call when you are running late. The later you are, the more excited dogs are to see you.
7. Dogs will forgive you for playing with other dogs.
8. Dogs don't notice if you call them by another dog's name.
9. Dogs are excited by rough play.
10. Dogs don't mind if you give their offspring away.
11. Dogs understand that farts are funny.
12. Dogs appreciate excessive body hair.
13. Anyone can say a dog is gorgeous.
14. Other dogs don't hate it when you leave lots of things on the floor.
15. They love red meat.
16. Dogs can get a good-looking dog.
17. Dogs don't shop.
18. A dog's disposition stays the same all month long.
19. Dogs never need to examine the relationship.
20. A dog's parents never visit.
21. Dogs love long car trips.
22. Dogs understand that instincts are better than asking for directions.
23. Dogs understand that all animals smaller than dogs were made to be hunted.
24. When a dog gets old and starts to snap at you incessantly, you can shoot it.
25. Dogs like beer.

26. Dogs don't hate their bodies.
27. No dog ever bought a Kenny G or Hootie the Blowfish album.
28. No dog ever put on 100 pounds after reaching adulthood.
29. Dogs never criticise.
30. Dogs agree that you have to raise your voice to get your point across.
31. Dogs never expect gifts.
32. It's legal to keep a dog chained up at your house.
33. Dogs don't worry about germs.
34. Dogs don't want to know about every other dog you ever had.
35. Dogs like to do their snooping outside as opposed to in your wallet, desk, and the back of your sock drawer.
36. Dogs don't let magazine articles guide their lives.
37. Dogs would rather have you buy them a hamburger dinner than a lobster one.
38. You never have to wait for a dog. They're ready to go 24 hours a day.
39. Dogs have no use for flowers, cards, or jewellery.
40. Dogs don't borrow your shirts.
41. Dogs never want a foot-rub.
42. Dogs enjoy heavy petting in public.
43. Dogs find you amusing when you're drunk.
44. Dogs can't talk.
45. Dogs aren't catty.

46.   Dogs seldom outlive you.

HOW DOGS AND WOMEN ARE ALIKE:

Both look stupid in hats. Both can eat 5 pounds of chocolate in one sitting. Both tend to have a Whips problems. Neither understand football. Both look good in a fur coat. Both are good at pretending that they're listening to every word you say. Neither can balance a chequebook. You can never tell what either of them is thinking. Both put too much value on kissing.

HOW WOMEN ARE BETTER THAN DOGS:

It is socially acceptable to have sexual relations with a woman. Women look good in sweaters. Women leave the room to fart. Though they only have two, women's breasts are far more interesting.

Subject: FW: Dalia Lama Personality Test.

This test is very exciting. It only has four (4) questions, and you'll be surprised about the results! Please do not scroll your screens to know the results before starting. The human mind is like an umbrella: it works better when it opens. It is fun to answer the questions, but please follow the instructions.

MAKE A WISH BEFORE STARTING THE TEST.

Caution! Answer the questions step by step. This test has only four questions, but if you see the answers before finishing, your results will not be honest or accurate. Scroll your screen slowly and write down your answers.

This questionnaire will tell you a lot about your inner self.

First, order the following animals according to your preference:

a) Cow; b) Tiger; c) Sheep; d) Horse; e) Pig.

Second, write a word that qualifies each of the following:

a) Dog; b) Cat; c) Rat; d) Coffee; e) Ocean.

Third, think about someone (who also knows you and is important to you,) that can be related to the following colours (do not repeat your answers.).

Name only one person per colour:

a) Yellow; b) Orange; c) Red; d) White; e) Green.

Finally, write down your favourite number, as well as your favourite weekday.

Did you finish? Verify that all your answers are accurate. Last chance to verify. Look at the answers below, but before make again your own wish.

This will define your priorities in life:

Cow: means career.

Tiger: means pride.

Sheep: means love.

Horse: means family.

Pig: means money.

Your description of Dog implies your own personality.

Your description of Cat implies your spouse or couple's personality.

Your description of Rat implies the personality of your enemies.

Your description of Coffee is how you interpret sex.

Your description of Ocean implies your own life.

Yellow: Someone you will never forget.

Orange: Someone you could consider a good friend.

Red: Someone you really love.

White: Your twin soul.

Green: Someone you will remember all your life.

INSTRUCTIONS FOR GIVING YOUR CAT A PILL:

1. Pick cat up and cradle it in the crook of your left arm as if holding a baby. Position right forefinger and thumb on either side of cat's mouth and gently apply pressure to cheeks while holding pill in right hand. As cat opens mouth, pop pill into mouth. Allow cat to close mouth and swallow.

2. Retrieve pill from floor and cat from behind sofa. Cradle cat in left arm and repeat process.

3. Retrieve cat from bedroom, and throw soggy pill away.

4. Take new pill from foil wrap, cradle cat in left arm holding rear paws tightly with left hand. Force jaws open and push pill to back of mouth with right forefinger. Hold mouth shut for a count of 10.

5. Retrieve pill from goldfish bowl and cat from top of wardrobe. Call spouse from garden.

6. Kneel on floor with cat wedged firmly between knees, holding front and rear paws. Ignore low growls emitted by cat. Get spouse to hold cat's head firmly with one hand while forcing wooden ruler into mouth. Drop pill down ruler and rub cat's throat vigorously.

7. Retrieve cat from curtain rail, get another pill from foil wrap. Make note to buy new ruler and repair curtains. Carefully sweep shattered figurines from floor and set to one side for gluing later.

8. Wrap cat in large towel and get spouse to lie on cat with its head just visible from below spouse's armpit. Put pill in end of drinking straw, force cat's mouth open with pencil and blow down drinking straw.

9. Check label to make sure pill not harmful to humans, drink glass of water to take taste away. Apply Band-Aid to spouse's forearm and remove blood from carpet with cold water and soap.

10. Retrieve cat from neighbour's shed. Get another pill. Place cat in cupboard and close door onto neck to leave head showing. Force mouth open with dessert spoon. Flick pill down throat with elastic band.

11. Fetch screwdriver from garage and put door back on hinges. Apply cold compress to cheek and check records for date of last tetanus shot. Throw T-shirt away and fetch new one from bedroom.

12. Ring fire brigade to retrieve cat from tree across the road. Apologise to neighbour who crashed into fence while swerving to avoid cat. Take last pill from foil wrap.

13. Tie cat's front paws to rear paws with garden twine and bind tightly to leg of dining table. Find heavy duty pruning gloves from shed. Force cat's mouth open with small spanner. Push pill into mouth followed by large piece of fillet steak. Hold head vertically and pour a pint of water down throat to wash pill down.

14. Get spouse to drive you to emergency room; sit quietly while doctor stitches fingers and forearm and removes pill remnants from right eye. Stop by furniture shop on way home to order new table.

15. Arrange for RSPCA to collect cat and call local pet shop to see if they have any hamsters.

So there's this penguin driving across the Nullarbor Plain and it's a *really* hot day—and that's bad news for a penguin. So, the penguin is driving and saying "Sheesh" a lot and wiping his brow with his flipper then the car starts acting up! Bumpity bumpity bump...

"Oh great", thinks the penguin. To his relief, there is a service station not too far further along. He drives in, parks his car, hops out and waddles over to the mechanic. "Can you have a look at my car?" says the penguin, "it's making a funny sound." "Sure" says the mechanic.

"Sheesh," thinks the penguin. "It's so hot! I think I'll go inside to the air conditioning." So he waddles over and goes inside. He mooches around, flicking through magazines, killing time. He decides he'll buy an ice cream to help him cool down. Then he goes back out to the car.

"Sheesh," he says as he waddles back over the tarmac. "It's really hot." And he's making a real mess of the ice cream, on account of it being so hot and him being a penguin and only being able to hold it with his flipper. He spills more of it over himself than he gets in his mouth. He gets back to the car and comes up to the mechanic who's leaning over the engine. The mechanic looks up at him and says "Hmm. Looks like you've blown a seal." "Oh no," laughs the penguin, "That's only ice cream."

David received a parrot for his birthday. The parrot was fully grown with a bad attitude and worse vocabulary.

Every other word was an expletive. Those that weren't expletives, were to say the least, rude.

David tried hard to change the bird's attitude and was constantly conversing polite with the parrot, playing gentle music, anything he could think of to set a good example...

Nothing worked. Then he yelled at the bird and the bird yelled back. He shook the bird and the bird try to bite his nose. Finally, in a moment of desperation, David put the parrot in the freezer.

For a few moments he heard the bird parrot squawk and kick and holler- then suddenly, there was quiet. David was frightened that he might have hurt the bird and quickly opened the freezer door. Not a sound for half a minute.

The parrot calmly stepped out onto David's extended arm and said, "I believe I may have offended you with my rude language and actions. I will endeavour at once to correct my behaviour. I really am truly sorry and beg your forgiveness."

David was astonished at the bird's change in attitude and was about to ask what had made such a dramatic change when the parrot continued, "May I ask what the chicken did?"

Frank was excited about his new rifle. So, he decided to go bear hunting. He spotted a small brown bear and shot it. There was then a tap on his shoulder, and he turned around to see a big black bear. The black bear said "You've got two choices. I either maul you to death or we have sex."

Frank decided to bend over. Even though he felt sore for two weeks, Frank soon recovered and vowed revenge. He headed out on another trip where he found the black bear and shot it.

There was another tap on his shoulder. This time a huge grizzly bear stood right next to him. The grizzly said "That was a huge mistake, Frank. You've got two choices. Either I maul you to death or we'll have rough sex. "

Again, Frank thought it was better to comply. Although he survived, it would take several months before Frank finally recovered. Outraged he headed back to the woods, managed to track down the grizzly and shot it. He felt sweet revenge, but then there was a tap on his shoulder.

He turned round to find a giant polar bear standing there. The polar bear said? "Admit it, Frank, you don't come here for the hunting, do you?"

This guy lived on his own and he was feeling a bit lonely, so he goes to the pet shop to get something to keep him company. The pet shop owner suggested an unusual pet, a talking millipede. OK, thought the man, I'll give it a go, so he bought one and took it home. That night he decided to test out his new pet, so he opened the box and said, "I'm going to the pub for a drink, do you want to come too?"

But there was no reply. He tried again, "Oi, millipede, want to come to the boozer with me?" Again, no response. So the man ranted and raved for a bit, but after a while decided to give it one more try before he took the thing back to the shop. So he took the lid off the box and repeated, "I said I'm going to the pub for a drink do you want to come?"

"For f#@k's sake, I heard you the first time" snapped the millipede, "I'm just putting my shoes on."

Late one night, a burglar broke into a house that he thought was empty. He tiptoed through the living room but suddenly he froze in his tracks when he heard a loud voice say: "Jesus is watching you!" the voice boomed again.

The burglar stopped dead again. He was frightened. Frantically, he looked all around. In a dark corner, he spotted a bird cage and in the cage was a parrot. He asked the parrot, "Was that you who said Jesus is watching me?" "Yes," said the parrot. The burglar breathed a sigh of relief, then he asked the parrot, "What's your name?" "Clarence," replied the bird.

"That's a dumb name for a parrot," sneered the burglar. "What idiot named you Clarence?" The parrot said, "The same idiot who named the Rottweiler Jesus."

A woman walked into the bar with a duck under her arm. One of the drunks at the bar looked over and commented, "That has got to be the ugliest pig I've ever seen." "That's not a pig, it's a duck," said the woman indignantly. The drunk explained, "I was talking to the duck."

A busload of politicians was driving down a country road, when suddenly the bus ran off the road and crashed into an old farmer's barn.

The old farmer got off his tractor and went to investigate. Soon he dug a hole and buried the politicians. A few days later, the local sheriff came out, saw the crashed bus and asked the old farmer where all the politicians had gone.

The old farmer told him he had buried them.

The sheriff asked the old farmer, "Lordy, were they all dead?"

The old farmer said, "Well, some of them said they weren't, but you know how them crooked politicians lie—I didn't believe them."

www.ingramcontent.com/pod-product-compliance
Lightning Source LLC
Chambersburg PA
CBHW050546160426
43199CB00015B/2553